INVISIBLE ATROCITIES

Invisible Atrocities assesses the role aesthetic factors play in shaping what forms of mass violence are viewed as international crimes. International criminal justice is, at its core, an anti-atrocity project. Yet just what an "atrocity" is remains undefined and undertheorized. This book examines how associations between atrocity commission and the production of horrific spectacles shape the processes through which international crimes are identified and conceptualized, leading to the foregrounding of certain forms of mass violence and the backgrounding or complete invisibilization of others. In doing so, it identifies various, seemingly banal, ways through which international crimes may be committed and demonstrates how the criminality of such forms of violence and abuse tends to be obfuscated. This book suggests that the failure to address these "invisible atrocities" represents a major flaw in the current international criminal justice system, one that produces a host of problematic repercussions and undermines the legal legitimacy of international criminal law itself.

RANDLE C. DEFALCO is an Assistant Professor of Law at the University of Hawai'i at Mānoa William S. Richardson School of Law.

INVISIBLE ATROCITIES

The Aesthetic Biases of International Criminal Justice

RANDLE C. DEFALCO
University of Hawaiʻi at Mānoa William S. Richardson School of Law

CAMBRIDGE
UNIVERSITY PRESS

CAMBRIDGE
UNIVERSITY PRESS

University Printing House, Cambridge CB2 8BS, United Kingdom

One Liberty Plaza, 20th Floor, New York, NY 10006, USA

477 Williamstown Road, Port Melbourne, VIC 3207, Australia

314–321, 3rd Floor, Plot 3, Splendor Forum, Jasola District Centre,
New Delhi – 110025, India

103 Penang Road, #05–06/07, Visioncrest Commercial, Singapore 238467

Cambridge University Press is part of the University of Cambridge.

It furthers the University's mission by disseminating knowledge in the pursuit of
education, learning, and research at the highest international levels of excellence.

www.cambridge.org
Information on this title: www.cambridge.org/9781108487412
DOI: 10.1017/9781108766692

First published 2022

A catalogue record for this publication is available from the British Library.

Library of Congress Cataloging-in-Publication Data
Names: DeFalco, Randle C., 1982– author.
Title: Invisible atrocities : the aesthetic biases of internationalcriminal justice / Randle C. DeFalco, University of Toronto.
Description: Cambridge, United Kingdom ; New York, NY : CambridgeUniversity Press, 2022. | Includes bibliographical references and index.
Identifiers: LCCN 2021044778 (print) | LCCN 2021044779 (ebook) | ISBN9781108487412 (hardback) | ISBN 9781108766692 (ebook)
Subjects: LCSH: Atrocities – Law and legislation. | Criminal justice,Administration of – International cooperation. | World War,1914-1918 – Atrocities. | International criminal law.
Classification: LCC KZ7145 .D44 2022 (print) | LCC KZ7145 (ebook) | DDC341.6/9–dc23/eng/20211223
LC record available at https://lccn.loc.gov/2021044778
LC ebook record available at https://lccn.loc.gov/2021044779

ISBN 978-1-108-48741-2 Hardback

CONTENTS

ACKNOWLEDGMENTS

Dedication: For Marquita and Amari

The cover of this book features a reproduction of Ceija Stojka's *Ohne Titel, Untitled, 15.3.2003*, which depicts the eyes of people in hiding. Stojka, a survivor of the World War II Roma Genocide, included text on the back of the original piece naming family members, referencing anxieties about food, and expressing fear of Nazi terror. The first lines of the text are especially relevant to the themes in this book. Translated into English, they read:

> Auschwitz a place without fruit
> Dear God where is the bread and sausage
> Bread
> And SAUSAGE
> There was none of that in Auschwitz.[1]

The focus on the lack of food helps crystallize the interconnectedness of various forms of oppression and violence, from the spectacular to the everyday, explored in this book. Combined with the striking image of obscured faces, hiding yet recognizable if we look closely, this emphasis on everyday experiences of atrocity violence encapsulates much of what I have tried to convey here: If only we were able to look more carefully, free from our aestheticized preconceptions regarding what "atrocity crimes" are, we may see certain overlooked forms of violence and oppression as potential international crimes. While Stojka herself was a survivor of perhaps the most paradigmatic atrocity of all – Nazi concentration camps – as a Roma woman, she was a member of a largely overlooked class of victims. The backgrounding of certain atrocities underscores the fact that, as individuals and societies, we choose what we see and how we interpret and prioritize harm and suffering. This book focuses on a subset

[1] Translation provided by the Ceija Stojka International Fund.

of other atrocity crimes that have remained largely obscured: those committed through means lacking the dramatic spectacles of violence associated with dominant social and legal understandings of atrocity and international crime. Ceija Stojka's art and her family's generosity in allowing its reproduction have provided me with an image I believe can help us to see and recognize how we often fail to see and recognize certain aesthetically unfamiliar atrocities, their victims, and their perpetrators. I thank the family again and Carina Kurta of the Ceija Stojka International Fund for entrusting me with this powerful image.

The thinking that led me to writing this book began during the time I spent between 2008 and 2012 at the Documentation Center of Cambodia (DC-Cam). In conversations with Youk Chhang, Anne Heindel, Dany Long, Savina Sirik, Soksreinith Ten, Farina So, Sokvisal Kimsroy, Vanthan Peoudara, Khamboly Dy, Terith Chy, and many others, and in engaging with survivors of the Khmer Rouge era, I became interested in questions related to international criminal law's relationship to everyday forms of violence and oppression. This interest and Anne's unfailing support and research guidance led me to explore these issues, especially in relation to famine and starvation, in greater depth, setting me on a path culminating in this book.

I am grateful to have learned from many generous academic mentors. Professors Karima Bennoune, Saul Mendlovitz, Penny Venetis, and Adil Haque all nurtured my interest in international law and justice issues. Jutta Brunnée has been a source of immense support and incisive feedback. Input from Stephen Toope, Vincent Chiao, Karen Knop, and the ever-enthusiastic Mark Drumbl was instrumental in moving this project forward. Christine Schwöbel-Patel also deserves special recognition for consistently pushing and challenging my thinking about what international criminal law is and what it actually does.

Conversations with colleagues, mentors, and friends have provided valuable opportunities to develop the ideas of this project. Workshops organized by Christine and Rob Knox were instrumental in my thinking, as was the feedback I received from Pádraig McAuliffe, Alex Batesmith, Immi Tallgren, Anne Neylon, Gerry Simpson, Tor Krever, and Sofia Stolk. Thanks to Zinaida Miller, Frédéric Mégret, Jocelyn Getgen-Kestenbaum, Margaret deGuzman, Haley Anderson, James Tyner, Y-Dang Troeung, Vinh Nguyen, Jordan Sheridan, Bridgette Conley, Alex de Waal, Catherine Lu, Wayne Jordash, Catriona Murdoch, Roger Clark, Linda Krieger, and many others for conversations that have moved my thinking forward in ways large and small.

The work of this project has been supported by a Fulbright Fellowship, and the Social Sciences and Humanities Research Council of Canada's Vanier Scholarship and Banting Fellowship programs. Support from my colleagues at the University of Hawai'i at Mānoa William S. Richardson School of Law was critical in finalizing this book and seeing it through to publication, especially faculty support specialists Kelly-Ann Hernandez and Keiralyn Pease.

Finally, I would like to thank my parents, Charlie DeFalco and Diane Stevens, for always nurturing my curiosity, and my siblings, Amelia and Tom, for their continued support. Thanks to Morris Hemmings for being the highlight of each of my research trips to England. Thanks to Kate DeFalco, Gwen Horne, Brittany Taylor, Chris Taylor, and Robert Hemmings for putting up with me. And, most importantly, my deepest thanks to Marquita Smith and Amari DeFalco, my two loves. Without Marquita's endless support, there is no way I could have written this book. I can't thank her enough. Amari, thanks for being a constant source of joy.

1

Introduction

Visible and Invisible Atrocity Crimes

From October 19 to 30, 1943, as the tide of World War II turned in favor of the Allies, representatives of the governments of the United States, United Kingdom, and Soviet Union met in Moscow to consider "measures to shorten the duration of the war against Hitlerite Germany and her Allies in Europe."[1] Following this conference, on November 1, the governments of the three countries issued a joint Protocol, signed the previous evening, concerning various matters relating to the conclusion of the war.[2] Among the documents annexed to the Protocol was a "Declaration of German Atrocities" drafted by Winston Churchill and signed by Churchill, Franklin Roosevelt, and Josef Stalin.[3] Referencing "atrocities, massacres and cold-blooded mass executions," the Declaration states that the United States, United Kingdom, and Soviet Union "solemnly declare and give full warning of their declaration" that at the conclusion of the war "those German officers and men and members of the Nazi party who have been responsible for or have taken a consenting part in the above atrocities, massacres and executions will be sent back to the countries in which their abominable deeds were done in order that they may be judged and punished."[4] The "above atrocities" mentioned are not described with greater specificity in the Declaration, nor the Moscow Protocol more generally. Instead, references are made to evidence of "atrocities, massacres and cold-blooded mass executions," along with "ruthless cruelties," and "monstrous crimes" that had been, and were continuing to be, committed by "Hitlerite forces."[5]

[1] USA–UK–USSR, Moscow Protocol, Moscow, USSR, October 30, 1943, in force November 1, 1943, 1943 For. Rel. (I) 749, para. 1.

[2] Moscow Protocol, Annex 10, "Declaration of German Atrocities."

[3] Gary Bass, *Stay the Hand of Vengeance: The Politics of War Crimes Tribunals* (Princeton University Press, 2014), 149.

[4] Moscow Protocol, "Declaration of German Atrocities."

[5] Ibid.

The relative vagueness of the criminal acts alleged in the Declaration was not lost on Churchill. While drafting the text that would become the Declaration, Churchill wrote to Roosevelt and Stalin that while "he was 'not particular about the phraseology,'" his hope was that the general warning of postwar prosecution might "'make some of these villains reluctant to be mixed up in butcheries now they realize they are going to be defeated.'"[6] While focusing on the potential deterrent effect the Declaration might have on the commission of further "butcheries" by the Nazis, neither in his correspondence, nor in the ultimate text of the Declaration, does Churchill specify what crimes the "villains" he refers to might be prosecuted for.[7] Instead, Churchill seems to assume that the "abominable deeds" and "monstrous crimes" referred to are so self-evident in nature that they require no further defining or description.

The stated intention to carry out postwar prosecutions was, of course, followed through on by the Allies, marking the birth of international criminal law (ICL). In the nearly eight decades since Churchill drafted the Declaration, ICL prosecutions have focused primarily on the kinds of highly visible forms of mass violence invoked in the Declaration – new manifestations of the "monstrous crimes" referenced in the Declaration. In describing these "abominable deeds," ICL actors have embraced terms such as atrocity and mass violence. The International Criminal Court's (ICC's) Rome Statute, for instance, refers to "unimaginable atrocities that deeply shock the conscience of humanity" in its preamble when referring to the general subject matter of ICL.[8] This language, the prosecutorial tendencies of ICL in its application, and the ways in which the trio of so-called core international crimes – genocide, crimes against humanity, and war crimes – have been interpreted, combine to suggest that the commission of these crimes inherently involves the production of highly visible spectacles of horrific violence. The "criminal" nature of such horrific spectacles is intuitively recognizable: piles of corpses greeting Allies at liberated concentration camps, rivers full of dead bodies in Rwanda, child soldiers and severed limbs in Sierra Leone, and literal piles of bones and skulls in Cambodia, to name but a handful of examples.

[6] Letter quoted in Bass, *Stay the Hand of Vengeance*, 149.

[7] According to Gary Bass, the wording of the Statement was also left intentionally vague to avoid potential reprisals against Allied prisoners of war. Ibid.

[8] Rome Statute of the International Criminal Court, Rome, July 17, 1998, in force July 1, 2002, 2187 UNTS 3, preamble.

This association between international crime commission and the production of horrific spectacles raises a host of questions concerning the nature, scope, and purposes of ICL. What role do aesthetic considerations play in shaping social and legal understandings of what international crimes are (and are not)? Is there something intrinsic to the substance or nature of ICL itself that demands all crimes involve such spectacles? If not, might certain international crimes be committed through unspectacular means, the criminality of which is not so self-evident? If so, given ICL's extreme selectivity in application, have such crimes been overlooked? What might the broader effects of this potential "invisibilization" of unspectacular forms of mass harms be, including for the legitimacy of ICL itself?

These are the questions at the heart of this book, which explores the roles aesthetics play in shaping how we conceptualize what international crimes are, and imagine how they might be committed. The significance of the normative associations between international crime and an aesthetics of spectacle remains understudied. This book attempts to rectify this oversight. It does so by examining the role aesthetic considerations play in the social construction of shared social and legal understandings of international crime and ICL. Attending to both individual and social processes of aesthetic perception and meaning-making to account for the complex ways in which they feed into one another, I argue that, within the realm of ICL, the net result of these processes has been, among other things, the construction, embedding, and reproduction over time of an assumption that real-world instances of genocide, crimes against humanity, and/or war crimes will necessarily conform to a particular aesthetic model of atrocities as highly visible, intuitively recognizable spectacles of horrific violence. I demonstrate that aesthetic considerations continue to play a significant role in shaping what forms of harm causation are viewed as potentially grounding ICL accountability. This reliance on the spectacular stems from the grounding of widely shared understandings of international crime in what I refer to as a dominant "atrocity aesthetic" model of international crime commission. Emerging from longstanding, widely shared understandings of mass violence, "atrocity," and international crime, this dominant, if largely unacknowledged, aesthetic model undergirds predominant understandings of genocide, crimes against humanity, and war crimes, as manifesting themselves exclusively through the commission of gruesome, horrific acts of violence and abuse.

These horrifically spectacular acts conform to preconceived notions of not only violence, but also harm, by resembling prior canonical atrocity crimes and thus resist innovation or broader understandings. Consequently, less aesthetically familiar processes of mass harm causation – those that are slow, banal, bureaucratic, attritive, or otherwise aesthetically unspectacular and unfamiliar in nature – tend to be assumed to fall outside the purview of ICL. These unspectacular forms of harm causation are consequently characterized as either not severe enough to warrant being characterized as international crimes, or as wholly forms of "structural violence" inherently situated outside the reach of criminal law generally, and ICL specifically. As this book, and the work of a growing cohort of scholars demonstrates, this characterization, however, is not always accurate. International crimes can be, and regularly are, committed through a wide variety of means, ranging from the spectacular to the banal, even mundane.

Moreover, the current myopic focus on familiar, spectacular forms of violence and harm causation within ICL helps obscure the reality that virtually all atrocities, including those conforming to the atrocity aesthetic, are complex social phenomena, involving the culpable production of overlapping, mutually reinforcing forms of harm causation by groups of actors working in unison. Even within broader atrocity situations conforming to the atrocity aesthetic, ICL's narrow focus on spectacular forms of killing and abuse may obscure other, comparably important harms. For example, as discussed in more detail in Chapter 5, the Khmer Rouge regime abused, killed, and traumatized Cambodians not only through the commission of extreme forms of physical violence, but also by placing victims in terrible living conditions where they were systematically overworked, underfed, denied access to basic health care, and forbidden from engaging in coping behaviors, such as foraging for food or cultivating subsistence gardens. In many cases, including that of Cambodia, such unspectacular, everyday forms of harm causation can involve suffering and death of a scale and magnitude comparable to even the most large-scale international crimes committed through traditional, spectacularly violent means. Less spectacular does not necessarily mean less serious or less harmful. Moreover, these relatively unspectacular forms of killing and abuse may be quite direct in terms of harms caused and the culpability of those involved, as I argue appears to be the case in the Cambodian context, where the regime's leaders continued to demand the rigid implementation of their mass death-producing policies even as the civilian population starved and died by the thousands.

More generally, there now exists a significant and growing literature identifying various novel and largely overlooked means of international crime commission, ranging from the enforcement of famine conditions, to sustained socioeconomic oppression. One common thread tying many otherwise disparate forms of routinely overlooked or ignored atrocity commission processes analyzed within this literature is a failure to conform to the atrocity aesthetic. I suggest that this shared tendency toward aesthetic unfamiliarity plays a significant, and largely overlooked role in the continued backgrounding of these harm causation processes within international criminal justice. In turn, the culpability of those responsible is obscured and the status of victim denied for those affected.

While the obfuscation of the criminality of certain unfamiliar forms of international crime commission is undoubtedly multicausal and tied up in politics and power relations, I nonetheless suggest that aesthetically unfamiliar forms of mass harm causation represent a distinctive *lacuna* in ICL. Aside from the usual manipulation of ICL to suit the preferences of powerful states and actors, as well as ICL's inherent inability to address wholly structural forms of violence and injustice, I suggest that aesthetic sensibilities and biases play a meaningful role in whether (and how) certain international crimes are recognized and branded as such. The net result is the narrowing of ICL from its potential, broad-based applicability, encompassing virtually any process through which individuals culpably participate in the infliction of large-scale harms on others, to focusing narrowly on familiar, spectacular processes of harm causation, the criminality of which is intuitively recognizable. Because this normative association between international crime and the production of horrific spectacle is itself unacknowledged, and fails to accurately reflect the actual boundaries of ICL, *de lege lata*, I frame this phenomenon as a distinctly aesthetic bias that, along with other factors, narrows the scope of ICL by rendering certain international crimes socially and legally invisible.

Spectacular and Invisible Atrocities: Why It Matters

This book grew out of a longstanding interest in studying intersections between ICL and novel, heretofore unprosecuted forms of mass killing, abuse, and oppression. As I researched this topic, I began to find that many scholars have considered ICL's potential applicability to forms of harm causation that are unlikely to immediately come to mind when one thinks of international crimes. Comparatively scant attention has been paid to the question of why these forms of harm causation not only go, like so many other potential atrocity crimes, unprosecuted, but also tend not even to be recognized as potentially grounding ICL liability in the first place.

While a small, but growing cohort of scholars have by now identified various heretofore ignored modalities of international crime commission, the question of why has remained a secondary one, with the primary assessment being a largely doctrinal one, of whether and how ICL might address previously ignored forms of atrocity. When opining as to why such potential forms of international crime commission have been largely overlooked, authors have tended to frame this practice gap as a political or structural choice. While, as with all aspects of ICL and international law more generally, politics and power dynamics play a major role in shaping what is and is not criminalized and who is and is not prosecuted, this book argues that one significant, and largely overlooked factor underwriting ICL's exclusionary tendencies is aesthetic in nature. That is, dominant understandings of international crime seem to be grounded in a particular aesthetic model of horrific spectacle. This aesthetic commitment leads us to associate atrocity and international crime with spectacular harms and rarely, if ever, to associate unspectacular suffering with atrocity or prosecution, even if occurring on a massive scale. Indeed, this commitment is often evident in pushback against the notion that ICL might be applied to novel, unspectacular forms of violence and harm causation.[9]

One salutary approach to understanding and explaining the dynamic whereby we recognize certain forms of atrocity violence quite easily, yet struggle to see others, is to excavate the aesthetic from the doctrinal, and in doing so demonstrate that the classification of international crimes and the inclusion/exclusion of specific acts, situations, places, people, and so on, are deeply influenced by aesthetic sensibilities relating to notions of atrocity and international crime, rather than produced strictly by legal considerations. While I conduct such an analysis in Chapters 4 and 5, this process does not reveal the deepest aspects and implications of the atrocity aesthetic. This is because such an analysis suggests that

[9] Hence, for example, what Evelyne Schmid refers to as the "legal impossibility argument" regarding the potential applicability of ICL to harms brought about through economic, social, and cultural human rights violations may be also partially grounded in an (unacknowledged) general feeling that such harms are inherently not "criminal" in nature. See Evelyne Schmid, *Taking Economic, Social and Cultural Rights Seriously in International Criminal Law* (Cambridge University Press, 2015), 22–40.

a simple reformist approach, one that encourages institutions such as the ICC to seek out new forms of international crime commission to investigate and prosecute, would likely be met with pushback and allegations "expanding" ICL improperly. One person's "expansion" of ICL doctrine may be merely the "application" of existing laws to new facts for another. Consequently, a reformist agenda might turn out to be a lot harder to follow than we think precisely because of how deep-seated, unquestioned, and foundational the atrocity aesthetic is when it comes to processes of recognizing potential international crimes.

As this book shows through its use of interactional legal theory, individual and social processes of constructing ideas are complex and intertwined, making it not only hard to reconceptualize what forms international crimes may take, but also to recognize the ways ICL shapes understandings of atrocious behavior in the world. It is this process, of "seeing" as a form of social recognition, that I am primarily interested in, as what we choose to see as an international crime has serious consequences beyond the realm of international criminal justice. Given that ICL's influence has grown to the point that international *criminal* justice has come to be routinely conflated with the much broader concept of *global* justice,[10] global justice resources are funneled first and foremost to acknowledged sites of atrocity. This funneling makes sense if one views international crimes as the worst forms of global injustice and believes that resources ought to be distributed by giving priority to the worst injustices.

As many commentators have warned, this seemingly ever-increasing fascination with atrocity and ICL may or may not be a net positive development in terms of prospects of actually improving global justice and the lives of the world's most vulnerable populations.[11] I share these concerns, and would add that the degree to which ICL draws attention

[10] For discussions of the ways in which ICL has begun to monopolize global justice and human rights discourses, see Sarah M. H. Nouwen and Wouter G. Werner, "Monopolizing Global Justice: International Criminal Law as Challenge to Human Diversity" (2015) 13 *Journal of International Criminal Justice* 157–176; Karen Engle, "Anti-Impunity and the Turn to Criminal Law in Human Rights" (2015) 100 *Cornell Law Review* 1069–1128. Along these lines Christine Schwöbel-Patel demonstrates how the branding of ICL has actively coopted the language of global justice. Christine Schwöbel-Patel, *Marketing Global Justice: The Political Economy of International Criminal Law* (Cambridge University Press, 2021).

[11] See, for example, Kamari Maxine Clarke, "'We Ask for Justice You Give Us Law': The Rule of Law, Economic Markets and the Reconfiguration of Victimhood," in Christian De Vos, Sara Kendall, and Carsten Stahn, eds., *Contested Justice: The Politics and Practice of International Criminal Court Interventions* (Cambridge University Press, 2015), 272–301; Engle, "Anti-Impunity."

away from certain pressing global justice issues, for example, the perpetuation and expansion of radical global wealth inequality, can only be compounded when we fail to see certain international crimes. Through this process, harms that are in actuality products of culpable, agentic actions are conceptually transformed into non-agentic structural injustices, which are then excused as inevitable or at least too complex to do anything about. Thus, direct violence becomes structural violence, which is then dismissed as nobody's fault and therefore impossible to stop.

Even when we may be able to see unspectacular atrocities as potentially implicating ICL, a similar dynamic operates to downgrade the perceived seriousness of such crimes. Given what scholars such as Margaret deGuzman have already demonstrated in terms of the amorphousness and malleability of "gravity" as a basis for assessing the relative seriousness of even the most paradigmatic international crimes,[12] we may easily fall into the trap of simplistically equivocating the most aesthetically horrific forms of violence with the most serious international crimes. Who makes up the "we" in this regard is also troubling, as assessments of what is and is not an international crime viewed as being authoritative are overwhelmingly made by elite technocrats (lawyers, judges, investigators, etc.) clustered in the Global North.[13] Thus, what is recognized as an international crime, and what are viewed as the most serious of these crimes warranting the bulk of our time and energy, may turn largely on what forms of harm causation distant elites in the Global North are most revulsed by, exposing ICL to further allegations of engaging in "distant" justice or falling prey to racist and/or neocolonial notions of where atrocities occur, who commits them, and who is victimized.[14]

[12] Margaret M. deGuzman, "Gravity and the Legitimacy of the International Criminal Court" (2009) 32 *Fordham International Law Journal* 1400–1465.

[13] On the question of who and what institutions make up the "we" so often invoked in mainstream ICL discourses, see Immi Tallgren, "Who are 'We' in International Criminal Law? On Critics and Membership," in Christine Schwöbel-Patel, ed., *Critical Approaches to International Criminal Law: An Introduction* (Routledge, 2014), 71–95. On the representational practices of ICL and the constituencies it seeks to speak on behalf of, see Sara Kendall and Sarah Nouwen, "Representational Practices at the International Criminal Court: The Gap between Juridified and Abstract Victimhood" (2014) 76 *Law and Contemporary Problems* 235–262; Frédéric Mégret, "In Whose Name? The ICC and the Search for Constituency," in Carsten Stahn, Sarah Kendall, and Christian M. de Vos, eds., *Contested Justice: The Politics and Practice of International Criminal Court Interventions* (Cambridge University Press, 2015), 23–45.

[14] See, for example, Phil Clark, *Distant Justice: The Impact of the International Criminal Court on African Politics* (Cambridge University Press, 2018); Sofia Stolk, "A Sophisticated Beast? On the Construction of an 'Ideal' Perpetrator in the Opening

Considering the distributional role ICL plays in labeling the "worst" global injustices,[15] adherence to the atrocity aesthetic risks rewarding powerful actors willing to kill and oppress creatively and through novel means, by removing them from the intense glare of what Larissa van den Herik describes as the "spotlight" effect of ICL.[16] Individuals accused of planning or participating in atrocity crimes may be branded, socially, if not legally, as *hostis humani generis* ("enemies of all humankind"), limiting their freedom of movement and ability to participate in various political arenas and organizations.[17] Peacebuilding, foreign aid, and transitional justice activities also tend to be funneled toward acknowledged sites of atrocity. Conversely, denial that atrocities were committed against members of a particular victim group often correlates with their continuing oppression, highlighting the importance of whether dominant historical narratives are couched in the language of atrocity and international crime.

Given these concerns, my motivation for engaging in this line of inquiry is less to advocate for the abolishment, continuation, or expansion of international criminal justice as a global project. Rather, given my ambivalence about the legitimacy and usefulness of ICL and its current institutions, my ambition is to contribute to a more nuanced understanding of what this body of law actually does and does not do, and perhaps more importantly, what it can and should do if it is to continue existing. Along these lines, I am of the view that, if ICL is going to continue to exist and attract the attention it does, this body of law should at least be used to highlight the gravity and culpability of a broader array of forms of violence, abuse, and oppression than it currently does. While we must remain vigilant to the risks of uncritically equating the criminal law prosecution of individuals with "doing justice," especially given the fact

Statements of International Criminal Trials" (2018) 29 *European Journal of International Law* 677–701; Randle C. DeFalco and Frédéric Mégret, "The Invisibility of Race at the ICC: Lessons from the US Criminal Justice System" (2019) 7 *London Review of International Law* 55–87; Clarke, "'We Ask for Justice You Give Us Law'"; Christine Schwöbel-Patel, "Spectacle in International Criminal Law: The Fundraising Image of Victimhood" (2016) 4 *London Review of International Law* 247–274.

15 Frédéric Mégret, "Practices of Stigmatization" (2013) 76 *Law and Contemporary Problems* 287–318; Nikolas M. Rajkovic, "What Is a 'Grave' International Crime? The Rome Statute, Durkheim and the Sociology of Ruling Outrages" (2020) 16 *Loyola University Chicago International Law Review* 65–86.

16 Larissa van den Herik, "International Criminal Law as a Spotlight and Black Holes as Constituents of Legacy" (2016) 110 *AJIL Unbound* 209–213.

17 On the more general neoliberal branding culture of ICL, see Schwöbel-Patel, *Marketing Global Justice*.

that criminal prosecutions and mass incarceration have done so much *in*justice – indeed in certain circumstances may themselves arguably be atrocity processes – I tentatively agree with Itamar Mann's assertion that "as long as we have prisons, let them be filled with those who have committed the worst of crimes."[18] Hence, I think it is imperative to carefully explore the outer boundaries of ICL and to point out that, while powerful actors may be able to better disguise the criminality of their actions by producing harms through seemingly banal, bureaucratic means, they remain culpable, and we may condemn their actions as "atrocious," just as we condemn other forms of violence committed through more familiar means.

Thus, even if one arrives at the conclusion that the kinds of reforms necessary to render ICL a worthwhile endeavor are so radical as to justify jettisoning the entire project of international criminal justice, it remains important to consider what ICL does do, while it continues to exist and operate. Of particular importance are the ways in which ICL shapes narratives, influences resource allocation, and selectively condemns certain forms of mass violence and abuse, while ignoring others. Consequently, in researching ICL's treatment of less obvious forms of large-scale harm causation, I remain primarily interested in the role(s) ICL plays in reflecting and (re)constructing socio-legal understandings of what mass violence and atrocity themselves are, as opposed to opining whether the international criminal justice project is worthwhile, or advocating for specific doctrinal interpretations.[19]

While undoubtedly various factors, especially politics and power (both direct and structural), continue to play important roles in dictating the substance and reach of ICL, I nonetheless suggest that power relations are both enabled, and subtly shaped by, aesthetic biases, especially when it comes to the identification of potential international crimes. Thus, in sum, this book demonstrates how aesthetically unfamiliar forms of mass harm causation – those that are slow, attritive, banal, and hence generally unspectacular in nature – have been relegated to the margins of international criminal justice; why this backgrounding is not always the

[18] Itamar Mann, "Border Violence as Crime" (2021) 42 *University of Pennsylvania Journal of International Law* 675–736, 723.

[19] That said, in terms of doctrinal interpretation, while I recognize the inherent limitations of ICL in terms of the forms of violence and oppression it can address given its foundational exclusive focus on individual culpability, I am of the view that ICL doctrine should be interpreted in a way that, as far as possible, encompasses all of the many ways in which individuals may culpably participate in large-scale harm causation.

product of the inherent limitations or doctrinal substance of ICL; how it compounds the broader invisibility of these forms of violence and oppression; and, from an interactional theoretical perspective, how this state of affairs undermines the legal legitimacy of ICL.

Ultimately, through this analysis, I conclude that there is a pressing need to question and reassess our assumptions concerning what international crimes are, how they are committed, and how they will manifest themselves. One critical component of such a process of reevaluation would be to more carefully assess the myriad and often banal ways in which power may be wielded to kill, abuse, and oppress, and how ICL might better address both spectacular *and* everyday forms of atrocity violence.

Defining Aesthetics: Sense Perception in Individual and Social Meaning-Making

At this juncture, a note on how the term "aesthetics" is deployed is necessary, given that the term has been defined in many ways, and applied in many disparate contexts. In a broad sense, the term aesthetics is typically used to "encompass the perception, production, and response to art, as well as interactions with objects and scenes that evoke an intense feeling, often of pleasure."[20] For the purposes of this book, in a general sense, the term aesthetics is understood to refer to both individual and social processes of the perception, production, and response to scenes evoking an intense emotional reaction, in this case a decidedly negative one, of horror, disgust, terror, or the like. More specifically, I am interested in aesthetics both as it may be used to refer to a particular style, model, or set of conventions (as in a cubist, or art deco "aesthetic"), and in relation to individual and social processes of sense perception (often referred to as "aesthetic perception").

In terms of *individual* processes of aesthetic perception, I borrow Ioannis Xenakis and Argyris Arnellos' "interactive affordance" model that situates aesthetic perception as an intuitive process that assists us in interacting with the world despite ever present, yet highly variable degrees of uncertainty. According to this model, for each of us a "particular perception should be considered 'aesthetic' when ... potential interactions ... are emotionally evaluated."[21] According to this

[20] Anjan Chatterjee, "Neuroaesthetics: A Coming of Age Story" (2010) 23 *Journal of Cognitive Neuroscience* 53–62: 53.

[21] Ioannis Xenakis and Argyris Arnellos, "Aesthetic Perception and Its Minimal Content: A Naturalistic Perspective" (2014) 5 *Frontiers in Psychology* 1–15: 11.

definition, "'the aesthetic' is nothing more than a way of interaction [that helps us] to cope with the environment."[22] While we may rely to some degree on aesthetic perception in virtually all of our daily interactions, from the banal to the extraordinary, the primary role aesthetic perception plays in this model is that of allowing us to act despite persistent, yet highly variable, degrees of uncertainty. We thus rely more heavily on the intuitive process of aesthetic perception "in situations that are mainly characterized by high degrees of uncertainty and minimal knowledge."[23]

As is made clear in Chapter 2, for various reasons, ICL represents an environment rife with uncertainty and lack of knowledge. Consequently, actors seeking to identify potential international crimes are apt to heavily rely, knowingly or not, on aesthetic perception to resolve ambiguity and fill in knowledge gaps. In other words, these actors are inclined to look for situations closely resembling widely acknowledged prior examples of international crimes when identifying potential new instances of genocide, crimes against humanity and/or war crimes.

While the interactive affordance model helps us to conceptualize the role aesthetic perception plays in individual notions of what is and is not a potential international crime, the question remains how these individual aestheticized processes of sense-making aggregate to influence socially constructed notions of atrocity, mass violence, international crime, genocide, and the like. To describe the *social* ramifications of the aggregation of individual processes of aesthetic perception as actors interact, and the production of dominant aesthetic forms, conventions, or models, this book borrows Jacques Rancière's concept of aesthetics as the "partition" or "distribution" of that which is "sensible" within a given society or social group, that is, the deeply political process of determining both who can speak and what can be spoken about legibly.[24] This is where various forms of power, both direct and structural, come into play in shaping how we perceive atrocity violence, as Rancière reminds us that not everyone is given an equal voice, nor allowed to speak in and through this distributive process. Rancière's framework is also highly compatible with the social constructivist foundations of interactional legal theory, as it allows for the partitioning of knowability to be understood as an ongoing process through which what is socially and politically sensible

22 Ibid.
23 Ibid., 12.
24 Jacques Rancière, *The Politics of Aesthetics: The Distribution of the Sensible*, trans. Gabriel Rockhill (Continuum, 2013).

(in this case as an "atrocity" or "international crime") is determined that is continual and perpetual.

These twin frameworks of individual and social sense-making processes as shaped by aesthetic factors, resulting over time in the construction of dominant aesthetic models, allow us to see how certain ways of conceptualizing international crimes and associated harms predominate over others. Many individuals may, and probably do, conceptualize various unspectacular, everyday forms of violence and abuse as crimes. For example, in interacting with rural Cambodian survivors of the Khmer Rouge regime, I was routinely asked whether the Extraordinary Chambers in the Courts of Cambodia (ECCC)[25] would prosecute those tried before it for "starving" them, or forcing them to live in terrible conditions separated from their loved ones. For at least these individuals, none of whom had any legal training to my knowledge, the distinction between traditional forms of (direct, physical) atrocity violence and other forms of abuse and oppression they suffered was nonexistent, or at least not significant. Indeed, it was these extended experiences of deprivation and suffering that were repeatedly highlighted by survivors, even as the Court itself focused predominantly on more traditional forms of atrocity (beatings, torture, executions, etc.) in its adjudication of the regime's crimes.

It is this dynamic, whereby that which is knowable ("sensible") is "partitioned," that I employ Rancière's concept of aesthetics as the "partition of the sensible" to describe. I view the processes through which such partition occurs as being multifaceted, deeply intertwined with power relations, and importantly, both the product of intentional and nonpurposive norm development processes. The net result of this partitioning process is that, through power dynamics and sociopolitical processes of dictating what is knowable, sayable, and understandable, in terms of what forms mass violence and abuse may take, what international crimes are, how they manifest themselves, who commits them, how they are committed, and who is victimized is established and maintained over time.

Thus, this book is interested both in the role intuitive processes of sense perception play in shaping how we interact with the world and, in doing so, identify abstract phenomena such as international crimes or

[25] The ECCC is a hybrid United Nations-Cambodian tribunal with jurisdiction over senior leaders and others most responsible for the commission of various international and domestic crimes in Cambodia from 1975 to 1979. On the ECCC generally, see John D. Ciorciari and Anne Heindel, *Hybrid Justice: The Extraordinary Chambers in the Courts of Cambodia* (University of Michigan Press, 2014).

atrocity violence, and also in how, over time, such individualized experiences feed into the construction and maintenance of dominant social understandings. In the case of ICL, I argue that a variety of factors, prime among them being the aesthetic spectacularity and self-evident nature of many (yet not all) atrocity crimes, combined with the continuing ambiguity of ICL normatively and doctrinally, and extreme selectivity in application, have combined to render certain potential international crimes non-"sensible" as such, at least to key actors.

It is this dynamic, tied up as it is in power and notions of what harms entail sufficient culpability and are of sufficient gravity to warrant being branded "international crimes" developed primarily by elites and technocrats, rather than those subject to oppression, precarity, and violence, that has resulted in the current myopic focus on horrific spectacle when conceptualizing international crime as a category of phenomena. To return to the example of Cambodia, an elite group of mostly international experts and later a mix of international and Cambodian legal professionals and investigators were able to prescribe and prioritize what actions amounted to international crimes during the Khmer Rouge era and determine how to prioritize among them. From the outset, what was sayable and knowable as a crime was largely preordained, not only by applicable law but also by deep-seated assumptions concerning the nature of causality, the feasibility of evidence collection and required proofs, and the relative severity and importance of various harms. Through this process, potentially novel instantiations of international crimes committed by the regime, in the form of the cumulative effects of sustained deprivation, overwork, and generalized mistreatment, were cordoned off and relegated to the background, as either unexplored potential crimes, or more often, by being framed as collateral causes or consequences of more aesthetically familiar, and hence more "real" in a legal sense, forms of atrocity violence.

Theoretical Framework: Interactional Legal Theory

To demonstrate the influential role aesthetics play in shaping dominant notions of what international crimes are, this book utilizes an interactional legal theory framework of social and legal norm development. Developed by Jutta Brunnée and Stephen Toope, interactional theory is a practice-based model of lawmaking, legitimacy, and legality at the international level, built on a merger of social constructivist international relations scholarship and Lon Fuller's work on the "internal morality" of law.[26] Social constructivists "focus attention upon the role that culture, ideas, institutions, discourse and social norms play in shaping identity and influencing behaviour."[27] Brunnée and Toope merge this approach to social norm development with legal theory, especially Fuller's well-known theory of legality, itself often used as a rule of law assessment tool. They do so by adapting Fuller's eight "criteria of legality" to the international level, where they contend a broad spectrum of actors, ranging from individuals to states, continually make, and refine (or unmake) international law as they interact with one another.[28]

Interactional legal theory views international law as consisting of a web of widely shared, socially constructed normative understandings that have been instantiated into law in substantial compliance with Fuller's eight criteria of legality, and thereafter sustained by practices of legality.[29] Fuller's legality criteria are:

1. generality;
2. promulgation;
3. nonretroactivity;
4. clarity;
5. noncontradiction;
6. possible to follow;
7. constancy (or stability); and
8. congruence between the law and official action.[30]

Fuller famously argued that only when rules substantially satisfy these characteristics can they properly be labeled "law."[31] Thus, for Fuller, rules purporting to be law that substantially depart from these criteria fail to exhibit the necessary basic characteristics of law, and hence represent some extra-legal form of rulemaking or exercise of power. Aside from

[26] Jutta Brunnée and Stephen J. Toope, *Legitimacy and Legality in International Law: An Interactional Account* (Cambridge University Press, 2010); Lon L. Fuller, *The Morality of Law* (Yale University Press, 1969).

[27] Jutta Brunnée and Stephen J. Toope, "Constructivism and International Law," in Jeffrey L. Dunoff and Mark A. Pollack, eds., *Interdisciplinary Perspectives on International Law and International Relations* (Cambridge University Press, 2012), 119–145.

[28] See Jutta Brunnée and Stephen J. Toope, "Interactional International Law: An Introduction" (2011) 3 *International Theory* 307–318: 309.

[29] See generally Brunnée and Toope, *Legitimacy and Legality in International Law*.

[30] Brunnée and Toope, "Interactional International Law," 310.

[31] See Fuller, *Morality of Law*. This legitimation as true "law" is, in turn, key for Brunnée and Toope because for them "true" (i.e., interactional) law attracts a special "sense of commitment among those to whom law is addressed." Ibid., 308; see also Brunnée and Toope, *Legitimacy and Legality in International Law*, 52–55.

mere issues of proper labeling, Fuller as well as Brunnée and Toope claim that only norms and rules properly labeled as "law" by substantially conforming to Fuller's eight criteria attract the unique value-added status of legality, that of habitual obeyance, which Fuller refers to as "fidelity" and Brunnée and Toope refer to as legal "obligation."[32] That is, only when rules and norms are instantiated into law in substantial accordance with Fuller's criteria of legality, and for Brunnée and Toope, are also thereafter supported by robust practices of legality, do such norms and rules create a sense of legal obligation, and can hence be accurately labeled as international "law" from the perspective of interactional legal theory.[33]

Whether a norm or rule is or is not properly labelable as "law," however, is not a binary yes or no assessment. Fuller himself claimed that each of his eight legality criteria may, both cumulatively and individually, be satisfied in degrees.[34] Accordingly, legality *exists* in degrees according to both Fuller, and Brunnée and Toope.[35] This view of legality as a continuum of degrees, along with their requirement of law being sustained through robust practices of legality, combines for Brunnée and Toope to create a view of international lawmaking (or unmaking) as a dynamic, ongoing process, rather than a sequential formula with a distinct beginning and end. The degree to which purported international legal norms are subject to widely shared understandings, have been instantiated into law in accordance with Fuller's criteria of legality, and are supported by robust practices of legality, therefore, dictates the degree to which Brunnée and Toope would characterize such norms as "interactional" international law. Thus, in the words of Brunnée and Toope, the "hard work" of international lawmaking is never done but represents a continual, dynamic, nonlinear enterprise.[36]

Interactional legal theory provides the overarching methodological framework through which norm development, lawmaking, and legal legitimacy are conceptualized in this book. As a social constructivist, practice-based theory, interactionalism is particularly useful as a methodological framework for exploring the normative epistemological forces underlying the current international criminal justice

[32] Brunnée and Toope, *Legitimacy and Legality in International Law*, 27.

[33] Ibid., 350–355.

[34] Fuller, *Morality of Law*.

[35] Fuller referred to this dynamic as law's ability to "half-exist." Ibid., 122–123; accord Brunnée and Toope, *Legitimacy and Legality in International Law*, 22–23.

[36] Brunnée and Toope, *Legitimacy and Legality in International Law*, 6–19, 72.

regime and for identifying how such forces influence the substance and practice of ICL itself. First, interactional theory, particularly its notion of "shared understandings," provides a helpful model for describing how the widely shared assumptions of social actors may influence the formation, interpretation, and evolution of ICL. As such, interactional legal theory helps to describe and articulate how widely shared assumptions concerning the means through which international crimes may be committed may help drive legal practices, and eventually even change the law. Through such processes, as Brunnée and Toope have argued, "power relations and even violence can be hidden or justified by new norms, including new legal norms."[37] Interactionalism thus helps elucidate how excessive reliance on intuitive processes of aesthetic perception in identifying atrocities may contribute to the social and legal invisibility of aesthetically unfamiliar international crimes. It also helps us to see the power dynamics underlying such invisibility.

Second, interactionalism also provides a method of analysis for differentiating between shared normative understandings that have, versus have not, been instantiated into international law. Only understandings that have been instantiated into law in substantial accordance with Fuller's criteria of legality may legitimately lay claim to the label of "law" per interactional theory. This framework thus facilitates an analysis of whether aesthetic considerations and associated politics of recognition *affect* the practice of ICL while remaining outside of the law, as opposed to having been instantiated into ICL itself. It is one thing for assumptions concerning the means through which international crimes may be committed to gradually shape the evolution of the doctrinal substance of ICL to focus narrowly and exclusively on such means. It is another thing for such assumptions to shape legal practices while themselves remaining extralegal and unacknowledged, as I argue is often the case when it comes to hidden forms of atrocity violence.

Regardless of the legal status of the normative assumptions underlying ICL's aesthetic biases, interactionalism provides a useful tool for assessing the broader ramifications of such biases for the legal legitimacy of ICL by facilitating an analysis of how aesthetic assumptions concerning the nature of international crime commission operate to encourage congruence or deviation from Fuller's criteria of legality in practice. I argue that, in the case of ICL, deep-seated expectations that international crimes will always and necessarily announce themselves in spectacular, self-evident

[37] Brunnée and Toope, "Constructivism and International Law," 137.

fashion continue to undergird widely shared normative understandings concerning the means through which international crimes may be committed and forms they may take. Critically, such expectations, despite their virtual ubiquity, have not in any meaningful way been instantiated into the actual doctrinal substance of ICL itself, which remains largely means-neutral and unspecific when it comes to the forms commission may take. Despite not being instantiated into ICL, such aestheticized understandings continue to influence legal practices associated with ICL, pushing spectacular crimes to the foreground and unspectacular ones to the background. Such influence undermines the generality and clarity of ICL in practice and widens the gap between ICL's potential applicability and its actual practice. Consequently, from an interactional perspective, I argue that the grounding of shared understandings of atrocity and international crime in an aesthetics of horrific spectacle undermines the legal legitimacy of ICL.

Chapter Overview

Chapter 2 explores shared understandings of the subject matter and purposes of ICL. I argue that the tendency to collectively describe genocide, crimes against humanity, and war crimes as crimes of "atrocity" or "mass violence" is indicative of an implicit aesthetic framing of these crimes as horrific spectacles. I make this argument in two parts. First, I identify atrocity as the general subject matter ICL is dominantly viewed as being tasked with addressing and compare various proposed definitions of atrocity. While these proposed definitions coalesce around a basic framing of atrocities as instances of large-scale culpable harm causation, in the second part, I argue that the deployment of the rhetoric of atrocity and mass violence also brings with it a set of aesthetic presumptions and sensibilities.

I do so by demonstrating how, as both a general concept and the presumed core subject matter of ICL, the concept of atrocity is grounded in an aesthetics of horrific spectacle. I then demonstrate how this dominant "atrocity aesthetic" model has both aided in garnering support for ICL and subtly shaped shared understandings of international crime. This chapter demonstrates that the association between atrocity (and later "atrocity crimes") and an aesthetics of horrific spectacle is both deep-seated and longstanding and has helped to uncritically embed the notion that all international crimes will manifest themselves as highly visible, intuitively recognizable harms in the social and legal imaginaries of international law and international criminal justice.

Chapter 3 considers why shared understandings of international crime appear to remain so deeply intertwined within the atrocity aesthetic, even as this normative linkage itself remains largely unacknowledged. Combining insights from social constructivist models of norm development and research on the role aesthetic perception plays in individual and social processes of identification and recognition, I theorize ICL as an especially ideal environment for aesthetic considerations to play a significant yet unacknowledged role in shaping shared understandings of what international crimes are over time. I do so by framing individual and social processes of meaning-making and norm development as relying more heavily on intuitive processes of aesthetic perception when occurring within a context of uncertainty and lack of knowledge. Defining individual processes of aesthetic perception as emotional, intuitive evaluative processes that are "aesthetic" in nature in that they involve assessments of "rightness" grounded in sensory experience, I argue that, through a persistent "know it when you see it" approach to identifying potential international crimes, understandings of atrocity and international crime have remained embedded in an aesthetics of horrific spectacle.

Chapter 4 assesses the degree to which the atrocity aesthetic accurately captures the full array of forms that genocide, crimes against humanity, and war crimes may actually take. This chapter argues that the current dominant atrocity aesthetic oversimplifies the highly complex nature of many processes of mass killing and abuse and misrepresents the boundaries of ICL in relation to such processes. The atrocity aesthetic fails to capture the complexity of mass harm causation processes, which are social phenomena that unfold dynamically over large expanses of time and space through a host of overlapping, mutually reinforcing means. Many such means, particularly those which are slow, attritive, and/or socioeconomic in nature, fail to conform to the atrocity aesthetic and, hence, tend not to be conceptualized as potential international crimes. While this exclusion from international criminal justice of unspectacular forms of violence is often presumed to be wholly attributable to limitations in the doctrinal substance of ICL or the intrinsic limitations of criminal law more generally, this chapter demonstrates that this is not always the case. It does so by identifying areas of apparent overlap between ICL and a variety of aesthetically unfamiliar modalities of atrocity commission, ranging from the enforcement of famine conditions to socioeconomic oppression.

Chapter 5 grounds the preceding analysis by providing examples of real-world situations involving the likely commission of genocide, crimes against humanity, and/or war crimes through means failing to conform to the atrocity aesthetic identified. Such situations have, predictably, been relegated to the margins of international criminal justice or been viewed as altogether beyond the purview of ICL. Examples discussed include the enforcement of famine conditions and everyday violence in Khmer Rouge-era Cambodia, the starvation of civilians in occupied Poland and other Axis-controlled territories during World War II, the slow, multifaceted genocidal processes experienced by Indigenous populations in North America and elsewhere, colonial-era atrocities attendant to wealth and resource extraction, and the longstanding persecution of minority groups in various locations ranging from the United States to Myanmar. Such examples demonstrate that a host of atrocity commission processes failing to conform to the atrocity aesthetic may violate ICL, *de lege lata*, yet continue to be dominantly viewed as structurally excluded from the purview of ICL.

Chapter 6 explores some of the broader implications of ICL's aesthetic biases. It does so by framing ICL as operating as a spotlight, one that highlights the wrongfulness and impact of certain forms of violence while obscuring the severity, wrongfulness, and criminality of other forms of violence. As such, ICL's aesthetic biases arguably not only impair the efficacy of international criminal justice as a bulwark against atrocity commission, but also entail negative consequences for historical memory, the distribution of human rights, transitional justice and peacebuilding resources, and help facilitate the ongoing oppression of groups who remain under-acknowledged as victims of past atrocity crimes and/or whose ongoing victimization fails to conform to the atrocity aesthetic. Moreover, ICL's aesthetic selectivity also arguably undermines the retributive, utilitarian, and expressive credentials of international criminal justice as a global project. In terms of retributive goals, ICL's aesthetic selectivity problematically inserts arguably irrelevant factors into determinations of what constitutes an international crime, who should be held accountable, and how the extremely scarce resources of international criminal justice should be allocated. In terms of utilitarian goals, aesthetic selectivity creates a risk that any deterrent effect ICL may have, presently or in the future, may be undermined by allowing powerful actors to enjoy impunity so long as they commit international crimes through unspectacular means. Finally, the expressive value of ICL is also undermined by the current preoccupation with visibility and spectacle. The salutary effects of ICL, of attaching social stigma to certain harmful behaviors, and those responsible therefor, and in recognizing the victimhood of those harmed, are all undermined by the continued message emanating from ICL that, so long as violence, oppression, and persecution do not shock our aesthetic sensibilities, they remain relatively tolerable from the perspective of international criminal justice, regardless of their potential scale and severity. Thus, as a global project, international criminal justice risks expressing the troubling norm that only when atrocities aesthetically manifest themselves in ways that offend the sensibilities of key constituencies clustered in the Global North, by confronting them with horrific spectacles of violence in faraway places, are they deemed worthy of recognition as international crimes and all that comes with such recognition. This state of affairs problematically renders those exposed to the horrors of atrocity violence as a kind of collateral class of quasi victims of international crimes. It also may play into tropes of the "savage" Global South, where atrocities seemingly exclusively occur, and the "civilized" Global North, where atrocities seemingly do not occur and where "justice" emanates from.[38] Pursuant to this deeply problematic narrative, racialized men in the Global South become the sole visible authors of an extreme, exoticized form of violent criminality. Meanwhile, the more banal, everyday forms of violence that disproportionately, though not solely, affect the lives of residents of the Global South, often along racial and gendered lines, is further relegated to the periphery of global justice concerns.

In addition to these problematic ramifications in terms of the traditional criminal law justifications for ICL, the aesthetic selectivity of international criminal justice also negatively affects historical memory and the distribution of global justice resources and aid. Histories of oppression and atrocity may be misremembered, and the culpability of those responsible obscured, by shifting the tenor of the language used in discussing such histories from that of criminal law, implying direct human causation and culpability, to more ambiguous language, such as the causally neutral language of "disaster," "tragedy," or "mistake." In terms of material repercussions, given ICL's highly influential position within the architecture of global justice, blind spots in ICL affect the

[38] Makau Mutua, "Savages, Victims, and Saviors: The Metaphor of Human Rights" (2001) 42 *Harvard International Law Journal* 201–245.

distribution of material resources earmarked as contributions to human rights, transitional justice, and peacebuilding. The tendency to not see aesthetically unfamiliar atrocities thus may prevent civil society actors and social justice activists from accessing certain resources and sources of funding if they are in a location where mass harms have been caused through means failing to conform to the atrocity aesthetic. Moreover, how historical narratives are framed also often have continuing material ramifications and may help to perpetuate the continuing oppression of groups who have experienced atrocities in the past. By masking the intentional, oft-criminal roots of violence that has, over time, become increasingly structural in nature, such structural forms of oppression and violence become easier to dismiss the importance of or deny the existence of altogether. Moreover, in postcolonial contexts, former colonial nations are more able to conceptually transform capital accumulated through long histories of atrocity commission into wealth acquired through means other than those involving the commission of atrocity crimes. Thus, the aesthetic selectivity of ICL may be seen as part of a broader obfuscation of the directness of the relationship between the current global distribution of wealth and capital and the role of atrocity commission in the initial capture and accumulation of such wealth.

Chapter 7, returning to interactional legal theory, considers the legal legitimacy ramifications of ICL's aesthetic biases. Using interactional legal theory's models of legality and legitimacy, I argue that the aesthetic biases identified in this book operating within international criminal justice undermine ICL's legal legitimacy. In doing so, I argue that such biases undermine key interactional criteria of legality, including generality, clarity, stability, and congruence between the substance and actual practice of the law. In particular, I argue that aesthetic biases distort practices of legality associated with ICL, jeopardizing the gains ICL has made toward legal legitimacy in terms of the instantiation of relevant legal norms.

Conclusion

The overarching argument advanced in this book is that there exists a dominant, longstanding assumption that international crimes will adhere to a specific, easily recognizable aesthetic model. This model combines elements of familiarity (visceral, intuitive recognizability) and spectacle (large-scale public acts of violence). Crucially, this model captures only a subset, albeit a large and highly visible one, of the many ways in which genocide, crimes against humanity, and war crimes may manifest themselves. As such, there exists a need to reconsider the forms mass atrocity may take and means through which international crimes may be committed. Specifically, greater acknowledgment is needed of the fact that, although genocide, crimes against humanity, and war crimes are extraordinary in terms of their scale and the collective nature of their perpetration, such extraordinariness does not always translate directly into the production of violent spectacles. Greater recognition is needed of the reality that one of the extraordinary characteristics of mass atrocities is that they may be committed through unspectacular means precisely *because* they are large-scale, collective endeavors perpetrated by powerful actors. Thus, just as Hannah Arendt famously described the potential "banality" of those who participate in, or even lead, atrocities, I argue that there exists a need to acknowledge and grapple with the consequences of the fact that one of the ways in which atrocity crimes are extraordinary is that they may be committed through seemingly ordinary, even banal means. Only by recognizing this reality can the role ICL can and should play in addressing atrocity violence be properly considered.

2

The Atrocity Aesthetic

International Crimes as Horrific Spectacles

> *... during this century millions of children, women and men have been victims of unimaginable atrocities that deeply shock the conscience of humanity*[1]
>
> Rome Statute of the International Criminal Court, Preamble

> *... Whereas the adoption of the Rome Statute, with the establishment of the ICC, was in and of itself a new tidal force that changed the status quo of the world for the better, two decades after the Rome Conference, the system of international criminal justice created by the Statute continues to make significant waves toward building a culture of accountability for atrocity crimes.*[2]
>
> Fatou Bensouda, Former ICC Prosecutor

This chapter assesses the role aesthetics play in the social construction of dominant shared understandings of the so-called core crimes of ICL: genocide, crimes against humanity, and war crimes. It demonstrates how, since the inception of ICL, widely shared understandings of these crimes have remained grounded in an aesthetics of horrific spectacle, which I refer to as the "atrocity aesthetic." First, I demonstrate how, since its very inception, ICL has been, and continues to be, broadly conceptualized as a body of law tasked with assigning criminal responsibility to individuals who contribute to harm production on a massive scale, situations often referred to as "atrocities" or instances of "mass violence." After demonstrating this framing of ICL as an anti-atrocity project, the normative foundations of the concept of atrocity itself are explored. Examining several proposed definitions of atrocity, I identify three main common elements: harm, culpability, and scale. Thus, in a general sense, definitions of atrocity usually encompass instances of culpable harm causation on a large (or "mass") scale.

[1] Rome Statute of the International Criminal Court, Rome, July 17, 1998, in force July 1, 2002, 2187 UNTS 3, preamble.

[2] Fatou Bensouda, "Remarks at the Commemoration of the 20th Anniversary of the Adoption of the Rome Statute of the International Criminal Court," July 17, 2018, www.icc-cpi.int/itemsDocuments/20180717-otp-speech.pdf, 2.

While this basic definition does accurately reflect the general thrust of ICL liability, and hence, is not intrinsically problematic, I further demonstrate that the tendency to refer to genocide, crimes against humanity, and war crimes collectively as "atrocity crimes" both reflects and helps reproduce deep-seated normative linkages between these crimes and an aesthetics of horrific spectacle. That is, shared understandings of both atrocity and international crime are associated with spectacular acts of horrific violence and abuse, reflecting deeply held, if rarely articulated, assumptions concerning how genocide, crimes against humanity, and war crimes will manifest themselves and the means through which they may be committed. It is this dominant "atrocity aesthetic" model of international crime commission that the remainder of this book considers the causes and consequences of.

International Crimes as "Atrocity" Crimes

ICL is conceived of primarily as an anti-atrocity project. That is, ICL was created to address (and perhaps even repress) crimes of large-scale violence (often referred to as "atrocities") through the technique of criminal prosecution. This normative framing of international crimes as "atrocity crimes," whether useful or not, has persisted since the inception of ICL itself at Nuremberg.[3] From the 1943 Moscow Declaration and its description of Nazi crimes as atrocities, subsequently quoted in the 1945 London Agreement establishing the International Military Tribunal (IMT) at Nuremberg, to decisions issued by the IMT and subsequent ICL courts and tribunals, the rhetoric of atrocity permeates discourses of international criminal justice.[4] For example, the IMT's judgment repeatedly describes acts of mass killing and abuse committed against Jews and other

[3] The mainstream view dates the inception of contemporary ICL to post-World War II prosecutions by the Allies. Many scholars, however, take issue with this framing as being overly simplistic and ignoring various earlier prosecutions of individuals for actions characterizable as "international crimes" in some way. See, for example, Ziv Bohrer, "International Criminal Law's Millennium of Forgotten History" (2016) 34 *Law and History Review* 393–485. As this book focuses on mainstream understandings of ICL and international crime, it emphasizes the post-World War II prosecutions as the founding of contemporary ICL.

[4] USA–UK–USSR, Moscow Protocol, Moscow, USSR, October 30, 1943, in force November 1, 1943, 1943 For. Rel. (I) 749; France–USSR–UK–USA, Agreement by the Government of the United Kingdom of Great Britain and Northern Ireland, the Government of the United States of America, the Provisional Government of the French Republic, and the Government of the Union of Soviet Socialist Republics for the prosecution and punishment of the major war criminals of the European Axis, London, UK, August 8, 1945, in force August 8, 1945, 82 UNTS 79, preamble.

civilians in Germany and German-occupied territories as "atrocities."[5] As with the Moscow Declaration and London Agreement, the term is used primarily descriptively in the judgment, serving to describe, as well as underscore the brutality of, crimes committed by the Nazis.

This dominant conceptual framing of ICL as an anti-atrocity project[6] has changed little since Nuremberg. ICL continues to be broadly understood as a body of law tasked with delineating when and how individuals who participate in atrocities can be criminally prosecuted. The language of atrocity is employed to describe the horrific nature of international crimes committed in Rwanda, the former Yugoslavia, Cambodia, and Sierra Leone, in the jurisprudence of the international and hybrid courts created to prosecute the international crimes committed in these countries.[7] The preamble of the ICC's Rome Statute, meanwhile, references the continuing prevalence of "unimaginable atrocities that deeply shock the conscience of humanity" as a primary reason why the ICC itself is needed, going so far as to directly equate atrocities with international crimes by immediately following its reference to "unimaginable atrocities" with the assertion that "*such grave crimes* threaten the peace, security and well-being of the world."[8] The very raison d'être of the ICC is thus linked to atrocity punishment and prevention, as the Statute declares that the State Parties to the ICC are motivated by a shared "[d]etermin[ation] to put an end to impunity for the perpetrators of *these crimes* and thus to contribute to the prevention of *such crimes*," with the "crimes" in question, again, clearly referencing the aforementioned "unimaginable atrocities."[9] The Rome Statute thereby explicitly frames international crimes as atrocities

[5] See International Military Tribunal, *Trial of the Major War Criminals before the International Military Tribunal, Nuremberg 14 November 1945–1 October 1946*, 42 vols. (International Military Tribunal, 1947), vol. 1, pp. 175, 251, 270–271, 275, 296, 298, 300, 303, 338.

[6] Some argue the same could largely be said for human rights law, which also emerged in the wake of World War II. For example, David Kennedy argues: "[m]odern human rights advocacy was born in a burst of energy after the Second World War to people who wanted to respond to nonmilitary atrocities that seemed unthinkable, incomprehensible, even banal; who wanted to know them, tame them, redeem them as civilized, name them 'genocide,' bring them into polite parlance." David Kennedy, "Spring Break" (1985) 63 *Texas Law Review* 1377–1423: 1413–1414.

[7] See, for example, *Prosecutor* v. *Karemera and Ngirumpatse, ICTR-98-44-A, September 29, 2014*, ICTR, paras. 333, 353, 698; *Prosecutor* v. *Karadžić, IT-95-5/18-T, March 24, 2016*, ICTY, paras. 550, 3348, 3519, 4238, 4814, 5825, 6112; *Prosecutor* v. *Taylor, SCSL-03-01-A, September 26, 2013*, SCSL, paras. 275, 305–306, 317–318, 335, 454, 530, 538, 560; *Case 002/01, 002/19-09-2007/ECCC/TC, August 7, 2014*, ECCC, paras. 856, 958.

[8] Rome Statute, preamble (emphasis added).

[9] Ibid (emphasis added).

and assigns the ICC the task of prosecuting individuals who participate in such atrocities. This framing is repeated in various policy documents and statements made by court officials framing the ICC's "primary mission" as "help[ing] put an end to impunity for mass atrocities."[10]

References to atrocity are also commonplace in ICL-related policy documents and scholarship. For example, in 2014, the UN Office on Genocide Prevention and the Responsibility to Protect issued a *Framework of Analysis for Atrocity Crimes* policy document that defines "atrocity crimes" as a term referring to "three legally defined international crimes: genocide, crimes against humanity and war crimes."[11] Prominent advocacy and legal groups, such as the Global Centre for the Responsibility to Protect, Global Action Against Mass Atrocity Crimes, and American Bar Association, also refer collectively to genocide, crimes against humanity, and war crimes as atrocities or "mass" atrocities.[12] The rhetoric of atrocity is also employed regularly by scholars to generally reference the subject matter of ICL.[13] Indeed, while scholars may sharply disagree concerning whether, for example, ICL adequately prevents and/or punishes atrocity, the notion that it is atrocities that are to be

[10] International Criminal Court, "Joining the International Criminal Court: Why Does It Matter?," 2018, www.icc-cpi.int/Publications/Joining-Rome-Statute-Matters.pdf; see also, for example, Chile Eboe-Osuji, "Remarks at Opening Ceremony: 55th Ordinary Session of the Authority of Heads of State and Government of the Economic Community of West African States (ECOWAS)," June 29, 2019, www.icc-cpi.int/itemsDocuments/190629-ICC-President-remarks-ECOWAS-Summit-ENG.pdf.

[11] United Nations Office on Genocide Prevention and the Responsibility to Protect, *Framework of Analysis for Atrocity Crimes* (United Nations, 2014), 1.

[12] See, for example, Global Centre for the Responsibility to Protect, "Defining the Four Mass Atrocity Crimes," August 15, 2018, www.globalr2p.org/publications/defining-the-four-mass-atrocity-crimes (listing genocide, war crimes, crimes against humanity, and ethnic cleansing as "mass atrocity crimes"); Global Action against Mass Atrocity Crimes, "Prevention of Atrocities," www.gaamac.org/prevention-of-atrocities ("The term atrocities refers to genocide, crimes against humanity, war crimes and ethnic cleansing."); American Bar Association, "Atrocity Crimes Initiative," www.americanbar.org/groups/human_rights/preventing-atrocities (describing the initiative's goal as working "to prevent genocide, war crimes, and crimes against humanity").

[13] See, for example, Payam Akhavan, "Beyond Impunity: Can International Criminal Justice Prevent Future Atrocities?" (2001) 95 *American Journal of International Law* 7–31; Mark A. Drumbl, "Collective Violence and Individual Punishment: The Criminality of Mass Atrocity" (2004) 99 *Northwestern University Law Review* 539–610; Kirsten Fisher, *Moral Accountability and International Criminal Law: Holding Agents of Atrocity Accountable to the World* (Routledge, 2013); Mark Osiel, *Making Sense of Mass Atrocity* (Cambridge University Press, 2009); Saira Mohamed, "Deviance, Aspiration, and the Stories We Tell: Reconciling Mass Atrocity and the Criminal Law" (2015) 124 *Yale Law Journal* 1628–1689; Hyeran Jo and Beth A. Simmons, "Can the International Criminal Court Deter Atrocity?" (2016) 70 *International Organization* 443–475.

prevented and/or punished by this body of law remains subject to near-universal acceptance.[14]

Despite the ubiquity of the rhetoric of atrocity in ICL discourses, the term has never been defined with any specificity as it pertains to ICL, or for that matter international law more generally. Instead, atrocities have been treated as self-evident phenomena. Thus, the term "atrocity" performs both descriptive and definitional functions, often simultaneously. Atrocities are commonly presented as the general subject matter of ICL in a descriptive sense. However, when one asks what an atrocity is, the answer provided is likely to refer to the substance of ICL itself. That is, international crimes are described as atrocities, while atrocities are described as international crimes. There similarly exists no clear, widely agreed-upon general definition of what the universal hallmarks of an international crime are.[15] This state of affairs has led Roger O'Keefe to conclude that "[t]he approach one adopts to the concept of an international crime is as much a matter of taste as of law," often based on a "know it when you see it" approach.[16]

Examining how the term "atrocity" is rhetorically deployed within ICL-related discourses provides similarly little in the way of insight into the range of situations this term is meant to refer to. For example, Gideon Boas describes atrocities as situations of "war, . . . the rupture of society and . . . systematised murder and persecution."[17] The term is also regularly used interchangeably with similarly dramatic and emotionally resonant, yet definitionally vague and malleable turns of phrase, such as "mass violence," "gross human rights violations," or "horrors of the most severe order."[18] Others use phrases such as "organizational criminality,"

[14] See, for example, Akhavan, "Beyond Impunity"; Jo and Simmons, "Can the International Criminal Court Deter Atrocity?"; Kate Cronin-Furman, "Managing Expectations: International Criminal Trials and the Prospects for Deterrence of Mass Atrocity" (2013) 7 *International Journal of Transitional Justice* 434–454; Mark A. Drumbl, *Atrocity, Punishment and International Law* (Cambridge University Press, 2007).

[15] See, for example, Kevin Jon Heller, "What Is an International Crime? (A Revisionist History)" (2017) 58 *Harvard International Law Journal* 353–420: 354.

[16] Roger O'Keefe, *International Criminal Law* (Oxford University Press, 2015), 66.

[17] Gideon Boas, "What Is International Criminal Justice?," in Gideon Boas, Michael P. Scharf, and William Schabas, eds., *International Criminal Justice: Legitimacy and Coherence* (Edward Elgar, 2012), 1–24: 1.

[18] See, for example, Mirjan Damaška, "What Is the Point of International Criminal Justice?" (2008) 83 *Chicago-Kent Law Review* 329–365: 334–335, 342. Damaška argues that international criminal courts are overburdened by an overabundance of objectives but nonetheless frames ICL as a response to "massive human rights violations." Ibid., 330. Moreover, in a 2013 speech, then-ICC President Judge Sang-Hyun Song referenced the problematic continued existence of atrocities and stated that "[b]y encouraging national

"collective violence," or "system criminality" to highlight the group dynamics of genocide, crimes against humanity, and war crimes.[19] Each of these phrases is similar to atrocity in that they evoke a notion of largeness in terms of the scale and severity of relevant harms but also tend to evoke a preexisting archive of real-world events, from the Holocaust to the Rwandan Genocide. Notions of massiveness, severity, horror, or what characterizes "gross" human rights violations are, like atrocity, inherently subjective and malleable. Terms such as "mass" and "gross" gesture toward largeness in terms of scale, but imprecisely, and what constitutes "violence" is subject to a protracted, widely divergent definitional debate.[20] Thus, like atrocity, other common descriptors of international crimes tend to be definitionally vague while evoking notions of horrific, large-scale harms.

The basic understanding of ICL as a body of law that criminalizes individual contributions to the production of large-scale harm is not inherently problematic, as such understanding does roughly approximate the kinds of situations ICL is indeed applicable to, albeit in a highly generalized sense. Yet, this is not the extent of the normative substance of widely shared understandings of international crime. ICL did not invent the notions of atrocity, gross violations, mass violence, or the like, but

implementation under the principle of complementarity, the Rome Statute helps the global entrenchment of legal and social norms prohibiting mass violence." Sang-Hyun Song, "Keynote Remarks at Human Rights Council Side Event 'The International Criminal Court after 15 Years: Prospects for the Future'," September 10, 2013, www.icc-cpi.int/Pages/item.aspx?name=2013-09-10-President-keynote-Geneva. Similarly, Mark Drumbl, in an influential article, states that "[t]he prevailing paradigm views *mass atrocity* as something greater than the sum of its parts, namely each of its ordinary constituent murders. Under this paradigm, *mass violence* is constructed as something extraordinarily transgressive of universal norms." Drumbl, "Collective Violence," 540 (emphasis added); see also, for example, Jaya Ramji and Beth Van Schaack, eds., *Bringing the Khmer Rouge to Justice: Prosecuting Mass Violence before the Cambodian Courts* (Mellen Press, 2005); Alette Smeulers and Fred Grünfeld, *International Crimes and Other Gross Human Rights Violations* (Brill Nijhoff, 2011); Martha Minow, "Naming Horror: Legal and Political Words for Mass Atrocities" (2007) 2 *Genocide Studies and Prevention* 37–41: 38.

19 Drumbl, "Collective Violence"; André Nollkaemper, "Systemic Effects of International Responsibility for International Crimes" (2010) 8 *Santa Clara Journal of International Law* 313–352; Julian Ku, "How System Criminality Could Exacerbate the Weaknesses of International Criminal Law" (2010) 8 *Santa Clara Journal of International Law* 365–372; Mark A. Drumbl, "Accountability for System Criminality" (2010) 8 *Santa Clara Journal of International Law* 373–382.

20 For an overview of the many widely ranging approaches to defining violence, see Eugene Aisenberg et al., "Defining Violence," in Todd I. Herrenkohl et al., eds., *Violence in Context: Current Evidence on Risk, Protection, and Prevention* (Oxford University Press, 2010), 13–22.

rather this body of law has been broadly viewed as a juridical response to these concepts as preexisting phenomena. The way in which the rhetoric of atrocity, in particular, is deployed within ICL discourses suggests that the term is not merely used as a placeholder to refer generally to international crimes but reflects deeply held ideas of what makes up the essence of these crimes. Over time, through social interaction among relevant actors within legal and other expert communities, communities of norm entrepreneurs, and more generally within communities of practice relevant to ICL, shared understandings of what international crimes are have remained normatively moored to atrocity as a concept, begging the question of how atrocity itself is generally understood and conceptualized.

Defining Atrocity: Large-Scale Culpable Harm Causation

While the term "atrocity" lacks any legal definition under international law, a handful of scholars have attempted to define the term in a more general sense. Claudia Card, David Scheffer, and Scott Straus stand out as exemplars within the fields of philosophy, law, and political science, respectively, who have sought to define atrocity.[21] While the substance of the respective definitions outlined by these and other scholars do differ in important ways, they also share three core elements: (1) culpability, (2) harm, and (3) scale. After identifying these core elements of atrocity as a normative and (pseudo) legal concept, I demonstrate how shared understandings of international "atrocity" crimes have always been, and continue to be, tied to deep-seated assumptions that large-scale culpable harm causation processes will manifest themselves as horrific spectacles whose criminality is intuitively recognizable.

Claudia Card: Atrocity as a Paradigm of Evil

A good place to start in attempts to understand and define atrocity is in the work of Claudia Card, who proposes the concept of atrocity as a paradigm for understanding evil (or in her framing, the plural,

[21] David Scheffer, "Genocide and Atrocity Crimes" (2006) 1 *Genocide Studies and Prevention* 229–250; Claudia Card, *The Atrocity Paradigm: A Theory of Evil* (Oxford University Press, 2002); Scott Straus, "What Is Being Prevented? Genocide, Mass Atrocity, and Conceptual Ambiguity in the Anti-Atrocity Movement," in Sheri P. Rosenberg, Tibi Galis, and Alex Zucker, eds., *Reconstructing Atrocity Prevention* (Oxford University Press, 2016), 17–30.

"evils") as a philosophical subject of inquiry.[22] For Card, there are two core elements of an atrocity: "wrongdoing and harm," meaning that atrocities are both "perpetrated and suffered," and consequently, there "is no such thing as an atrocity that just happens or an atrocity that hurts no one."[23] Thus, for Card, the core features of evils are agency, causation, and culpability (i.e. wrongdoing and harm). While she presents wrongdoing and harm as the core elements of any atrocity, Card adds another element of scale to her proposed definition by stating that atrocities are situations where wrongdoing and harm occur "writ large."[24]

Card's conception of atrocities as evils evokes the work of Hannah Arendt, who, in *The Human Condition*, refers to atrocities, such as those committed by the Nazis, as "those offenses which, since Kant, we call 'radical evil' and about whose nature so little is known, even to us who have been exposed to one of their rare outbursts on the public scene."[25] While Card herself adopts a rather broad view of relevant harms, for instance, allowing for nonhuman victims, her basic definition of atrocities as the combination of the three indispensable ingredients of wrongdoing, harm, and scale remains a helpful starting point for ruminations on the concept of atrocity.[26]

David Scheffer: Atrocity Crimes and Atrocity Law

While Card uses the concept of atrocity as an entrance point for a philosophical exploration of the concept of evil, former US Ambassador-at-Large for War Crimes Issues David Scheffer provides a more specific, decidedly legalistic definition of atrocity. Arguing that there exists a need to move away from overusing the rhetoric of genocide to refer to all instances of mass crime, Scheffer advocates for a shift in language to the use of the term "atrocity crimes" to generally refer to the types of serious

22 Card, *Atrocity Paradigm*, 4.

23 Ibid., 9.

24 Ibid.

25 Hannah Arendt, *The Human Condition*, 2nd ed. (University of Chicago Press, 1958), 241. Arendt goes on to state that "[a]ll we know is that we can neither punish nor forgive such offenses and that they therefore transcend the realm of human affairs and the potentialities of human power, both of which they radically destroy wherever they make their appearance." Ibid.

26 Card mentions such nontraditional atrocity modalities as "the domestic terrorism of prolonged battery, stalking, and child abuse," capital punishment, and "evils done to animals who are raised on factory farms and butchered in mass-production slaughterhouses" as examples of "atrocities" as a paradigm of evils that may strain more conservative conceptions of both atrocity and evil. Card is clear, however, that she adopts a particularly broad view of what amounts to an atrocity. Card, *Atrocity Paradigm*, 8–9.

international crimes that have traditionally been prosecuted at international criminal justice institutions.[27] Scheffer describes atrocities in terms of their "high-impact" on victims, "severe gravity," "orchestrated character," and ability to "shock the conscience of humankind."[28] This description, like Card's invocation of evil, evokes a commonly held sentiment famously voiced by Arendt – the notion that international crimes transcend the scope of domestic legal systems because of their sheer scale, which injures not only individual victims, but all of humanity as such.[29]

Scheffer views such crimes as being "of such magnitude and destructive character as to be particularly prominent and logically inconsistent with the protection of human rights and the maintenance of international peace and security."[30] He also references the "shocking" nature and high visibility of atrocity crimes, describing them as situations "that one would expect the international media and the international community to focus on as meriting an international response holding the lead perpetrators accountable before a competent court of law."[31] Ultimately, Scheffer defines "atrocity crimes" as consisting of five elements:

1. The crime must be of *significant magnitude*, meaning that its commission is widespread or systematic or occurs as part of a large-scale commission of such crimes. The crime must involve a relatively large number of victims (e.g. a fairly significant number of deaths or casualties), or impose other very severe injury upon noncombatant populations (e.g. massive destruction of private property), or subject a large number of combatants or prisoners of war to violations of the laws and customs of war.
2. The crime may occur in time of war, or in time of peace, or in time of violent societal upheaval of some organized character, and may be either international or non-international in character.
3. The crime must be identifiable in conventional international criminal law.

27 Scheffer, "Genocide and Atrocity Crimes," 230.
28 Ibid., 238.
29 In an oft-cited formulation of this idea of international crimes transcending the boundaries of domestic legal jurisdictions, Hannah Arendt, observing the Eichmann trial noticed that "[i]nsofar as the victims were Jews, it was right and proper that a Jewish court should sit in judgment; but insofar as the [Holocaust] was a crime against humanity, it needed an international tribunal to do justice to it." Hannah Arendt, *Eichmann in Jerusalem: A Report on the Banality of Evil* (Penguin Classics, 2006), 269.
30 Scheffer, "Genocide and Atrocity Crimes," 238.
31 Ibid., 239.

4. The crime must have been led, in its execution, by a ruling or otherwise powerful elite in society . . . who planned the commission of the crime and were the leading perpetrators of the crime.
5. The law applicable to such crime, . . . [is] regarded under customary international law as holding *individuals criminally liable* for the commission of such crime, thus enabling the prosecution of such individuals before a court duly constituted for such purpose.[32]

Thus, while much more detailed and legalistic than Card's, Scheffer's proposed definition of "atrocity crimes" retains Card's three core elements of wrongdoing (Scheffer's elements 3 and 5), harm (Scheffer's element 1), and scale (Scheffer's elements 1 and 4). Scheffer also views legal responses to atrocity as not being limited to ICL, instead advocating for the acknowledgment of a specific body of "atrocity law" drawn from a composite of ICL, international humanitarian law, international human rights law, and the law of war.[33] Scheffer argues that it is this composite body of "atrocity law," not solely ICL, which modern international criminal tribunals, including the ICC, apply.[34]

At first glance, Scheffer's proposed definition appears much more substantive and detailed than Card's basic combination of wrongdoing, harm, and scale. Yet, upon close reading, Scheffer's definition merely attaches legal requirements to Card's basic definition of atrocity by utilizing the label "atrocity *crimes*." Otherwise, Scheffer's definition closely tracks that of Card, as his requirement of "magnitude" is comparable to Card's "writ large" qualifier. Meanwhile, his requirement that relevant atrocity acts violate law that provides for the criminal prosecution of individuals clearly imports with it (a perhaps more stringent version of) Card's element of "wrongdoing" by requiring law providing for individual criminal culpability.

Beyond these similar elements, Scheffer merely limits his definition of atrocity crimes to an apparent subset of international crimes. He notes that international crimes may now be committed within any societal context, be it a period of peace, armed conflict, or social upheaval. Scheffer also notes that applicable law (i.e. ICL) must provide for individual criminal responsibility and requires involvement of local elites in the commission of such crimes. These requirements also merely reflect

32 Ibid., 238–239.
33 Ibid., 245.
34 In this vein, Scheffer identifies various international crimes that clearly do not amount to atrocities according to this definition. Ibid., 244–246.

the substance of ICL itself, which provides solely for the prosecution of individuals, and the reality that only large-scale groups or other powerful group actors are able to actually commit genocide, crimes against humanity, and/or war crimes in the vast majority of cases. Of course, this excludes, for Scheffer, violence carried out by individual, non-elite actors, such as so-called lone wolf terrorists. However, this omission may be largely attributable to the fact that Scheffer proposed this definition of atrocity in 2006, predating many of the recent spate of uncoordinated yet large-scale terrorist attacks that have occurred in recent years.

Moreover, despite its seeming specificity, Scheffer's "atrocity crimes" definition provides only a rough outline of what an "atrocity" itself is. The elements of magnitude and commission by powerful actors gesture toward both a fundamental largeness in terms of the scope, size, and structure of atrocities and the harms suffered therefrom. The second element, that atrocities must be committed in "time of war, or in time of peace, or in time of violent societal upheaval of some organized character, and may be either international or non-international in character," adds little, if anything substantively, to Scheffer's definition, but merely confirms that international crimes can be committed in the midst of war or peace, or any other state of affairs for that matter.[35]

Finally, the third and fifth elements, that atrocity crimes violate ICL and the law provides for individual criminal responsibility, respectively, merely reference the elements of specific international crimes/modes of liability and the ICL principle of individual culpability, reflecting Scheffer's specific interest in atrocity "crimes."[36] This definition fails to

[35] Ibid., 238. It is unclear what state a society may be in other than being at war, at peace, or in violent upheaval. As such, this element appears to merely remind the reader that atrocity crimes can be committed within any social context but are not limited to periods of war. Moreover, this reference reminds the reader that whether and how ICL and various other areas of atrocity law apply to a situation, continues to fluctuate based on whether a state of armed conflict exists, and whether such armed conflict is international in nature or not.

[36] This is not to disparage the importance of these elements or the general utility of a shift in the language used to discuss ICL to one that revolves around the language of "atrocity," especially as a replacement for the unfortunate and incoherent use of the language of "genocide" in popular discourses to refer to ICL as a whole. Many important international actors, especially those with an interest of ICL who are not legal practitioners or scholars, benefit from the distinctions drawn by Scheffer, which summarize key developments within ICL that have removed previous, rather arbitrary barriers to international prosecutions, such as the former requirement that crimes against humanity and war crimes could solely be committed during periods of armed conflict legally characterized as international in nature.

delve into the complexities that can be involved in linking the acts of a perpetrator group sufficiently to both a harm suffered by the victim group and to an individual accused. As such, Scheffer limits his definition of atrocities to a subset of international crimes, but does little to elucidate the common characteristics such crimes share with one another, or to provide examples of noncriminal atrocities or non-atrocity international crimes (though he does gesture toward certain war crimes in this regard), thereby adding little in the way of substance, to discussions concerning the normative features of the subject matter he attempts to affix a label to.

Ultimately, Scheffer describes atrocity crimes in much the same way as Card defines atrocity itself, by focusing on individual culpability (i.e. wrongdoing) and the production of harm on a large scale (i.e. of a particular "magnitude" in Scheffer's words). By adding the qualifier "crimes" to that of atrocity, Scheffer, however, adds legal limitations to his definition, requiring the commission of acts "prohibited by recognizable" international law.[37] Thus, both Card and Scheffer arrive at relatively open-ended definitions of atrocities, which can seemingly encompass a broad spectrum of large-scale, culpable harm-causing behaviors.

Scott Straus: Atrocities as Large-Scale, Systematic Violence against Civilians

A more recent attempt to define atrocity is that of political scientist and prominent genocide studies scholar Scott Straus, who asserts that, while "mass atrocities and atrocities have no formal, legal definition, they usually refer to genocide, [crimes against humanity], war crimes, and ethnic cleansing," noting the common usage of the rhetoric of atrocity within the Responsibility to Protect (R2P) discursive framework.[38] Pursuant to an assessment of the general characteristics of these legal categories, Straus concludes that the protection of civilian and noncombatant populations from large-scale violence is a prominent, recurring theme common to the law of genocide, crimes against humanity, war crimes, and ethnic cleansing, while the R2P framework itself references more generally the protection of "populations."[39] As such, Straus proposes that atrocities be defined as instances of "large-scale, systematic violence against civilian populations" as a subject of public policy and scholarly

37 Scheffer, "Genocide and Atrocity Crimes," 238.
38 Straus, "What Is Being Prevented?," 23.
39 Ibid., 27.

study.[40] Straus' "large-scale, systematic violence" definition combines elements of scale, organization, violence and civilian victimhood, predicated on an underlying understanding of the term "civilian" as referring to any noncombatant.[41] Straus summarizes this definition thusly:

> The idea of large-scale, systematic implies that the violence is organized, repeated over time and space in a regular fashion, coordinated, widespread, and sustained. Violence includes killing but also includes other forms of deliberate harm being inflicted, such as rape, starvation, and population removal. As conceptualized here, civilians means noncombatants and combatants removed from conflict (e.g. prisoners of war).[42]

Straus views the term atrocity, as he defines it, as superior to other proposed labels, such as "mass killing" because "in contrast to mass atrocity, mass killing is exclusively about killing rather than a range of violence including starvation, attacks on shelter or water supplies, sexual violence, and other forms of violence."[43] Thus, in sum, Straus' proposed definition of atrocity contains elements of culpable harm causation (in the requirement of "deliberate" harm infliction), and scale (in the requirement of organized violence repeated over time), while also further limiting the class of victims to civilians (albeit based on an intentionally broad definition of civilian), and also requires a degree of organization in the commission of atrocities (in the requirements of violence being "coordinated"). Straus' definition also largely overlaps with that proposed by Bridget Conley and Alex de Waal, who use the term "mass atrocities" to refer to "widespread and systematic violence that results in the deaths of 50,000 or more civilians within a five-year period."[44] Like Straus, Conley and de Waal encompass within this definition "both killing as well as instances of the creation of conditions that bring about high levels of dying."[45] The most notable differences between these definitions being that, unlike Straus, Conley and de Waal focus

[40] Ibid., 18.
[41] Ibid., 27.
[42] Ibid., 29.
[43] Ibid., 27. This statement provides an implicit definition of what constitutes "violence" within Straus' proposed definition, which encompasses forms of harm causation beyond the direct physical application of force. Accordingly, Straus views his proposed definition of atrocity as synonymous with the concept of "mass violence," another term commonly used to describe the general subject matter of ICL. Ibid., 28.
[44] Bridget Conley-Zilkic and Alex de Waal, "Setting the Agenda for Evidence-Based Research on Ending Mass Atrocities" (2014) 16 *Journal of Genocide Research* 55–76: 57.
[45] Ibid., 57, note 10.

exclusively on harms resulting in victim deaths and set a numerical threshold in terms of number of victims.

Definitional Themes: Wrongdoing, Harm, and Scale

Despite the significant variation among the proposed definitions of atrocity suggested by Card, Scheffer, Straus, and Conley and de Waal, some basic commonalities do exist. On a basic level, each of these efforts to define atrocity references three key elements: wrongdoing, harm, and scale, albeit using differing terminology. In terms of wrongdoing, each definition refers in some way to blameworthy human agency as the driving factor behind atrocities. Card refers to this as "wrongdoing," while Scheffer references individual criminal culpability, and Straus refers to "deliberate harm being inflicted."[46] These definitions thus exclude harms caused primarily by nonhuman forces, such as those associated with unforeseen natural disasters such as hurricanes, tsunamis, earthquakes, and the like, as well as mere human error and run-of-the-mill negligence, thereby omitting tragic, yet unintentional accidents, such as airplane crashes or the like, which do not involve a sufficient degree of culpable human wrongdoing in their causation.[47]

Second, perhaps the most obvious and least contested element of atrocity is that of human suffering. All the proposed definitions discussed earlier reference the fact that atrocities have victims, who directly and acutely suffer. As Card pithily puts it, "there is no such thing as . . . an atrocity that hurts no one,"[48] while Scheffer and Straus both specify that atrocities involve the production of harm among civilian or otherwise

[46] Card, *Atrocity Paradigm*, 9; Scheffer, "Genocide and Atrocity Crimes," 239; Straus, "What Is Being Prevented?," 29.

[47] While this distinction is often quite clear, significant gray areas in terms of causation do exist. For example, when a government neglects to adequately respond to a natural disaster, exacerbating the suffering and death produced by it, such as occurred in Burma in 2008 in the aftermath of Cyclone Nargis, culpability for harm causation may be attributed to a complex mix of natural and human causes. For an analysis of the Myanmar Government's potential criminal responsibility for its failure to respond adequately to Nargis, see Stuart Ford, "Is the Failure to Respond Appropriately to a Natural Disaster a Crime against Humanity? The Responsibility to Protect and Individual Criminal Responsibility in the Aftermath of Cyclone Nargis" (2010) 38 *Denver Journal of International Law & Policy* 227–276.

[48] Card, *Atrocity Paradigm*, 9. It is worth noting that Card would include harms suffered by nonhuman animals, such as "evils done to animals who are raised on factory farms and butchered in mass-production slaughterhouses" and egregious environmental harms as falling within her avowedly expansive definition of atrocity as a model of evils. Ibid., 8–9.

noncombatant (human) populations.[49] While Card's broad philosophical paradigm of atrocity does not parse between categories of victims, she does acknowledge that in a traditional sense, atrocities are understood to have human victims, although she herself does not prescribe to this view.[50] Conley and de Waal, meanwhile, define atrocities in terms of a threshold of civilian deaths over a five-year period.

The third and final universal element of atrocity is that of scale, in terms of number of victims affected and the severity of such suffering. Indeed, a certain threshold of seriousness is heavily implied, but not explicitly required, by the ordinary dictionary definition of atrocity, which references acts that are "extremely wicked, brutal or cruel ... appalling, horrifying [or] utterly revolting: abominable."[51] Presumably, acts only rise to such a high level of egregiousness or extreme wickedness when they involve the production of harm on a large scale. Card, Scheffer, and Straus all explicitly include qualitative scale requirements in their respective definitions.[52] In contrast, Conley and de Waal propose a numerical threshold specifically in terms of civilian deaths, that of 50,000 excess deaths over a five-year period, for their working definition of atrocity.[53]

While, in many instances, references to scale and gravity tend to equate atrocity with mass killing,[54] one can easily imagine situations of mass harm causation not necessarily involving killing, such as the large-scale commission of sexual violence, or torture, that could rise to a level of severity sufficient to be labeled an atrocity as defined by Card, Scheffer, and Straus, along with conforming to the basic dictionary definition of

49 Scheffer, "Genocide and Atrocity Crimes," 238; Straus, "What Is Being Prevented?," 29.

50 Card intentionally leaves open the question of whether situations she views as contemporary evils, such as large-scale factory farming involving the ill-treatment and subsequent mass slaughter of nonhuman animals, may be considered "atrocities." Card, *Atrocity Paradigm*, 8–9.

51 See *Merriam-Webster Dictionary*, "atrocious" (defining the adjective atrocious alternatively as "extremely wicked, brutal, or cruel: barbaric" ... "appalling, horrifying" or "utterly revolting: abominable"); see also similar formulations in the *Oxford English Dictionary*. Oxford University Press, *Oxford English Dictionary*, www.oed.com, "atrocious."

52 Card notes that atrocities involve wrongdoing and harm "writ large." Card, *Atrocity Paradigm*, 9. Scheffer repeatedly references the scale of atrocity crimes, referring to their "high-impact" on victims, "severe gravity," "orchestrated character," and ability to "shock the conscience of humankind." Scheffer, "Genocide and Atrocity Crimes," 238. Straus, meanwhile, explicitly requires a threshold of scale in defining atrocities as "large-scale, systematic violence." Straus, "What Is Being Prevented?," 18.

53 Conley-Zilkic and de Waal, "Setting the Agenda," 57.

54 Ibid.

atrocity, although such a situation would be excluded from Conley and de Waal's working definition. This scale requirement typically serves a dual purpose, referring to both the severity of harm suffered by individual victims and to the number of victims affected.[55]

While some scale requirement is included in each definition of atrocity, aside from Conley and de Waal's definition, the threshold where this element is satisfied tends to be described in qualitative, rather than quantitative terms, as there exists a general unease with formulating a precise combination of severity of harm and number of victims necessary for a situation to be labeled an atrocity.[56] In addition to these three common elements, other recurring themes include the notions that atrocities involve coordinated action by groups and often involve some degree of complicity or involvement by state or other similarly powerful actors. These qualifiers, however, tend to relate back to the three core elements of atrocity, as they describe the kinds of actors who possess sufficient power and influence to cause harm on a massive scale, and the kinds of situations, such as armed conflict or periods of social breakdown, during which atrocities tend to occur.

When one considers the proposed definitions of atrocity provided by Card, Scheffer, Straus, and Conley and de Waal together, it is clear that, while the relatively amorphous concept of atrocity may defy any attempt at arriving at a singular, precise definition subject to universal agreement, in a general sense the term gestures toward situations wherein harms are culpably caused on a large or massive scale. Thus, in the most general sense one may describe atrocities as situations involving culpable mass harm causation, and which are likely to involve the commission of genocide, crimes against humanity, and/or war crimes. This basic definition of atrocity is not necessarily inaccurate or problematic in any way. Indeed, in some ways, even this quite general definition serves a useful function, that of providing a similarly pithy and emotionally resonant replacement for the overused term "genocide" to refer to all instances of mass killing and abuse, thereby escaping what Scheffer refers to as the "g-word" problem.[57] Beyond

55 This element of massiveness, in terms of severity of harm inflicted and number of victims affect, helps to explain the routine inclusion use of the term "mass atrocity," in a manner undifferentiated from that of atrocity alone. For an example of such a usage, see, for example, Straus, "What Is Being Prevented?," 17–18.

56 Efforts to set a specific numeric threshold, such as the approach adopted by Conley-Zilkic and de Waal, requiring 50,000 civilian deaths within a five-year period, are clearly efforts to use a numerical placeholder to approximate the threshold of massiveness. See Conley-Zilkic and de Waal, "Setting the Agenda."

57 See Scheffer, "Genocide and Atrocity Crimes."

serving this particular function, however, the rhetorical turn to the language of atrocity does little to help us understand and conceptualize what kinds of situations ICL can (or should) apply to, and what is distinctive about international crimes.[58]

Atrocities as Horrific Spectacles

Thus far, this chapter has demonstrated the centrality of atrocities as the general subject matter ICL is dominantly framed as being tasked with addressing, and that, in a rough sense, proposed definitions of atrocity focus on situations involving culpable harm causation on a massive scale. Such rough definitions, combining elements of culpability, harm causation, and scale, while not necessarily inaccurate or problematic, do little in describing current dominant shared social understandings concerning how international crimes manifest themselves. The remainder of this chapter attempts to delve more deeply into the substance of such understandings by identifying a longstanding, if rarely acknowledged, association between "atrocities" and later, international crimes, and an aesthetics of horrific spectacle. The association is both deep-seated and longstanding, and has helped to embed the notion that all international crimes will manifest themselves as intuitively recognizable spectacles of horrific violence and abuse in the social and legal imaginaries of international law and international criminal justice.

Martha Minow describes the task of describing, in a general sense, the core subject matter of international criminal justice, as an exercise in "naming horror."[59] While Minow acknowledges the "incommensurability of human language and responses to the horrors" ICL deals with, she nonetheless concludes that as a "general term" used to describe genocide, crimes against humanity, and war crimes, "'atrocity' may be as good as any."[60] Minow's comments reflect a foundational belief, discussed previously in this chapter, that undergirds the international criminal justice movement as a global project. This belief is that, at its very core, this project represents an effort to combat the "horrors" of atrocity through the technique of criminally prosecuting individuals. This section considers the

[58] This definitional ambiguity has been pointed out by several scholars. See, for example, Minow, "Naming Horror," 39–40; Straus, "What Is Being Prevented?"; Margaret M. deGuzman, "Gravity and the Legitimacy of the International Criminal Court" (2009) 32 *Fordham International Law Journal* 1400–1465: 1400–1402.

[59] Minow, "Naming Horror."

[60] Ibid., 40.

implications of this belief for ICL itself, particularly in relation to notions of the perceptibility and relative visibility of atrocity violence and how this has facilitated the development of a deeply aestheticized understanding of genocide, crimes against humanity, and war crimes.

As Susan Sontag asserts, atrocities have long been associated with the production of horrific spectacles that shock and appall us, yet somewhat paradoxically, attract our attention and intrigue us.[61] Connections between atrocity and brutal acts of violence can be traced back to the term's Latin roots. In Latin, atrōcitās, from the root atrōx, connotes actions marked by their "fierceness; savageness, cruelty; [or] severity."[62] According to Mark Osiel, under Roman military law, the language of atrocity was employed to describe a "subset of offenses, those legally inexcusable despite having been performed under orders," although the term never had any specific, legally defined meaning in Roman law itself.[63] The contemporary term atrocity has not much changed from its Latin roots and continues to be defined in largely moral, emotional, and aesthetic terms. The Oxford English Dictionary, for example, defines "atrocity" as either "[s]avage enormity, horrible or heinous wickedness" or "[a]n atrocious deed; an act of extreme cruelty and heinousness."[64] "Atrociousness," meanwhile, is defined as "extremely wicked, brutal or cruel ... appalling, horrifying [or] utterly revolting: abominable."[65] These definitions oscillate between focusing on the nature of relevant "atrocious" actions, and the visceral emotional responses elicited by such actions.

Human history is, of course, replete with acts of such extreme cruelty and heinousness, many of which have involved the commission of acts that, if committed now, would undoubtedly involve the commission of genocide, crimes against humanity, and/or war crimes.[66] The way such events have been described and remembered, even before contemporary ICL came into existence, tend to highlight their manifest horror and wrongfulness. For example, in a 1919 article entitled "Atrocities in Greek Warfare," Helen Law draws comparisons between "atrocities" committed during the Greek wars of antiquity and those committed

[61] Susan Sontag, *Regarding the Pain of Others* (Farrar, Straus and Giroux, 2003).
[62] *Oxford English Dictionary*, "Atrōcitās," "Atrōx."
[63] Ibid.
[64] *Oxford English Dictionary*, "Atrocity."
[65] *Oxford English Dictionary*, "Atrocious" (defining the adjective atrocious alternatively as "extremely wicked, brutal, or cruel: barbaric" ... "appalling, horrifying" or "utterly revolting: abominable").
[66] See, for example, generally Ben Kiernan, *Blood and Soil: A World History of Genocide and Extermination from Sparta to Darfur* (Yale University Press, 2007).

during World War I.[67] Referencing various atrocities committed during the Greek wars, Law singles out the Thracian attack on Mycalessus during the Peloponnesian war as the "most dreadful atrocity committed during that war."[68] This atrocity was so especially "dreadful" because "the women and children were not spared, as they ordinarily were. The Thracians, bursting in, sacked the houses and temples and butchered the inhabitants, sparing neither youth nor age but killing all they fell in with, even children and women."[69] Clearly, the mass killing of civilians by the Thracians, as described by Law, would amount to prototypical war crimes, and perhaps also crimes against humanity under contemporary ICL.

The rhetoric of atrocity has been similarly deployed to convey the severity of instances of mass killing and abuse in a wide variety of settings prior to the inception of contemporary ICL. A brief list of relatively recent examples ranges from massacres in colonial India and the Congo in the early nineteenth and twentieth centuries, respectively; to the conditions in Siberian gulags in the late nineteenth century; to what has come to be known as the Armenian Genocide of 1915–1917. The massacres in India and the Congo involved instances of mass killing, while torture and abuse were also systematically committed. Meanwhile, the mass killing of Armenians and other members of minority groups in Turkey is now generally regarded as an early twentieth-century example of conduct now criminalized as genocide. Conditions in Siberian gulags, often used as a means of punishing political dissidents, are comparable to conditions in internment camps in places such as the former Yugoslavia, later prosecuted as international crimes. Even though when they were committed, ICL, at least as we now know it, did not exist, each of these situations was described using the language of atrocity in contemporaneous writings.[70]

These examples demonstrate the evocative power of the term atrocity as a descriptive turn of phrase, along with its association with acts currently characterizable as international crimes. Such events, while being near-universally derided as awful and morally condemnable in the strongest terms, also seem to capture our attention and pique our

67 Helen H. Law, "Atrocities in Greek Warfare" (1919) 15 *The Classical Journal* 132–147.

68 Ibid., 139.

69 Ibid.

70 See, for example, The Independent, "Atrocities in Congo" (1902) 1 *The Journal of Geography* 228–229; "British Atrocities in India" (February 1809) *Irish Magazine and Monthly Asylum for Neglected Biography* 52–54; "The Sanitary Phase of the Siberian Atrocities" (12 April 1890) 135 *The Lancet* 820; Clarence Ussher, "The Armenian Atrocities and the Jihad" (1916) 6 *The Muslim World* 140–143.

interest. Even as we condemn, we may find it difficult to look away. Whether this social fascination with atrocity stems from empathy or mere prurient voyeurism is the subject of longstanding debate.[71] Regardless, however, of why atrocities fascinate us, this fascination itself is undeniable, and is reflected in the fact that war and atrocity have always been major news events and subjects of the arts. Indeed, much of our knowledge of ancient histories is based on surviving accounts of various wars, atrocities, and genocides.

While acts of mass killing and abuse, especially of civilians, has not always been framed as necessarily being criminal in nature, the very act of framing an event as an atrocity does bring with it a high degree of moral condemnation. This condemnatory power has been harnessed by various anti-war and anti-atrocity activists in efforts to garner support for the eradication of mass violence through its visceral depiction.[72] Two well-known examples of such a strategy include the work of Francisco Goya, especially his "The Disasters of War" series (see Figure 2.1), and Ernst Friedrich's "War against War" (*Krieg dem Kriege*), a booklet containing numerous grisly images depicting the horrors of World War I.[73]

While the allure of atrocity as a subject able to capture our attention is not new, the degree to which realistic, even actual depictions of atrocity, in the form of photographs and video recordings, are able to be captured has expanded rapidly since the invention of photographic technologies. Indeed, war, violence, and atrocity are the subject matter of many early iconic photographs. By now, technology has also progressed to the point that Sontag argues we have come to expect photographic evidence in order for atrocities themselves to be made "real" to remote audiences.[74]

Yet, even as our ability to document atrocities as they unfold has steadily progressed to a state of affairs wherein virtually anyone with a smartphone can document atrocities and human rights abuses in real-time, an overarching tendency to disseminate images conforming to preexisting notions of what atrocity violence itself is has persisted. Thus, even as Sontag critiques our potentially voyeuristic and unproductive fascination with atrocity images, she does so while assuming that such imagery will itself conform to a set of aesthetic conventions, referring to "the mounds of skulls in Pol Pot's Cambodia, [and] the mass graves in Guatemala and El

[71] See, for example, Sontag, *Regarding the Pain of Others*.
[72] See generally, for example, Ibid.
[73] Ernst Friedrich, *War against War*, trans. Douglas Kellner, 3rd ed. (Spokesman Press, 2014).
[74] Sontag, *Regarding the Pain of Others*, 7, 21, 26.

Figure 2.1 Plate 26 from Goya's *The Disasters of War* (Los Desastres de la Guerra): "*One can't look*" (No se puede mirar)[75]

Salvador, Bosnia and Kosovo" as expected "evidence" establishing the "realness" of recent atrocities.[76]

While the tendency to associate atrocities with spectacular acts of horrific violence long predated photographic technologies, it has also survived, and even been seemingly reaffirmed by such technologies. This association between atrocity and an aesthetics of spectacular, viscerally horrific imagery is evident in the fact that some of the earliest, most well-known atrocity photographs were altered or staged to highlight the ferocity of the violence involved. For example, Roger Fenton's *Valley of the Shadow of Death* (1855) (Figure 2.2), Felice Beato's *Interior of the Secundra Bagh after the Slaughter of 2,000 Rebels* (1858) (Figure 2.3), and many widely circulated images of the United States Civil War were staged or altered to enhance the drama and visceral quality of the violence and killing they sought to capture.

Fenton's photograph, produced shortly after the ill-fated 1854 charge of the British light brigade during the Crimean War, famously recounted in Tennyson's poem, depicts a valley pockmarked with cannonballs. The

[75] Image in public domain. Image file courtesy of the Metropolitan Museum of Art, available at: www.metmuseum.org/art/collection/search/361851.

[76] Sontag, *Regarding the Pain of Others*, 83.

Figure 2.2 Roger Fenton, *Valley of the Shadow of Death* (1855)[77]

valley shown in the photograph, however, was not the actual valley where the ill-fated charge had taken place, but rather another one nearby. Moreover, before producing the image that would ultimately become iconic, Fenton had additional cannonballs strewn across the roadway depicted in the photograph, serving to highlight the intensity of the cannon fire that had cut down the British cavalry.[78] Of course, the addition of the cannonballs also helps to visually connect the photograph to Tennyson's famous poem, wherein the sheer volume of the cannon fire faced by the charging brigade is a central feature:

Cannon to right of them,
Cannon to left of them,
Cannon in front of them
Volleyed and thundered;
Stormed at with shot and shell,

[77] Digital image courtesy of the Getty's Open Content Program. https://www.getty.edu/about/whatwedo/opencontent.html.

[78] Sontag, *Regarding the Pain of Others*, 52–56.

Boldly they rode and well,
Into the jaws of Death,
Into the mouth of hell
Rode the six hundred.[79]

Similarly, Beato, whose iconic image depicts the courtyard of a devastated palace in India where approximately 2,000 rebels had been massacred by British troops several months prior, is believed to have arranged for the corpses of victims to be exhumed from a nearby mass grave and their bones strewn across the courtyard before taking his well-known photograph.[80]

Figure 2.3 Felice Beato, *Interior of the Secundra Bagh after the Slaughter of 2,000 Rebels, Lucknow* (1858)[81]

[79] Lord Alfred Tennyson, "The Charge of the Light Brigade," in Lord Alfred Tennyson, ed., *The Charge of the Light Brigade and Other Poems* (Dover, 1992), 52.

[80] Ateya Khorakiwala, "Staging the Modern Ruin: Beato's 'Sikander Bagh, Lucknow'" (2013) 41 *Thresholds: Journal of the MIT Department of Architecture* 138–145.

[81] Digital image courtesy of the Getty's Open Content Program, https://www.getty.edu /about/whatwedo/opencontent.html.

Finally, many of the iconic photographs produced by Alexander Gardner and his team of assistants during the Civil War, such as the iconic *Home of a Rebel Sharpshooter*, which depicts a single dead Confederate soldier in a "sharpshooter's den" in the aftermath of the battle of Gettysburg, are also believed to have been staged in order to "intensify [their] emotional effect."[82]

As technology progressed, photographers became able to capture the horrors of war and atrocity in increasing detail and with increasing realism. For example, Robert Capa's *The Falling Soldier* (1936) appears to, for the first time, capture the very moment a combatant is shot and killed during the Spanish Civil War, while H. S. Wong's *Bloody Saturday* (1937) depicts a dirtied infant crying amid rubble and burning fires in the immediate aftermath of a Japanese bombing raid on Shanghai.[83]

These and many other early photographic depictions of war and atrocity both reflect and have helped to normatively solidify a preexisting association between atrocity and spectacular acts of horrific violence. The horrors of war and atrocity that had previously been depicted solely in stories, histories, paintings, and other mediums became graphically visible to us through photography and film. Yet, until roughly World War II, due to technological limitations and lack of access to sites of war and atrocity, photographs of atrocities remained limited mostly to especially large-scale events, such as World War I. Only a handful of images depicting lesser-known atrocities, such as the Armenian or Herrero Genocides, were produced and distributed globally. Thus, in the words of *TIME* magazine, early iconic photos of war and atrocity "revealed to the general public the reality of the lifeless desolation left in the wake of senseless slaughter."[84]

The scale of production of photographs, and later video recordings, capturing atrocities as they unfolded escalated rapidly as technology progressed. These videos, images, and the like both reflected and helped reproduce the notion that atrocities are appalling events, and, eventually,

[82] Alexander Gardner, "Home of a Rebel Sharpshooter, Gettysburg," in *Gardner's Photographic Sketchbook of the War* (Museum of Modern Art, 1865), www.moma.org/learn/moma_learning/alexander-gardner-home-of-a-rebel-sharpshooter-gettysburg-from-gardners-photographic-sketchbook-of-the-war-1865.

[83] Both of these photos are on *TIME* magazine's list of the one hundred "Most Influential Images of All Time." TIME, *Time 100 Photographs: The Most Influential Images of All Time* (Time Inc. Books, 2016).

[84] TIME, *Time 100 Photographs: The Most Influential Images of All Time* (Time Inc. Books, 2016), 174.

that such events merit criminal prosecutions. For example, the graphic images of World War II atrocities that circulated in news media, most notably images of recently liberated Nazi concentration camps (see e.g. Figure 2.4), undoubtedly played a role in garnering support for postwar prosecutions. Indeed, the IMT began operations in 1945, in the wake of years of the widespread publication of photos and videos depicting the horrors of the war and, beginning in early 1945, the publication of a steady stream of graphic photographs of Nazi "atrocities."[85]

The scale of production of photographs, and later video recordings, capturing atrocities as they unfolded escalated precipitously as technology

Figure 2.4 *Life* magazine photographer Margaret Bourke-White prepares to take a photograph of a wagon piled with corpses in the newly liberated Buchenwald concentration camp[86]

[85] Sontag, *Regarding the Pain of Others*, 24–25. Indeed, Sontag argues that "[i]f there was one year when the power of photographs to define, not merely record, the most abominable realities trumped all the complex narratives, surely it was 1945" citing the publication of photographs of concentration camps and the atomic bombings. Ibid., 24–25. Of course, the horrors of the manifestly illegal use of atomic weapons by the United States were deemphasized by the Allies.

[86] Credit: United States Holocaust Memorial Museum, courtesy of Patricia A. Yingst. Photograph taken by Lt. Col Parke Yingst, April 1945, Buchenwald Concentration Camp, Thuringia, Germany, https://collections.ushmm.org/search/catalog/pa1150895.

progressed. World War II and, later, the Vietnam War were both key moments in the increasing visual documentation of war and atrocities as they unfolded in near real-time. Discussions of these events invariably bring to mind iconic images, such as photos of soldiers storming the beaches of Normandy or raising the US flag at Iwo Jima, or the iconic photo of "napalm girl" in Vietnam, whose clothes had been burned off by napalm, or the photo depicting the very moment a South Vietnamese officer is executed by being shot in the head. In the contemporary moment, we continue to be inundated with these kinds of familiar representations of atrocity, as conflict and mass violence occur continually all over the globe.

Yet, in seeing the dispiriting continued proliferation of atrocity violence worldwide, we continue to look backward, to familiar reference points, in order to make sense of what is happening and to parse between "real" atrocities involving the commission of international crimes, and "mere" run-of-the-mill human right violations or other noncriminal forms of oppression and injustice. In looking back, canonical genocides and atrocities, especially the Holocaust, operate as implicit aesthetic reference points that are relied on in the recognition of new atrocities. Accordingly, describing a situation as an atrocity has come to be associated with a particular aesthetics of horrific spectacle. That is, atrocity crimes are expected to manifest themselves as highly visible, shocking displays that capture our attention, resemble previous well-known atrocities, and elicit a host of negative emotional reactions (horror, disgust, sadness, etc.). The more a real-world situation exhibits these aesthetic characteristics, the more recognizable it becomes as an atrocity and, in turn, an apparent manifestation of genocide, crimes against humanity, and/or war crimes.

A close examination of spectacle itself, as it is defined and understood, helps elucidate the nature of the aesthetic grounding of shared understandings of atrocity and international crime. The term "spectacle" is "derived from the Latin *spectaculum*, meaning 'a show', . . . coming from the verb *spectare* 'to view'."[87] Currently, the term spectacle can be defined as either a "specially prepared or arranged display of a more or less public nature (esp. one on a large scale), forming an impressive or interesting show or entertainment for those viewing it" or a "person or thing exhibited to, or set before, the public gaze as an object either of curiosity or contempt, or of marvel or admiration."[88] The adjective "spectacular" is defined as

[87] Christine Schwöbel-Patel, "Spectacle in International Criminal Law: The Fundraising Image of Victimhood" (2016) 4 *London Review of International Law* 247–274: 249.
[88] *Oxford English Dictionary*, "spectacle."

describing a person, place, or thing that is "of the nature of a spectacle or show; striking or imposing as a display" or "[t]hat which appeals to the eye."[89] Thus, as Christine Schwöbel-Patel helpfully summarizes, the core "idea of spectacle . . . concerns the social construction of people and events in order to make a striking impression."[90] Atrocities, at least as they tend to be described as massive, real-world manifestations of evil that assault our senses, are a prime example of spectacles, in that they demand attention and make a striking impression on those exposed to them. Formulated thusly, public fascination with atrocities is a prime example of a broader fascination with spectacles.

The basic notion that we are drawn to spectacular arrangements of sensory inputs is ancient, dating back at least to ancient Greek philosophy.[91] While clearly the fact that humans are drawn to spectacular, or otherwise aesthetically engaging arrangements of sensory inputs, and the notion that such attraction may mediate social relations and interactions is not itself new, the sheer volume of spectacular imagery produced and circulated has escalated precipitously since the industrial revolution. It is the resultant saturation of society with spectacles that is the subject of Guy Debord's *Society of the Spectacle*, in which he provocatively claims that "[t]he whole life of those societies in which modern conditions of

89 *Oxford English Dictionary*, "spectacular."

90 Schwöbel-Patel, "Spectacle in International Criminal Law," 249.

91 For example, in *Poetics*, Aristotle defines tragedy as "an imitation of an important and complete action, possessing a certain degree of magnitude, in ornamented language, having its forms distinct in their respective parts, by the representation of persons acting, and not by narration, effecting through the means of pity and terror, the purgation of such passions." Aristotle, *The Poetic of Aristotle*, trans. Henry James Pye (John Stockton Piccadilly, 1788), 32–33. Within this definition, Aristotle includes the "decorations of the theatre" among six elements that "must be considered as a principal part of tragedy." Ibid., 34. Aristotle's six essential elements of tragedy are: "the apparatus of the theatre, the music, the fable, the manners, the language, and the sentiment." Ibid., 36. Often, such "decorations" are described as the element of "spectacle." See, for example, Leslie Kan, "Spectacle," in *The University of Chicago Theories of Media Keyword Glossary*, https://csmt.uchicago.edu/glossary2004/spectacle.htm. However, some scholars quibble with the equivocation of the phrase "decorations of the theater" with the term "spectacle." See, for example, Aristotle, George Whalley, John Baxter, and Patrick Atherton, *Aristotle's Poetics* (McGill-Queen's University Press, 1997). According to Aristotle, we are drawn to the tragic form, including its spectacle, or "ornamented language," by the promise of the pleasurable experience of catharsis, which is the "beneficial transformation of painful emotions through absorbed contemplation of a powerfully moving work of art." Stephen Halliwell, "Katharsis," in Donald M. Borchert, ed., *The Encyclopedia of Philosophy*, 2nd ed. (Macmillan Reference, 2006), 44. This attraction to the tragic form has engendered much scholarly debate. See Anthony D. Nuttall, *Why Does Tragedy Give Pleasure?* (Oxford University Press, 2001), 1–28.

production prevail presents itself as an immense accumulation of spectacles. All that once was directly lived has become mere representation."[92] Such concerns are also present in the work of theorists such as Michel Foucault, who presents the spectacular and ever-present nature of modern surveillance technologies as central facets of their panoptic nature, which he views as central to processes of social disciplining and the automatic functioning of power.[93]

While Debord, Foucault, and many others have voiced concern regarding how spectacles affect the ordering of contemporary society, comparably scant attention has been paid to the role(s) spectacles may play in shaping the international legal order. Among the handful of scholars who have considered the role spectacle plays in this arena, the work of Wendy Hesford and Schwöbel-Patel, who use spectacle as an analytic to assess the fields of human rights and ICL, respectively, stands out as particularly applicable. Hesford focuses on how and what she characterizes as modernist "ocular epistemologies" (i.e. seeing is believing paradigms) shape "discourses of vision and violation within the normative frameworks of a human rights internationalism."[94] Schwöbel-Patel, meanwhile, argues that visual spectacles play a significant role in the social construction of victimhood and the branding and marketing successes of ICL.[95]

While Hesford and Schwöbel-Patel focus most closely on the relationship between spectacle and human subjectivity within the realms of human rights and ICL, much less attention has been paid to the roles spectacle may play in mediating shared normative understandings of the forms that human rights violations and international crimes

92 Guy Debord, *The Society of the Spectacle*, trans. Donald Nicholson-Smith (Zone Books, 1994), 7.

93 Michel Foucault, *Discipline and Punish: The Birth of the Prison*, trans. Alan Sheridan, 2nd ed. (Vintage Books, 1995). Indeed, Foucault views the modern reality that we are each in a near-constant state of being potentially surveilled by the state, and acutely aware of this reality as having replaced the social disciplinary roles previously occupied by more direct spectacles of authority and punishment, such as public executions.

94 Wendy S. Hesford, *Spectacular Rhetorics: Human Rights Visions, Recognitions, Feminisms* (Duke University Press, 2011), 7; see also ibid., 29, 52. Hesford employs the phrase "human rights spectacle" to "refer to the incorporation of subjects (individuals, communities, nations) through imaging technologies and discourses of vision and violation into the normative frameworks of a human rights internationalism based on United Nations (UN) documents and treaties." Ibid., 7.

95 Schwöbel-Patel, "Spectacle in International Criminal Law"; see also Christine Schwöbel-Patel, "The 'Ideal' Victim of International Criminal Law" (2018) 29 *European Journal of International Law* 703–724; Christine Schwöbel-Patel, *Marketing Global Justice: The Political Economy of International Criminal Law* (Cambridge University Press, 2021).

themselves may take.[96] Certain other scholars, such as Hilary Charlesworth, in her theorization of public international law as a "discipline of crisis," and Larissa van den Herik's suggestion that ICL prosecutions "spotlight" certain harms, victims, and perpetrators, while rendering others invisible, have gestured toward the roles spectacle and aesthetic politics may play in shaping international legal discourses relevant to ICL, but only indirectly.[97]

Although international crimes are associated with tragic spectacles of human suffering and death, situations involving such spectacles regularly occur that are not socially or legally conceptualized within the rubrics of atrocity or ICL. Earthquakes, tsunamis, and other natural disasters are one such example. The squalor and suffering associated with widespread global poverty is another. These and other situations may involve spectacles of human suffering and death, and yet tend to be viewed as lacking the degrees of causation and/or culpability demanded by criminal law. Consequently, instead of being viewed as "atrocities," environmental disasters or global poverty are primarily associated with nonhuman or wholly structural causation.[98] As such, despite the spectacularity of such events, and the fact that some of them are highly visible news events, they tend to not be viewed as atrocities.

This fact raises the second, perhaps less obvious, component of the atrocity aesthetic, that of a kind of horrific familiarity. This element describes the aesthetic characteristics of the subset of spectacles of human misery and death that tend to be understood as falling within the purview of ICL. Atrocities are so heinous because they are perpetrated; they do not just occur in the absence of culpable human behavior. Thus, an expectation exists that atrocities should not only upset us, but should outrage us, we should feel, intuitively, that *someone* is to blame for the horrors of an atrocity we are exposed to, even if who is responsible may not be readily apparent.

[96] Of course, constructed notions of who the perpetrators and victims of human rights violations and international crimes are play a significant role in shaping notions of what such violations and crimes themselves are. If one focuses on violence narrowly perpetrated by a particular set of paradigmatic actors against paradigmatic victims, this shifts one's gaze from the outset toward certain forms of violence and harm causation.

[97] Hilary Charlesworth, "International Law: A Discipline of Crisis" (2002) 65 *Modern Law Review* 377–392; Larissa van den Herik, "International Criminal Law as a Spotlight and Black Holes as Constituents of Legacy" (2016) 110 *AJIL Unbound* 209–213.

[98] This is not to suggest that all such sources of harm causation are spectacular in nature. Indeed, as Rob Nixon points out, many of the worst environmental harms are slow and unspectacular in nature, obscuring their violence. See Rob Nixon, *Slow Violence and the Environmentalism of the Poor* (Harvard University Press, 2011).

Outside of these limited references, the possibility that spectacle and aesthetics more generally shape understandings of mass atrocity and international crime themselves has, thus far, only been touched on in passing within scholarship. Most of this literature involves examinations of specific examples of overlooked potential international crimes. Sonja Starr, for example, in discussing potential ICL accountability in relation to large-scale corruption, gestures toward aesthetic considerations by mentioning the romantic tendencies of many ICL scholars, who write against the background of a "thundering and bloody history" while critiquing the lack of attention paid to international crimes perpetrated outside the context of crises.[99] Diana Sankey similarly notes that deprivations of basic human subsistence needs tend to be less visible than other forms of violence within ICL and other transitional justice practices in arguing that such "subsistence harms" deserve far more attention.[100] Meanwhile, Sheri Rosenberg, in calling for a greater acknowledgment of the "processorial" nature of mass atrocity and genocide, argues that slow, attritive processes of killing are more difficult to conceptualize as international crimes than killing processes involving the "immediate unleashing of violent death."[101] More recently, Schwöbel-Patel frames the spectacularized nature of international crimes as a major facet of the highly successful marketing of ICL and the anti-impunity movement.[102]

These and other scholars thus identify what seems to be a common discomfort with conceptualizing forms of harm causation that are slow, attritive, or otherwise appear banal in nature as human rights violations, let alone international crimes. This discomfort suggests that associations between international crime and the production horrific spectacles goes beyond mere descriptive flourish, and may be at the core of shared understandings of what the essence of international crimes are. Indeed, the full definition of a spectacle as "something exhibited to view as unusual, notable, or entertaining; especially: an eye-catching or dramatic public display; an object of curiosity or contempt" appears to neatly encapsulate a major facet of shared understandings of atrocity crimes;

99 Sonja Starr, "Extraordinary Crimes at Ordinary Times: International Justice Beyond Crisis Situations" (2007) 101 *Northwestern University Law Review* 1257–1314: 1265–1266.

100 Diana Sankey, "Toward Recognition of Subsistence Harms: Reassessing Approaches to Socioeconomic Forms of Violence in Transitional Justice" (2014) 8 *International Journal of Transitional Justice* 121–140.

101 Sheri P. Rosenberg, "Genocide Is a Process, Not an Event" (2012) 7 *Genocide Studies and Prevention* 16–23.

102 Schwöbel-Patel, *Marketing Global Justice.*

specifically the notion that atrocities are highly visible, unusual, notable, and even perversely entertaining phenomena that fascinate, yet horrify us.[103] That is, atrocities are objects of both curiosity *and* contempt.

In this regard, atrocities may be viewed as contemporary, real-world tragedies, that is, spectacular examples of human suffering and wrongdoing that capture our attention and elicit strong emotional responses.[104] It is this notion, of atrocities as tragic, yet visually engrossing public spectacles, that Justice La Forest of the Canadian Supreme Court captures when observing that atrocities "assault our eyes," which permeates the dramatic opening statements of ICL prosecutors, and grounds the emotionally charged language used to describe the kinds of situations ICL is applicable to.[105]

The Atrocity Aesthetic and Shared Understandings of International Crime

The aesthetic connotations attached to the broad conceptualization of ICL as a body of law tasked with providing the tools necessary to prosecute those who plan and carry out atrocities has undoubtedly played a significant role in ICL's relatively rapid development, especially since the early 1990s. The visceral horror depicted in iconic images of the Holocaust and other World War II atrocities[106] helped ground the lofty rhetoric of Justice Jackson's iconic opening statement at Nuremberg and buttressed the ability of the Tribunal to brush aside the glaringly ex post facto nature of certain aspects of ICL at that time, by declaring that it would be "unjust" to *not* prosecute individuals who participated in such horrific, self-evidently criminal atrocities.[107] Had the IMT lacked the ability to

[103] *Merriam-Webster Dictionary*, "Spectacle."

[104] In this regard, on the tragic form, see Aristotle, *Poetic*. For analyses of Aristotle's poetics, including his definition of tragedy, see Nuttall, *Why Does Tragedy Give Pleasure?*; Dana LaCourse Munteanu, "Introduction," in Dana LaCourse Munteanu, ed., *Tragic Pathos: Pity and Fear in Greek Philosophy and Tragedy* (Cambridge University Press, 2011), 1–26.

[105] *R.* v. *Finta*, [1994] 1 SCR 701: 775.

[106] For examples of such images, see, for example, Dmitri Baltermants, "Grief" (1942) In TIME, *Time 100 Photographs*, 104. Alan Taylor, "World War II: The Holocaust" (16 October 2011) *The Atlantic*, www.theatlantic.com/photo/2011/10/world-war-ii-the-holocaust/100170.

[107] International Military Tribunal, *Trial of the Major War Criminals*, vol. 1, p. 219 ("To assert that it is unjust to punish those who in defiance of treaties and assurances have attacked neighboring states without warning is obviously untrue, for in such circumstances the attacker must know that he is doing wrong, and so far from it being unjust to punish him, it would be unjust if his wrong were allowed to go unpunished.").

prosecute crimes against humanity, the horrors depicted in the images of the Holocaust and other civilian massacres not able to be characterized as war crimes would have been rendered largely noncriminal in nature.[108] How could such horrors *not* be criminal? Clearly, the photographs and newsreels depicting emaciated concentration camp internees and masses of dead civilian bodies strewn about and piled in mass graves were a testament to the criminality of those responsible, even if the Tribunal failed to prosecute many of the crimes most directly associated with these horrific images by largely skirting the criminality of the Holocaust itself.

The same can be said for other atrocities that have resulted in ICL prosecutions in places such as the former Yugoslavia, Rwanda, Cambodia, and Sierra Leone.[109] Each of these situations has involved the production and wide dissemination of images graphically depicting viscerally appalling acts of violence and abuse or their aftermath. For example, a now-iconic image of emaciated concentration camp internees in the former Yugoslavia, closely resembling images of emaciated victims in Nazi concentration camps, appeared on the August 17, 1992, cover of *TIME* magazine.[110] The intertwined normative and aesthetic connections made between ongoing abuses in the Balkans with Nazi-era concentration camps undoubtedly helped to not only raise awareness and mobilize opposition to the camps, but also to frame the abuses as international crimes, meriting, even demanding, the prosecution of those individuals responsible for setting up and running the camps.

The publication of this and other such shocking images, along with the report of a UN-appointed Commission of Experts documenting evidence of "horrific crimes" in the Balkans, helped galvanize support for the creation of the International Criminal Tribunal for the former

[108] Of course, the IMT spent very little effort addressing crimes specific to the Holocaust and lacked jurisdiction over crimes committed against German Jews before the onset of armed conflict.

[109] For example, Getty Images has numerous "stock" photos depicting the Rwandan Genocide. Most of the images depict horrific violence or its aftermath in the form of mutilated bodies or mass graves. Getty Images, "Rwanda Genocide Stock Photos and Pictures," www.gettyimages.com/photos/rwanda-genocide?sort=mostpopular&mediatype=photography&phrase=rwanda%20genocide. The same can be said for the most widely circulated images of the Bosnian War. See, for example, Massimo Calabresi, "20 Years Later: The Bosnian Conflict in Photographs," *TIME* magazine, http://time.com/3787440/bosnia.

[110] *TIME* magazine, "The Story of this Shocking Image from a Prison Camp in Bosnia Continues 25 Years Later," November 22, 2017, https://time.com/5034826/fikret-alic-time-cover-bosnia.

Yugoslavia (ICTY).[111] Images of Rwandan rivers swollen with corpses, the dramatic capturing of an actual killing of civilians on film in Kigali, literal mounds of the skulls and bones of Khmer Rouge victims in Cambodia, and of child soldiers brandishing weapons and victims missing limbs in Sierra Leone, all similarly played important roles in garnering support for the International Criminal Tribunal for Rwanda (ICTR), Special Court for Sierra Leone (SCSL), and ECCC, respectively. The dominant catalogue of images from each of these, and many other, widely acknowledged recent atrocity events, conform neatly to preexisting, widely shared, deeply aestheticized understandings of what international crimes are, and how they will manifest themselves.

This representation of international crimes as dramatic, highly visible, self-apparent events is not limited to visual forms of representation, but is also evident within the rhetoric of international criminal justice itself.[112] Typically, such rhetoric evokes visually arresting, graphic scenes of death and destruction.[113] The opening statements of ICL prosecutors, for example, tend to present international crimes as epic dramas of breathtaking evil.[114] The opening statement delivered by David Crane in the case of

[111] ICTY, "The Tribunal – Establishment," www.icty.org/en/about/tribunal/establishment.

[112] For example, Mark Drumbl describes atrocities as being "characterized as crimes against the world community or, more emotively, as offenses against us all." Drumbl, "Collective Violence," 540. On the topic of the so-called core crimes of ICL, Alexander Greenwalt observes that "[ICL practice from the 1990s onwards] focus on a core trio of ICL offenses: genocide, crimes against humanity, and war crimes." Alexander K. A. Greenwalt, "The Pluralism of International Criminal Law" (2011) 86 *Indiana Law Journal* 1063–1130: 1073. Sometimes the crime of aggression is added to this trio. See, for example, Heller, "What Is an International Crime?," 354–420.

[113] Examples of such dramatic turns of phrase include those such as "unimaginable atrocities," "mass violence," or "horrors of the worst order."

[114] For example, Sofia Stolk, in observing the prosecution's opening statement in the *Lubanga* case at the International Criminal Court, notes that the prosecution uses "[e]xplicit accounts and many metaphors help us to imagine what is hard to describe; black pools of blood, cascades of bullets, kids dragging rifles because they are too small to carry the weapons." Sofia Stolk, "Ntaganda at the ICC–Some Observations from the Public Gallery" (14 September 2015) *Vrije Universiteit Amsterdam School of Law Center for International Criminal Justice*, https://cicj.org/2015/09/the-opening-of-the-ntaganda-trial-at-the-icc-some-observations-from-the-public-gallery; see also Sofia Stolk, *The Opening Statement of the Prosecution in International Criminal Trials: A Solemn Tale of Horror* (Routledge, 2021); Sofia Stolk, "A Sophisticated Beast? On the Construction of an 'Ideal' Perpetrator in the Opening Statements of International Criminal Trials" (2018) 29 *European Journal of International Law* 677–701. Similarly, in his opening statement in a case against the most senior former Khmer Rouge leaders still alive at the time, then-ECCC Co-Prosecutor Andrew Cayley describes the Khmer Rouge regime as creating a "system of brutality that defies belief to the present day." *Case 002/01, 002/19-09-2007-ECCC/TC, November 21, 2011*, Transcript of Trial Proceedings, 16, lines 5–6.

Prosecutor v. *Sesay et al.* at the SCSL is emblematic in this regard. In his statement to the Court, Crane describes the accused as the "evil spawn of [an] unholy union" and "commanders of an army of evil, a corps of destroyers, a brigade of executioners bent on the criminal takeover of Sierra Leone," claiming further that "the pure evil of the[relevant] deeds of destruction are so horrific, terrible, and devastating in their scope, words in any language do not describe the offences committed."[115] While such flair for drama and hyperbole is perhaps expected within the context of opening statements in criminal trials, such dramatic rhetoric permeates ICL discourses. Many scholars, for example, also tend toward the dramatic in characterizing the kinds of situations that are the subject matter of ICL.[116] Even international judges routinely resort to dramatic rhetorical flourishes to describe the scale and nature of many international crimes.[117]

In many scenarios, of course, such dramatic, emotionally charged rhetoric accurately reflects realities on the ground. Situations involving the production of severe human suffering and/or death on a massive scale frequently involve the production of horrific spectacles of violence. Such spectacles are intuitively recognizable as contemporary international crimes. So too are many other paradigmatic atrocities, such as the Holocaust and Rwandan Genocide, to name but two of many instantly recognizable examples. Indeed, efforts to gain recognition of historical events, such as the Armenian Genocide, *as atrocities* invariably involve a heavy emphasis on the brutality and horror of relevant acts of violence.

The normative origins of this expectation can be traced back to the peculiarities of ICL's historical development. Since Nuremberg, ICL has evolved in fits and starts, alternately spurred on in reaction to cataclysmic events such as the Holocaust, and dramatic violence in Rwanda and the former Yugoslavia in the early 1990s, or impeded by Cold War or other

[115] *Prosecutor* v. *Sesay, Kallon, and Gbao, SCSL-2004–15-PT, July 5, 2004,* The Opening Statement of Prosecutor David M. Crane with Mr. Abdul Tejan-Cole, Trial Attorney, 4, 14.

[116] For example, David Scheffer, in advocating the adoption of the term "atrocity crimes" as a means of generally referring to the core set of crimes international courts and tribunals are concerned with, describes atrocity crimes as "a basket of particularly heinous crimes" that are "collectively executed crimes of such magnitude and destructive character as to be particularly prominent and logically inconsistent with the protection of human rights and the maintenance of international peace and security in an increasingly interdependent and sophisticated global society." Scheffer, "Genocide and Atrocity Crimes," 238.

[117] For example, the judgment of the International Military Tribunal at Nuremberg describes the crimes of the Nazi regime as being of "a scale larger and more shocking than the world has ever had the misfortune to know." International Military Tribunal, *Trial of the Major War Criminals*, vol. 1, p. 279.

political realities. The Rwandan Genocide, Holocaust, and other paradigmatic atrocity events elicited a certain degree of shock and disbelief among key global constituencies, spurring new legal developments, such as the introduction of the concepts of crimes against humanity and genocide. Yet, despite being created to address such decidedly extraordinary events, ICL has itself been constructed mainly through the importation of criminal law principles from domestic jurisdictions, which have been mixed, often clumsily, with international law.[118]

This process of importation is also partially attributable to the fact that most of the lawyers and judges who populate ICL institutions have been drawn from epistemic communities of domestic criminal lawyers.[119] Given that ICL has developed reactively, straining to adapt to each new situation it is applied to, while being driven by actors with deeply engrained notions of what constitutes a crime drawn from their experiences within domestic legal regimes, the reliance on familiarity in identifying atrocities is unsurprising. The ebb and flow of the substance of ICL has clearly moved in relation to discrete real-world challenges presented by the evolving nature of armed conflict, technological advances in weaponry, and the like.[120] Thus, in a certain sense, ICL is a fundamentally backward-looking discipline, and there exists a concomitant tendency to compare contemporary atrocities with historical ones, particularly well-recognized ones such as the Holocaust, or the Rwandan Genocide.[121]

In addition to this tendency to identify contemporary atrocities through aesthetic comparison, there exists a tendency to draw analogies between international crimes and their domestic counterparts, especially in terms of means of commission. This tendency to analogize stems from the fact

[118] Mark Drumbl has referred to this process as the construction of ICL on the "borrowed stilts" of domestic criminal law. Drumbl, *Atrocity, Punishment and International Law*, 44.

[119] Drumbl, "Collective Violence," 567 (describing ICL as a "nascent field constituted essentially in reaction to cataclysmic events" within which "most of the individuals building [ICL] hail from the epistemic community of domestic criminal lawyers.").

[120] For example, criticisms of the exclusion in the Nuremberg Judgment of any discussion of prewar atrocities against Jews and others in Nazi Germany helped lead to a gradual erosion of the armed conflict "nexus" requirement for crimes against humanity applicability, and the prevalence of civil wars, complex insurgencies, and other non-international, or nontraditional armed conflicts has clearly fed into the erosion of the classical distinction between international and non-international armed conflicts in terms of war crimes applicability.

[121] In regard to the role of the Holocaust in shaping the social imaginary in relation to genocide, see Rebecca Jinks, *Representing Genocide: The Holocaust as Paradigm?* (Bloomsbury, 2016).

that forms of harm causation that resemble well-established domestic forms of criminality (e.g. run-of-the-mill assaults or homicides) are easier to conceptualize as being "criminal" in nature, especially for lawyers whose primary expertise lies in domestic criminal law. The tendency toward analogy helps explain the relative ease with which certain new international crimes, for example, crimes involving sexual violence, or the abuse of children, have been adopted, while other international crimes without clear domestic corollaries, such as the crime of aggression, or the proposed direct criminalization of large-scale corruption via ICL, have been comparatively unsuccessful in gaining widespread support and recognition, despite routinely involving suffering and death on a comparably large scale to more familiar forms of international criminality.[122] Sexual violence and child abuse are familiar subjects of domestic criminal law regimes, while aggression has no such direct and clear domestic corollary. Large-scale corruption is a more complicated example, yet nonetheless still follows this pattern. Many domestic legal regimes criminalize corrupt acts, although often such crimes are notoriously under-prosecuted. The common thread is that certain forms of mass harm causation involving the production of spectacles of human suffering are intuitively identifiable as "criminal" in nature, while others fail to fit within widely shared notions of what crimes are expected to look like.

Conclusion

From the Nuremberg prosecutions of 1945 to the present day, ICL has benefitted from the circulation of horrific images depicting the "real" violence and carnage of war and atrocity. Over time, a massive corpus of stereotypical representations of atrocity has been amassed. From World War II, to the "killing fields" of Cambodia, Rwandan Genocide, Sierra

[122] This observation is not meant to suggest in any way that sexual violence and the abuse of children should not form part of ICL. For examples of proposed international crimes predicated on grand corruption, see Ndiva Kofele-Kale, "Patrimonicide: The International Economic Crime of Indigenous Spoliation" (1995) 28 *Vanderbilt Journal of Transnational Law* 45–118; Paul D. Ocheje, "Refocusing International Law on the Quest for Accountability in Africa: The Case against the 'Other' Impunity" (2002) 15 *Leiden Journal of International Law* 749–779; Chile Eboe-Osuji, "Kleptocracy: A Desired Subject of International Criminal Law that Is in Dire Need of Prosecution by Universal Jurisdiction," in Evelyn A. Ankumah and Edward K. Kwakwa, eds., *African Perspectives on International Criminal Justice* (Africa Legal Aid, 2005), 121–132; Ben Bloom, "Criminalizing Kleptocracy? The ICC as a Viable Tool in the Fight against Grand Corruption" (2014) 29 *American University International Law Review* 627–671.

Leonean civil war, Balkan conflicts of the 1990s, wars in Iraq and Afghanistan, and recent or ongoing violence and strife in places such as Syria, Myanmar, Iraq, Afghanistan, Yemen, Darfur, South Sudan, Central African Republic, Democratic Republic of the Congo, and elsewhere, reports of acts of mass killing and abuse have invariably been accompanied by quite visceral images depicting suffering, death, and violence. Rebecca Jinks describes the resultant dominant iconography of atrocity and genocide as a prevailing "Genocide imaginary."[123] This imagined association – between atrocity and an aesthetics of horrific spectacle – has become so embedded in dominant understandings of genocide, atrocity, and international crime that, according to Sontag, the very notion of atrocity has come to be "associated with the expectation of photographic evidence" in order to be believed by distant publics.[124]

The problem, as it were, of existing dominant generalized, nonspecific definitions and understandings of atrocity is not in their focus on large-scale harm causation, but in deep-seated, highly aestheticized notions of the ways in which such harm causation processes may manifest themselves. When discourses shift from general definitions of atrocity to descriptions of actual, real-world instances of atrocity violence, the "know it when you see it" approach resurfaces. This approach is grounded in expectations that processes of mass culpable harm causation will necessarily produce highly visible horrific spectacles whose heinousness and criminality are self-evident in nature. This assumption is evident in the rhetoric of international criminal justice, such as the preambular description of atrocities in the Rome Statute as being "unimaginable" events that "shock" the conscience of (an undefined) "humanity."[125] Such rhetorical flair suggests the existence of a widely shared assumption that situations involving mass harm causation will, because of their extraordinary scale, manifest themselves in ways that are extraordinarily visible and intuitively identifiable as atrocity crimes.

This intuitive, aestheticized approach to identifying atrocities is at least partially attributable to the fact that the very notion of atrocity, as defined both generally and as employed in the rhetoric of international criminal justice, is grounded in sensory experiences and emotional responses. That is, we know what acts we view as being especially "heinous," "abominable," or "wicked" by experiencing a host of negative emotions (horror, disgust,

[123] Jinks, *Representing Genocide*.
[124] Sontag, *Regarding the Pain of Others*, 83.
[125] Rome Statute, preamble.

revulsion, anger, etc.) when we are exposed to such acts, be it visually or in narrative form. As such, the language of atrocity (along with other similar terms, such as "mass violence" or "gross human rights violations") provides an evocative, emotionally affective, yet free-floating label, which can be affixed to horrific events that capture the public imagination, with very little in the way of hard definitional edges. Hence, an atrocity (i.e. an international crime) becomes that which captures our attention and horrifies or appalls us.[126] From the perspective of interactional legal theory, the notion that international crimes will manifest themselves as familiar horrific spectacles appears to be situated at the core of shared understandings of ICL and its genesis as part of a project to stamp out the scourge of atrocity. Over time, the operation of ICL itself has seemed to legally confirm that atrocities are, by their very nature, events that need not be sought out, but will affirmatively demand our attention.

The remainder of this book explores why ICL, in its structure and practice, continues to encourage reliance on a "know it when you see it" approach to identifying potential real-world manifestations of genocide, crimes against humanity, or war crimes, and assesses the ramifications of this reliance on aesthetics in the recognition and acknowledgment of such crimes. In Chapter 3, I explain why aesthetics play a relatively large role in shaping shared understandings of international crimes, by theorizing ICL as encouraging reliance on aesthetic perception in the identification of potential international crimes due to its various areas of ambiguity and extreme selectivity. In subsequent chapters, I argue that the assumption that *all* serious international crimes will necessarily conform to the atrocity aesthetic is both inaccurate and deeply problematic, as it further backgrounds certain forms of harm causation and further impairs the

[126] In this context the relevant "us" being "humanity," which itself is a social construct whose identity, beliefs, and values reflect deep global power imbalances and are in a constant state of flux. This raises the troubling question of *whose* conscience must be shocked in order for a situation to be viewed as an atrocity. Much has been written on the deeply problematic implications of whose *suffering*, or even lives, matter that can be instructive in this regard. See, for example, Judith Butler, *Frames of War: When Is Life Grievable?* (Verso, 2009); Ratna Kapur, "Precarious Desires and Ungrievable Lives: Human Rights and Postcolonial Critiques of Legal Justice" (2015) 3 *London Review of International Law* 267–294. However, the flipside of this question is that of whose *outrage* matters? In respect to ICL, whether or not a situation provokes moral outrage among key constituencies clustered in the Global North has deep ramifications for the distributive politics of international criminal justice. On such politics, see generally Frédéric Mégret, "Practices of Stigmatization" (2013) 76 *Law and Contemporary Problems* 287–318; Frédéric Mégret, "What Sort of Global Justice is 'International Criminal Justice'?" (2015) 13 *Journal of International Criminal Justice* 77–96.

already tenuous legal legitimacy of ICL through the insertion of an additional, unacknowledged layer of aesthetic bias in its application. Ultimately, I conclude that, if ICL is to continue to lay claim to being a project of criminalizing culpable individual contributions to especially large-scale harm causation processes, there is a need to step back and recognize the wide array of forms such processes may take, ranging from familiar spectacles of violence, to unfamiliar, unspectacular forms of killing and abusing through more banal, yet no less culpable, means.

3

Maintaining Invisibility

Aesthetic Perception and the Recognition of International Crimes

The previous chapter argued that shared understandings of international crimes are, among other things, embedded in an aesthetic of horrific spectacle, which I refer to as the atrocity aesthetic. This chapter provides an account of why and how this aesthetic model has persisted, despite remaining itself grounded in unstated and untested assumptions concerning the fundamental nature of the causal dynamics of mass harm causation. It does so by examining the substance, structure, and application of ICL in light of insights from social constructivist norm development theories, and research on the role aesthetic considerations play in individual and social meaning-making processes.

I argue that a variety of factors operate within the substance and practice of ICL that encourage actors to rely heavily on aesthetic perception when identifying potential international crimes and assessing their relative gravity. These factors include: the complexity of many atrocity situations; the continued presence of considerable zones of ambiguity within ICL; the extreme selectivity of ICL investigations and prosecutions; and the spectacular visibility and self-evident nature of many historical, recent and ongoing situations involving the commission of genocide, crimes against humanity, and/or war crimes. Moreover, because only a tiny fraction of even the most aesthetically paradigmatic international crimes are ever investigated, let alone prosecuted, there is little incentive for international criminal justice actors to affirmatively seek out novel manifestations of these crimes, as to do so would merely broaden the already wide "impunity gap" when it comes to accountability for participating in atrocities. The net result of this reliance on aesthetic perception in the identification of international crimes has been the reproduction and further embedding of shared understandings of international crime in the atrocity aesthetic described in the previous chapter.

Interactional Legal Theory and Social Constructivist Norm Development Models

One of the premises underlying interactional legal theory is the notion that "collectively held background knowledge, norms or practices," which Brunnée and Toope refer to as "shared understandings," constitute the raw material out of which international law is created.[1] Such understandings "do not simply exist, or miraculously emerge as agreed among actors . . . [but are] generated and maintained through social interaction."[2] This notion, of the centrality of social interaction in norm development processes, is rooted in social constructivism, a core premise of which is the notion that "[t]hings – including even nature – are not simply given, revealed, fully determined, and as such, unalterable. Rather, things are made, and made up, in and through diverse social and cultural processes, practices, and actions."[3] Thus, constructivism "represents a way of thinking which explicitly thematizes cognitive operations and social practices as processes of construction."[4]

Social constructivism's recognition of the broad array of inputs that contribute to social norm development is integral to interactional theory. Brunnée and Toope adopt an inclusive view of what actors and institutions participate in international norm development and lawmaking processes, arguing that "existing patterns of participation in international law-making where norms, although formally sanctioned by states alone, in fact are influenced strongly by a diversity of actors."[5] This insight rings particularly true within the realm of ICL. While states negotiate the conventions and treaties that outline the elements of certain international crimes, and create ICL institutions such as the various ad hoc tribunals and the ICC, a much broader array of actors are involved in collecting evidence, creating the necessary political willpower to investigate and prosecute crimes, developing the doctrinal substance of ICL itself, and influencing crucial policy choices, such as what situations to investigate, what potential crimes to focus on, and whom to prosecute.[6]

[1] Jutta Brunnée and Stephen J. Toope, *Legitimacy and Legality in International Law: An Interactional Account* (Cambridge University Press, 2010), 64.

[2] Ibid.

[3] Joseph W. Schneider, "Social Constructionism," in George Ritzer, ed., *Encyclopedia of Social Theory* (Sage, 2005), 724–729: 724.

[4] Armin Nassehi, "Social Constructivism," in Austin Harrington, Barbara L. Marshall, and Hans-Peter Müller, eds., *Encyclopedia of Social Theory* (Routledge, 2006), 98–100: 99.

[5] Brunnée and Toope, *Legitimacy and Legality*, 36.

[6] For example, the International Law Commission has been integral to the development of ICL, especially through the production of various draft codes. Civil society actors and nongovernmental organizations (NGOs), meanwhile, have been integral to advocacy for

For the most part, Brunnée and Toope remain agnostic concerning the pathways through which shared understandings relevant to international law may emerge.[7] Regardless of their ultimate genesis, what is important from an interactional perspective is the basic social constructivist premise that shared understandings "emerge, evolve or fade through processes of social learning."[8] Given that, from this perspective, social learning is a perpetual, nonlinear enterprise, norm development and lawmaking are also viewed by Brunnée and Toope as open-ended enterprises, subject to continual processes of revision, (re)negotiation, and calibration.

Despite their agnosticism concerning the pathways through which shared understandings emerge, Brunnée and Toope do highlight three theories of norm development as especially salient, in their view, to the development of international legal norms, as each spotlights the role of particular actors in social learning processes.[9] First, the "norm cycle" model, developed by Martha Finnemore and Kathryn Sikkink, is grounded in the notion that "norm entrepreneurs," encompassing states, nongovernmental organizations, and individuals, work to establish "new logic[s] of appropriateness" that gain social traction over time.[10] As such "logics" gain traction, they gradually achieve social acceptance and, hence, normative force. Second, the "epistemic community" approach focuses on the role of expertise within "knowledge-based networks," which tend to be "focused on technical matters" and whose members tend to be viewed as relatively impartial experts.[11] The technocrats who populate such epistemic communities interactively develop their own specialized languages and background understandings in order to facilitate more efficient interactions. In the process, new norms emerge, which over time, may be adopted more broadly outside the confines of the epistemic communities themselves.

While Brunnée and Toope acknowledge the importance of these two theories and the roles of norm entrepreneurs and epistemic communities in social norm development processes relevant to international law, it is

the advancement of various legal norms related to ICL, such as the Responsibility to Protect (R2P), and development of new international crimes to provide greater coverage over sexual and gender-based crimes, and crimes against children. Furthermore, much of the substance of contemporary ICL was developed within the jurisprudence of the various ad hoc UN courts and tribunals.

7 See generally Brunnée and Toope, *Legitimacy and Legality*, 57–62.
8 Ibid., 65.
9 Ibid., 57–65.
10 Ibid., 57.
11 Ibid., 59.

the third, nonlinear social learning theory they discuss that they view as best encompassing the diverse range of social interactions through which international legal norms are generated. These theories are grounded in social norm development processes involving what Étienne Wenger describes as the "continuous negotiation of collective meanings" within social communities involved in "relations of mutual engagement."[12] According to this approach, actors within such "communities of practice," defined as "knowledge-based networks," continually develop shared understandings, while simultaneously refining the structure of the communities themselves.[13] Brunnée and Toope agree with Wenger that "learning is not simply a discrete activity through which individuals acquire knowledge, but is part and parcel of everyday life and occurs through continuing social engagement."[14] Within communities of practice, social relations are guided by "particular norms or procedures," which provide "reference points in the ongoing negotiation of meanings."[15] Such communities of practice need not be formal or even recognized by the actors operating within them, but can develop organically as actors interact. Furthermore, the actors within such communities need not even be aware of their role in developing new social norms, as such norms may emerge organically, as actors communicate with one another and share ideas.[16]

Brunnée and Toope's emphasis on international legal norms developed within communities of practice is evident in their concluding comments on the concept of shared understandings, which they view as "inherently interactional, created through communities of practice that shape the mutual engagement of various actors in international society[,] engagement [that] is framed by existing norms and social structures, and the active participation of actors in turn maintains and reshapes both norms and structures."[17] Thus, both the substance of shared understandings and the structure of the communities of practice within which they are developed are fluid and continually evolving, per interactionalism.

[12] Ibid., 63, citing Étienne Wenger, *Communities of Practice: Learning, Meaning, and Identity* (Cambridge University Press, 1998), 73.
[13] Brunnée and Toope, *Legitimacy and Legality*, 62.
[14] Ibid.
[15] Ibid.
[16] See ibid., 57–87.
[17] Ibid., 86.

Given interactionalism's expansive view of the social processes through which shared understandings are developed and evolve over time, a virtually unlimited set of factors arguably play some role in influencing such understandings. Thus, one can imagine that sources of norms that may influence international lawmaking are nearly without limit, encompassing all the factors that go into the social development of ideas and ways of thinking. The remainder of this chapter argues that, given the realities of ICL as it is constructed and practiced currently, relevant actors participating in communities of practice within which shared understandings of genocide, crimes against humanity, and war crimes are developed and refined, operate within normative environments conducive to an especially high degree of reliance on aesthetic perception in the recognition of potential instances of these crimes.

ICL, as a fulcrum point around which various communities of practice are loosely organized, represents an environment especially conducive to reliance on aesthetic considerations in the development of shared understandings of what constitutes an atrocity crime. ICL is such a favorable environment because actors within ICL-related epistemic communities and broader communities of practice, such as diplomats, international lawyers and judges, ICL institutions, advocacy groups, NGOs, academics, journalists, human rights and transitional justice activists, and the like, are especially apt to rely on intuitive processes of aesthetic perception when identifying potential international crimes. From an interactional legal theory perspective, these "reference points" or "shortcuts" play a key role in the continual "negotiation of meanings" and construction of shared understandings.[18] Thus, a constellation of aesthetic reference points concerning what actors are talking about when generally discussing socially constructed concepts such as "atrocities," "mass violence," and "international crimes" have emerged, facilitating interaction among such actors within various communities of practice. Rather than describing what they are talking about when they generally refer to atrocity crimes, such actors are able to simply use terms such as "atrocity" and various specialized acronyms[19] to generally refer to a commonly understood general subject matter with which ICL is concerned. These

[18] See ibid., 62.

[19] Examples of common ICL acronyms include "SGBV" (sexual and gender-based violence), "JCE" (joint criminal enterprise"), "IHL" (international humanitarian law), "IAC" (international armed conflict), "NIAC" (non-international armed conflict), and various other specialized terms.

established shorthand practices facilitate more efficient interaction between such actors, who are able to rely on a preestablished lexicon.

The usage of commonplace shorthand descriptors of international crimes, however, implicitly assumes a degree of clarity, specificity, and access to evidence that remains the exception, rather than the rule when it comes to ICL and real-world instances of large-scale harm causation. For example, as discussed in the previous chapter, when we describe a situation as an atrocity or instance of mass violence, it is not clear what precise category of phenomena we are referring to, except a vague reference to ICL itself. ICL, meanwhile, continues to suffer from ambiguity, extreme selectivity in application, complexity in terms of both law and factual scenarios, and political contestation. Over time, the widely assumed aesthetic obviousness of international crimes stemming from this combination of factors has allowed aesthetic connotations to be subtly woven into the substance of shared understandings of the essence of international crimes. Thus, when we refer to atrocities, we are referring to, among other things, a certain kind of easy to recognize, visceral aesthetic experience of being exposed to a horrific spectacle.

Given interactional legal theory's broad and inclusive approach to the array of factors and actors that influence the development of norms related to international law, it follows that one could argue that aesthetics, as well as any number of other factors, necessarily play *some* role in influencing shared understandings relevant to all areas of international law, including ICL. This brings me to two important caveats regarding the arguments advanced in this book.

First, the argument I advance in this book is that aesthetic considerations are neither the sole nor even dominant factor in shaping shared understandings of international crimes, to the exclusion of any number of other factors, including the influence of powerful states and other actors, and the operation of structural biases and power dynamics. The argument I do advance is much more modest. What I *do* argue is that aesthetic considerations play a significant and generally overlooked role in influencing what harms are broadly conceptualized, socially as well as legally, as potential instantiations of genocide, crimes against humanity, and/or war crimes. Although I consider some of the broader implications of this bias toward horrific spectacle in Chapter 6, and raise some additional ones in the conclusion (Chapter 8), I leave a fulsome analysis of the interplay *between* the particular aesthetic biases identified in this book and various other factors shaping international criminal justice for future research.

Second, at this juncture, a note on vagueness, indeterminacy, and distinctions between ICL and other legal regimes, especially domestic criminal law systems, is warranted. The argument presented in this book generally and the specific framing of ICL as an environment especially conducive to reliance on the aesthetic perception of potential international crimes outlined in this chapter are wholly intended as relative assessments. That is, all legal regimes are, to some extent, indeterminate and vague, and these realities and the discretion they necessarily confer, create prime entry points for various forms of biases, prejudices, and the like to stealthily creep into legal practices. There is no such thing as a completely clear, fully determined legal regime, somehow "objective" in its sources and methods, and fully free from subjective biases. Indeed, indeterminacy has been a major theme in critical legal scholarship for quite some time, including that analyzing international law. While there is undoubtedly merit in exploring ICL and especially its selective recognition of certain forms of violence to the exclusion of others, through the lens of the broad critiques of international law advanced by such well-known scholars as David Kennedy and Martti Koskenniemi, this is not what this book sets out to do.[20] Instead, this book describes one arguably overlooked source of ambiguity and indeterminacy within ICL: that of an unstated preference for an aesthetics of horrific spectacle.

Along these lines, I envision this book primarily as in internal critique of ICL, one with the goal of pointing out that, while ICL and its champions tend to claim this area of law as one committed to prosecuting individuals who culpably participate in the large-scale abuse of others, in reality, the primary thrust of ICL is to prosecute (or at least shame) a subset of individuals who participate in the production of spectacular harms. As such, where this book converges with other strains of critical scholarship is in the assertion that external biases creep into law surreptitiously. Rather than attempting to make any grand pronouncement about all of the various biases afflicting ICL (and inherent in ICL taking up the mantle of "international justice"), this book seeks to explore one particular form of bias operating, unseen and unacknowledged, within ICL: a tendency to only recognize certain forms of violence.

[20] See, for example, generally, David Kennedy, "Spring Break" (1985) 63 *Texas Law Review* 1377–1423: 1417–1423 (describing the various strains of critical legal scholarship relating to the alleged indeterminacy of law, including international law); Martti Koskenniemi, *From Apology to Utopia: The Structure of International Legal Argument* (Cambridge University Press, 2005).

These arguments, of course, can also be made in relation to domestic legal regimes, especially criminal law regimes, which are rife with injustice, bias, and selectivity the world over. Some of these biases can also be inflected by aesthetics, modulated by power dynamics, such as the systemic failure to prosecute economic crimes, or treat them as being as serious as other forms of criminality, despite their often devastating consequences. Again, I do not mean to suggest that aesthetic biases do not form part of the picture in influencing other legal regimes, both domestic and international, but rather I frame ICL as a prime environment for aesthetic biases to flourish within, and, hence, have an especially large degree of influence in shaping legal norms and practices. As such, as the following analysis demonstrates, the degree to which actors interacting through the rubric of ICL are apt to rely on aesthetic considerations is arguably greater within ICL than many other criminal and international legal arenas.

With these caveats in mind, the contention that shared understandings of international crime remain grounded in, among other things, a predominant aesthetics of horrific spectacle, as argued in Chapter 2, raises questions as to how and why. How have aesthetic considerations become embedded in collectively held notions of what international crimes are? If aesthetic considerations have played such a significant role, is this role more significant than that which aesthetics play in shaping other areas of law, especially international law, and, if so, why? It is these questions that the remainder of this chapter attempts to answer. I argue that a combination of factors have combined to encourage a relatively high degree of reliance on aesthetic familiarity in the identification of potential international crimes since the inception of ICL. The construction and embedding of the atrocity aesthetic within shared understandings of what international crimes are is one of the results of this tendency toward aesthetic perception.

Individual and Social Processes of Aesthetic Perception

As indicated in Chapter 1, this book is interested in aesthetics as the term relates to both individual and social processes of sense perception and meaning-making. As such, this book is interested in both how and when individual actors rely on aesthetic perception in identifying international crimes, and how over time these individual aesthetic experiences factor into the production of widely shared social understandings of atrocity and international crime commission. The concept of aesthetics is thus, used as a method of both referring to individual processes of sense perception and the social dynamics of delineating what is and is not recognizable (or "sensible").

The origins of the word "aesthetic" can be traced back to the ancient Greek term aisthētikos (αἰσθητικός), which roughly translates to "of, or relating to sense perception."[21] This reference to sense perception underscores that aesthetic philosophy is grounded in the twin realities that cognitive processes of sensory perception mediate all of our interactions with the world, and that certain arrangements of sensory inputs attract and hold our attention more so than others, especially those eliciting strong emotional responses.[22] In addition to their role in capturing attention and eliciting emotional responses, sensory experiences also play a role in processes of individual perception and social interaction, by shaping intuitive assessments of the "rightness" of an object or state of affairs.[23] Within the realm of aesthetic scholarship, such assessments of rightness are referred to as the aesthetic "experience" or "perception," in relation to an object, concept, or state of affairs.[24]

While early research on aesthetic perception tended to focus on human experiences of the arts, more recently, scientific researchers have pioneered the relatively new field of neuroaesthetics, branching out to investigate the cognitive functions involved in aesthetic experiences.[25] Within the resultant field of neuroaesthetics, "[t]he term aesthetics is used broadly to encompass the perception, production, and response to art, as well as interactions with objects and scenes that evoke

[21] James Shelley, "The Concept of the Aesthetic," in Edward N. Zalta, ed., *Stanford Encyclopedia of Philosophy* (2015), https://plato.stanford.edu/archives/win2015/entries/aesthetic-concept; Oxford University Press, *The Oxford English Dictionary*, www.oed.com, *sub verbo*, "aesthetic." Though the etymological roots of term aesthetic date back to the Greeks, the term was not regularly used as a philosophical term of art until deployed thusly by Alexander Gottlieb Baumgarten in his 1735 thesis, *Philosophical Meditations Pertaining to Some Matters Concerning Poetry*. See Dana LaCourse Munteanu, "Introduction," in Dana LaCourse Munteanu, ed., *Tragic Pathos: Pity and Fear in Greek Philosophy and Tragedy* (Cambridge University Press, 2011), 1–26: 21.

[22] See Munteanu, "Introduction."

[23] For a helpful overview of the notion of aesthetic perception, see Ioannis Xenakis and Argyris Arnellos, "Aesthetic Perception and Its Minimal Content: A Naturalistic Perspective" (2014) 5 *Frontiers in Psychology* 1–15: 1–3.

[24] See, for example, ibid.

[25] See, for example, Anjan Chatterjee, "Prospects for a Cognitive Neuroscience of Visual Aesthetics" (2004) 4 *Bulletin of Psychology and the Arts* 55–59; Anjan Chatterjee, "Neuroaesthetics: A Coming of Age Story" (2011) 23 *Journal of Cognitive Neuroscience* 53–62.

an intense feeling."[26] The term "neuroaesthetics" itself is used to broadly describe anything that has "to do with properties of the brain as it engages in aesthetics" as the term is described in the preceding sentence.[27] It is these definitions of aesthetics, as a term relating to sense perception, especially when such perception elicits intense feelings, and "aesthetic perception" as a means of referring to sense perception and sense-making, that are utilized in this book. I propose that thinking about aesthetics in this twin manner, as a descriptor of an intuitive cognitive process we rely on more or less depending on the circumstances, helps us to see the conditions under which we are apt to rely more so on aesthetic familiarity as a means of identifying potential international crimes.

It may seem counterintuitive to look at atrocity crimes, which tend to be associated with ugliness and horror, rather than beauty and pleasure, through the lens of aesthetics. However, when one considers recent developments in understandings of aesthetics and aesthetic perception in light of the strong emotional responses exposure to mass killing and abuse tend to elicit, the value of aesthetics as an analytic framework for understanding notions of atrocity and international crime becomes evident. Recent research has undermined certain assumptions embedded within classical aesthetic philosophy. One such assumption that has been largely debunked has been the binary categorization of experiences as being either intrinsically aesthetic or non-aesthetic in nature, depending on the qualities of what is being perceived.[28] For example, according to outdated binary approaches, certain objects, performances, and the like can be categorized as "aesthetic" in nature, while others not. Thus, a carefully crafted vase could be considered an aesthetic object, while an empty jar designed to transport foodstuffs in a wholly utilitarian manner would likely be viewed as non-aesthetic in nature.

This presumed dichotomy of experience has been called into question through research demonstrating that to some degree, aesthetics and aesthetic perception shape all of our interactions with the world. For example, according to a recent study, neuroimaging data suggests that

26 Chatterjee, "Neuroaesthetics," 53.

27 Ibid., 53.

28 This traditional Kantian view may be summarized as the notion that "aesthetic objects are valued for their own sake and that the evaluation of beauty in objects is independent of desire (liking without wanting) and other utilitarian goals, or in other words, 'disinterested'." Veena Chattaraman et al., "Form 'Defines' Function: Neural Connectivity between Aesthetic Perception and Product Purchase Decisions in an fMRI Study" (2016) 15 *Journal of Consumer Behaviour* 335–347, citing Immanuel Kant, *Critique of Judgment*, trans. J. H. Bernard (Hafner, 1951).

a consumer's aesthetic experience of a product not only factors into purchasing decision-making processes but also influences the consumer's overall experience of a product, including assessments of the product's utilitarian functionality.[29] On a neural level, meanwhile, "brain areas activated in response to artworks overlap with those activated during the aesthetic appraisal of other objects of evolutionary importance, such as food and potential mates . . . emphasiz[ing] the utilitarian goals of aesthetic appraisals."[30] Consequently, the researchers who carried out this study conclude that "object beauty is of critical importance in consumer products because it triggers emotions and utilitarian motivations such as the 'desire to use' products, which drive the decision to purchase or own the product."[31] This is but one example of the erosion of the notion that aesthetics are the exclusive domain of artistic expression.

One upshot of research demonstrating our reliance on aesthetic appraisals in a wide array of decision-making processes is that aesthetic considerations are apt to play a role in virtually all social learning processes to some degree. The question thus, becomes that of under what circumstances such considerations play a more or less prominent role. In considering this question within the context of the recognition of instantiations of genocide, crimes against humanity, and/or war crimes, various individual cognitive and social processes of experience and recognition are relevant.

The remainder of this chapter frames ICL as a normative environment especially conducive to the insertion of aesthetic considerations into shared understandings of international crimes. ICL is so conducive to reliance on aesthetics because actors are apt to rely more heavily on intuitive processes of sense perception when interacting amid uncertainty and lack of information, and ICL represents a prime example of such an environment. This reality, combined with the extreme selectivity of ICL in practice and the spectacular visibility of international crimes conforming to the atrocity aesthetic, including many that go unprosecuted, encourages continued reliance on a "know if when you see it" approach to identifying potential ICL violations.

I make this argument in two parts. First, I provide an overview of general research on the role of familiarity and aesthetics in decision-making processes and social meaning-making, by weaving together

29 Chattaraman et al., "Form 'Defines' Function," 345.
30 Ibid., 335.
31 Ibid.

insights from Ioannis Xenakis and Argyris Arnellos' "interactive affordance" model of aesthetic perception, Amos Tversky and Daniel Kahneman's "representativeness heuristic" theory of decision-making amid uncertainty, Paul Slovic's work on "psychic numbing," the social phenomenon of "compassion fatigue," and Jacques Rancière's theorization of aesthetics as the "partition of the sensible."[32] The interactive affordance model of aesthetic perception and the representativeness heuristic both help us to explain why, as individual actors, we are apt to rely more heavily on intuitive processes of aesthetic perception when making decisions amid uncertainty, and/or are faced with a lack of knowledge or information, or high levels of complexity. When we are confronted by such a conundrum, yet need to act, the identification of familiar clusters of sensory experiences helps us to identify, name, and categorize objects and situations we interact with. The phenomena of psychic numbing and compassion fatigue help us to see how ICL actors and activist groups are incentivized to frame atrocities as horrific spectacles, with representative victims who have suffered gruesome injuries, in order to establish the seriousness and urgency of international crimes.

Over time, as we interact while being continually inundated with representations of international crimes closely conforming to the atrocity aesthetic, this aesthetic model has come to be the unstated standard when it comes to international crime commission. In turn, it has become a key factor in determining whether a given form of mass harm causation is recognized as a potential international crime. In sum, the labels affixed to and the ideas associated with international crime, combine to form an overarching, widely shared, yet rarely defined, imaginary of what international crimes are and how they will manifest themselves.[33]

After explaining the role aesthetic perception plays in individual and social processes of recognition and meaning-making, and how this role is increased within environments marked by uncertainty, lack of

[32] Xenakis and Arnellos, "Aesthetic Perception and Its Minimal Content"; Amos Tversky and Daniel Kahneman, "Judgment under Uncertainty: Heuristics and Biases" (1974) 185 *Science* 1124–1131; Paul Slovic, "'If I Look at the Mass I will Never Act': Psychic Numbing and Genocide" (2007) 2 *Judgment and Decision Making* 79–95; Susan Moeller, *Compassion Fatigue: How the Media Sell Disease, Famine, War and Death* (Routledge, 1999).

[33] See also Rebecca Jinks' argument that a dominant social "Genocide imaginary," largely predicated on the Holocaust as paradigmatic example, exists and helps structure how we think about genocide and mass atrocity. See Rebecca Jinks, *Representing Genocide: The Holocaust as Paradigm?* (Bloomsbury, 2016).

information and easily recognizable paradigmatic representative examples, I theorize ICL as a prime example of such an environment. Consequently, I conclude that ICL, in its structure and highly selective application, encourages actors seeking to identify international crimes to rely heavily on intuitive processes of aesthetic perception. In doing so, international criminal justice actors tend to compare current situations, aesthetically, to past paradigmatic atrocities, such as the Holocaust, Rwandan Genocide, or other high-profile, so-called canonical atrocities and genocides.[34] Over time, this has led to a self-replicating representativeness feedback loop, the net result of which has been that when seeking to identify potential manifestations of genocide, crimes against humanity, or war crimes, we are apt to do so largely by comparing potential crimes to representative past crimes.

Aesthetics, Uncertainty, and the Partition of the Sensible in Social Meaning-Making

What is aesthetic perception, and when do we rely on it? Xenakis and Arnellos define aesthetic perception as a certain kind of cognitive process, wherein "an emotional evaluation with anticipatory features assigns values to interactive indications (interactive affordances)."[35] They posit that individual actors are more apt to rely on such processes of emotional evaluation "in situations that are mainly characterized by high degrees of uncertainty and minimal knowledge."[36] As such, according to Xenakis and Arnellos' "interactive affordance" model, intuitive, emotionally driven processes of aesthetic perception serve as a cognitive mechanism that helps us to "better understand[] the world by reducing the

[34] See, for example, Donald Bloxham and A. Dirk Moses, "Editors' Introduction: Changing Themes in the Study of Genocide," in Donald Bloxham and A. Dirk Moses, eds., *The Oxford Handbook of Genocide Studies* (Oxford University Press, 2010), 1–16: 4 (identifying a "tendency in university syllabi, textbooks, and the mantras of public commemoration of genocide to focus upon a few instances of genocide that, for a variety of reasons, have qualified for the canon of general acceptance: alongside the Holocaust, Armenia, Cambodia, Rwanda, and the former Yugoslavia, and now Darfur tend to be included, but virtually no other cases."); see also Alexander Laban Hinton, "Critical Genocide Studies" (2012) 7 *Genocide Studies and Prevention* 4–14 (dividing the "genocide studies canon" into various categories based on their recognition, acknowledgment, and social visibility). While Bloxham, Moses, and Hinton refer to canonical "genocides," they use the term in a nonlegal manner to describe instances of targeted mass violence and killing.

[35] Xenakis and Arnellos, "Aesthetic Perception and Its Minimal Content," 12.

[36] Ibid.

uncertainty of interaction."[37] Thus, what actors "may perceive as aesthetic . . . is any combination of indications that could aid them in reducing their uncertainty of interaction and to accordingly feel like they are clearing their path toward a successful choice for an optimal interaction."[38] Put another way, Xenakis and Arnellos view aesthetic perception as a specific *kind* of cognitive process, one that we rely on in order to make decisions despite uncertainty.

Rare is the case where any person acts completely free from uncertainty and with perfect knowledge. Hence, one of the implications of the interactive affordance model is that aesthetic perception must play *some* role in virtually all decision-making processes, even if it is a largely subsidiary one in situations generally marked by certainty and a strong baseline of relevant knowledge. Hence, Xenakis and Arnellos' assertions further lend support to the general notion that there are not aesthetic and non-aesthetic objects, experiences, or processes of perception, but rather situations that provoke more or less reliance on a certain kind of intuitive reasoning relying on aesthetic familiarity. Conceptualized as such, aesthetic perception may be characterized as performing a sort of cognitive shortcut or triage, one which allows each of us to act amid uncertainty or without perfect knowledge.

The interactive affordance model is similar in terms of the cognitive function sensory experience, intuition, and emotions play in decision-making to that of the "representativeness heuristic" described by Tversky and Kahneman in the 1970s.[39] According to Tversky and Kahneman, individuals faced with uncertainty are apt to rely, knowingly or unknowingly, heavily on processes of largely aesthetic comparison in resolving uncertainty in order to act.[40] Thus, when assessing "the probability that object A belongs to class B" Tversky and Kahneman found that "people typically rely on the representativeness heuristic, in which probabilities are evaluated by the degree to which A is representative of B, that is, by the degree to which A resembles [prior examples of] B."[41] Thus, according to both Xenakis and Arnellos, and Tversky and Kahneman, we are apt to rely more heavily on such intuitive perceptive processes when we are faced with the need to resolve uncertainty.

[37] Ibid.
[38] Ibid.
[39] Tversky and Kahneman, "Judgment under Uncertainty."
[40] Ibid.
[41] Ibid., 1124.

If one accepts that, as individuals, we are apt to rely more so on intuitive processes of aesthetic perception under certain conditions, when it comes to the *social* construction of dominant notions of what international crimes are, the question becomes one of how, in aggregate, such individual practices shape collective ideas and social norms. This shift, from the individual to the social, in terms of the role aesthetics play in shaping how we recognize and conceptualize international crimes, brings us to Jacques Rancière's notion of aesthetics as the "partition of the sensible" and Paul Slovic's work on the phenomenon of "psychic numbing." Rancière helps us to conceptually delineate when and how, over time, individual instances of sense-making relying on aesthetic representativeness may influence the development of shared understandings and to understand how this process is inherently political in that it dictates what is knowable or sayable in a given social grouping. Slovic's work, meanwhile, helps us to see how actors are incentivized to represent atrocities themselves as individualized acts of horrific violence, rather than relying on more abstract representations, such as in the form of numbers and statistics.

Rancière defines aesthetics as the "reigning configuration between perception and meaning," or the "partition/distribution" of the "sensible" (*partage du sensible*).[42] Rancière's formulation of aesthetics as a form of politics that dictate the boundaries of acceptable, even recognizable, topics of social discourse helps highlight the "tension between a specific act of perception and its implicit reliance on preconstituted objects deemed worthy of perception."[43] It is in this social preconstitution of deeming what is, and is not worthy of perception that power dynamics, both direct and structural, come into play. Rancière describes resistance to dominant partitions of social sensibility as a strategy or politics of "dissensus," or, in the words of Davide Panagia, political action that "is aesthetic in that it requires a reconfiguration of the conditions of sense perception so that the reigning configuration between perception and meaning is disrupted by those elements, groups or individuals in society that demand not only to exist but indeed to be perceived."[44] The ultimate political goal is thus "a reconfiguration of

[42] Jacques Rancière, *The Politics of Aesthetics: The Distribution of the Sensible*, trans. Gabriel Rockhill (Continuum, 2013); Davide Panagia, "'Partage du Sensible': The Distribution of the Sensible," in Jean-Phillipe Deranty, ed., *Jacques Rancière: Key Concepts* (Routledge, 2014), 95–103: 96.

[43] Panagia, "'Partage du Sensible'," 95.

[44] Ibid., 96.

the perceptual disposition of sights and sounds by those who are excluded from the fields of the visible and of the sayable."[45]

While Rancière's primary focus is on *who* is excluded from a given society and its political discourse, his general arguments nonetheless can be applied to questions of what forms of mass killing and abuse are "visible" as potential international crimes within the realm of international criminal justice. Indeed, what forms of harm causation are visible directly relates to who are visible, as both perpetrators and victims of relevant harms. This is where Paul Slovic's pioneering research on the cognitive phenomenon of "psychic numbing" becomes relevant. Slovic uses the terms "psychic" or "psychosocial" "numbing" to refer to the reality that human "cognitive and perceptual systems seem designed to sensitize us to small changes in our environment, possibly at the expense of making us less able to detect and respond to large changes."[46] Consequently, "constant increases in the physical magnitude of a stimulus typically evoke smaller and smaller changes in response. Applying this principle to the valuing of human life suggests that a form of *psychophysical numbing* may result from our inability to appreciate losses of life as they become larger."[47] Applied to the realm of atrocity, genocide, and mass violence, Slovic theorizes that "affect," defined as "the positive and negative feelings that combine with reasoned analysis to guide our judgments," represents one "fundamental mechanism that may play a role in many, if not all, episodes of mass murder neglect."[48] One upshot of Slovic's claims is that, as individuals, we are cognitively primed to be more emotionally affected by, and hence focus our energies on, small-scale, relatively simple forms of violence and injustice. We are consequently relatively unmoved by figures and statistics of mass suffering and death, which we struggle to relate to. This reality, combined with the intense competition for resources and attention within the global justice marketplace, incentivizes international human rights and criminal justice actors to peddle in attention-grabbing imagery, often through the use of shocking, graphic images of violence and its aftermath.[49]

[45] Ibid., 102.

[46] Slovic, "'If I Look at the Mass I will Never Act'," 85; see also Paul Slovic, David Zionts, Andrew K. Woods, Ryan Goodman, and Derek Jinks, "Psychic Numbing and Mass Atrocity," in Eldar Shafir, ed., *The Behavioral Foundations of Public Policy* (Princeton University Press, 2013), 126–142: 129.

[47] Slovic, "'If I Look at the Mass I will Never Act'," 85 (emphasis in original).

[48] Ibid., 80.

[49] On this market incentivization dynamic and the tropes and stereotypes reproduced thereby, see generally Christine Schwöbel, "The Market and Marketing Culture of

On a broader, social level, the dynamic of psychic numbing that Slovic describes can be seen as contributing to the phenomenon known as "compassion fatigue," whereby entire societies inundated with news and images of suffering and violence become desensitized to such horrors.[50] The result is a continuing incentive to transform instances of mass killing and abuse from being expressed as statistics and abstract ideas, to concrete aesthetic experiences, ones evocative of paradigmatic prior atrocity events and which elicit the proper affective response among those exposed to them – one of visceral horror and outrage. Otherwise, such instances risk being ignored or rendered invisible as potential international crimes, that is, excluded from the partition of what is, socially and legally, "sensible" (i.e. recognizable, or understandable) as an atrocity.

Thus, in sum, as individuals, we are cognitively primed to rely on aesthetic familiarity (or "representativeness") when facing uncertainty and/or lacking knowledge. Additionally, because of the phenomena of psychic numbing and compassion fatigue, we are more apt to react strongly to simple, familiar harms that are individualized, rather than abstract recitations of statistics. Over time, as we interact with our environments and one another, that which is "sensible" is socially partitioned. The remainder of this chapter demonstrates how the realities of ICL, especially its normative and doctrinal zones of ambiguity and extreme selectivity, create a prime environment for aesthetic factors to play an outsized, if largely unacknowledged, role in the partition of what forms of mass harm causation, violence, and oppression are and *are not* sensible, socially and legally, as potential international crimes. The net result of this (ongoing) process is a grounding of the "reigning configuration between perception and meaning" in the atrocity aesthetic, as described in the previous chapter.

International Criminal Law," in Christine Schwöbel, ed., *Critical Approaches to International Criminal Law: An Introduction* (Routledge, 2014), 264–280; Wendy S. Hesford, *Spectacular Rhetorics: Human Rights Visions, Recognitions, Feminisms* (Duke University Press, 2011); Christine Schwöbel-Patel, "Spectacle in International Criminal Law: The Fundraising Image of Victimhood" (2016) 4 *London Review of International Law* 247–274; Sara Kendall, "Donors' Justice: Recasting International Criminal Accountability" (2011) 24 *Leiden Journal of International Law* 585–606; Sofia Stolk, "A Sophisticated Beast? On the Construction of an 'Ideal' Perpetrator in the Opening Statements of International Criminal Trials" (2018) 29 *European Journal of International Law* 677–701.

50 See Moeller, *Compassion Fatigue.*

The Structure of International Criminal Law: Ambiguity and Selectivity

This chapter has thus far argued that aesthetic considerations play a role in all human interaction with the world and, hence, play a role in social norm development, especially within environments marked by "high degrees of uncertainty and minimal knowledge."[51] The remainder of this chapter considers the substance, structure, and practice of ICL in light of this insight. Through this analysis, I frame ICL as a normative and social environment especially conducive to a high degree of reliance on aesthetic perception in the recognition of potential international crimes. Consequently, over time, constructed understandings of genocide, crimes against humanity, and war crimes have remained aesthetically configured as intuitively recognizable, highly visible horrific spectacles.

Normative Ambiguity: What Is an International Crime?

One of the reasons actors are encouraged to rely on aesthetic perception in identifying potential international crimes is that, in a general sense, a clear, widely agreed-on definition of what international crimes are remains lacking. In a strict sense, "an act qualifies as an international crime only if that act is universally criminal under international law."[52] As noted by Kevin Jon Heller, this requirement of universal criminalization, at least for "true" international crimes, refers to criminalization through international law and not merely universal domestic criminalization.[53] Thus, at a "most basic level international crimes are distinctive from purely national crimes insofar as the origin of the norm is found in international law and/or it is not entirely left to states to decide whether or not the conduct should be criminalised domestically."[54]

51 Panagia, "'Partage du Sensible'," 102.

52 Kevin Jon Heller, "What Is an International Crime? (A Revisionist History)" (2017) 58 *Harvard International Law Journal* 353–420: 354.

53 Ibid.

54 Evelyne Schmid, *Taking Economic, Social and Cultural Rights Seriously in International Criminal Law* (Cambridge University Press, 2015), 62. Accordingly, genocide, crimes against humanity, war crimes, and aggression, which are all directly criminalized by public international law, are the paradigmatic examples of true international crimes. There is disagreement in both the practice and literature of international law concerning whether additional offences, such as terrorism, torture, and various others universally (or at least near-universally) prohibited acts, qualify as true international crimes. This ongoing debate is outside the scope of the current inquiry, which is concerned solely with genocide, crimes against humanity, and war crimes, which are all well-established

Beyond this thin definition of international crimes as conduct rendered criminal directly by international law, attempts to arrive at an accurate descriptive general definition of international crime invariably end in a mix of vagueness and contestation. While certain individual international crimes are now subject to detailed definitions after being refined through processes of adjudication and codification, there is no universally agreed-upon common thread that ties together all international crimes, or even the so-called core crimes of genocide, crimes against humanity, and war crimes. Instead, as discussed in the previous chapter, terms such as "atrocity" or "mass violence" are commonly used as shorthand methods of referring to the primary subject matter the international criminal justice regime is concerned with.[55] Yet, nowhere in international law are these terms defined, and underlying concepts, such as those of atrociousness, violence, and massiveness, tend to be themselves definitionally vague, aside from gesturing toward harm causation of a relatively large scale.[56]

Beyond these vague concepts, there exist a large and growing number of proposed normative and descriptive theories of ICL, and its constituent subparts, such as genocide and crimes against humanity.[57] While

international crimes. For an overview of this debate, see ibid., 62–67. Furthermore, while individual states cannot unilaterally declare a particular course of conduct to not be an international crime, states may choose not to incorporate ICL into domestic criminal law and as such, may avoid prosecuting any international crimes in domestic courts. While this undermines the enforcement of ICL significantly, it does not alter the fact that international crimes are directly criminalized under international law.

55 These terms are employed regularly by scholars as a method of referring to the kinds of situations that international criminal justice is concerned with. For usage of the term "atrocity" see, for example, Mark A. Drumbl, *Atrocity, Punishment and International Law* (Cambridge University Press, 2007); Gideon Boas, "What Is International Criminal Justice?," in Gideon Boas, Michael P. Scharf, and William Schabas, eds., *International Criminal Justice: Legitimacy and Coherence* (Edward Elgar, 2012), 1–24. For usage of the term "mass violence" see, for example, Margaret M. deGuzman, "Choosing to Prosecute: Expressive Selection at the International Criminal Court" (2012) 33 *Michigan Journal of International Law* 265–320: 312 ("As currently configured, the ICC does not have the resources or proximity to local populations to make significant direct contributions to restoring victims or communities that have suffered mass violence."); Martha Minow, *Between Vengeance and Forgiveness: Facing History after Genocide and Mass Violence* (Beacon Press, 1998).

56 See *Oxford English Dictionary*, *sub verbis*, "atrocity," "atrocious," "mass," "violence"; see also Eugene Aisenberg et al., "Defining Violence," in Todd I. Herrenkohl et al., eds., *Violence in Context: Current Evidence on Risk, Protection, and Prevention* (Oxford University Press, 2010), 13–22.

57 See Sarah Nouwen, "International Criminal Law: Theory All Over the Place," in Anne Orford, Florian Hoffmann, and Martin Clark, eds., *The Oxford Handbook of the*

a full overview of the numerous proposed normative and descriptive theories of ICL is outside the scope of the present inquiry, a few examples suffice to demonstrate the wide variation in their substance. For instance, Adil Haque proposes a "group retributivist" theory of ICL, according to which the "relational structure of retributive justice" is applied to groups rather than individuals, which challenges the legitimacy of the state, and thereby explains and justifies international intervention.[58] Frédéric Mégret, meanwhile, proposes a distributive theory of international criminal justice, whereby the international community, through ICL, selectively distributes heightened stigma to certain types of behavior.[59] Alejandro Chehtman, in turn, argues that the "defining feature of an international crime is that it confers jurisdiction over it also upon an extraterritorial authority with no traditional link to the crime, the perpetrator(s), or the victim(s)."[60] These are but three of a large number of proposed descriptive and/or normative theories of international crime and ICL.

Additional layers of normative muddiness concerning the justifications for and purposes of ICL are added by the numerous competing theories of ICL's constituent parts. Theories of genocide, crimes against humanity, war crimes, aggression, other proposed international crimes,

Theory of International Law (Oxford University Press, 2016), 738–761. For examples of proposed theories of ICL and its constituent parts, such as crimes against humanity, see, for example, David Luban, "A Theory of Crimes against Humanity" (2004) 29 *Yale Journal of International Law* 85–167; Larry May, *Crimes against Humanity: A Normative Account* (Cambridge University Press, 2005); Alejandro Chehtman, "Contemporary Approaches to the Philosophy of Crimes against Humanity" (2014) 14 *International Criminal Law Review* 813–835; Kai Ambos, "The Overall Function of International Criminal Law: Striking the Right Balance between the Rechtsgut and the Harm Principles: A Second Contribution Toward a Consistent Theory of ICL" (2015) 9 *Criminal Law and Philosophy* 301–329; Frédéric Mégret, "In Defense of Hybridity: Toward a Representational Theory of International Criminal Justice" (2005) 38 *Cornell International Law Journal* 725–751; Richard Vernon, "What Is a Crime against Humanity?" (2002) 10 *Journal of Political Philosophy* 231–249; Christopher Roberts, "On the Definition of Crimes against Humanity and Other Widespread or Systematic Human Rights Violations" (2017) 20 *University of Pennsylvania Journal of Law and Social Change* 1–27; Heller, "What Is an International Crime?"

58 Adil Ahmad Haque, "Group Violence and Group Vengeance: Toward a Retributivist Theory of International Criminal Law" (2005) 9 *Buffalo Criminal Law Review* 273–328.

59 Frédéric Mégret, "Practices of Stigmatization" (2013) 76 *Law and Contemporary Problems* 287–318.

60 Alejandro Chehtman, "A Theory of International Crimes: Conceptual and Normative Issues," in Kevin Jon Heller, Frédéric Mégret, Sarah MH Nouwen, Jens David Ohlin, and Darryl Robinson, eds., *The Oxford Handbook of International Criminal Law* (Oxford University Press, 2020), 317–340: 328.

and the modes of liability through which such crimes are prosecuted abound. For example, the normative foundations and basic elements of crimes against humanity remain unclear and contested. Hannah Arendt, for instance, famously defines the essence of crimes against humanity as the fact that they represent an "attack upon human diversity as such."[61] Larry May proposes a gravity-based "international harm principle," which justifies the existence of crimes against humanity by positing that such crimes are of a scale that harms the international community as a whole.[62] The gravity and harm-based theories of scholars such as Arendt and May can be contrasted with theories grounded in the perceived political nature of crimes against humanity, proposed by scholars such as David Luban and Richard Vernon. Luban characterizes crimes against humanity as "politics gone horribly wrong,"[63] while Vernon views them "as an abuse of state power involving a systematic inversion of the jurisdictional resources of the state."[64] Again, additional, widely divergent competing theories abound.

This small sample of some of the competing theories of ICL and its constituent parts demonstrates the basic fact that the normative values and underlying commitments of ICL itself, and international criminal justice as a global project, remain very much up for grabs.[65] The upshot of this combination of normative vagueness and contestation is that a widely shared, general understanding of what the essential elements of an international crime are simply does not exist.

Doctrinal Ambiguity

The ambiguity concerning the normative foundations of ICL both contributes to, and is a consequence of, the fact that, doctrinally, ICL arguably remains firmly in its formative stages and, hence, continues to lack specificity and clarity in certain important areas. While the mountain of jurisprudence churned out by the various ad hoc UN courts and tribunals, and the increasing codification of ICL in instruments such as the

61 Hannah Arendt, *Eichmann in Jerusalem: A Report on the Banality of Evil* (Penguin Classics, 2006), 268–269.

62 May, *Crimes against Humanity*.

63 Luban, "A Theory of Crimes against Humanity," 108.

64 Vernon, "What Is a Crime against Humanity?," 242.

65 See, for example, Nouwen, "International Criminal Law." On the increasing awareness of the brittleness of the normative assumptions upon which ICL has been constructed and the ramifications of such awareness, see Frédéric Mégret, "The Anxieties of International Criminal Justice" (2016) 29 *Leiden Journal of International Law* 197–221.

Rome Statute have led to increased clarity in many areas, ICL doctrine continues to be far from settled. Many of the areas within ICL that remain unclear and/or unsettled touch on issues that may affect fundamental questions of guilt or innocence or be determinative of ICL's very applicability to certain situations.

One example of an important doctrinal question that remains unclear concerns the precise set of prerequisites for crimes against humanity to be applicable to a given situation. In a general sense, as a legal term of art, the phrase "crimes against humanity" refers to a set of individual crimes that are considered crimes against humanity when committed as part of a "widespread or systematic attack against a civilian population."[66] This definition, however, remains subject to areas of ambiguity and contestation. The meaning of the term "attack" in this context, for example, remains unclear and unsettled.[67] In particular, it is unclear whether the requisite attack must involve the commission of acts of violence, and, if so, how "violence" is defined within this context.[68]

The applicability of crimes against humanity is further complicated at the ICC by the insertion in the Rome Statute of the requirement that crimes against humanity be committed "pursuant to or in furtherance of a State or organizational policy to commit [the requisite] attack."[69] It is unclear whether and to what degree this "policy" element narrows the applicability of crimes against humanity at the ICC.[70] For example, it is unclear whether a policy document or announcement must exist evincing an explicit policy to commit international crimes, or whether the

66 See, for example, Rome Statute of the International Criminal Court, Rome, July 17, 1998, in force July 1, 2002, 2187 UNTS 3, Art. 7(1); see also generally Luban, "A Theory of Crimes against Humanity"; May, *Crimes against Humanity*; Chehtman, "Contemporary Approaches."

67 For example, in relation to the meaning of the term "attack" as codified in the Rome Statute, see, for example, Schmid, *Taking Economic, Social and Cultural Rights Seriously*, 76–80. The Rome Statute does state that the phrase "'[a]ttack directed against any civilian population' means a course of conduct involving the multiple commission of acts [constituting the *actus reus* of the various individual crimes against humanity listed in the Rome Statute] against any civilian population, pursuant to or in furtherance of a State or organizational policy to commit such attack." Rome Statute, Art. 7(2)(a). However, this definition provides little in the way of clarification, as its plain language suggests that the requisite "attack" simply requires the commission of multiple individual crimes against humanity.

68 See generally, Schmid, *Taking Economic, Social and Cultural Rights Seriously*, 76–80.

69 Rome Statute, Art. 7(2)(a).

70 Tilman Rodenhäuser, *Organizing Rebellion: Non-State Armed Groups under International Humanitarian Law, Human Rights Law, and International Criminal Law* (Oxford University Press, 2018), 250.

commission of crimes may be an incidental, yet foreseeable consequence of an otherwise noncriminal policy. It is also unclear whether non-state "organizations" must resemble states, and, if so, how and to what degree they must be "state-like."[71] As the determination of these questions will, in many cases, decide whether crimes against humanity are applicable to an entire situation, their interpretation will ultimately contribute significantly to dictating the outer boundaries of crimes against humanity applicability at the ICC.

Another area of ambiguity and contestation is that of ICL's distinctive "modes of liability." In many cases, legal findings concerning these modes of liability are determinative of guilt or innocence, as they are the means through which individuals are held accountable for collectively perpetrated crimes. The ad hoc tribunals utilized a variety of modes of liability to prosecute individuals for their contributions to collective crimes. One of the most controversial of these modes has been that of the joint criminal enterprise (JCE), which was held by the ICTY, ICTR, SCSL, and ECCC to be a mode of "commission," though not without variation in terms of the doctrine's specific requirements. In any event, JCE has been subject to a steady stream of criticism,[72] and the precise requirements of JCE have also fluctuated over time and remain somewhat unsettled, including in terms of critically important issues such as the minimum *actus reus* required.[73] In formulating JCE in the *Tadić* Appeal Judgment, the ICTY Appeals Chamber held that an accused must "contribute" to a group operating with a common criminal purpose; however, such contribution "need not involve commission of a specific crime . . .

[71] A fulsome discussion of these issues is outside the scope of the present inquiry. For a helpful discussion of issues related to the so-called policy element of crimes against humanity in the Rome Statute, see Darryl Robinson, "Crimes against Humanity: A Better Policy on 'Policy'," in Carsten Stahn, ed., *The Law and Practice of the International Criminal Court* (Oxford University Press, 2014), 705–730.

[72] For an overview of JCE and its historical antecedents in post-World War II ICL jurisprudence, see Jared L. Watkins and Randle C. DeFalco, "Joint Criminal Enterprise and the Jurisdiction of the Extraordinary Chambers in the Courts of Cambodia" (2010) 63 *Rutgers Law Review* 193–273: 206–263. For examples of criticism of JCE, see, for example, Allison Marston Danner and Jenny S. Martinez, "Guilty Associations: Joint Criminal Enterprise, Command Responsibility, and the Development of International Criminal Law" (2005) 93 *California Law Review* 75–169; Jens David Ohlin, "Three Conceptual Problems with the Doctrine of Joint Criminal Enterprise" (2005) 5 *Journal of International Criminal Justice* 69–90.

[73] On the fluctuation of the *actus reus* required under JCE liability, see Randle C. DeFalco, "Contextualizing Actus Reus under Article 25(3)(d) of the ICC Statute: Thresholds of Contribution" (2013) 11 *Journal of International Criminal Justice* 715–735: 718–721.

but may take the form of assistance in, or contribution to, the execution of the common plan or purpose."[74] Subsequent decisions, recognizing that virtually any act, no matter how insignificant, might be characterized as a "contribution" to a criminal enterprise, inserted the qualifier that individual contributions must be "significant" in order to suffice under JCE, although such jurisprudence has been uneven and what counts as "significant" remains imprecise.[75]

As JCE was first formulated by the Appeals Chamber of the ICTY in 1999, shortly after the 1998 Rome Conference, the concept was not included in the Rome Statute and has not been adopted by the ICC. Instead, the ICC adopted certain preexisting ICL modes of liability, such as superior responsibility, and outlined its own generally applicable modes of liability in Article 25 of the Rome Statute.[76] Although the ICC skirted the controversy associated with JCE by declining to adopt it as a mode of commission, Article 25(3)(d) of the Rome Statute nonetheless provides for liability in situations wherein an accused "[i]n any other way contributes to the commission or attempted commission of [a charged] crime by a group of persons acting with a common purpose."[77] The phrase "in any other way" within Article 25(3)(d) seemingly encompasses all contributions to group crimes that are not captured elsewhere within Article 25, and the inclusion of the qualifier "any" suggests a very low *actus reus* threshold.[78] Predictably, the threshold *actus reus* required under Article 25(3)(d) has been a contentious issue at the ICC. Several chambers have expressed opinions on this issue, with some judges favoring borrowing the "significant act" threshold of JCE, while others favoring alternative approaches.[79] As of yet, the ICC Appeals Chamber has not issued any final opinion on the matter, leaving the outer boundaries of individual liability at the ICC hazy in the process.

[74] *Prosecutor* v. *Tadić, IT-94-1-A, July 15, 1999*, ICTY, para. 227.

[75] For an overview of this body of jurisprudence, see DeFalco, "Contextualizing Actus Reus," 718–721.

[76] Rome Statute, Art. 25.

[77] Ibid., Art. 25(3)(d).

[78] For analyses of article 25(3)(d) liability, see generally: DeFalco, "Contextualizing Actus Reus"; Kai Ambos, "The ICC and Common Purpose: What Contribution Is Required under Article 25 (3)(d)?," in Carsten Stahn, ed., *The Law and Practice of the International Criminal Court* (Oxford University Press, 2015), 592–607; Zurab Sanikidze, "The Level of 'Contribution' Required under Article 25(3)(D) of the Rome Statute of the International Criminal Court" (2012) 83 *Revue Internationale de Droit Pénal* 221–232.

[79] DeFalco, "Contextualizing Actus Reus," 721–734.

The doctrinal ambiguity concerning the applicability of crimes against humanity and the minimum *actus reus* requirements of JCE and Article 25(3)(d) "contribution" liability at the ICC touch on issues that are routinely critical to questions of ICL's applicability to a situation and the guilt or innocence of specific accused. These determinations are but two of many fundamental doctrinal ICL questions that remain unsettled and at least somewhat ambiguous.[80] In many domestic legal regimes, such questions would be progressively addressed and clarified through litigation and/or the passing of new codes or statutes. This is not the case when it comes to ICL. Multilateral treaty processes are slow, laborious, and rare. Moreover, as discussed in the following section, ICL remains highly selective in its application, greatly slowing processes of clarification through adjudication. Indeed, ICL is so selective that ICL actors wielding discretionary decision-making powers typically face little, if any, pressure to consider ICL's potential applicability to situations other than those involving paradigmatic international crimes, allowing questions concerning the boundaries of ICL liability to remain unexplored and, hence, undefined.

Layers of Selectivity

Since its inception, and to this day, ICL continues to be extremely selective, in terms of the small number of international crimes that are prosecuted compared to the total number of such crimes committed.[81] This extreme selectivity represents perhaps the most fundamental challenge to the legitimacy of ICL, as one need not be a legal theorist to grasp why it may be problematic for a legal regime that purports to apply everywhere and to everyone to be only actually applied to a tiny subset of situations and individuals that it declares itself applicable to. This selectivity is especially pernicious because it directly undermines the intrinsically universalist ambitions of ICL.[82]

[80] Other examples of areas of ICL that remain unclear are defenses, other modes of liability, and how serious crimes must be to quality under the ICC's gravity threshold.

[81] On the topic of ICL's selectivity, see generally Timothy L.H. McCormack, "Selective Reaction to Atrocity: War Crimes and the Development of International Criminal Law" (1996) 60 *Albany Law Review* 681–732; Robert Cryer, *Prosecuting International Crimes: Selectivity and the International Criminal Law Regime* (Cambridge University Press, 2005).

[82] One of the foundational claims made by ICL is that it is a body of law that has global geographic and personal jurisdiction. This renders ICL a deeply cosmopolitan project. On

The effects of ICL's selectivity are compounded by the multifaceted nature of such selectivity, which operates in numerous ways and on numerous levels. First, ICL is jurisdictionally selective. International crimes regularly occur in jurisdictional gaps. Such gaps vary in nature, as they may be geographic, temporal, subject matter, or personal, in terms of the nature of the jurisdictional element(s) lacking in order for such crimes to be investigated and prosecuted by a competent authority. For example, there exists no legal institution with standing jurisdiction over international crimes committed prior to July 1, 2002, when the ICC began operations, aside from the limited pockets of jurisdiction conferred on the various ad hoc tribunals. The forward-looking temporal jurisdiction of the ICC immediately leaves a litany of mass atrocity situations that occurred before 2002, without any clear legal forum to pursue prosecutions within.[83] Similarly, all of the ad hoc tribunals have had explicit temporal limits placed on their jurisdiction, preventing certain atrocities from being investigated and adjudicated.[84]

In addition to temporal limitations, many ICL courts and tribunals have limitations placed on the ambit of their personal jurisdiction,[85] and,

this subject, see Darryl Robinson, "A Cosmopolitan Liberal Account of International Criminal Law" (2013) 26 *Leiden Journal of International Law* 127–153.

83 See Rome Statute, Art. 11. While theoretically states with personal jurisdiction over a suspect involved in one such international crime could invoke the doctrine of universal jurisdiction, such invocations remain very much the exception rather than the rule.

84 For example, the illegal bombing of Cambodia by the United States under the Nixon administration from 1975 to 1979 appears to have involved the quite clear commission of war crimes and/or crimes against humanity and was integral to the Khmer Rouge's rise to power. See generally Burt Neuborne, "The Legality of the American Bombing of Cambodia–The ACLU Position" (1973) 40 *Brooklyn Law Review* 1–34; Taylor Owen and Ben Kiernan, "Bombs over Cambodia" (October 2006) *The Walrus* 62–69; World Peace Foundation, "Cambodia: U.S. Bombing and Civil War," August 7, 2014, https://sites.tufts.edu/atrocityendings/2015/08/07/cambodia-u-s-bombing-civil-war-khmer-rouge. Despite the importance of the civil war and US bombing campaign to atrocity commission in 1970s Cambodia, the temporal jurisdiction of the ECCC is limited to the time between April 1975 and January 1979, the specific time frame during which the Khmer Rouge held power. See United Nations-Cambodia Agreement between the United Nations and the Royal Government of Cambodia Concerning the Prosecution under Cambodian Law of Crimes committed during the Period of Democratic Kampuchea, June 6, 2003, in force April 29, 2005, 2329 UNTS 117.

85 For example, the ECCC and Special Court for Sierra Leone (SCSL) have limited their prosecutions to a handful of suspects. The ECCC is limited to prosecuting either "senior leaders" or individuals otherwise "most responsible" for crimes committed during the Khmer Rouge era, while the SCSL was mandated "to prosecute persons who bear the greatest responsibility for serious violations of international humanitarian law and Sierra Leonean law committed in the territory of Sierra Leone since 30 November 1996." See United Nations-

in policy documents, the ICC Office of the Prosecutor has stated its intention to pursue only suspects it considers most responsible for relevant crimes, given its scarce resources.[86] Moreover, the ICC itself, despite its very name being suggestive of its having global jurisdiction, only has standing jurisdiction over crimes committed either on the territory of a state party, or by a national of a state party.[87] Otherwise the Court is powerless to investigate past or ongoing atrocity crimes, absent the extraordinary measure of a UN Security Council referral.[88]

In addition to falling within one of the various jurisdictional *lacunae* of ICL outlined earlier, many international crimes remain unprosecuted because of resource limitations and political realities. The scale and collective nature of most international crimes create unique practical challenges in terms of the selection of cases and suspects to pursue, even when an institution is conferred with unlimited jurisdiction in terms of how many individuals it is permitted to investigate and prosecute. The number of individuals complicit in the commission of mass atrocity crimes may run into the hundreds or thousands, rendering the prosecution of all suspects functionally impossible. This was the case in Rwanda in the wake of the 1994 genocide, as the new government's pledge to pursue full accountability against all individuals involved in the genocide quickly proved impossible from a practical standpoint.[89]

Cambodia, Agreement, Art. 1; Sierra Leone-UN, Agreement between the United Nations and the Government of Sierra Leone on the establishment of a Special Court for Sierra Leone, January 16, 2002, in force April 13, 2002, 2178 UNTS 137, Art. 1. These requirements are ultimately quite similar, as the language "most responsible" was also considered for the SCSL Statute. For a discussion of these terms and their similarities, see Randle C. DeFalco, "Cases 003 and 004 at the Khmer Rouge Tribunal: The Definition of 'Most Responsible' Individuals According to International Criminal Law" (2014) 8 *Genocide Studies and Prevention* 45–65: 45–53.

86 ICC Office of the Prosecutor, "Prosecutorial Strategy 2009–2012," February 1, 2010, www.icc-cpi.int/Pages/item.aspx?name=otp-rep-strategy-2010, para. 19.

87 Rome Statute, Art. 12.

88 Ibid., Arts. 12–13.

89 For example, in the wake of the 1994 Rwandan Genocide and following the creation of the ICTR, "over 120,000 lower-level suspects remained in Rwandan prisons, and the government soon realized it would take its dilapidated domestic judicial system over 200 years to try all cases" leading to the creation of a local quasi-judicial mechanism referred to as "Gacaca Courts." Shannon E. Powers, "Rwanda's Gacaca Courts: Implications for International Criminal Law and Transitional Justice" (2011) 15 *American Society of International Law Insights*, www.asil.org/insights. Of course, this pledge at "full" accountability did not encompass any of the numerous alleged atrocities committed by the Rwandan Patriotic Front (RPF) forces led by current Rwandan President Paul Kagame, who militarily ended the genocide in 1994. See Victor Peskin, "Victor's Justice Revisited: Rwandan Patriotic Front Crimes and the Prosecutorial Endgame at the ICTR," in

Thus, even in situations where full accountability is pledged, difficult prosecutorial selection decisions must be made. Such decisions typically necessitate triaging out even quite serious cases.

Political realities also narrow the practical jurisdictional reach of institutions tasked with investigating and prosecuting international crimes. Because such institutions depend on the cooperation of states in gathering evidence and apprehending suspects, political realities often stymie investigations, or prevent the effectuation of arrest warrants. The ICC, for example, has struggled in many cases to gather evidence, due to poor security conditions in areas where investigation sites are located or lack of local political support. For instance, the ICC saw cases related to the postelection violence that occurred in Kenya from late 2007 to early 2008 collapse.[90] The suspects in those cases included current Kenyan President Uhuru Kenyatta, whose case was indefinitely stayed due to lack of evidence in 2014, along with Deputy President William Ruto and former broadcaster, Joshua Sang, who were co-accused in a case dismissed for lack of evidence.[91] Serious acts of witness tampering, including the commission of acts of violence against witnesses, were reported as the cases deteriorated.[92]

Another example of political power frustrating efforts to prosecute international crimes is the ICC's failure to effectuate the arrest warrant it issued against former Sudanese President Omar al-Bashir and several of his associates in 2009 on various charges related to atrocities committed in the Darfur region and other areas of Sudan.[93] Al-Bashir visited numerous countries while the warrant has been valid, including various ICC state parties, all of which failed to execute the warrant.[94] Recently, the possibility of al-Bashir being prosecuted for international crimes, by the ICC, domestic courts, or another body, has increased.[95] However, the renewed

Scott Straus and Lars Waldorf, eds., *Remaking Rwanda: State Building and Human Rights after Mass Violence* (University of Wisconsin Press, 2011), 173–183.

90 Human Rights Watch, "ICC: Kenya Deputy President's Case Ends," April 5, 2016, www.hrw.org/news/2016/04/05/icc-kenya-deputy-presidents-case-ends.

91 Ibid.

92 Ibid.

93 For an overview of the charges against al-Bashir, see *Prosecutor* v. *al Bashir, ICC-02/05–01/09, Second Warrant of Arrest for Omar Hassan Ahmad Al Bashir, July 12, 2010*, ICC.

94 For example, al-Bashir visited Jordan on March 29, 2017, to attend the 28th summit of the Arab League. See Human Rights Watch, "Jordan: Bar Entry or Arrest Sudan's Bashir," March 26, 2017, www.hrw.org/news/2017/03/26/jordan-bar-entry-or-arrest-sudans-bashir; Sudan Tribune, "Sudan's Bashir Arrives in Jordan for Arab Summit," March 28, 2017, www.sudantribune.com/spip.php?article62037.

95 Randle DeFalco, "Sudan Announces Intention to Have al-Bashir and Others 'Appear' before the ICC" (February 13, 2020) *Just Security*, www.justsecurity.org/68643.

prospect of such a prosecution occurring is primarily attributable to political factors, most notably, the ouster of al-Bashir from power in Sudan, rather than any renewed commitment to universality or the mandates of the Rome Statute. Another example of such power politics is the ongoing efforts by the United States to block the ICC's ongoing investigation of alleged crimes related to the conflict in Afghanistan, including allegations of crimes committed by the US citizens.[96]

These various jurisdictional, practical, and political limitations on the reach of ICL create overlapping forms of selectivity. This selectivity progressively narrows the number of total situations, cases, suspects, and charges that are ever investigated and prosecuted. First, many large-scale international crimes occur each year in jurisdictional gaps, where, absent extraordinary action, such as a Security Council referral to the ICC, or a domestic judiciary invoking universal jurisdiction, there simply is no competent adjudicative body with jurisdiction over such crimes. Second, in the event that international crimes occur and an institution, such as the ICC, has jurisdiction, such institutions lack the resources to investigate more than a handful of situations at a time. Third, even if an institution such as the ICC has jurisdiction and sufficient desire to investigate exists, there is no guarantee that such investigation will be permitted to proceed and be successful in gathering evidence. Fourth, even in situations where evidence is available, the security situation and political climate permit its gathering, and relevant authorities faithfully execute arrest warrants, prosecuting authorities still must engage in triage. Because of the massive scale of such crimes, prosecutors must make difficult decisions concerning where to investigate, whom to investigate, and ultimately, what charges to bring.

Selectivity thus operates on multiple levels and in multiple ways within ICL. Such selectivity (or, perhaps more accurately, selectivities) both

[96] The most recent, and extreme, example of such efforts was the issuing of an Executive Order by the Trump Administration attempting to sanction specific ICC staff members and other individuals who may participate in the Court's Afghanistan investigation. On these sanctions, their questionable legality, and global reactions, see Randle DeFalco, "Is Pompeo Unintentionally Helping Out the International Criminal Court?" (March 25, 2020) *Just Security*, www.justsecurity.org/69362; Adam M. Smith, "Dissecting the Executive Order on Int'l Criminal Court Sanctions: Scope, Effectiveness, and Tradeoffs" (June 15, 2020) *Just Security*, www.justsecurity.org/70779; Beth Van Schaack, "The Int'l Criminal Court Executive Order: Global Reactions Compiled" (September 1, 2020) *Just Security*, www.justsecurity.org/72256; Haley S. Anderson, "Why Them? On the U.S. Sanctions against Int'l Criminal Court Officials" (September 2, 2020) *Just Security*, www.justsecurity.org/72275.

perpetuates the uncertainty of ICL's normative commitments and doctrinal substance, and confers considerable discretionary powers on ICL actors in terms of how they allocate their extremely scarce resources. Unsurprisingly, within this environment, the selection of whom to investigate has been subject to persistent controversy and contestation within ICL.[97]

Aesthetic Perception and International Criminal Law Norm Development

The ambiguity and selectivity of ICL inject uncertainty into assessments of ICL's applicability to real-world situations. Furthermore, due to the complex, politically contentious nature of most atrocity situations, norm entrepreneurs, technocratic experts, and other actors, all must routinely make factual and legal assessments while lacking knowledge of key facts and potential forms of evidence. Moreover, situations amid which atrocities are perpetrated tend to be complex and may change rapidly. Factions in conflict with one another are apt to actively hide evidence of their wrongdoing, or to falsely accuse their opponents of committing atrocities. Efforts to independently verify such claims are also often hampered by lack of access for journalists, investigators, and the like, due to security concerns or outright restrictions on travel.

It is against this backdrop of uncertainty and lack of knowledge that various actors interact with one another through the rubric of ICL, and in doing so, develop and refine relevant shared understandings related to atrocity and international crime. Such uncertainty, combined with the spectacular visibility of many (perhaps most) international crimes, leads ICL actors to focus their time and efforts addressing international crimes that are aesthetically familiar.[98]

All three social constructivist social learning models highlighted within interactional legal theory – norm entrepreneurship, epistemic

[97] See, for example, Cryer, *Prosecuting International Crimes*; deGuzman, "Choosing to Prosecute," 69; Ifeonu Eberechi, "'Rounding Up the Usual Suspects': Exclusion, Selectivity, and Impunity in the Enforcement of International Criminal Justice and the African Union's Emerging Resistance" (2011) 4 *African Journal of Legal Studies* 51–84; DeFalco, "Cases 003 and 004."

[98] As will be discussed in the following chapters, this tendency to aesthetically perceive atrocity crimes is further encouraged by the highly visible, easily recognizable ways in which many atrocities manifest themselves.

communities, and communities of practice – are influenced by aesthetic factors within the realm of ICL. Shared understandings relevant to ICL are developed most visibly within epistemic communities of legal experts. These experts interact in a variety of fora. The most obvious such fora are the various institutions, such as the ad hoc tribunals and ICC, explicitly empowered to investigate and prosecute international crimes. These institutions create environments within which large groups of actors with legal and other forms of expertise (investigators, translators, judicial assistants, etc.) engage in sustained interactions with one another. While the direct purpose of such institutions is the investigation and adjudication of international crimes, from the perspective of interactional legal theory, such institutions also serve as environments for social interaction and norm development.

Epistemic communities relevant to ICL are, however, not strictly limited to adjudicatory institutions such as the ICC. Actors with expertise relevant to ICL also fill the ranks of state departments throughout the globe and interact regularly at various functions and meetings, both large and small. Other organizations, such as the International Law Commission, and communities of experts, such as academics, also operate as epistemic communities, generating and refining shared understandings through interaction within communities of specialized expertise. Such communities have been integral to the development of ICL, as experts have been deeply involved in designing treaties such as the Genocide Convention and the Rome Statute, and further developing the substance of ICL through adjudication.

The rather soft legal edges of ICL, and the jurisdictional, political, and resource limitations that combine to limit the reach of the ICC and other international criminal justice institutions, present legal experts within such epistemic communities with considerable uncertainty and lack of knowledge. Crucial areas of law may be unsettled or ambiguous, evidence may be difficult to access, and political cooperation may not be forthcoming. Consequently, ICL's applicability, both generally and within a specific institutional setting, may be difficult for relevant actors, even ones possessing a great deal of expertise and training, to assess. Moreover, the resources such actors have at their disposal are typically quite limited. Given these circumstances, such actors must quite carefully select which situations and suspects to pursue, even within the potentially narrow ambit of their jurisdictional and practical abilities.

Consequently, even ICL legal experts, such as judges, prosecutors, or defense lawyers, who may be perceived as technocrats relatively detached from the often highly emotional subject matter ICL deals with, are apt to seek out familiar forms of violence and criminality when identifying potential international crimes. Such reliance may be entirely subconscious, but may still significantly, if subtly, influence how they interact with one another through the rubric of ICL and how they perceive the subject matter this body of law deals with. Over time, through the repetition of such individual interactions, patterns concerning the forms atrocity crimes may take begin to emerge, and actors are apt to actively look for such patterns to avoid or reduce uncertainty and fill in knowledge gaps. As such individuals interact with one another, in both legal and nonlegal settings, and discuss matters related to ICL, a distinctive language and set of normative understandings imbued with aesthetic considerations has emerged and become widely shared.

A similar, yet differently incentivized tendency to rely on aesthetic perception plays out within communities of norm entrepreneurs, which themselves often incorporate actors, such as legal scholars, or international lawyers, who are also members of epistemic communities.[99] The most visible norm entrepreneurs are advocacy groups and nongovernmental organizations (NGOs) such as Amnesty International and Human Rights Watch, which often quite openly advocate for the development of new legal norms relevant to ICL, including advocacy for new international crimes themselves.[100] The ranks of such organizations tend to be filled with international lawyers, or other individuals with specialized training relevant to ICL, lending credibility to their advocacy through affiliation with expert communities. Such organizations also

[99] Academics, for example, often fall within this category. While technocratic experts in some regards, academics may themselves openly champion new norms and have had a significant role in shaping the trajectory of ICL. For example, scholar Raphael Lemkin relentlessly advocated for the adoption of genocide as an international crime, while Cambridge Professor Hersch Lauterpacht was integral to the normative and legal development of crimes against humanity. For discussions of Lemkin and Lauterpacht's contributions to ICL, see Phillipe Sands, *East West Street: On the Origins of "Genocide" and "Crimes against Humanity"* (Knopf, 2016). As a more recent example, a group of legal academics, including members such as M. Cherif Bassiouni and Leila Sadat, have advocated for the creation of a crimes against humanity convention for years. See M. Cherif Bassiouni, "Crimes against Humanity: The Need for a Specialized Convention" (1994) 31 *Columbia Journal of Transnational Law* 457–494; Leila Nadya Sadat, ed., *Forging a Convention for Crimes against Humanity* (Cambridge University Press, 2011); Leila Nadya Sadat, "Crimes against Humanity in the Modern Age" (2013) 107 *American Journal of International Law* 334–377.

[100] For example, NGOs and other advocacy groups have championed the development of norms such as the responsibility to protect and greater recognition of sexual and gender-based violence within ICL.

create informal social networks within which they interact and promote select norms, often quite strategically. In addition to interacting with one another, ICL norm entrepreneurs actively engage in public advocacy utilizing sophisticated marketing and social media campaigns to broadly promote their respective agendas, at times with great success.[101]

Aesthetic considerations also influence the decision-making of ICL norm entrepreneurs, albeit in a slightly different way than they shape understandings within epistemic communities. Because norm entrepreneurs are actively engaged in what can be described as the "marketing" of new norms, they are incentivized to operate according to marketing practices in order to gain attention and increase receptivity to their messaging.[102] Within ICL and associated areas of law and politics, such as those of human rights, transitional justice, and humanitarian law, the standard method of promoting new norms is to appeal to public sympathy, while combatting compassion fatigue and the psychic numbing effect of abstract numbers and statistics, by highlighting the extreme harms associated with the commission of atrocity crimes and large-scale human rights violations, and seeking to personalize such harms through accounts and depictions of individual victim experiences.[103] Consequently, there is an incentive for norm entrepreneurs to highlight the most dramatic and horrific aspects of atrocity situations, in order to gain support for new norms, which are themselves marketed as being able to reduce, or even eliminate such horrors. This incentive leads to the creation and perpetuation of a particular, shocking style of representing international crimes grounded in graphic depictions of violence and its effects on individual victims.

It is relatively clear that experts and norm entrepreneurs play integral roles in the development of ICL. It is hard to argue that legal experts who have helped draft foundational ICL documents, such as the Genocide Convention or Rome Statute, and who serve as judges and lawyers at ICL institutions, such as the ICC, have not had a major hand in developing relevant legal norms. So too have norm entrepreneurs, from individuals such as Raphael Lemkin and Hersch Lauterpacht, to NGOs, such as Human Rights Watch, Amnesty International, or the Coalition for the

[101] Prominent relatively recent examples include the Save Darfur Coalition and the Kony 2012 marketing campaign.

[102] Within the realm of ICL in this regard, see generally Schwöbel, "Market and Marketing Culture."

[103] On this standard marketing narrative generally in relation to ICL, see ibid; see also Schwöbel-Patel, "Spectacle in International Criminal Law"; Kendall, "Donors' Justice."

ICC, also clearly shaped the trajectory of ICL. Such entrepreneurs have shaped ICL by doggedly advocating for new ICL norms, for example, pushing for acceptance of universal jurisdiction and greater recognition of sexual and gender-based violence. Often, much like other areas of international law, along with states themselves, such experts and activists are viewed as the only actors with the ability to shape the trajectory of ICL. As previously indicated, Brunnée and Toope reject such a narrow understanding of the pathways through which international legal norms are formed and evolve. Interactional theory instead adopts a quite broad and inclusive view of who and what institutions qualify as actors who contribute to the development of shared understandings relevant to international law, through more diffuse, less purposive processes of social interaction.[104]

This broader view of norm development and lawmaking is well-suited to account for how ICL has developed, as the language of mass atrocity and international crime is regularly employed outside the confines of traditional ICL fora, such as courts or in foreign relations, to describe a wide variety of situations and actions. The clear majority of such situations will never be subjected to any form of legal adjudication; however, ICL's applicability to real world events is assessed by actors such as scholars, NGOs, journalists, and the like, far more often than it is actually determined through legal adjudication. Thus, one ramification of ICL's selectivity is a large role for nontraditional actors to engage with ICL and make arguments concerning its applicability. While some may view the effect of such actors on the law itself as nil, Brunnée and Toope view such actors, and the communities within which they interact with one another, as participating in the development of shared understandings, and, potentially over time, of new legal norms.[105]

[104] For example, Brunnée and Toope argue that in the wake of the terrorist attacks of 9/11 the Bush administration actively sought to undermine the prohibition on torture under international law. However, Brunnée and Toope also argue that such efforts at undermining this legal norm were met with "vigorous efforts to uphold the rule on the prohibition of torture." Brunnée and Toope, *Legitimacy and Legality*, 102. Brunnée and Toope argue that the actors involved in such efforts were quite diverse, including "international organizations, individual diplomats and politicians, government lawyers, high-ranking military officers, nongovernmental organizations, academics, journalists, and the proverbial person in the street protesting against attempts to weaken the prohibition." Moreover, the "spaces in which these interactions occurred were equally diverse, ranging from UN meetings to domestic legislatures, and courts to national media, to the internet, and more."

[105] Brunnée and Toope, *Legitimacy and Legality*.

The ambiguity and malleability of the substance of ICL, meanwhile, facilitates the insertion of aesthetic considerations into these norm development processes as well. Actors, ranging from those far removed from relevant harms to local activists and grassroots organizations, typically arrive at preliminary conclusions concerning ICL's applicability to a given situation amid uncertainty and while lacking reliable factual knowledge. For instance, people may come to understand recent events in Darfur through the rubric of ICL as a "genocide" because they are exposed to various sources of information using that label. The same can be said for various other situations, such as the Rwandan Genocide or Khmer Rouge "killing fields," which have both come to be socially understood as emblematic examples of what atrocities are, and are also associated with a catalogue of horrific stories and depictions of suffering, abuse, and violence that are by now, integral aspects of social understandings of such events.

When an individual person, or actors within communities of practice relevant to ICL, interact with the world and one another through the medium of ICL, they do so while using a common language and set of normative reference points. This language and these reference points are often deeply aesthetic in nature, as actors interact with one another through the continual, if largely implicit, referencing of prior atrocities. Moreover, when presented with uncertainty concerning ICL's applicability, these actors are especially apt to resort to processes of aesthetic perception, as they typically lack complete knowledge concerning the actual substance of ICL and the full dynamics at play in a given situation involving the infliction of harm on a massive scale.

Conclusion

Aesthetic perception and the representativeness heuristic are integral to how each of us makes sense of an uncertain, complicated world. If aesthetic perception operates as a process of intuitive, emotional evaluation, one can see how exposure to the horrors of atrocity create a situation conducive to individual, and in turn, shared understandings of international crimes being grounded in a particular set of sensory and emotional experiences. If one accepts the central insight of constructivism that "things are made, and made up, in and through diverse social and cultural processes, practices, and actions"[106] and the assertion that

[106] Schneider, "Social Constructionism," 724.

aesthetic considerations – that is, sensory experiences and the thoughts and emotions triggered by them – influence how each of us interacts with the world and one another, then it follows that aesthetic considerations play some role in all processes of individual, and in turn, social meaning-making. Indeed, this conclusion may seem obvious to the point of triteness.

Beyond these seemingly self-evident realities of human experience and social interaction, what this chapter has set out to elucidate are the factors that tend to encourage *more or less* reliance on aesthetic perception and to assess the implications for norm development processes relevant to ICL. Generally, individuals tend to rely more so on aesthetic perception, or a "know it when you see it" approach, when faced by uncertainty and/or lack of knowledge. Because ICL is awash in uncertainty and lack of knowledge, it follows that individuals interacting through the rubric of ICL to identify potential international crimes are apt to rely, consciously or not, significantly on aesthetic perception and the representative heuristic when doing so. Over time, through this dynamic, widely shared understandings of international crime have become imbued with aesthetic substance. To paraphrase Rancière, that which is socially and legally identifiable, knowable, or "sensible" as a potential manifestation of genocide, a crime against humanity, or a war crime, has been "distributed" or "partitioned" in conformance with, among other things, a particular aesthetic paradigm or model. As described in Chapter 2, the net result of this reliance on aesthetics has been the grounding of shared understandings of international crimes in an aesthetic of horrific spectacle. The remainder of this book considers whether ICL, *de lege lata*, might be applicable to mass harms committed through means deviating from the atrocity aesthetic, and explores some of the social, legal, and political ramifications of ICL's myopic focus on horrific spectacles.

4

Unspectacular Atrocities and International Criminal Law

The previous two chapters sought to describe what this book argues is an unstated, yet dominant aesthetic model of international crime commission and to offer some thoughts on how this model came to be so embedded while remaining unacknowledged, even invisible. Chapter 2 argued that shared understandings of international crimes are grounded in, among other things, an aesthetic of horrific spectacle, which I refer to as the "atrocity aesthetic." Chapter 3 offered a theory as to why this is the case and how this notion seems to have been uncritically reproduced without even being acknowledged in most cases, arguing that the combination of the spectacularly visible, self-evident nature of many forms of international crime commission, along with the continuing normative and doctrinal ambiguity of ICL, and various forms of selectivity operating to limit the reach of ICL institutions combine to create an environment especially conducive to reliance on aesthetic perception in the identification and assessment of the relative gravity of potential international crimes.

One may well agree with the main assertions made thus far in this book and yet find this to be, at best, slightly interesting, yet otherwise inconsequential. Over the years, in presenting various aspects of the research that went into this book, this is the response I have encountered many times. This kind of dismissive response is often couched in some variation of the following argument. Yes, when we think of international crimes, we think of appalling spectacles of harm causation. However, this is because, as crimes of mass violence, international crimes – at least the most serious ones, involving the most victims suffering the most serious harms – necessarily involve the production of such spectacles. After all, each of the three categories of "core" international crimes – genocide, crimes against humanity, and war crimes – contains at least some element, either contextual or substantive, requiring harm causation on a quite large scale. It seems logical that acts committed with the intention of destroying a "substantial part" of an entire racial, ethnic, national, or religious group (i.e. genocidal acts), a "widespread or systematic attack on a civilian population" (i.e. crimes against humanity), or crimes connected to an armed conflict (i.e. war crimes) will announce themselves in spectacular fashion.[1]

According to this line of reasoning, we associate international crimes with horrific spectacles because these crimes *necessarily* produce such spectacles. Consequently, the atrocity aesthetic merely describes the intrinsic aesthetic characteristics of genocide, crimes against humanity, and war crimes. Moreover, because ICL is fundamentally a body of *criminal* law, and, as such, is bounded by certain inherent traditional liberal criminal law limitations, most notably stringent requirements of causation, *mens rea*, and *actus reus*, it cannot be "expanded" to address subjects such as famine, corruption, or socioeconomic oppression. These topics, while clearly involving suffering, including potentially on a massive scale, simply lack the causal dynamics and high individual degrees of culpability demanded by criminal law. Evelyne Schmid, writing within the context of an assessment of ICL's potential applicability to harms also characterizable as economic, social, and cultural human rights violations, refers to this assumption as the "legal impossibility argument."[2]

This chapter addresses the contention that ICL practice focuses myopically on horrific spectacles because all, or at least the most serious,

[1] The crime of genocide involves acts committed with the intention of destroying at least a "substantial part" of an entire racial, ethnic, national, or religious group. Convention on the Prevention and Punishment of the Crime of Genocide, Paris, December 9, 1948, in force January 12, 1951, 78 UNTS 277. Jurisprudence establishes that, regarding efforts to destroy only a "part" of a protected group, such part must be "substantial" in relation to the overall group itself. See, for example, *Prosecutor* v. *Krstić, IT-98-33-T, August 2, 2001*, ICTY, para. 634 (holding that genocide requires "an intent to destroy only part of the group must nevertheless concern a substantial part thereof, either numerically or qualitatively."). Crimes against humanity can only be committed as part of a "widespread or systematic attack on a civilian population." See, for example, Rome Statute of the International Criminal Court, Rome, July 17, 1998, in force July 1, 2002, 2187 UNTS 3, Art. 7(1). Finally, while certain war crimes may be relatively minor in terms of their severity and may be committed against a single victim, and as such clearly would not amount to atrocities in and of themselves, all war crimes must nonetheless have a "nexus" to an armed conflict, which itself is the paradigmatic example of a situation involving mass violence. For example, "[w]ilfully depriving a prisoner of war or other protected person of the rights of fair and regular trial" is a war crime and does not necessarily involve any degree of mass harm causation, as the harm itself may not be especially severe (e.g. depriving a prisoner of war accused of a minor crime of a fair trial) and may be committed against a single victim. See ibid., Art. 8(2)(vi).

[2] Evelyne Schmid, *Taking Economic, Social and Cultural Rights Seriously in International Criminal Law* (Cambridge University Press, 2015), 22–40.

international crimes necessarily involve the production of such spectacles. It does so by demonstrating that ICL, *de lege lata*, appears capable of addressing forms of harm causation significantly different in nature and aesthetic familiarity than those it has overwhelmingly been applied to in the past. While certain harms are indeed situated wholly outside the reach of ICL (and indeed, in some cases, inherently outside the reach of criminal law more generally), this chapter challenges the notion that *all* situations involving the commission of genocide, crimes against humanity, and/or war crimes will necessarily conform to the atrocity aesthetic. This notion is not actually dictated by the doctrinal substance of ICL, and is predicated on an overly narrow view of the forms atrocities and associated individual culpability may take.

To demonstrate that ICL is not necessarily limited to any specified means of commission, and indeed, may be applicable to a much wider array of situations and harm causation processes than typically assumed, this chapter proceeds in two parts. First, it considers scholarship that examines how genocide, atrocity, and mass violence actually manifest and unfold. Within this literature, that atrocities are complex social phenomena that regularly involve harm production through a wide variety of overlapping, mutually reinforcing means, including many failing to conform to the atrocity aesthetic, is increasingly acknowledged.

After considering the causal dynamics of atrocities as a general class of social phenomena involving large-scale harm causation, this chapter examines the degree to which the doctrinal substance of ICL could account for the causal heterogeneity and complexity of atrocities. Through this analysis, this chapter demonstrates that, in theory, ICL could be applied to a variety of harm causation modalities failing to conform to the atrocity aesthetic. I identify four distinct (though oft-overlapping) examples of modalities of mass harm causation tending not to conform to the atrocity aesthetic, through which genocide, crimes against humanity, and/or war crimes could be (and perhaps have been) committed. These are: the creation/enforcement of famine conditions, extreme forms of corruption, aid interference, and socioeconomic oppression. Each of these four forms of harm causation tends to involve the production of harm through means that, at first glance, appear largely bureaucratic or otherwise banal in nature, and unfold over significant expanses of time. Consequently, such forms of harm causation, in most instances, fail to involve the production of discrete, temporally contained eruptions of spectacular violence, and as such, fail to manifest themselves in accordance with shared understandings of international criminality grounded in the atrocity aesthetic. Based on this analysis, this chapter concludes that there is a need to reassess our assumptions concerning what international crimes are, how they will be committed, who participates in such crimes, what such participation looks like, who is victimized, and how those who suffer are victimized, in order to better align ICL with the diverse array of forms mass harm causation processes may take.

Atrocities as Complex Processes

While, within the discourse and practice of ICL, atrocities tend to be rather simplistically conceptualized as spectacular outbursts of interpersonal violence, the large-scale production of human suffering and/or death may take a wide variety of forms. This fact is increasingly reflected in scholarly literature exploring the causal dynamics of atrocity and mass killing. Scholars have demonstrated that even paradigmatic atrocity events, such as the Rwandan Genocide, are often much longer-term processes that build up "beneath the threshold of visibility" until exploding spectacularly.[3] Moreover, certain key harms, in terms of their proportionate impact on victims, may remain hidden, even when occurring alongside more familiar forms of atrocity violence. For example, Marijke Verpoorten identifies various forms of what she refers to as "hidden violence" in the form of counterinsurgency campaigns and the creation of a refugee crisis that were integral to the production of mass death before, during, and after the 1994 Rwandan Genocide.[4] These harms were not addressed in any significant way by the ICTR, and, as noted by Larissa van den Herik, one legacy of the tribunal has been the "spotlighting" of certain harms and the relegation of others to "black holes" of obscurity.[5]

The increasingly acknowledged dynamic nature of the various stages and harm causation processes involved in genocides and other mass killing events has facilitated a movement toward understanding such phenomena as complex processes, rather than discrete events necessarily

[3] Norbert Finzsch, "War, Violence, and Population: Making the Body Count" (2011) 13 *Journal of Genocide Research* 187–189: 188 (book review) ("The Rwanda genocide is an important example of a long-term process that takes place mostly beneath the threshold of visibility, until it finally explodes in a rampage of violence that appears unfathomable.").

[4] Marijke Verpoorten, "Detecting Hidden Violence: The Spatial Distribution of Excess Mortality in Rwanda" (2012) 31 *Political Geography* 44–56.

[5] Larissa van den Herik, "International Criminal Law as a Spotlight and Black Holes as Constituents of Legacy" (2016) 110 *AJIL Unbound* 209–213.

following a predictable, linear model.[6] Consequently, genocide, atrocity, and mass killing are increasingly described as "dynamic processes" rather than "static" "events" or "outcomes."[7] Such process-based approaches tend to view atrocities as dense webs of complex, interactive methods of harm causation that, in the words of Sheri Rosenberg, amount to a "collective cataclysm" of suffering and death.[8]

Critical to the present analysis, many of the methods of bringing about mass suffering and death increasingly recognized as integral aspects of atrocity processes need not conform to the atrocity aesthetic. Scholars writing on these novel, oft-overlooked large-scale harm causation processes propose a wide range of descriptive nomenclature, referring to them as "cold" or "slow" forms of genocide, "genocide by attrition," "nonviolent crimes against humanity," "subsistence harms," "displacement atrocities," or "economic violence."[9] These and other labels are

6 See generally Verpoorten, "Detecting Hidden Violence"; Sheri P. Rosenberg, "Genocide Is a Process, Not an Event" (2012) 7 *Genocide Studies and Prevention* 16–23.

7 Sheri Rosenberg argues specifically that processes of genocide and mass killing are better conceptualized as "processes" rather than "events." Rosenberg, "Genocide Is a Process." Various other scholars, meanwhile, describe genocide, atrocity, and mass killing in processorial terms. See, for example, Martin Shaw, "From Comparative to International Genocide Studies: The International Production of Genocide in 20th-Century Europe" (2012) 18 *European Journal of International Relations* 645–668: 658 (referring to "dynamic genocidal processes"); Kjell Anderson, "Colonialism and Cold Genocide: The Case of West Papua" (2015) 9 *Genocide Studies and Prevention* 9–25 (distinguishing between "hot" more rapid forms of genocide and "cold" or "slow-motion genocide, where the destruction of the group may occur over generations" through complex processes of domination and subordination); Peter B. Owens, Yang Su, and David A. Snow, "Social Scientific Inquiry into Genocide and Mass Killing: From Unitary Outcome to Complex Processes" (2013) 39 *Annual Review of Sociology* 69–84; Benjamin Lieberman, "From Definition to Process: The Effects and Roots of Genocide," in Adam Jones, ed., *New Directions in Genocide Research* (Routledge, 2012), 3–17.

8 Rosenberg, "Genocide Is a Process," 18.

9 Anderson, "Colonialism and Cold Genocide" ("cold" genocide); Kiera L. Ladner, "Political Genocide: Killing Nations through Legislation and Slow-Moving Poison," in Andrew Woolford, Jeff Benvenuto, and Alexander Laban Hinton, eds., *Colonial Genocide in Indigenous North America* (Duke University Press, 2014), 226–245 ("slow" genocide); Maung Zarni and Alice Cowley, "The Slow-Burning Genocide of Myanmar's Rohingya" (2014) 23 *Pacific Rim Law and Policy Journal* 683–752 ("slow" genocide); Helen Fein, "Genocide by Attrition 1939–1993: The Warsaw Ghetto, Cambodia, and Sudan: Links between Human Rights, Health, and Mass Death" (1997) 2 *Health and Human Rights* 10–45 (genocide "by attrition"); Eamon Aloyo, "Improving Global Accountability: The ICC and Nonviolent Crimes against Humanity" (2013) 2 *Global Constitutionalism* 498–530 ("nonviolent" atrocity crimes); Diana Sankey, "Toward Recognition of Subsistence Harms: Reassessing Approaches to Socioeconomic Forms of Violence in Transitional Justice" (2014) 8 *International Journal of Transitional Justice* 121–140

employed in attempts to describe the causal dynamics involved in situations wherein large-scale suffering and/or death is brought about through complex sets of contributing causal factors that interact and unfold dynamically over time and space. In a more general sense, such atrocities can be framed as especially severe and causally direct manifestations of what Rob Nixon refers to as "slow violence" defined as "a violence that occurs gradually and out of sight, a violence of delayed destruction that is dispersed across time and space, an attritional violence that is typically not viewed as violence at all."[10] Nixon himself notes the relative un-spectacularity and resultant invisibility of such forms of violence, noting that while "[v]iolence is customarily conceived as an event or action that is immediate in time, explosive and spectacular in space, and as erupting into instant sensational visibility," slow violence "is neither spectacular nor instantaneous, but rather incremental and accretive, its calamitous repercussions playing out across a range of temporal scales."[11]

One alternative framing of atrocity and mass killing that quite effectively conveys the nature of large-scale slow violence is that of "genocide by attrition," proposed by Helen Fein.[12] Fein defines genocide by attrition as occurring when "a group is stripped of its human rights, political, civil and economic[,] lead[ing] to deprivation of conditions essential for maintaining health, thereby producing mass death."[13] Fein argues that processes of killing by attrition typically follow a pattern, whereby the "violation of political and civil rights leads to violation of economic and health rights and life-integrity rights, jeopardizing the life of group members on the basis of their real or perceived membership in the group."[14] These relatively slow and multifaceted attritive processes are, according to Fein, frequently ignored within genocide studies because "the historiography of genocide often focuses on the numbers directly killed – by execution, gassing, or burning in mass graves," despite the reality that "many victims die from starvation and disease induced by

("subsistence harms"); Dustin N. Sharp, ed., *Justice and Economic Violence in Transition* (Springer, 2014) ("economic violence").

10 Rob Nixon, *Slow Violence and the Environmentalism of the Poor* (Harvard University Press, 2011), 2.

11 Ibid.

12 Fein, "Genocide by Attrition."

13 Ibid., 10.

14 Ibid., 13.

elevated vulnerability following deportation (usually under harsh conditions) and enforced concentration."[15] Fein argues that conditions in the Warsaw Ghetto (1939–1943), Khmer Rouge-era Cambodia (1975–1979), and Sudan (1983–1993) all involved genocide by attrition alongside more paradigmatic forms of atrocity violence.[16]

In recent years, scholars have begun to both build on Fein's theory of genocide by attrition and to use it as a framework for understanding contemporary and historical atrocity situations. Sheri Rosenberg, for example, uses the concept of genocide by attrition as the foundation of her argument that "the social phenomenon of genocide" is best understood and analyzed "as a process rather than as the outcome of a process."[17] According to Rosenberg, outdated, "static" approaches to conceptualizing genocidal violence ignore the reality that such violence is best understood as a "process, a collective cataclysm that relies more heavily – than currently appreciated – on indirect methods of destruction for its success."[18]

[15] Ibid., 12. Fein provides the example of conditions in Jewish ghettos preceding the commencement of Nazi Germany's mass extermination Final Solution plan. Ibid., 14. Stating that:

> approximately one of every five Jews in the ghetto (whose population was constantly increasing due to the influx of refugees between 1939 and 1942) had already died by July 1942, before mass deportation. They died from starvation, tuberculosis, typhus, and undetermined causes, impossible to classify with any reliability because the greatest number of dead were dumped on the streets, picked up by wagons, and buried in mass graves after a simple count. The underlying causes of their death were German policies: expulsion of Jews from territory incorporated into the Reich to the General-Government; segregation and concentration in a walled ghetto with extreme overcrowding (68,000 persons per square kilometer); deprivation of its inhabitants of customary livelihoods and subsequent pauperization; enforcement of arduous labor for males; and denial of food, fuel, and medicines. (internal citations omitted).

Fein also references conditions in Cambodia under the Khmer Rouge (1975–1979) and in Sudan (1983–1993). Ibid., 18–31. Fein argues that there was "widespread agreement by 1978 that genocide was occurring" in Cambodia under the Khmer Rouge. Ibid., 22. This assertion is based on a nonlegal and controversial concept of "autogenocide." Nonetheless, Fein's more general argument concerning abuse and killing through attrition remains a vital contribution to understandings of processes of mass killing and abuse generally.

[16] Ibid., 14–31.

[17] Rosenberg, "Genocide Is a Process," 17.

[18] Ibid., 18. Rosenberg sees the marginalization of attritive processes within genocide studies as due to an "excessive focus on violent deaths" and a "preoccupation with the numbers of victims [which] have obscured alternative means of annihilation." Ibid. According to

Rosenberg and Everita Silina highlight the roles time and space play in facilitating the production of mass death through attritive means.[19] They note that relevant processes of killing through attrition tend to manifest themselves as a "slow process of annihilation that reflects the unfolding phenomenon of mass murder ... rather than the immediate unleashing of violence and death."[20] Rosenberg and Silina provide the examples of forced displacement, denial of health care, denial of food, and sexual violence as means through which genocidal policies may be pursued through attrition, noting that understanding genocidal processes in this dynamic way highlights the "interdependence between the series of human rights violations that create conditions of life that bring about physical destruction and eventual mass deaths."[21]

A host of other approaches to understanding genocide and mass atrocity generally follow Fein, Rosenberg, and Silina's approaches of treating instances of mass killing and abuse as complex, long-term processes, rather than short-term spectacular eruptions of violence. For example, Andrew Basso posits that "processes of forced population displacement and systemic deprivations of vital human needs (i.e. food, water, clothing, shelter, and medical care)" are integral components of broader, structural processes of mass killing beyond immediate and direct physical violence, referring to such processes as "displacement atrocities."[22] Diana Sankey makes a similar argument, using the label "subsistence harms," to refer to what she views as a "discrete type of violence, centred on attacking or showing total disregard for human

Rosenberg, this limited understanding of genocide (and more general mass killing processes) "ignores many victims of historical genocides died from slower, 'indirect', and less immediately deadly methods than outright murder." Ibid. While there is a tendency to conflate "indirectness" with a lack of proximate causation, the two are not necessarily one and the same.

[19] Sheri P. Rosenberg and Everita Silina, "Genocide by Attrition: Silent and Efficient," in Joyce Apsel and Ernesto Verdeja, eds., *Genocide Matters: Ongoing Issues and Emerging Perspectives* (Routledge, 2013), 106–126: 110 ("Interpreting genocide as a complex process of attrition draws attention to the link between direct and indirect means of annihilation and reveals the interdependence between the series of human rights violations that create conditions of life that bring about physical destruction and eventual mass deaths.").

[20] Ibid., 107. Again, Rosenberg and Silina challenge the accuracy of "linear models" of genocide. Ibid., 110.

[21] Ibid., 107, 110.

[22] Andrew Basso, "Toward a Theory of Displacement Atrocities: The Cherokee Trail of Tears, The Herero Genocide, and The Pontic Greek Genocide" (2016) 10 *Genocide Studies and Prevention* 5–29: 6.

subsistence."[23] Eamon Aloyo, meanwhile, refers to a similar set of situations, wherein mass harm is produced over time, through unfamiliar means, as "nonviolent crimes against humanity."[24] Further examples include terms such as "slow-moving," "slow-burning," or "cold" forms of genocide and atrocity commission.[25]

The notion that processes of mass killing and abuse are routinely much more causally complex and multifaceted than traditionally conceptualized, involving numerous processes beyond the direct infliction of physical violence by perpetrators against victims, has gained significant traction within scholarly discourses concerning atrocity, genocide, and mass killing. For example, in a 2013 article reviewing trends in social scientific literature on genocide and mass killing, the authors identify what they characterize as a:

> promising recent movement in the literature away from explaining episodes of genocide and mass killing as holistic events and toward the disaggregation and explanation of different causal processes and mechanisms at various levels of analysis that play a role in constituting such episodes [which recognizes that] Genocides are massively complex social phenomena that incorporate many moving parts at all levels of analysis.[26]

[23] Sankey, "Toward Recognition of Subsistence Harms." Sankey defines "subsistence harms" as "deprivations of the physical, mental and social needs of human subsistence, perpetrated against individuals or populations in situations of armed conflict or as an act of political repression, where the perpetrator acts with intent or with knowledge of the inevitable consequences of such deprivations." Ibid., 122. Sankey "introduces the term 'subsistence harms' as a way of gathering up and highlighting deprivations of subsistence needs as a discrete type of violence, centred on attacking or showing total disregard for human subsistence." Ibid.

[24] Aloyo, "Improving Global Accountability," 498 (arguing that "nonviolent harms can be just as morally wrong as violent ones."). Both Aloyo and Sankey focus on similar sources of harm, such as famine. Ibid., 505–506; Sankey, "Toward Recognition of Subsistence Harms," 124–127. Aloyo's analysis is based on an underlying conceptualization of such events as being typified by their nonviolent nature, while Sankey argues that similar or the same events are best conceptualized as a distinctive form of violence. Aloyo, "Improving Global Accountability"; cf. Sankey, "Toward Recognition of Subsistence Harms," 122. As such, while both Aloyo and Sankey call for greater engagement with substantially the same set of issues, they disagree as to the underlying conceptualization of the problem. Aloyo calls for greater engagement with nonviolent acts, while Sankey calls for an expanded conceptualization of violence itself. Both, however, agree that certain instances of the harms they discuss can and should be prosecuted as international crimes.

[25] Ladner, "Political Genocide" ("slow-moving"); Zarni and Cowley, "Slow-Burning Genocide" ("slow-burning"); Anderson, "Colonialism and Cold Genocide" ("cold").

[26] Owens, Su, and Snow, "Social Scientific Inquiry," 70.

The authors further find "encouraging evidence that the social science of genocide and mass killing is moving from initial engagement with genocide as a holistic dependent variable" and toward "analytic disaggregation and engagement with a diversity of contributing dynamics, processes, and outcomes."[27]

Thus, in sum, a contingent of scholars of genocide and mass atrocity have begun a movement away from linear, "static" understandings of genocide and other forms of atrocity, and toward more dynamic, process-based ones. Such "processorial" models of mass killing intentionally do not differentiate between forms of harm causation based on their familiarity or aesthetic characteristics, but explicitly recognize that situations wherein powerful actors cause harm on a massive scale tend to be complex social phenomena involving various, interactive processes of harm production. Clearly, many such forms of harm causation, particularly those which do not involve the commission of spectacular acts of violence, and/or unfold relatively slowly over significant expanses of time and space, are apt to manifest themselves in ways that deviate from the expected atrocity aesthetic.

While this reality is increasingly recognized within the academic study of genocide, atrocity, and mass killing generally, it has failed to gain a comparable degree of recognition within legal scholarship and discourse, especially in relation to ICL. Indeed, many scholars who have advocated for broader understandings of the causal modalities through which atrocities may be committed have blamed the narrow scope of ICL and international law more generally for the persistence of outdated, static understandings of genocide and atrocity.[28] Relatedly, there seems to be little incentive for actors committed to the anti-impunity movement and its emphasis on ICL to acknowledge the complexity of atrocity situations, as doing so could further expose ICL's fundamental inability to address the complexity and nuances of atrocity situations as they occur in the real world, while widening the already expansive impunity gap.[29]

The remainder of this chapter demonstrates that the inherent limitations of ICL are not always wholly to blame for this tendency toward oversimplified, static understandings of atrocity, as there is nothing in the substance of ICL that limits the modalities through which the vast majority of international crimes may be committed. Indeed, as it is

[27] Ibid., 72.

[28] See, for example, Rosenberg, "Genocide Is a Process," 17, 19.

[29] On the general inabilities of ICL to account for the complexity of real-world atrocity situations, see, for example, Mark A. Drumbl, *Atrocity, Punishment and International Law* (Cambridge University Press, 2007).

currently structured, ICL allows for many international crimes to be committed through a virtually unlimited set of means, many of which may deviate from the atrocity aesthetic.

Unspectacular Harms and International Criminal Law

While there may be a discernible shift in the general study of genocide and mass atrocity away from static, linear models of causation and toward more nuanced ones, a concomitant shift has not, as of yet, occurred within the realm of ICL. Instead, understandings of atrocity within ICL tend to frame atrocity processes within outdated, relatively simplistic models of causality and commission. As demonstrated previously, such models emphasize the production of harm through means that are highly visible and intuitively recognizable as "criminal" in nature. Even in situations where it is acknowledged that atrocities themselves may be more complex than commonly recognized, the standard assumption is that ICL is simply ill-equipped to delve into such complexities, relegating unfamiliar harms to the realm of noncriminal root causes or collateral consequences of atrocities, rather than means of perpetrating them.[30]

At first glance, this seems to be a roughly accurate characterization of the subject matter boundaries of ICL, as attempts to address the complex deeper causal realities of atrocity appear to run afoul of basic liberal criminal law principles of individual culpability and proximate causation. However, as the remainder of this chapter demonstrates, the notion that ICL simply lacks the ability to address novel forms of harm causation is not true in all cases. Not all forms of harm causation failing to conform to the atrocity aesthetic are purely structural in nature, and even the most paradigmatic atrocities routinely present practical challenges related to causal overdetermination and complex group action.[31] Moreover,

[30] ICL's status as an expression of liberal criminal law predicated on binary assessments of guilt and innocence and grounded in individualized culpability is often cited as one of the main factors contributing to the persistence of outdated, oversimplified understandings of the forms atrocity and human rights violations may take in the first place. See, for example, Sarah M.H. Nouwen and Wouter G. Werner, "Monopolizing Global Justice: International Criminal Law as Challenge to Human Diversity" (2015) 13 *Journal of International Criminal Justice* 157–176; Karen Engle, "Anti-Impunity and the Turn to Criminal Law in Human Rights" (2015) 100 *Cornell Law Review* 1069–1128; Adam Jones, "Genocide and Structural Violence: Charting the Terrain," in Adam Jones, ed., *New Directions in Genocide Research* (Routledge, 2012), 132–152.

[31] Indeed, causal overdetermination and group perpetration have both been referred to as leitmotifs of international crime. See, for example, James G. Stewart, "Overdetermined

nothing in the doctrinal substance of ICL explicitly limits its applicability to mass harms brought about through any specific set of means. To the contrary, while the applicability of the concept of "continuous" crimes, which involve "an ongoing breach [of ICL] or a series of repeated breaches which continue in time" remains unclear within ICL,[32] more well-established provisions contain various crimes and modes of liability that combine to criminalize individual contributions to the production of mass harm through a virtually unlimited set of means, making ICL, in actuality, relatively well equipped to address the factual and legal challenges presented by atrocities committed through unorthodox means.[33]

The Structure and Substance of International Criminal Law

Despite the widespread tendency to assume that all international crimes will be committed exclusively through the commission of spectacular acts of violence and abuse, nothing in the actual substance of ICL limits the array of means through which most international crimes may be committed. After all, as observed by Frédéric Mégret, criminal justice itself "is, in the end, nothing more than . . . a particular technique, a means to an end rather than an end in itself" and, accordingly, no set of transgressions or normative aims are necessarily "presupposed by the very idea of criminal law."[34] As such, given that the bulk of ICL is, in the words of Roger Clark, "weapons neutral," in terms of relevant means of commission, an assessment of ICL's general applicability and subject matter boundaries can only be made through an examination of the substance of the law itself, combined with careful analyses of relevant factual scenarios.[35] Given that a number of scholars, myself included, have conducted such analyses in relation to specific forms of harm causation

Atrocities" (2012) 10 *Journal of International Criminal Justice* 1189–1218; Jens David Ohlin, "Group Think: The Law of Conspiracy and Collective Reason" (2007) 98 *Journal of Criminal Law and Criminology* 147–206.

32 Matthias Neuner, "The Notion of Continuous or Continuing Crimes in International Criminal Law," in Morten Bergsmo, Wolfgang Kaleck, and Kyaw Yin Hlaing, eds., *Colonial Wrongs and Access to International Law* (Torkel Opsahl Academic EPublisher, 2020), 123–174: 130.

33 By this, I mean roughly as well equipped as ICL is to address the realities of *any* instantiation of mass harm.

34 Frédéric Mégret, "What Sort of Global Justice Is 'International Criminal Justice'?" (2015) 13 *Journal of International Criminal Justice* 77–96: 80–81.

35 See Roger S. Clark, "Weapons of Mass Destruction," in Dinah L. Shelton, ed., *Encyclopedia of Genocide and Crimes against Humanity* (Macmillan Reference, 2005), 1151–1155.

and/or real world scenarios tending not to conform to the atrocity aesthetic already,[36] the following is intended as an overview, rather than exhaustive analysis of all of ICL in terms of its theoretical applicability to unspectacular atrocities. Nonetheless, the following overview demonstrates that ICL, as currently constructed, includes various crimes and modes of liability that combine to provide potential pathways for pursuing individual criminal accountability for novel forms of harm causation.

Genocide

The crime of genocide consists of "any of the following acts committed with intent to destroy, in whole or in part, a national, ethnical, racial or religious group, as such:

(a) Killing members of the group;
(b) Causing serious bodily or mental harm to members of the group;
(c) Deliberately inflicting on the group conditions of life calculated to bring about its physical destruction in whole or in part;
(d) Imposing measures intended to prevent births within the group;
(e) Forcibly transferring children of the group to another group."[37]

Where only a "part" of a protected group is targeted, jurisprudence has consistently held that at least a "substantial portion" of the overall group population must be targeted for destruction for relevant acts to qualify as genocidal.[38] Accordingly, in *Prosecutor* v. *Musema*, the ICTR Appeals

[36] See, for example, Ilias Bantekas, "Corruption as an International Crime and Crime against Humanity: An Outline of Supplementary Criminal Justice Policies" (2006) 4 *Journal of International Criminal Justice* 466–484; Sonja Starr, "Extraordinary Crimes at Ordinary Times: International Justice Beyond Crisis Situations" (2007) 101 *Northwestern University Law Review* 1257–1314; Randle C. DeFalco, "Accounting for Famine at the Extraordinary Chambers in the Courts of Cambodia: The Crimes against Humanity of Extermination, Inhumane Acts and Persecution" (2011) 5 *International Journal of Transitional Justice* 142–158; Schmid, *Taking Economic, Social and Cultural Rights Seriously*; Ben Bloom, "Criminalizing Kleptocracy? The ICC as a Viable Tool in the Fight against Grand Corruption" (2014) 29 *American University International Law Review* 627–671.

[37] Genocide Convention, Art. II; see also Rome Statute, Art. 6.

[38] See, for example, *Prosecutor* v. *Krstić, IT-98-33-A, April 19, 2004*, ICTY, para. 8; *Prosecutor* v. *Jelisić, IT-95-10-T, December 14, 1999*, ICTY, para. 82; *Bosnia and Herzegovina* v. *Serbia and Montenegro, February 26, 2007*, ICJ, para. 198. This requirement may be numerically or qualitatively satisfied. See *Prosecutor* v. *Krstić, IT-98-33-T, August 2, 2001*, ICTY, para. 634 (holding that genocide requires "an intent to destroy only part of the group must nevertheless concern a substantial part thereof, either numerically

Chamber held that the crime of genocide consists of three essential elements: (1) commission of an enumerated act; (2) against a recognized protected class, "specifically targeted as such"; and (3) committed with the intent to destroy the protected group in whole or in part (i.e. the *mens rea* of "*dolus specialis*").[39]

Nothing in the language enumerating the *actus rei* through which genocide may be committed gives any indication that the crime can only be committed through a limited set of means, or that such means must conform to any specific archetype, aesthetic, or otherwise.[40] To the contrary, each of the enumerated means through which genocide can be committed, by their plain language, is quite expansive, rather than restrictive, in terms of the means through which the destruction of a protected group may be pursued. In this regard, the *actus rei* of killing members of the group; causing "serious bodily or mental harm" to members of the group; and "deliberately inflicting on the group conditions of life calculated to bring about its physical destruction," stand out in terms of their ability to encompass forms of genocide that occur over time, through attritive, socioeconomic, or other non-paradigmatic means.[41]

For example, regarding the genocidal *actus reus* of the deliberate infliction of "conditions of life . . . calculated to bring about" the destruction of a protected group, the Preparatory Commission for the ICC interpreted this provision as consisting of five distinct elements:

1. The perpetrator inflicted certain conditions of life upon one or more persons.
2. Such person or persons belonged to a particular national, ethnical, racial, or religious group.
3. The perpetrator intended to destroy, in whole or in part, the national, ethnical, racial or religious group, as such.

or qualitatively"). However, "the part targeted must be significant enough to have an impact on the group as a whole." *Prosecutor* v. *Krstić, IT-98-33-A, April 19, 2004*, ICTY, para. 8.

39 *Prosecutor* v. *Musema, ICTR-96-13-A, January 27, 2000*, ICTR, para. 154.

40 See Michelle Jarvis and Alan Tieger, "Applying the Genocide Convention at the ICTY: The Influence of Paradigms Past" (2016) 14 *Journal of International Criminal Justice* 857–877: 859 ("Confronted with the question of responsibility . . . the ICTY was not called upon to determine the extent to which these events resembled a particular factual paradigm. Instead, it was required to determine whether any of the genocidal acts specified in the Convention . . . had been committed with the intent to destroy the Bosnian Muslims in whole or in part.").

41 Genocide Convention, Art. II; Rome Statute, Art. 6.

4. The conditions of life were calculated to bring about the physical destruction of that group, in whole or in part.
5. The conduct took place in the context of a manifest pattern of similar conduct directed against that group or was conduct that could itself effect such destruction.[42]

These elements, while providing greater clarity, nonetheless continue to provide for a near-unlimited set of means through which relevant "conditions of life" may be produced, so long as the conditions themselves, alone or as part of a "manifest pattern of similar conduct," could actually destroy, in a physical sense, a substantial portion of the relevant group.[43]

The ICTR Trial Chamber adopted a similarly open-ended approach concerning the production of conditions of life calculated to destroy a protected group, holding in *Prosecutor* v. *Akayesu* that Article 2(c) of the Genocide Convention encompasses "methods of destruction by which the perpetrator does not immediately kill the members of the group, but which, ultimately, seek their physical destruction."[44] Similarly, in *Prosecutor* v. *Kayishema*, the same chamber opined that the Genocide Convention "allows for the punishment of the perpetrator for the infliction of substandard conditions of life which, if left to run their course, could bring about the physical destruction of the group."[45] Examples of specific means through which such conditions of life could be inflicted provided by the *Kayishema* Trial Chamber include "rape, the starving of a group of people, reducing required medical services below a minimum, and withholding sufficient living accommodation for a reasonable period, provided the above would lead to the destruction of the group in whole or in part."[46] Thus, the plain language of the Genocide Convention, especially Article 2(c), appears to quite readily accommodate the commission of genocide through means other than those conforming to the atrocity aesthetic. The same can be said of the *actus rei* of killing members of a targeted

[42] Preparatory Commission for the International Criminal Court, Report of the Preparatory Commission for the International Criminal Court, Addendum Part II, Finalized Draft Text of the Elements of Crimes, UN Doc. PCNICC/2000/1/Add.2, November 2, 2000, p. 7, Art. 6(c).
[43] Ibid.
[44] *Prosecutor* v. *Akayesu, ICTR-96-4-T, September 2, 1998*, ICTR, para. 505.
[45] *Prosecutor* v. *Kayishema, ICTR-95-1-T, May 21, 1999*, ICTR, para. 116.
[46] Ibid.

group, and that of causing serious bodily or mental harm to members of a targeted group.[47]

Crimes against Humanity

Crimes against humanity are an enumerated set of criminal offenses forming part of a widespread or systematic attack against a civilian population.[48] Like genocide, crimes against humanity may be committed through a virtually unlimited set of means, so long as such means satisfy the elements of an individual crime against humanity and are sufficiently connected to the requisite attack. Lists of specific crimes against humanity vary from jurisdiction to jurisdiction, although the Rome Statute contains a generally inclusive list of contemporary crimes against humanity, including:

(a) murder;
(b) extermination;
(c) enslavement;
(d) deportation or forcible transfer of population;
(e) imprisonment or other severe deprivation of physical liberty in violation of fundamental rules of international law;

[47] The ICTY and ICTR held that the term "killing" in this context to be akin to that of "murder," that is, "[h]omicide committed with intent to cause death." See *Prosecutor* v. *Akayesu, ICTR-96-4-T, September 2, 1998*, ICTR, para. 500. Clearly, intentional homicides can be committed through various means. Moreover, citing the *Akayesu* Trial Judgment, the ICTY Trial Chamber in *Krstić* stated that for the purposes of committing genocide, all the *actus reus* of inflicting "serious bodily or mental harm [requires] is an intentional act or omission causing serious bodily or mental suffering. The gravity of the suffering must be assessed on a case by case basis and with due regard for the particular circumstances." *Prosecutor* v. *Krstić, IT-98-33-T, August 2, 2001*, ICTY, para. 513. Moreover, such "serious harm need not cause permanent and irremediable harm, but it must involve harm that goes beyond temporary unhappiness, embarrassment or humiliation. It must be harm that results in a grave and long-term disadvantage to a person's ability to lead a normal and constructive life." Ibid. For additional analysis on this subject, see Schmid, *Taking Economic, Social and Cultural Rights Seriously*, 229–230.

[48] While this definition varies slightly from jurisdiction to jurisdiction, the requirement of the existence of a widespread or systematic attack against a civilian population is universally required and presumably amounts to customary international law. See generally Leila Nadya Sadat, "Crimes against Humanity in the Modern Age" (2013) 107 *American Journal of International Law* 334–377. As noted previously, the Rome Statute adds the unique requirement that such attack be committed pursuant to a "state or organizational policy." Rome Statute, Art. 7(1). The precise meaning of this requirement remains unclear. See generally Darryl Robinson, "Crimes against Humanity: A Better Policy on 'Policy'," in Carsten Stahn, ed., *The Law and Practice of the International Criminal Court* (Oxford University Press, 2014), 705–730.

(f) torture;
(g) rape, sexual slavery, enforced prostitution, forced pregnancy, enforced sterilization, or any other form of sexual violence of comparable gravity;
(h) persecution against any identifiable group or collectivity on political, racial, national, ethnic, cultural, religious, gender . . ., or other grounds that are universally recognized as impermissible under international law, in connection with any act referred to in this paragraph or any crime within the jurisdiction of the [ICC];
(i) enforced disappearance of persons;
(j) the crime of apartheid; and
(k) other inhumane acts of a similar character intentionally causing great suffering, or serious injury to body or to mental or physical health.[49]

Both the general, "*chapeau*" requirements of crimes against humanity, and the elements of various individual crimes provide a significant degree of coverage over forms of mass harm causation that may fail to conform to the atrocity aesthetic. In terms of *chapeau* elements, the qualifiers "widespread or systematic" refer to the scale, or highly organized nature of the requisite attack. Less clear is precisely what forms the requisite "attack" itself can take and whether such attack must necessarily involve the commission of acts of physical violence.[50] There exists a common tendency to assume that such attacks must involve the commission of acts of violence, in a narrow sense of the word.[51] This assumption,

[49] Rome Statute, Art. 7(1).

[50] Schmid, *Taking Economic, Social and Cultural Rights Seriously*, 76 (internal citation omitted). Within the context of the ICC, according to Tilman Rodenhäuser, "the understanding of attack as spelled out in the ICC Statute requires groups to be able to orchestrate a campaign or operation that involves the multiple commissions of crimes, which follows an organizational policy." Tilman Rodenhäuser, "Beyond State Crimes: Non-State Entities and Crimes against Humanity" (2014) 27 *Leiden Journal of International Law* 913–926: 924. For additional analysis, see Dermot Groome, "The Church Abuse Scandal: Were Crimes against Humanity Committed?" (2011) 11 *Chicago Journal of International Law* 439–503.

[51] See, for example, David Luban, "A Theory of Crimes against Humanity," 29 *Yale Journal of International Law* 85-167, 103 (Luban argues that, if attacks could be committed nonviolently, then "a system of laws prohibiting the use of foreign languages in official documents and traffic signs, if designed to force immigrant groups to learn the native language of a country, could constitute crimes against humanity of the persecution type. Regardless of what one thinks of the wisdom of such language laws, labeling them crimes against humanity is absurd."). Conversely, see Chile Eboe-Osuji, "Crimes against Humanity: Directing Attacks against a Civilian Population" (2006) 2 *African Journal of*

however, is not grounded in any law, but in preconceptions of the forms harm causation will take. As former ICC President Chile Eboe-Osuji contends, the:

> range of mistreatments recognised as crimes against humanity (such as enslavement, deportation, imprisonment, persecutions, apartheid) do not always connote the commission of violence against the victims, although they most often do. It is for this reason that the case law has taken a view of "attack" as encompassing "any mistreatment" of the civilian population.[52]

This approach is well supported in case law. For example, the case cited by Eboe-Osuji in making this assertion is that of *Prosecutor* v. *Kunarac, Kovac and Vukovic*, wherein the ICTY Appeals Chamber held that "the attack in the context of a crime against humanity . . . encompasses any mistreatment of the civilian population."[53]

Disputes over whether the requisite attack for crimes against humanity must be violent or not, moreover, remain highly contingent on underlying notions of what constitutes violence itself, which remains highly contested.[54] For example, Evelyne Schmid argues that, despite statements

Legal Studies 118–129: 119 ("Typically, an attack would entail violence against the victims. This, however, need not be so in all cases of crimes against humanity.").

52 Eboe-Osuji, "Crimes against Humanity," 119; see also Stuart Ford, "Is the Failure to Respond Appropriately to a Natural Disaster a Crime against Humanity? The Responsibility to Protect and Individual Criminal Responsibility in the Aftermath of Cyclone Nargis" (2010) 38 *Denver Journal of International Law and Policy* 227–276: 257 ("While the underlying acts that can constitute the attack are often carried out through violence, the attack does not have to be violent and may involve other inhumane mistreatment of the civilian population.").

53 *Prosecutor* v. *Kunarac, Kovac and Vukovic, IT-96–23-A and IT-96–23/1-A, June 12, 2002*, ICTY, para. 86. The ICTR Trial Chamber expressed a similar sentiment in *Akayesu*, opining that:

> The concept of "attack" may be defined as a unlawful act of the kind enumerated in [the ICTR Statute's provision on crimes against humanity], like murder, extermination, enslavement, etc. An attack may also be non violent in nature, like imposing a system of apartheid, which is declared a crime against humanity in Article 1 of the Apartheid Convention of 1973, or exerting pressure on the population to act in a particular manner, may come under the purview of an attack, if orchestrated on a massive scale or in a systematic manner.

Prosecutor v. *Akayesu, ICTR-96-4-T, September 2, 1998*, ICTR, para. 581; see also *Prosecutor* v. *Vasiljević, IT-98-32-T, November 29, 2002*, ICTY, paras. 29–30 ("In the context of a crime against humanity, the phrase 'attack' is not limited to the use of armed force; it also encompasses any mistreatment of the civilian population.").

54 For a discussion of the entrenched definitional debate concerning the meaning of the term violence, see Eugene Aisenberg et al., "Defining Violence," in Todd I. Herrenkohl

to the contrary in case law, the very "notion of an attack would lose its function to limit the scope of crimes against humanity if it was interpreted to encompass nonviolent measures alone."[55] However, Schmid also argues that the term violence should be understood broadly, to encompass "abusive policies that do not directly kill or maim immediately," including various forms of economic, social, and cultural human rights violations.[56] Thus, the disagreement between Schmid, who believes that the requisite attack within the context of crimes against humanity must be "violent" in nature, and others, such as Eboe-Osuji and scholar Stuart Ford, who argue that such attacks may be nonviolent, appears to be mostly grounded in differing underlying conceptualizations of what constitutes violence itself, rather than fundamental disagreements concerning the scope of crimes against humanity. What Eboe-Osuji may consider a "nonviolent" attack against a civilian population, Schmid would likely view as merely a form of violence that happens to not involve the direct and immediate physical application of force against victims. Thus, there seems to be a consensus, albeit a tentative one, that requisite widespread or systematic attacks can take many forms, including those which produce harms attritively over time or otherwise may not conform to the dominant atrocity aesthetic.

In terms of individual crimes against humanity, many crimes are defined in such a way as to allow their commission through an open-ended set of means. For instance, within the context of crimes against humanity involving killing, the ICC Preparatory Commission views the term "killing" as "interchangeable with the term 'caused death'."[57] Moreover, various individual crimes against humanity are constructed in a manner evincing the clear aim of maintaining flexibility in terms of means of commission. A prime example of such flexibility is the crime against humanity of extermination. A crime of mass killing, extermination, like genocide, explicitly "encompasses the intentional infliction of conditions of life, *inter alia*, the deprivation of access to food and medicine, calculated to bring about the destruction of part of

et al., eds., *Violence in Context: Current Evidence on Risk, Protection, and Prevention* (Oxford University Press, 2010), 13–22.

55 Schmid, *Taking Economic, Social and Cultural Rights Seriously*, 77.

56 Ibid; Scott Straus, "What Is Being Prevented? Genocide, Mass Atrocity, and Conceptual Ambiguity in the Anti-Atrocity Movement," in Sheri P. Rosenberg, Tibi Galis, and Alex Zucker, eds., *Reconstructing Atrocity Prevention* (Oxford University Press, 2016), 17–30: 29.

57 Preparatory Commission, UN Doc. PCNICC/2000/1/Add.2, p. 5, note 7.

a population."[58] The ICC Preparatory Commission lists the first element of extermination as requiring that the "perpetrator killed one or more persons, including by inflicting conditions of life calculated to bring about the destruction of part of a population," further noting that such "conduct could be committed by different methods of killing, either directly or indirectly."[59] While the enforcement of harsh "conditions of life" must be "calculated" to actually cause mass death, it remains unclear whether the term calculated is meant to imply a subjective intent or merely a "calculated assessment" that the conditions being inflicted will cause mass death (i.e. a form of knowledge).[60] The precise meaning of the "calculated" in this context has yet to be clarified, standing as another example of the fact that ICL remains in its formative stages, subject to ambiguity in many key areas. Regardless of the ultimate resolution of this *mens rea* issue, the fact remains that, in terms of *actus reus* requirements, the crime against humanity of extermination can clearly be committed through a wide variety of causal modalities.

Various other crimes against humanity, such as those of murder, enslavement, deportation, forcible transfer, torture, persecution,

[58] Rome Statute, Art. 7(2)(b). While the quoted definition of extermination is from the Rome Statute, it accords with how the crime has been defined more generally within ICL. For example, the ICTR and ICTY have held that extermination may be committed by "subjecting a number of people to conditions of living that would inevitably lead to death." *Prosecutor* v. *Ntakirutimana and Ntakirutimana, ICTR-96-10-A and ICTR-96-17-A, December 13, 2004*, ICTR, para. 522; see also *Prosecutor* v. *Stakić, IT-97-24-A, March 22, 2006*, ICTY, para. 259.

[59] Preparatory Commission, UN Doc. PCNICC/2000/1/Add.2, p. 6.

[60] Evelyne Schmid, for example, asserts that the "verb 'calculated' implies that the [alleged means through which mass death is caused, such as] deprivation of access to basic socio-economic rights must have been intended as a mechanism to bring about the destruction of part of a population." Schmid, *Taking Economic, Social and Cultural Rights Seriously*, 155. However, such an interpretation necessarily renders an accused's subjective motive for causing mass death a substantive element of the crime, which is quite rare within criminal law generally, due to the difficulty of proving subjective intent and its marginal role in the moral culpability of an accused, who otherwise was fully aware of the nature and consequences of his actions. More often, motive is treated as probative of knowledge or intent if proved, or as an aggravating factor at sentencing, such as is the case for most hate crimes. Furthermore, Schmid does acknowledge that a UN Commission of Inquiry for North Korea stated that in its view the "calculated" element of extermination requires only "the calculated assessment [by the accused] that the infliction of the particular conditions of life will in the ordinary course of events result in mass killing, even though this might not be the perpetrator's subjective purpose." Ibid., 155, note 418, citing United Nations Commission of Inquiry on Human Rights in the Democratic People's Republic of Korea, Report of the Commission of Inquiry on Human Rights in the Democratic People's Republic of Korea, UN Doc. A/HRC/25/CRP.1, February 7, 2014, p. 324, note 1558.

apartheid, and other inhumane acts, similarly allow for commission through a near-unlimited set of means.[61] For example, murder is a crime against humanity when forming part of a widespread or systematic attack against a civilian population.[62] According to the ICC Preparatory Commission, the crime against humanity of murder consists of three elements:

1. The perpetrator killed one or more persons.
2. The conduct was committed as part of a widespread or systematic attack directed against a civilian population.
3. The perpetrator knew that the conduct was part of or intended the conduct to be part of a widespread or systematic attack against a civilian population.[63]

As referenced previously, the Commission is also of the opinion that within the context of murder in the Rome Statute, the "term 'killed' is interchangeable with the term 'caused death'."[64] Thus, as with extermination, one can envision a multitude of processes through which a perpetrator, alone or with others, could intentionally cause the death of a victim.

Similarly, the crime against humanity of enslavement occurs when a perpetrator exercises "any or all of the powers attaching to the right of ownership over one or more persons, such as by purchasing, selling, lending or bartering such a person or persons, or by imposing on them a similar deprivation of liberty."[65] The Preparatory Commission views enslavement as encompassing forced labor and human trafficking, which can themselves take many forms.[66]

The crimes of persecution and other inhumane acts also follow a similar pattern of using general language to prohibit actions causing specific harmful outcomes for victims, while allowing for commission through any number of means. According to the Preparatory

[61] See generally, Schmid, *Taking Economic, Social and Cultural Rights Seriously*; Rome Statute, Art. 7(1)–(2); Preparatory Commission, UN Doc. PCNICC/2000/1/Add.2, pp. 74–165; Randle C. DeFalco, "Conceptualizing Famine as a Subject of International Criminal Justice: Toward a Modality-Based Approach" (2017) 38 *University of Pennsylvania Journal of International Law* 1113–1187; Aloyo, "Improving Global Accountability"; Clark, "Weapons of Mass Destruction"; Ford, "Failure to Respond."

[62] See, for example, Rome Statute, Art. 7(1)(a).

[63] Preparatory Commission, UN Doc. PCNICC/2000/1/Add.2, p. 9.

[64] Ibid., 9, note 7.

[65] Ibid., 10.

[66] Ibid., 10, note 11.

Commission, persecution occurs when victims are deprived of a fundamental right because of their "political, racial, national, ethnic, cultural, religious, [or] gender" identity or on "other grounds that are universally recognized as impermissible under international law."[67] The requisite "fundamental rights" violation is not limited to civil and political human rights violations, but may also involve the violation of a variety of economic, social, and cultural rights.[68]

The crime against humanity of other inhumane acts, meanwhile, is a residual, catch-all crime that, according to the ICTY Trial Chamber, "was deliberately designed as a residual category, as it was felt to be undesirable for this category to be exhaustively enumerated[, because any] exhaustive categorization would merely create opportunities for evasion of the letter of the prohibition."[69] This intentionally broad crime encompasses the "inflict[ion of] great suffering, or serious injury to body or to mental or physical health, by means of an inhumane act . . . of a character similar to any other" crime against humanity.[70] According to the Preparatory Commission, the term "'character' refers to the nature and gravity of the act."[71] Individuals have been convicted of other inhumane acts for a wide variety of forms of mistreatment, ranging from "beatings, torture, sexual violence, humiliation, harassment, psychological abuses, and confinement in inhumane conditions,"[72] to injuries sustained during forced labor,[73] and general physical assaults causing injury.[74] Scholars and experts have theorized the applicability of other inhumane acts to a large number of additional scenarios, ranging from the enforcement of famine conditions by the Government of North Korea, to the refusal of the junta government in Myanmar to allow humanitarian relief efforts in the wake of Cyclone Nargis, to the systemic commission of sexual abuse within the Catholic Church, to the abuse of migrants by border patrol agents.[75] Thus, in sum, much like genocide,

67 Ibid., 15.
68 See Schmid, *Taking Economic, Social and Cultural Rights Seriously*, 124–139.
69 *Prosecutor* v. *Kupreškić, IT-95-16-T, January 14, 2000*, ICTY, para. 563.
70 Preparatory Commission, UN Doc. PCNICC/2000/1/Add.2, p. 17.
71 Ibid., 17, note 30.
72 *Prosecutor* v. *Kvočka, IT-98-30/1-T, November 2, 2001*, ICTY, para. 209.
73 *Prosecutor* v. *Naletilić, IT-98-34-T, March 31, 2003*, ICTY, para 271.
74 See e.g. *Prosecutor* v. *Tadić, IT-94-1-T, May 7, 1997*, ICTY, para. 697 (beatings of six prisoners).
75 See UN Commission of Inquiry on Human Rights in the Democratic People's Republic of Korea, "Report of the Detailed Findings of the Commission of Inquiry on Human Rights in the Democratic People's Republic of Korea," UN Doc. A/HRC/25/CRP.1, February 7,

crimes against humanity may be committed through a virtually unlimited array of means which may, or may not, conform to the atrocity aesthetic.

War Crimes

War crimes are serious violations of international humanitarian law entailing individual criminal responsibility.[76] Due to their grounding in the law of war, many war crimes are quite specific in their application.[77] The universal requirement for all war crimes is that each individual crime must have a "nexus" to an armed conflict.[78] The applicability of certain war crimes depends on whether the requisite armed conflict is legally determined to be "international" in character or not.[79] Aside from this requirement that war crimes have a connection to armed conflict, certain war crimes may involve harms of a gravity much less serious than most forms of crimes against humanity or genocide. This potential lack of seriousness has led David Scheffer to cite specific war crimes as examples of non-atrocity-based international crimes.[80]

Regardless of whether select war crimes are properly considered within the rubric of atrocity, as with genocide and crimes against humanity, many war crimes provisions allow for commission through a wide variety of means. For example, war crimes derived from Common Article 3 of the 1949 Geneva Conventions, such as those of "wilful killing," "torture or inhuman treatment," "wilfully causing great suffering, or serious injury to body or health," and the "extensive destruction and appropriation of property, not justified by military necessity and carried out

2014; Ford, "Failure to Respond"; Groome, "Church Abuse Scandal"; Ioannis Kalpouzos and Itamar Mann, "Banal Crimes against Humanity: The Case of Asylum Seekers in Greece" (2015) 16 *Melbourne Journal of International Law* 1–28.

[76] See generally Antonio Cassese, *International Criminal Law*, 2nd ed. (Oxford University Press, 2008), 81.

[77] This is because many war crimes are grounded in underlying legal prohibitions on often quite specific prohibitions outlawing specific weapons or forms of warfare.

[78] For discussions of this "nexus" requirement, see, for example, Antonio Cassese, "The Nexus Requirement for War Crimes" (2012) 10 *Journal of International Criminal Justice* 1395–1417; *Prosecutor* v. *Kunarac, Kovac and Vukovic, IT-96-23-A and IT-96-23/1-A, June 12, 2002*, ICTY, para. 58.

[79] For example, the Rome Statute contains two separate lists of war crimes, divided into those applicable to international armed conflicts, and a shorter list of those applicable to non-international armed conflicts. Rome Statute, Art. 8(2).

[80] See, for example, David Scheffer, "Genocide and Atrocity Crimes" (2006) 1 *Genocide Studies and Prevention* 229–250: 244–246.

unlawfully and wantonly," all remain silent regarding the means through which they may be committed, merely referring to particular processes and outcomes that could take innumerable forms.[81] Other war crimes are similarly broadly worded. For example, the war crimes of "committing outrages upon personal dignity, in particular humiliating and degrading treatment" and "intentionally using starvation of civilians as a method of warfare by depriving them of objects indispensable to their survival" could both clearly be committed through a wide variety of means.[82]

The coverage of war crimes during non-international armed conflicts is much narrower than international conflicts. However, even during periods of non-international armed conflict, "violence to life and person, in particular murder of all kinds, mutilation, cruel treatment and torture," and "committing outrages upon personal dignity, in particular humiliating and degrading treatment," remain war crimes.[83] As with genocide and crimes against humanity, again one can easily envision many such forms of abuse that would fail to conform to the atrocity aesthetic, yet amount to such "outrages upon personal dignity" or other war crimes.[84]

Modes of Liability

Establishing that one or more international crimes occurred is but the first step in obtaining a conviction under ICL. Prosecutors must also prove beyond a reasonable doubt that the accused participated in such

81 See Rome Statute, Art. 8(2)(a); see also Geneva Convention for the Amelioration of the Condition of the Wounded and Sick in Armed Forces in the Field, Geneva, August 12, 1949, in force October 21, 1950, 75 UNTS 31; Geneva Convention for the Amelioration of the Condition of Wounded, Sick and Shipwrecked Members of Armed Forces at Sea, Geneva, August 12, 1949, in force October 21, 1950, 75 UNTS 85; Geneva Convention Relative to the Treatment of Prisoners of War, Geneva, August 12, 1949, in force October 21, 1950, 75 UNTS 135; Geneva Convention Relative to the Protection of Civilian Persons in Time of War; Geneva, August 12, 1949, in force October 21, 1950, 75 UNTS 287.

82 Rome Statute, Arts. 8(2)(b)(xxi), (xxv). For a discussion of Geneva Convention provisions related to the provision of relief supplies during periods of armed conflict, see Randle C. DeFalco, "The Right to Food in Gaza: Israel's Obligations under International Law" (2009) 35 *Rutgers Law Record* 11–22: 17–21.

83 See Rome Statute, Art. art 8(2)(c)(i)–(ii).

84 For example, Schmid identifies a long list of war crimes that can be, and, in some cases, have been, committed through violations of economic, social, and cultural human rights. See Evelyne Schmid, "War Crimes Related to Violations of Economic, Social and Cultural Rights" (2011) 71 *Heidelberg Journal of International Law* 523–540; Schmid, *Taking Economic, Social and Cultural Rights Seriously*, 166–206.

crime in a manner sufficient to ground individual criminal liability. Because virtually all international crimes are perpetrated collectively by groups, rather than by individuals, rare is the case where an accused physically perpetrates the entirety of the crime they are charged with. Indeed, individuals considered to be among those most responsible for the commission of atrocity crimes are often far removed from their physical perpetration. To account for this phenomenon, ICL has adopted its own specialized modes of liability that provide for various culpable forms of participation in group crimes.[85]

Such modes of liability represent an area of ICL commonly overlooked in assessments of its potential reach. Because ICL's modes of liability are designed to address individual contributions to crimes covering potentially vast expanses of time and space, and perpetrated by large numbers of individuals working in concert, they have been tailored to be flexible enough to encompass a diverse array of contributions to group crimes. Two examples of such flexible modes of liability are joint criminal enterprise, a doctrine used extensively by the various ad hoc UN tribunals, and "contribution" liability at the ICC.[86]

Joint criminal enterprise has been utilized by all of the ad hoc tribunals, but has been rejected thus far by the ICC after engendering considerable controversy.[87] This doctrine provides for individual liability when an

[85] For a general overview of these modes of liability, see Neha Jain, *Perpetrators and Accessories in International Criminal Law: Individual Modes of Responsibility for Collective Crimes* (Hart, 2014).

[86] The doctrine of joint criminal enterprise was first laid out in by the ICTY in the *Tadić* Appeal Judgment. *Prosecutor* v. *Tadić, Case No. IT-94-1-A, July 15, 1999*, ICTY, paras. 185–229 (laying out the elements of joint criminal enterprise for the first time). For an overview of joint criminal enterprise liability, see, for example, Jared L. Watkins and Randle C. DeFalco, "Joint Criminal Enterprise and the Jurisdiction of the Extraordinary Chambers in the Courts of Cambodia" (2010) 63 *Rutgers Law Review* 193–273. For an overview of the elements of superior and command responsibility, see, for example, Rome Statute, Art. 28. For the basic elements of "contribution" liability and other modes of liability at the ICC, see Rome Statute, Art. 25. For analyses of "contribution" liability under Article 25(3)(d) specifically, see Randle C. DeFalco, "Contextualizing Actus Reus under Article 25(3)(d) of the ICC Statute: Thresholds of Contribution" (2013) 11 *Journal of International Criminal Justice* 715–735; Kai Ambos, "The ICC and Common Purpose: What Contribution is Required under Article 25 (3)(d)?," in Carsten Stahn, ed., *The Law and Practice of the International Criminal Court* (Oxford University Press, 2015), 592–607; Zurab Sanikidze, "The Level of 'Contribution' Required under Article 25(3) (D) of the Rome Statute of the International Criminal Court" (2012) 83 *Revue Internationale de Droit Pénal* 221–232.

[87] For examples of criticisms of joint criminal enterprise, see Allison Marston Danner and Jenny S. Martinez, "Guilty Associations: Joint Criminal Enterprise, Command Responsibility, and the Development of International Criminal Law" (2005) 93

individual accused joins a criminal enterprise by agreeing to a group plan involving the commission of at least one international crime and thereafter, makes a "significant" contribution to the execution of such plan.[88] Such contribution must be made while the accused possesses knowledge of the criminal nature of the plan and the nature of their contribution thereto, or at least is advertently reckless in this regard.[89] Joint criminal enterprise provides a flexible mechanism for addressing the many forms atrocities, and contributions thereto, may take. Criminal enterprises may be large or small, consisting of several members operating exclusively within a small geographic area, or massive numbers of members spread widely across vast expanses of territory. Joint criminal enterprises may also be nested within one another, with various groups of individuals forming webs of interrelated, but mutually exclusive criminal enterprises.[90]

For example, in the context of the Khmer Rouge regime, in *Case 002/01*, the ECCC Trial Chamber held that a joint criminal enterprise "to rapidly build and defend the country through a socialist revolution, based on the principles of secrecy, independence-sovereignty, democratic centralism, self-reliance and collectivisation, was firmly established [by members of the Khmer Rouge] by June 1974 and continued at least until December 1977."[91] The Chamber found that, although the overall

California Law Review 75–169; Jens David Ohlin, "Three Conceptual Problems with the Doctrine of Joint Criminal Enterprise" (2005) 5 *Journal of International Criminal Justice* 69–90.

88 See, for example, *Prosecutor* v. *Tadić, Case No. IT-94-1-A, July 15, 1999*, ICTY, para. 220; *Prosecutor* v. *Brđanin, IT-99–36-A, April 3, 2007*, ICTY, para. 371; *Prosecutor* v. *Kvočka, IT-98-30/1-T, November 2, 2001*, ICTY, para. 309 ("The participation in the [joint criminal] enterprise must be significant. By significant, the Trial Chamber means an act or omission that makes an enterprise efficient or effective; e.g., a participation that enables the system to run more smoothly or without disruption."). It should be noted that the "significant" contribution *actus reus* threshold is far from settled.

89 This form of recklessness is referred to as the *mens rea* of "*dolus eventualis.*" See *Prosecutor* v. *Tadić, Case No. IT-94-1-A, July 15, 1999*, ICTY, paras. 220, 228.

90 For example, the ICTY Trial Chamber has held that an "overarching" joint criminal enterprise aimed at "the permanent removal of the Bosnian Muslims and Bosnian Croats from Bosnian Serb claimed territory" existed in the former Yugoslavia during the Tribunal's temporal jurisdiction along with other smaller criminal enterprises. *Prosecutor* v. *Karadžić, IT-95–5/18-T, March 24, 2016*, ICTY, para. 3505.

91 *Case 002/01, 002/19–09–2007/ECCC/TC, August 7, 2014*, ECCC, para. 777. It is worth noting that, because *Case 002* was bifurcated into multiple trials, and *Case 002/01* concerned only events prior occurring prior to 1977, the Chamber did not issue a holding as to whether this (or other) joint criminal enterprise(s) continued to exist from 1978 onward until the Khmer Rouge were ousted from power in January 1979.

"common purpose was not in itself necessarily or entirely criminal ... participants implemented the common purpose through [policies] which resulted in and/or involved crimes."[92] This criminal enterprise involved various members of the Khmer Rouge regime and extended across the entirety of Cambodia.[93] In other circumstances, such enterprises may be smaller, such as in ECCC *Case 001*, wherein accused Kaing Guek Eav (better known by his revolutionary alias, "Duch") was convicted of participating in a criminal enterprise limited to the operation of a specific prison where detainees were systematically tortured and subsequently executed.[94]

Although the ICC has thus far rejected the doctrine of joint criminal enterprise, the Court nonetheless provides for individual liability predicated on an accused's contributions to collective crimes in various ways, including through Article 25 of the Rome Statute, which states:

> a person shall be criminally responsible and liable for punishment for a crime within the jurisdiction of the Court if that person:

(a) Commits such a crime, whether as an individual, jointly with another or through another person, regardless of whether that other person is criminally responsible;
(b) Orders, solicits or induces the commission of such a crime which in fact occurs or is attempted;
(c) For the purpose of facilitating the commission of such a crime, aids, abets or otherwise assists in its commission or its attempted commission, including providing the means for its commission;
(d) In any other way contributes to the commission or attempted commission of such a crime by a group of persons acting with a common purpose. Such contribution shall be intentional and shall either:
   (i) Be made with the aim of furthering the criminal activity or criminal purpose of the group, where such activity or purpose involves the commission of a crime within the jurisdiction of the Court; or
   (ii) Be made in the knowledge of the intention of the group to commit the crime.[95]

Article 25 appears to provide for the broadest liability under subsection (3)(d), as this provision establishes liability for an accused who

[92] Ibid., para. 778.
[93] Ibid., para. 777.
[94] *Case 001, Case No. 001/18-07-2007/ECCC/TC, July 26, 2010*, ECCC, para. 514.
[95] Rome Statute, Art. 25.

contributes to a group crime "in any other way" than those enumerated elsewhere in Article 25. Subsection (3)(d), however, has yet to be fully clarified, and it remains unclear what the threshold degree of such contribution must be. The ICC Pre-Trial Chamber stated in *Prosecutor* v. *Mbarushimana* that an accused's contribution to the common criminal purpose must be "significant," which is the same *actus reus* threshold required under most joint criminal enterprise jurisprudence.[96] This assertion, however, was *obiter dicta*, as a majority of the Chamber found that the prosecution failed to adduce sufficient evidence that the relevant group, the Democratic Forces for the Liberation of Rwanda (FDLR) operating in the Democratic Republic of the Congo, constituted a common criminal purpose at all and that, regardless of whether this was true, Mbarushimana himself "did not provide *any* contribution to the commission" of the crimes alleged to have been committed by the FDLR.[97]

Although the prosecution appealed the decision, the Appeals Chamber did not need to address the question of the minimum degree of contribution legally required under Article 25(3)(d) and declined to express its opinion on the matter.[98] However, Appeals Chamber Judge Silvia Fernández de Gurmendi appended a separate opinion advocating for the adoption of a "normative and causal links" test to determine whether the acts of an accused legally qualify as a "contribution" to a group crime under Article 25(3)(d).[99] How Fernández de Gurmendi's proposed normative and causal links test would materially differ from the significant act test remains unclear, as does the precise legal characterization of the threshold *actus reus* requirement for contribution liability at the ICC at this time.[100] Regardless of the ultimate determination made by the ICC Appeals Chamber concerning how to legally characterize the minimum

[96] *Prosecutor* v. *Mbarushimana, Decision on Confirmation of Charges, December 16, 2011, ICC-01/04-01/10*, ICC, para. 285. For similar holdings concerning the threshold *actus reus* required for joint criminal enterprise liability to attach, see *Prosecutor* v. *Brđanin, IT-99-36-A, April 3, 2007*, ICTY, para. 371; *Prosecutor* v. *Kvočka, IT-98-30/1-T, November 2, 2001*, ICTY, para. 309.

[97] *Prosecutor* v. *Mbarushimana, Decision on Confirmation of Charges, December 16, 2011, ICC-01/04-01/10*, ICC, paras. 291–292 (emphasis added).

[98] *Prosecutor* v. *Mbarushimana, Judgment on the Appeal of the Prosecutor against the Decision of Pre-Trial Chamber I of 16 December 2011 entitled "Decision on the Confirmation of Charges," ICC-01/04-01/10 OA4, May 30, 2012*, ICC, paras. 64–69.

[99] *Prosecutor* v. *Mbarushimana, ICC-01/04-01/10 OA4, Separate Opinion of Judge Silvia Fernández de Gurmendi, May 30, 2012*, ICC.

[100] For analyses of *Mbarushimana* and the lack of clarity in terms of Article 25(3)(d) of the Rome Statute, see DeFalco, "Contextualizing Actus Reus"; Ambos, "ICC and Common Purpose"; Sanikidze, "Level of 'Contribution' Required."

threshold of contribution to ground liability under Article 25(3)(d), it is unlikely that specific limitations will be put on the *forms* such contributions may take.[101]

Thus, while the ICC has rejected the doctrine of joint criminal enterprise, under Article 25, the prosecution may still prove an accused's culpability through their participation in a group that has a common criminal purpose. Joint criminal enterprise jurisprudence at the ICTY and ECCC, meanwhile, demonstrate that groups forming a common criminal purpose or criminal enterprise may be relatively small and tight-knit, or vast organizations spanning entire countries or even crossing over national borders.[102] Especially large and powerful criminal groups are able to kill and abuse victims through means unavailable to ordinary, domestic criminal organizations, or even smaller criminal enterprises that commit international crimes. Significant, or for that matter, "substantial" contributions to massive criminal organizations may also take many forms, ranging from familiar forms of violence, such as hands-on killing, to bureaucratic functions.[103] Indeed, in many cases, the contributions of those who physically perpetrate even the most horrific crimes, such as those perpetrated in concentration camps during the Holocaust, may be relatively minor in comparison to the seemingly much more banal, bureaucratic contributions of others.[104] This seeming paradox is

[101] For example, in a situation where a group causes mass death through means deviating from the atrocity aesthetic, such as by diverting resources away from a population in severe need, an accused may be considered liable for contributing to such deprivation in a wide variety of ways, ranging from direct misappropriation of such resources, or by actively preventing the victim population from accessing such resources. Whether such contributions are "significant" or have sufficient "normative and causal links" to relevant harms will fluctuate depending on the overall size of the perpetrator group and the nature of his or her contribution.

[102] For example, the ICTY found that an "overarching" criminal enterprise with the common purpose of expelling non-Serbs from designated territories by any means necessary existed in the former Yugoslavia during the 1990s, and the ECCC found that a common criminal purpose existed amongst members of the Khmer Rouge leadership in *Case 002/01* encompassing the entirety of Cambodia's territory and society. See *Prosecutor* v. *Karadžić, IT-95-5/18-T, March 24, 2016*, ICTY, para. 3505; *Case 002/01, 002/19-09-2007/ECCC/TC, August 7, 2014*, ECCC, paras. 777–778.

[103] Of course, the recognition of the potential culpability of bureaucrats, businesspeople, and the like for their roles in the commission of international crimes is not new, dating back to Nuremberg itself, as well as the trial of Adolph Eichmann in Jerusalem. See Hannah Arendt, *Eichmann in Jerusalem: A Report on the Banality of Evil* (Penguin Classics, 2006); see also, for example, Kalpouzos and Mann, "Banal Crimes against Humanity."

[104] Consider, for example, the relative culpability of an individual concentration camp guard versus that of Adolph Eichmann, or various other relatively high-level Nazi bureaucrats who may not have committed any individual acts of violence. Another

personified in individuals such as Adolph Eichmann, the quintessential bureaucrat who oversaw the systematic murder of millions of victims from behind a desk.[105]

Of course, the ICC is not limited to prosecuting individuals for their contributions to group crimes exclusively via Article 25(3)(d). Indeed, as noted earlier, the ICC Office of the Prosecutor has mainly relied on other modes of liability in its prosecutions to date. Article 25 also provides for liability for crimes committed by an "individual, jointly with another or through another person, regardless of whether that other person is criminally responsible,"[106] and the Rome Statute contains other modes of liability, such as ordering, instigating, and incitement to commit genocide.[107] Article 28 of the Rome Statute, for instance, provides for liability through command and superior responsibility, ICL-specific doctrines used to hold military and civilian authority figures responsible for failing to prevent or punish crimes committed by their subordinates.[108] Command responsibility provides for the liability of military commanders who fail to prevent or punish international crimes committed by subordinates under their "effective command and control."[109] Superior responsibility, meanwhile, provides corollary liability for nonmilitary authority figures for the crimes of subordinates over whom they wield "effective authority and control" and attaches liability when such authority figure "fail[s] to take all necessary and reasonable measures within his or her power to prevent or repress" the commission of relevant crimes, or "to submit the matter to the competent authorities for investigation and prosecution."[110]

similar example would be the culpability of individual guards at Khmer Rouge prisons in Cambodia, including *Tuol Sleng* prison, compared to that of individual prison commanders, such as *Tuol Sleng* commandant Kaing Guek Eav alias Duch, or high-level Khmer Rouge officials, such as Pol Pot and Nuon Chea, who were the intellectual and bureaucratic architects of the country's nationwide system of prisons and torture centers.

105 On Eichmann's role in the Holocaust and its bureaucratic nature, see *Attorney General v. Eichmann, Criminal Case No. 40/61, December 11, 1961,* District Court of Jerusalem; see also Arendt, *Eichmann in Jerusalem.*

106 Rome Statute, Art. 25(3)(a).

107 See generally ibid., Art. 25. For a more detailed analysis of ICL modes of liability, see Jain, *Perpetrators and Accessories.*

108 Command and superior responsibility have, like joint criminal enterprise, been subject to considerable controversy concerning the scope of their applicability. See, for example, Danner and Martinez, "Guilty Associations." For a detailed analysis of superior responsibility, see Darryl Robinson, *Justice in Extreme Cases: Criminal Law Theory Meets International Criminal Law* (Cambridge University Press, 2020).

109 Rome Statute, Art. 28(a).

110 Ibid., Art. 28(b).

The flexibility and potential reach of joint criminal enterprise, contribution liability, command and superior responsibility, and various other ICL modes of liability, has engendered significant controversy.[111] Nevertheless, the basic need to account for individual contributions to group crimes is accepted by even some of the most strident critics of ICL's current modes of liability.[112] Controversy aside, the upshot of these specialized ICL modes of liability for the present inquiry is that they are designed to address the group nature of international crimes and as such, provide means through which individuals may be held responsible for their contributions to collectively perpetrated offenses.[113] Thus, while clearly not without their flaws, such modalities do provide opportunities to capture the complex nuances of international crime commission. Yet, despite this doctrinal flexibility and capaciousness, ICL continues to be dominantly viewed as a body of law concerned narrowly with spectacular outbreaks of extreme violence.

Four Examples of Aesthetically Unfamiliar Atrocity Modalities

The foregoing analysis has demonstrated that atrocities themselves are complex processes of mass killing and abuse, and that ICL does not appear doctrinally limited to any enumerated subset of such processes,

111 For a sampling of critiques of ICL modes of liability, see, for example, Danner and Martinez, "Guilty Associations"; Ohlin, "Three Conceptual Problems"; Robinson, *Justice in Extreme Cases.*

112 For example, Jens Ohlin has rather strongly critiqued joint criminal enterprise. See Ohlin, "Three Conceptual Problems." Yet, Ohlin nonetheless argues elsewhere that "[i]f we insist on individual blameworthiness to the point of ignoring the reality of collective conduct, then we have enforced a fallacious fidelity to the principle of culpability that is blind to the reality of human collaboration." Jens David Ohlin, "Organizational Criminality," in Elies van Sliedregt and Sergey Vasiliev, eds., *Pluralism in International Criminal Law* (Oxford University Press, 2014), 107–127: 117. To a significant degree, ICL may be merely caught in a perpetual dilemma, between accounting for the fundamentally collective causal realities attendant to processes of atrocity, and the strictures of liberal criminal law traditions grounded in the myth of the fully free-willed individual moral agent.

113 While the general summarization of ICL modes of liability as providing for individual penal responsibility predicated on each accused's contribution to a collectively perpetrated crime represents somewhat of an overgeneralization, a detailed analysis of all ICL modes of liability predicated on collective perpetration, and critiques thereof, is outside the scope of the present analysis. For further information on such modes of liability, see generally Jain, *Perpetrators and Accessories.* For a discussion of the collective nature of the vast majority of international crimes and the implications of this reality for the imputation of individual responsibility, see, for example, Ohlin, "Organizational Criminality."

but, in fact, contains provisions providing it with the ability to address a wide variety of manifestations of mass harm causation. The remainder of this chapter provides an overview of four (non-exhaustive) examples of the kinds of slow, attritive, or otherwise aesthetically unfamiliar means through which genocide, crimes against humanity, and/or war crimes may be committed: famine causation; large-scale corruption; humanitarian aid interference; and socioeconomic oppression. Scholars have identified significant areas of potential overlap between the harms associated with each of these harm causation processes and ICL. While there continues to be disagreement concerning how ICL might apply to relevant harms, and which crimes may be implicated, a general consensus is discernible that international crimes *may* be committed through these means.

Famine and Starvation Causation

Famine is perhaps the most-studied form of nontraditional potential means of atrocity commission, and for good reason. In a technological sense, famine[114] and starvation[115] have been fully preventable for well over a century, yet during this time some of the worst famines in human history occurred.[116] This seeming paradox has led certain scholars to increasingly theorize famine as a largely predictable product of human actions, rather than as an unpredictable natural disaster or product of overpopulation or aggregate food supply shocks.[117] Yet, ICL does not

[114] There are many different understandings of the term famine. I use the term famine to refer to instances where lack of access to food among an affected population results in a significant increase in mortality rates. For overviews of the dynamics of famine and various definitions, see generally Cormac Ó Gráda, *Famine: A Short History* (Princeton University Press, 2009); Stephen Devereux, ed., *The New Famines: Why Famines Persist in an Era of Globalization* (Routledge, 2006).

[115] Whereas the term famine refers to large-scale suffering from lack of food, the term starvation refers to the status of suffering from a complete lack of nutrition, eventually leading to death if unaddressed. See, for example, Ó Gráda, *Famine*; Amartya Sen, "Ingredients of Famine Analysis: Availability and Entitlements" (1981) 96 *The Quarterly Journal of Economics* 433–464: 434 (observing that "starvation is a matter of some people not having enough food to eat, and not a matter of there being not enough food to eat.").

[116] See generally Sen, "Ingredients of Famine Analysis"; Ó Gráda, *Famine*; Devereux, *New Famines*.

[117] To be sure, there remains a significant amount of disagreement among famine studies scholars concerning the root causes of famine and how they interact with natural conditions, especially within the realm of situations of food insecurity not rising to the level of a famine emergency. For the purposes of the current inquiry, it is sufficient,

explicitly address famine causation or mass starvation in any systematic way. While intentionally using starvation of civilians as a method of warfare is a longstanding, if under-prosecuted, war crime,[118] the specialized nature of war crimes, being limited to periods of armed conflict, along with the required strategic instrumentalization of starvation and the current applicability of this crime solely to periods of international armed conflicts, render this crime inapplicable to many famine scenarios.[119]

Nonetheless, in a broader sense, ICL does provide significant coverage over aspects of famine causation and from time to time, famine has been discussed at the periphery of ICL practice. For example, famine and starvation were addressed, albeit in a limited fashion, in the Judgment of the IMT,[120] wherein defendants such as Hermann Göring, Hans Frank, and Walther Funk were convicted of war crimes and crimes against humanity partially for their roles in, inter alia, the economic

however, to note that there is general agreement among famine experts that famines should not be understood as unforeseeable or so-called natural disasters but flow predictably from human activities. For overviews of current famine scholarship, see generally Devereux, *New Famines*; Ó Gráda, *Famine*. Amartya Sen's oft-referenced "entitlements" approach to famine dynamics is a particularly useful lens through which to examine famine as a subject of legal regimes, as the approach concentrates on the "ability of different sections of the population to establish command over food using the entitlement relations operation in that society depending on its legal, economic, political, and social characteristics." Sen, "Ingredients of Famine Analysis," 459; see also Alex de Waal, "A Re-assessment of Entitlement Theory in the Light of the Recent Famines in Africa" (1990) 21 *Development and Change* 469–490. De Waal argues that "entitlements themselves form only part of a larger account of famine. Some aspects of a revised account include coping strategies of famine-affected people, social disruption, and violence. In this account, less severe famine is not theoretically distinct from acute poverty, and severe famine is distinct largely because of the severity of social collapse." Ibid., 469. De Waal's critique of Sen's entitlement theory only serves to further underscore the existence of linkages between law, criminal justice, and famine.

118 For one formulation of this crime, see, for example, Rome Statute, Art. 8(2)(b)(xxv).

119 See Global Rights Compliance, "The Crime of Starvation and Methods of Prosecution and Accountability," June 13, 2019, https://sites.tufts.edu/wpf/files/2019/06/The-Crimes-of-Starvation-and-Methods-of-Prosecution-and-Accountability.pdf. The limitation of this war crime to international armed conflicts was recently removed within the context of the ICC through a 2019 amendment to the Rome Statute. This amendment, however, will take some to be fully applicable to the work of the ICC. See Kevin Jon Heller, "The Rome Statute's Flawed Amendment Regime – Starvation in NIAC Edition," December 7, 2019, www.opiniojuris.org/2019/12/07/the-rome-statutes-flawed-amendment-regime-starvation-in-niac-edition.

120 International Military Tribunal, *Trial of the Major War Criminals before the International Military Tribunal, Nuremberg 14 November 1945–1 October 1946*, 42 vols. (International Military Tribunal, 1947), 279–282, 296–301, 304–310.

exploitation of occupied territories, which in turn resulted in famine and mass starvation, especially in occupied Poland.[121] The IMT found that:

> agricultural products, raw materials needed by German factories, machine tools, transportation equipment, other finished products, and even foreign securities and holdings of foreign exchange were all requisitioned and sent to Germany. These resources were requisitioned in a manner out of all proportion to the economic resources of those countries, and resulted in famine, inflation, and an active black market.[122]

The IMT judgment, however, failed to clearly elucidate precisely how the enforcement of famine conditions satisfied the elements of specific crimes against humanity. For example, the IMT simply found Hans Frank guilty of various crimes against humanity based on his contributions to a variety of methods of abuse and killing utilized by the Nazi Party against Jews and Poles placed under his authority, without connecting specific harms to specific crimes against humanity.[123]

A similar analysis led Raphael Lemkin to conclude that the Ukrainian *Holodomor* ("extermination by hunger") famine of 1932–1933[124] formed a key part of a larger, genocidal "Russification" plan carried out by the Soviet Union in an effort to destroy the Ukrainian national identity.[125]

[121] Ibid., 240. The *Eichmann* Judgment also discussed starvation conditions as part of the overall Final Solution plan of the Nazis. *Attorney General* v. *Eichmann, Criminal Case No. 40/61, December 11, 1961,* District Court of Jerusalem. Recent international prosecutions have largely limited analysis of famine/starvation situations to conditions in prisons. See Diana Kearney, "Food Deprivations as Crimes against Humanity" (2013) 46 *New York University Journal of International Law and Politics* 207–289: 256–257.

[122] International Military Tribunal, *Trial of the Major War Criminals*, vol. 1, p. 240.

[123] Ibid., 296–301.

[124] For a historical account of this famine, see Robert Conquest, *The Harvest of Sorrow: Soviet Collectivization and the Terror-Famine*, reprint ed. (Oxford University Press, 1987); see also David Marcus, "Famine Crimes in International Law" (2003) 97 *American Journal of International Law* 245–281: 252–255.

[125] Roman Serbyn and Raphael Lemkin, "Lemkin on Genocide of Nations" (2009) 7 *Journal of International Criminal Justice* 123–130: 128 (Lemkin's unpublished essay argued that the "third prong of the Soviet plan" to destroy the Ukrainian nation "was aimed at the farmers, the large mass of independent peasants who are the repository of the tradition, folklore and music, the national language and literature, the national spirit, of Ukraine. The weapon used against this body is perhaps the most terrible of all – starvation. Between 1932 and 1933, 5,000,000 Ukrainians starved to death." In his analysis, Lemkin describes starvation as a "weapon" wielded by the Soviet Union against Ukrainian peasant farmers.).

Moreover, the judgment against Adolph Eichmann in Jerusalem also discussed the infliction of starvation conditions in ghettos and concentration camps as part of the overall Final Solution plan of the Nazis.[126]

Yet, despite these early engagements with famine as a subject of ICL, the notion that the creation of famine and starvation situations could form the *actus reus* of certain forms of genocide, crimes against humanity, or war crimes has remained undeveloped. As ICL became more codified and viewed as more scrupulously "legal" in nature during the 1990s, prosecutions have largely limited analysis of famine and starvation situations to the more familiar realm of prison and concentration camp contexts.[127]

The issue of potential intersections between ICL and famine was taken up in 2003 by David Marcus, who argues that extant ICL at the time provided only "patch-work" coverage of what he defined as "faminogenic" (i.e. famine-causing) behavior, in the form of certain crimes against humanity.[128] Marcus called for the codification of new crimes in a famine-specific convention designed to expand ICL liability for faminogenic acts.[129] To date, there has been no appreciable movement toward the adoption of famine-specific international crimes, aside from extension of the longstanding war crime of intentionally using starvation

[126] *Attorney General* v. *Eichmann, Criminal Case No. 40/61, December 11, 1961,* District Court of Jerusalem.

[127] Kearney, "Food Deprivations," 256–257.

[128] Marcus, "Famine Crimes," 247 (concluding that "[ICL] already criminalizes certain faminogenic conduct, but the legal doctrine that penalizes this behavior resembles the 'patch-work coverage' that typifies the customary law of crimes against humanity.").

[129] Ibid. Jlateh Vincent Jappah and Danielle Taana Smith similarly advocate for the codification of "politically induced famine" as a crime against humanity and use the term "state sponsored famine" to "reflect the conceptualization of famine as not merely nature-induced but also as a willfully orchestrated state policy." Jlateh Vincent Jappah and Danielle Taana Smith, "State Sponsored Famine: Conceptualizing Politically Induced Famine as a Crime against Humanity" (2012) 4 *Journal of International and Global Studies* 17–31: 17. Rhoda Howard-Hassmann echoes calls for the codification of new ICL provisions, proposing the term "state-induced famine" be used in order to "clarify that faminogenesis is often a state activity." Rhoda E. Howard-Hassmann, "State-Induced Famine and Penal Starvation in North Korea" (2012) 7 *Genocide Studies and Prevention* 147–165: 147; Rhoda E. Howard-Hassmann, "Mugabe's Zimbabwe, 2000–2009: Massive Human Rights Violations and the Failure to Protect" (2010) 32 *Human Rights Quarterly* 898–920: 908–909.

as a method of warfare to cover both international and non-international armed conflicts.[130]

Other scholars, myself included, have since also argued that famines are appropriately conceptualized through the rubric of atrocity, international crime, and/or human rights violations.[131] Certain of these scholars have approached the issue from the perspective of the human right to food,[132] or as part of a larger critique of the boundaries of transitional justice efforts.[133] Along with these general analyses, scholars have also argued that specific real-world famines have involved actions presumptively characterizable as international crimes. Eamon Aloyo, in

[130] International Criminal Court Assembly of State Parties Working Group on Amendments, "Report of the Working Group on Amendments," Doc. ICC-ASP/17/35, November 29, 2018, ICC, paras. 9–11.

[131] For example, Alex de Waal, *Mass Starvation: The History and Future of Famine* (Policy Press, 2017), 14–35 (chapter framing "famines as atrocities"); Jenny Edkins, "The Criminalization of Mass Starvations: From Natural Disaster to Crime against Humanity," in Stephen Devereux, ed., *The New Famines: Why Famines Persist in an Era of Globalization* (Routledge, 2007), 50–65 (arguing that the attendant shift in the vocabulary used to discuss famine would bring famine more in line with current understandings of its dynamics by removing the outmoded language of natural disaster that currently predominates popular discourses); DeFalco, "Conceptualizing Famine."

[132] For example, Larissa van den Herik contends that especially severe violations of the right to food resulting in mass famine and starvation, can potentially satisfy the *actus rei* requirements of genocide and/or the crime against humanity of extermination. Larissa van den Herik, "Economic, Social, and Cultural Rights: International Criminal Law's Blind Spot?," in Eibe H. Riedel, Gilles Giacca, and Christophe Golay, eds., *Economic, Social, and Cultural Rights in International Law: Contemporary Issues and Challenges* (Oxford University Press, 2014), 343–366: 351 (concluding that, at the ICC, "mass starvation in a famine could be captured [under ICL] but only if proven that there was a certain deliberateness involved" and noting that the ICC Office of the Prosecutor has included famine issues in its filings related to the situation in Darfur). Van den Herik generally concludes that, although there is "ample opportunity" to include socioeconomic and cultural concerns in ICL practice, the role of ICL in addressing economic, social, and cultural rights violations is "rather marginal," though "not necessarily redundant or inconsequential." Ibid., 366.

[133] See, for example, Amanda Cahill-Ripley, "Foregrounding Socio-Economic Rights in Transitional Justice: Realising Justice for Violations of Economic and Social Rights" (2014) 32 *Netherlands Quarterly of Human Rights* 183–213: 197–201 (arguing that ICL practice should pay greater attention to socioeconomic rights violations, noting as examples the blocking of food aid in Sudan and famine in Zimbabwe and stating that "[i]t is clear that systematic and large scale abuse of such rights can meet the threshold required to constitute a crime against humanity, war crimes or even genocide."); Sankey, "Toward Recognition of Subsistence Harms," 132–136. Sankey states that ICL provides some coverage over famine and starvation conditions currently but argues that this coverage is insufficient because it fails to comprehensively address what she terms "subsistence harms," which includes famine suffering.

an article advocating for the prosecution of what he refers to as "nonviolent crimes against humanity," cites the famines in the Ukraine, China, Ethiopia, and Zimbabwe as examples of the types of famine situations he argues merit such prosecutorial efforts.[134] Sigrun Skogly and others similarly argue that, at times, famine conditions in Darfur may have amounted to the crime against humanity of other inhumane acts in relation to acts of affirmatively blocking food aid.[135] Several authors, including myself, argue that the Khmer Rouge-era famine in Cambodia merits greater attention within international criminal justice.[136] Grace Kang and others have made similar arguments in regard to recurring famine conditions in North Korea in recent decades.[137] Conditions in Zimbabwe from 2000 to 2009[138] and Somalia over the past

[134] Aloyo, "Improving Global Accountability," 505–506.

[135] Sigrun I. Skogly, "Crimes against Humanity – Revisited: Is There a Role for Economic and Social Rights?" (2001) 5 *International Journal of Human Rights* 58–80: 68–71 (concluding, at page 71, that regarding the right to food "one could relatively easily establish that when a government or other organisation deliberately and intentionally blocks food aid from reaching people in immediate danger of starvation, this would be an act that would [qualify as a crime against humanity under] the ICC Statute."). Despite his reservations concerning the practical implications of doing so, Alex de Waal also argues that famine conditions in Darfur should be conceptualized as crimes against humanity. Alex de Waal, "Reflections on the Difficulties of Defining Darfur's Crisis as Genocide" (2007) 20 *Harvard Human Rights Journal* 25–33: 30 (advocating for the merging of scholarship on Sudan's civil wars and humanitarian crises and genocide studies and concluding that one implication of such a merger would be, "given the importance of the destruction of livelihoods and obstruction of relief to the Darfur genocide determination, ... a sharper conceptualization of the creation of famine as a crime against humanity."). De Waal does have reservations concerning the potential practical implications of the international criminalization of famine/starvation. See Alex de Waal, "On Famine Crimes and Tragedies" (2008) 372 *The Lancet* 1538–1539.

[136] See, for example, J. Solomon Bashi, "Prosecuting Starvation in the Extraordinary Chambers in the Courts of Cambodia" (2011) 29 *Wisconsin International Law Journal* 34–69: 69 (arguing that the ECCC has a "duty" to prosecute the "crime" of "starvation" in the form of crimes against humanity, but remaining skeptical as to the ultimate likelihood that convictions would result). I have similarly argued that, if the ECCC is to provide a fulsome accounting of the crimes of the Khmer Rouge in Cambodia, it is imperative that the Court address the issue of famine. Unlike Bashi, I view convictions as being reasonably obtainable, if aggressively pursued by the prosecution. See DeFalco, "Accounting for Famine," 144, 158.

[137] Grace M. Kang, "A Case for the Prosecution of Kim Jong Il for Crimes against Humanity, Genocide, and War Crimes" (2006) 38 *Columbia Human Rights Law Review* 51–114: 67 ("The charge of extermination as a crime against humanity for [North Korea's] policies that have led to mass starvation, for example, would mark new ground for a crime that has occurred repeatedly and will undoubtedly appear again on the international stage."), citing Marcus, "Famine Crimes."

[138] Howard-Hassmann, "Mugabe's Zimbabwe," 906–909.

decade[139] have also been cited as examples of famine situations involving apparent atrocity crimes. Questions of potential ICL accountability for famine and mass starvation have again arisen more recently in relation to reports of famine and instances of starvation in South Sudan, Syria, and Yemen.[140] Moreover, the ouster of Omar al-Bashir from power in Sudan has led to a renewed possibility that he and/or certain of his key associates may be prosecuted for crimes related to enforcing famine conditions in Darfur by the ICC or another court.

Corruption

Harms caused by large-scale corruption represent another issue that has been proposed as a worthy, yet largely ignored subject of ICL.[141] As with famine-related ICL scholarship, there exists a divide between scholars who see the current lack of accountability for harms flowing from large-scale corruption as a problem of a lack of suitable law versus a problem of enforcement of existing provisions of ICL. Also, as with famine, new issue-specific international crimes, using labels such as "patrimonicide," "indigenous spoliation," or "political corruption," have been proposed as

[139] Jens David Ohlin, "Somalia Famine 'Crime against Humanity'?," August 12, 2011, www.cnn.com/2011/OPINION/08/12/ohlin.somalia.crimes/index.html; Matt Bryden, "Somalia's Famine is Not Just a Catastrophe, It's a Crime" (October 2011) *Enough Project*, https://enoughproject.org/files/Bryden_SomaliaFamine%20Brief_final_0.pdf. While these analyses are brief, they do suggest that ICL accountability may be appropriate. For reports on conditions in Somalia during this period, see Wairagala Wakabi, "Health and Humanitarian Situation worsens in Somalia" (2007) 370 *The Lancet* 1201–1202.

[140] See, for example, Independent International Commission of Inquiry on the Syrian Arab Republic, "Sieges as Weapons of War: Encircle, Starve, Surrender, Evacuate," May 29, 2018, www.ohchr.org/Documents/HRBodies/HRCouncil/CoISyria/PolicyPaperSieges_29May2018.pdf; UN High Commissioner for Human Rights, "Report of the United Nations High Commissioner for Human Rights Containing the Findings of the Group of Independent Eminent International and Regional Experts: Situation of Human Rights in Yemen, Including Violations and Abuses since September 2014," UN Doc. A/HRC/39/43, August 17, 2018, pp. 7–10, paras. 46–64; UN Human Rights Council, "Report of the Commission on South Sudan," UN Doc. A/HRC/37/71, March 13, 2018, p. 5, para. 25.

[141] It should be noted that part of the arguments for the international criminalization of corruption-related issues is based on sources of law outside of ICL itself. While these steps are significant within the realm of international anti-corruption law, a fulsome analysis of their efficacy and criminal aspects is outside the scope of the current inquiry, which is limited to ICL. For an overview of these alternative legal efforts to suppress corruption, see, for example, Bantekas, "Corruption as an International Crime," 468–474.

methods of directly bringing corruption within the purview of ICL.[142] Ndiva Kofele-Kale argues that:

> the word 'patrimonicide' seems appropriate for this new international economic crime [because t]he word comes from combining the Latin words 'patrimonium,' meaning '[t]he estate or property belonging by ancient right to an institution, corporation, or class [and] 'cide', meaning killing. This term is fitting because indigenous spoliation is the destruction of the sum total of a state's endowment, the laying waste of the wealth and resources belonging by right to her citizens, and the denial of their heritage.[143]

Although Kofele-Kale argues "indigenous spoliation" should be prosecuted as an international crime, he offers no analysis of whether extant ICL could be used to address these twin phenomena.[144] Others, such as Ben Bloom, Sonja Starr, and Ilias Bantekas, have addressed this question

[142] See, for example, Ndiva Kofele-Kale, "Patrimonicide: The International Economic Crime of Indigenous Spoliation" (1995) 28 *Vanderbilt Journal of Transnational Law* 45–118: 57–58; see also Brian C. Harms, "Holding Public Officials Accountable in the International Realm: A New Multi-Layered Strategy to Combat Corruption" (2000) 33 *Cornell International Law Journal* 159–209. Harms appears to call for codification of a new corruption-specific crime against humanity but does not explicitly state as much, arguing that, if "persecution of citizens by misappropriating the resources and wealth of a country can fit within the definition of 'crimes against humanity', then corruption falls within the jurisdiction of the [ICC]." Ibid., 202. This language suggests that Harms may believe that corruption-related activities could amount to the crime against humanity of persecution; however, the general thrust of Harms' argument appears to call for codification, in line with Kofele-Kale. Ibid., 209 (concluding that the codification of a treaty "criminalizing indigenous despoliation" would be a positive step forward in the global struggle against corruption). Paul Ocheje also builds on the work of Kofele-Kale, calling for the creation of a new international crime of "political corruption." Paul D. Ocheje, "Refocusing International Law on the Quest for Accountability in Africa: The Case against the 'Other' Impunity" (2002) 15 *Leiden Journal of International Law* 749–779: 776. Ocheje links what he perceives to be the total lack of coverage within ICL over large-scale corruption as symptomatic of the larger prioritization of civil and political rights over social and economic rights within human rights and international law generally. Ibid., 779. Former ICC President Chile Eboe-Osuji has also added his voice to those arguing that the Rome Statute should be amended to include corruption as a stand-alone crime against humanity. Chile Eboe-Osuji, "Kleptocracy: A Desired Subject of International Criminal Law that is in Dire Need of Prosecution by Universal Jurisdiction," in Evelyn A. Ankumah and Edward K. Kwakwa, eds., *African Perspectives on International Criminal Justice* (Africa Legal Aid, 2005), 121–132. Not all scholars, however, view codification as a feasible, or necessary step toward the prosecution of large-scale corrupt acts as international crimes. See, for example, Bloom, "Criminalizing Kleptocracy?"; Starr, "Extraordinary Crimes"; Bantekas, "Corruption as an International Crime."

[143] Kofele-Kale, "Patrimonicide," 58 (internal citation omitted).

[144] Ibid., 117.

of the theoretical feasibility of applying ICL, *de lege lata*, to extreme forms of corruption producing mass harms. These three authors argue existing ICL provides a significant degree of coverage over corruption harms.[145] Bloom, Starr, and Bantekas also agree corrupt acts are best addressed as crimes against humanity,[146] while others advocating for the creation of new corruption-specific crimes also propose that such a crime be under the aegis of crimes against humanity.[147]

Meanwhile, some commentators address the issue of corruption by theorizing the lack of ICL accountability as a manifestation of a bias in favor of the prosecution of violations of civil and political human rights over economic, social, and cultural human rights violations.[148] For example, Sonya Starr argues that ICL is not commonly viewed as being capable of addressing "entrenched, longer-term abuses" such as large-scale corruption.[149] While acknowledging that ICL cannot and should not address all forms of petty corruption, Starr argues that "large-scale ransacking of treasuries" causing "extreme poverty and decimated government services, resulting in widespread deaths" may implicate the crime against humanity of other inhumane acts.[150] This sentiment is shared by Ilias

145 Bloom, "Criminalizing Kleptocracy?," 668 (concluding that the "existing ICC framework already provides a working foundation to prosecute egregious cases of grand corruption."); see also Starr, "Extraordinary Crimes"; Bantekas, "Corruption as an International Crime."

146 Bloom, "Criminalizing Kleptocracy?," 671 ("grand corruption constitutes an 'other inhumane act' under Article 7(1)(k); it also satisfies the contextual requirements for crimes against humanity due to its scope, widespread consequences, and underlying intentionality"); see also Starr, "Extraordinary Crimes," 1257 (concluding that there is "a fairly strong case that the worst cases of grand corruption . . . can be prosecuted as crimes against humanity, even with no link to crisis situations"); Bantekas, "Corruption as an International Crime," 484 ("there is no reason why a crime against humanity cannot be perpetrated against a civilian population by means of corruption").

147 Ndiva Kofele-Kale, "The Right to a Corruption-Free Society as an Individual and Collective Human Right: Elevating Official Corruption to a Crime under International Law" (2000) 34 *International Lawyer* 149–178: 173–174. Kofele-Kale identifies what he argues is an emerging norm of customary international law of treating large-scale corruption as criminal in nature, but fails to clearly elucidate whether existing ICL provisions at the time could be used to prosecute specific acts associated with large-scale corruption, instead averring only generally to the *chapeau* requirements for crimes against humanity. Ibid., 173–174. Subsequently, within the context of discussing enforcement issues, Kofele-Kale makes it clear that he advocates for the creation of a new corruption-specific international crime. Ibid., 174.

148 Ocheje, "Refocusing International Law," 778 (contending that the "lack of regard for the complementarity of human rights casts an unseemly blight on the otherwise impressive progress of human civilization exemplified by the establishment of the ICC.").

149 Starr, "Extraordinary Crimes," 1257.

150 Ibid., 1259.

Bantekas, who similarly argues that certain corruption scenarios should be prosecuted as crimes against humanity, including the crime of extermination in extreme situations wherein corrupt acts cause mass death.[151] Bantekas links corrupt practices to resulting harms and argues that corrupt acts should be understood as a means through which crimes against humanity can be committed, particularly where such acts "culminate[] in famine, disease and lack of medical care that leads to death."[152]

Issues related to corruption, kleptocratic governance and despoliation, and their relation to ICL, have also been taken up within transitional justice scholarship. Again, much of this scholarship forms part of a larger critique concerning the marginalization of socioeconomic justice issues within dominant prevailing transitional justice practices.[153] This scholarship tends to highlight the centrality of socioeconomic rights to the lives of vulnerable populations, often viewing this importance as incongruous with the current dearth of attention paid to these issues within prevailing paradigms of international justice-seeking.[154] Often, the turn

[151] Bantekas provides the example of a situation wherein a "corrupted government forcibly displace[s] a local community without measures for their subsequent welfare" rendering "access to food and medicine for the civilian population for the next 10 years almost impossible." Bantekas, "Corruption as an International Crime," 474.

[152] Ibid., 484. Unlike Starr, however, Bantekas focuses primarily on the crime against humanity of extermination in his legal analysis. Ibid., 474–475; cf. Starr, "Extraordinary Crimes," 1259.

[153] For example, Ruben Carranza argues that the "prevailing assumption" within transitional justice is that the discipline is meant to "engage mainly, if not exclusively, with civil and political rights violations that involve either physical integrity or personal freedom, and not with violations of economic and social rights, including such crimes as large-scale corruption and despoliation." Ruben Carranza, "Plunder and Pain: Should Transitional Justice Engage with Corruption and Economic Crimes?" (2008) 2 *International Journal of Transitional Justice* 310–330. Carranza further argues that transitional justice, as a field, "compartmentalizes the unresolved legacies faced by transitioning societies, particularly in developing countries. It constructs one compartment for human rights violations and another for economic crimes and corruption." Ibid., 314–315; see also Evelyne Schmid and Aoife Nolan, "'Do No Harm'? Exploring the Scope of Economic and Social Rights in Transitional Justice" (2014) 8 *International Journal of Transitional Justice* 362–382; Louise Arbour, "Economic and Social Justice for Societies in Transition" (2007) 40 *New York University Journal of International Law and Politics* 1–27.

[154] For example, Dustin Sharp argues that, despite a recent groundswell of support for the creation of transitional justice mechanisms in post-conflict societies, the proper role of transitional justice in addressing "economic violence" is "far less certain." Dustin Sharp, "Addressing Economic Violence in Times of Transition: Toward a Positive-Peace Paradigm for Transitional Justice" (2011) 35 *Fordham International Law Journal* 780–814: 792. Sharp defines "economic violence" as encompassing "violations of economic and social rights, corruption, and plunder of natural resources." Ibid. Sharp

to ICL as the preferred, at times sole, mechanism through which transitional justice is pursued is blamed as a driving force behind the neglect of corruption, reflecting the dominant, yet legally unsubstantiated perception that ICL is categorically inapplicable to all socioeconomic issues.

Aid Interference

As with both famine and corruption, a small, but lively scholarly discourse has emerged concerning potential intersections between ICL and the interference with, or outright denial of, humanitarian aid during periods of acute need.[155] As with starvation, a specific war crime exists that explicitly criminalizes certain forms of aid interference.[156] As is also the case with famine, the specificity of this crime and war crimes in general limit the utility of this crime. Outside of the context of direct attacks on aid workers and infrastructure, which must be committed during recognized periods of armed conflict, ICL coverage becomes much murkier regarding actions that deny, delay, or redirect aid.

further observes that "historically, economic violence and economic justice have sat at the periphery of transitional justice work" and, to the extent that these concerns have been addressed within transitional justice practice, they have "been treated as little more than useful context in which to understand the perpetration of physical violence." Ibid. The concept of "positive peace" used by Sharp is drawn from the work of Johan Galtung. Johan Galtung, "Violence, Peace and Peace Research" (1969) 6 *Journal of Peace Research* 167–191. According to Galtung, the term "positive peace" refers the absence of both direct and indirect violence, including various forms of "structural violence" such as poverty, hunger, and other forms of social injustice. In contrast, the term "negative peace" refers solely to the absence of direct physical violence. Ibid. Others have echoed the arguments of Carranza and Sharp concerning the need to foreground economic and social issues that are often intimately associated with corruption, within transitional justice efforts. For example, Zinaida Miller, "Effects of Invisibility: In Search of the 'Economic' in Transitional Justice" (2008) 2 *International Journal of Transitional Justice* 266–291.

155 "Humanitarian aid" can be a very broad term, encompassing both emergency life-saving undertakings and longer-term development projects. Within this book, the term is used to refer solely to situations where urgent action is needed to avert imminent large-scale suffering and/or excess deaths. For a discussion of the wide variety of forms that humanitarian aid may take, see Josh Scheinert, "Refusal to Save Lives: A Perspective from International Criminal Law" (2013) 13 *International Criminal Law Review* 627–663: 629–630.

156 It is a war crime to intentionally direct attacks against personnel, installations, material, units or vehicles involved in humanitarian assistance efforts during both international and non-international armed conflicts. See, for example, Rome Statute, Arts. 8(2)(b)(iii), 8(2)(e)(iii).

Part of the challenge in protecting the flow of humanitarian aid through ICL is one of definition, as aid interference can take many different forms, ranging from flat-out denial to more subtle methods, such as misappropriation or redirection. Christa Rottensteiner defines the denial of humanitarian assistance broadly as "a situation where, as a result of the intentional behaviour of certain persons, humanitarian assistance does not reach its intended beneficiaries."[157] The results of such varied actions, however, remain themselves quite predictable, involving the deterioration of living conditions, leading to the spread of famine, disease, and, in turn, widespread death. Like other scholars, such as Starr and Bantekas within the context of corruption, Rottensteiner connects acts that block or redirect aid with their eventual outcomes, including the spread of disease and extreme poverty.[158] This pattern, of aid interference followed by the spread of hunger, disease, and the like, has played out in various real-world situations, such as the aftermath of Cyclone Nargis in Myanmar,[159] South Africa's refusal to accept prenatal HIV/AIDS drugs,[160] and the Mugabe Government's restrictions on and manipulation of aid to Zimbabwe in the 2000s,[161] to name only a few examples referenced in the literature. More recently, the actions of the Trump administration in the United States and certain other governments that actively misled the populations under their authority concerning the nature and severity of the COVID-19 pandemic, and/or actively prevented necessary public health measures, such as by, for example, halting the distribution of face masks, raise a similar set of

[157] Christa Rottensteiner, "The Denial of Humanitarian Assistance as a Crime under International Law" (1999) 81 *International Review of the Red Cross* 555–582: 559.

[158] See generally ibid; Starr, "Extraordinary Crimes."

[159] See generally Ford, "Failure to Respond"; Scheinert, "Refusal to Save Lives"; J. Benton Heath, "Disasters, Relief, and Neglect: The Duty to Accept Humanitarian Assistance and the Work of the International Law Commission" (2010) 43 *New York University Journal of International Law and Policy* 419–477.

[160] Scheinert, "Refusal to Save Lives."

[161] Howard-Hassmann, "Mugabe's Zimbabwe" (arguing that the Mugabe Government committed the crime against humanity of other inhumane acts during the 2000s in Zimbabwe by inducing famine conditions through, inter alia, blocking and manipulating humanitarian assistance efforts, by refusing to accept certain sources of aid and manipulating the delivery of aid in order to prevent it from being distributed in areas perceived to be political opposition strongholds); see also John D. Kraemer, Dhrubajyoti Bhattacharya, and Lawrence O. Gostin, "Blocking Humanitarian Assistance: A Crime against Humanity?" (2008) 372 *The Lancet* 1203–1205 (arguing that acts that block humanitarian aid, including those actions by Mugabe where he "cut off international assistance, apparently to manipulate an election but leaving millions without food aid or medical care," may rise to the level of crimes against humanity).

questions concerning the appropriateness and legal feasibility of individual criminal sanctions, including under ICL.

Due to the narrow specificity of the war crime of directing attacks against humanitarian targets and the often widespread or systematic nature of mass harm causing aid interference, as with famine and corruption, scholars have focused predominantly on crimes against humanity as a potential entry point for the pursuit of ICL accountability predicated on aid interference. For example, Stuart Ford argues that certain acts by Myanmar's junta government in the immediate aftermath of the landfall of Cyclone Nargis in 2008, including the outright rejection of aid offers, diversion of aid from its intended beneficiaries, and the forcible eviction of civilians from aid camps, appear to have amounted to crimes against humanity.[162] Although he refrains from forecasting the ultimate guilt of specific junta leaders, Ford does conclude that available evidence "gives rise to a reasonable belief that the underlying criminal acts of a crime against humanity, including murder, extermination and inhumane acts, were occurring" in Myanmar in the immediate aftermath of Nargis' landfall.[163]

Other scholars have made similar arguments in relation to both post-Nargis Myanmar and other locations, such as South Africa, but, unlike Ford, have focused their analyses exclusively on the crime against humanity of other inhumane acts.[164] Eric Reeves makes similar arguments in relation to conditions in the Sudan over the past two decades,

[162] Ford, "Failure to Respond."

[163] Ibid., 255. Ford consequently concludes that it appears that the crimes against humanity of murder, extermination, and other inhumane acts appear to have occurred in the aftermath of Cyclone Nargis in Burma. Ibid., 261. This conclusion is based on the interpretations of crimes against humanity that Ford persuasively argues fall "well within" prevailing ICL jurisprudence. Ibid., 274. Ford concludes that, as a result, crimes against humanity could be "seamlessly applied to a government's failure to respond appropriately to a natural disaster." Ibid.

[164] For example, Scheinert argues that the South African Government's refusal to accept prenatal HIV/AIDS drugs and the behavior of Myanmar's junta leadership in the aftermath of Cyclone Nargis should be conceptualized as crimes against humanity. Scheinert, "Refusal to Save Lives." Scheinert defines humanitarian aid as "aid that on an objective standard stands to mitigate critical threats to the physical life of an individual or group." Ibid., 630. Scheinert broadly agrees with Ford that the challenge of bringing such scenarios within the purview of ICL is "more conceptual than actual" and argues that the lack of attention to date is due to the fact that the relevant circumstances "bear little or no resemblance to what one associates with ICL." Ibid., 629. Scheinert departs from Ford's analysis, however, by concluding that solely the crime against humanity of other inhumane acts is applicable to the South African and Myanmar scenarios and that other crimes against humanity could not be pursued in

during which time he argues that the Sudanese Government "deliberately and systematically denied, obstructed, destroyed, or attacked humanitarian facilities and personnel."[165] Reeves outlines the various ways in which he alleges the government interfered or manipulated aid efforts during this period,[166] contending that its military operations and denial of humanitarian assistance moved in "perfect concert in a campaign of destruction that clearly targeted ethnic groups, although the two parts of the war were rarely connected as mutually reinforcing crimes against humanity."[167]

Rhoda Howard-Hassmann makes similar arguments concerning the potential ICL culpability of deceased former president Robert Mugabe in relation to aid manipulation in Zimbabwe from 2000 to 2009.[168] Howard-Hassmann specifically notes that, in the midst of a burgeoning famine, while the world "called on Mugabe to allow humanitarian agencies access to all of Zimbabwe, he continued to block distribution of food to those who he thought supported the opposition."[169] It is these and other similar policies enacted and enforced by Mugabe and his inner

relation to the aftermath of Cyclone Nargis. This disagreement turns largely on the authors' varying interpretations of fine line *mens rea* distinctions between motive, intent, and knowledge within the Rome Statute and in ICL more generally. Ibid., 652–653; cf. Ford, "Failure to Respond," 241–242, 246–247. Eamon Aloyo also mentions the aftermath of Cyclone Nargis in Burma as one example of a situation likely involving the commission of nonviolent crimes against humanity. Aloyo, "Improving Global Accountability," 506. Like Scheinert, Aloyo argues solely for the prosecution of the crime against humanity of other inhumane acts.

165 Eric Reeves, "Humanitarian Obstruction as a Crime against Humanity: The Example of Sudan" (2011) 54 *African Studies Review* 165–174: 172.

166 Ibid., 169, summarizing as follows:

> The means of obstruction include the denial of visas and travel permits for humanitarian personnel; denial of humanitarian access to key areas for reasons unrelated to security; the halting of essential humanitarian supplies in Port Sudan; the gratuitous and incompetent testing of medical supplies; refusal to accept food deliveries on spurious grounds; the limiting of the transport capacity from Port Sudan and Khartoum to Darfur; contrived insecurity to prevent the movement of humanitarian personnel; arrests of humanitarian personnel as well as beatings and other threats; confiscation of humanitarian assets; and most dramatically, the expulsion from Darfur of thirteen international NGOs and humanitarian organizations, ... in March 2009.

167 Ibid., 170. Although Reeves fails to go into specifics regarding how acts by Sudanese leaders that have interfered with the delivery of much-needed humanitarian aid can and/or should be legally characterized as crimes against humanity.

168 Howard-Hassmann, "Mugabe's Zimbabwe," 898.

169 Ibid., 902.

circle, which Howard-Hassmann argues satisfies the *actus reus* requirement for the crime against humanity of other inhumane acts.[170]

Socioeconomic Oppression and Rights Violations

Scholars have also argued that international crimes may be committed through the cumulative effects of the sustained socioeconomic oppression of victims, including through multiple economic, social, and cultural human rights violations.[171] Although certain ICL provisions explicitly reference economic and social rights issues, such as the right to food and the right to health care, the notion persists that, in terms of human rights violations, ICL overlaps almost exclusively with violations of certain civil and political rights.[172] This assumption is powerfully challenged by Schmid in her recent book on the relationship between economic, social, and cultural rights and ICL.[173] Schmid concludes that "many types of abusive conduct depriving people of their rights to health, water, education, participation in cultural life, food or other [economic, social, and cultural rights,] are properly considered to be within the ambit of ICL."[174] Other scholars such as Larissa van den Herik and Sigrun Skogly have reached similar conclusions, identifying significant areas of legal overlap between particularly egregious forms of economic, social, and cultural rights violations and extant ICL.[175]

170 Ibid., 909.

171 Van den Herik, "Economic, Social, and Cultural Rights"; Schmid, *Taking Economic, Social and Cultural Rights Seriously*. This body of scholarship is closely related to the much broader ongoing debate concerning the justiciability of economic, social, and cultural rights within human rights law itself. A discussion of the justiciability of economic, social, and cultural rights generally is outside the scope of this the present inquiry. For discussions of this issue and its relation to transitional justice work, see, for example, Arbour, "Economic and Social Justice," 10–14; Schmid and Nolan, "'Do No Harm'?."

172 See, for example, Rome Statute, Art. 7(2)(b) (defining the crime against humanity of extermination as "include[ing] the intentional infliction of conditions of life, *inter alia*, the deprivation of access to food and medicine, calculated to bring about the destruction of part of a population"). For an in-depth critique of this lack of engagement, see Schmid, *Taking Economic, Social and Cultural Rights Seriously*.

173 Schmid, *Taking Economic, Social and Cultural Rights Seriously*, 77.

174 Ibid., 312.

175 For example, Evelyne Schmid identifies a "considerable area of overlap" between certain economic, social, and cultural rights violations and the elements of certain war crimes, concluding that, although "how abuses should be prioritised in a post-conflict context is a difficult question," there are "no legal reasons to conclude *a priori* that [economic, social and cultural rights] violations should not or cannot be addressed by attempts to

Within actual ICL practice, however, economic, social, and cultural rights violations and socioeconomic questions more generally, tend to be addressed solely as collateral causes or consequences of more familiar crimes more closely conforming to the atrocity aesthetic and primarily implicating civil and political rights violations.[176] This process, of foregrounding civil and political rights and backgrounding economic and

deal with a legacy of war crimes." Schmid, "War Crimes," 540–541. Schmid makes similar arguments more generally in relation to economic, social, and cultural rights violations and ICL. Schmid, *Taking Economic, Social and Cultural Rights Seriously*, 311–336. Similarly, Sigrun Skogly argues that certain situations involving economic, social, and cultural rights violations, such as "deliberate starvation" or forced evictions, could qualify as crimes against humanity. Skogly, "Crimes against Humanity." Skogly specifically mentions interference with food aid in the Sudan and forced evictions in Kosovo as examples of the types of acts that could be both conceptualized as involving mass economic, social, and cultural rights violations and the commission of international crimes. Ibid., 59. Like many other scholars, Skogly identifies the crime against humanity of other inhumane acts as the most suitable ICL entry point. Ibid., 70–72. Larissa van den Herik adopts a similar approach to Skogly, arguing that there is "ample opportunity to include socio-economic and cultural concerns in mainstream criminal justice modalities." Van den Herik, "Economic, Social, and Cultural Rights," 365. Van den Herik highlights the crimes against humanity of persecution and other inhumane acts as suitable entry points for doing so. Ibid., 352 ("In particular the broad crime definitions of persecution and other inhumane acts as crimes against humanity offered some leeway to import socio-economic human rights notions."). For van den Herik, the proper role of ICL in addressing economic, social, and cultural rights violations is "rather marginal, but not necessarily redundant or inconsequential" in that international prosecutions can help increase the visibility of such violations and thereby "reduce the overall blind spot on socio-economic abuses" by fostering a "more encompassing conflict discourse." Ibid., 366.

176 For example, at Nuremberg, the IMT considered not only the Final Plan to exterminate all Jews from Europe as involving various international crimes, but also held that the conditions in places such as the Warsaw Ghetto, prior to the commencement of the Nazi Final Plan, resulting in famine, spread of disease, overcrowding and excess deaths, to involve international criminal acts by certain Nazi figures. See generally International Military Tribunal, *Trial of the Major War Criminals*, vol. 1, pp. 171–342; see also Fein, "Genocide by Attrition"; Rosenberg, "Genocide Is a Process." Meanwhile, Mark Drumbl has observed that "[b]y and large, the reach of international criminal law is limited to serious violations of core civil and political rights. Therefore, notwithstanding certain exceptions where violations of social, economic, and environmental rights have become implicated, the focus of judicialization efforts remains limited to core civil and political rights." Mark A. Drumbl, "Accountability for Property Crimes and Environmental War Crimes: Prosecution, Litigation, and Development" (April 4, 2009) *International Center for Transitional Justice* 4. Drumbl further states that while there is "much to celebrate in the enforcement of international criminal law; there also is much to critique and improve upon. Part of the improvement project involves recognizing that criminal prosecutions and civil litigation concerning violations of core civil and political rights offer only a *partial print of justice*. Ever since the divide effected in international human rights law in the 1960s, economic, social, cultural, and environmental rights have mixed quite

social ones, has also been critiqued by a number of transitional justice and ICL experts, including notably Louise Arbour in a widely cited 2007 address.[177] Many such scholars view this tendency to foreground civil and political rights within ICL as reflective of a deeply problematic broader systemic prioritization of civil and political rights within human rights and global justice discourses.[178]

Conclusion

Rather than sudden, spectacular eruptions of extreme violence, atrocities are better understood as complex, multifaceted instances of large-scale harm causation that unfold and evolve dynamically over time and space. The production of harms through unspectacular, seemingly banal or bureaucratic means, are often key facets of such processes. These "slow," "attritive," or "cold" means of atrocity commission tend to be much less visible and more difficult to conceptualize as "criminal" in nature, especially when compared to the spectacular visibility and visceral wrongfulness of paradigmatic atrocities.

This chapter has demonstrated, however, that, despite failing to aesthetically conform to dominant shared understandings of international crime commission, certain forms of unspectacular, unfamiliar harm causation may involve the commission of genocide, crimes against humanity, and/or war crimes. As such, there is arguably no clear doctrinal explanation for the seeming systemic backgrounding of harms brought about through means such as the enforcement of famine conditions, extreme corruption, aid interference, socioeconomic oppression, or other similarly banal-seeming methods of harm causation. Given the otherwise disparate nature of the

uneasily with third-party criminal or civil enforcement strategies." Ibid., 4 (emphasis in original).

177 See, for example, Arbour, "Economic and Social Justice"; Cahill-Ripley, "Foregrounding Socio-Economic Rights."

178 See, for example, Arbour, "Economic and Social Justice," 4–9; see also Benjamin Authers and Hilary Charlesworth, "The Crisis and the Quotidian in International Human Rights Law" (2013) 44 *Netherlands Yearbook of International Law* 19–39 (arguing that failure to engage with everyday structural socioeconomic injustices impoverishes international human rights law). For an alternate view, see, for example, Kenneth Roth, "Defending Economic, Social and Cultural Rights: Practical Issues Faced by an International Human Rights Organization" (2004) 26 *Human Rights Quarterly* 63–72 (arguing that the process of "naming and shaming" that is central to current human rights work renders it more difficult to achieve results in relation to economic, social, and cultural rights violations, which typically arise from complex relationships and thus lack individuals who can be named and shamed).

harm causation processes discussed in this chapter, aside from their uniformly aesthetic unfamiliarity, I suggest that their systemic backgrounding both lends support to the assertion that aesthetic considerations figure into dominant shared understandings of international crime, and that aesthetic familiarity plays a role in determining what harms will and will not be viewed as potentially transgressing ICL. This is not to say that aesthetic considerations and, more specifically, the degree to which relevant harm causation modalities conform to the atrocity aesthetic are always the sole, or even most important factor figuring into sociopolitical processes of recognizing potential ICL violations. There are surely a host of factors, social, political, and otherwise, that figure into what harms are, and are not, widely conceptualized as international crimes. Biases and power dynamics are sure to affect many, if not all of these factors. Such are the politics of recognition and naming, especially in international law and relations.

Nonetheless, there does seem to be something distinctly aesthetic about the knee-jerk hostility one often encounters at the mere suggestion that international crimes might be able to be committed through novel, seemingly mundane means. The notion that the radical evils ICL deals with might be committed insidiously, closer to home, and by banal-seeming bureaucrats, politicians, and the like seems to discomfort many people deeply invested in human rights, international criminal justice, and the anti-impunity movement. The source of this discomfort remains unclear. Perhaps it is the possibility that international crimes may not be so extraordinary after all. Perhaps recognition of a broader array of forms of mass violence and subjugation may create a sense of hopelessness by expanding the already enormous global impunity gap. Perhaps it is the potential for us (in the Global North) to feel implicated in atrocities ourselves, if not directly, then as bystanders or beneficiaries. Perhaps it pushes us toward an uncomfortable reckoning with our own racialized exoticism of international crimes as horrific events occurring in a distant "uncivilized" part of the world (that we are fully separated from). These are but a handful of the many "anxieties" of international criminal justice that may be implicated by the recognition of banal, everyday atrocity processes.[179] Whatever the factors may be that combine to create hostility to the notion that international crimes might take more forms than we previously imagined, the reality continues to be that there is sustained

[179] Frédéric Mégret, "The Anxieties of International Criminal Justice" (2016) 29 *Leiden Journal of International Law* 197–221.

resistance to the very notion that the prosecution of unspectacular forms of large-scale violence and abuse through ICL may be feasible and warranted.

The following chapter looks at some real-world examples of atrocity processes failing to conform neatly to the atrocity aesthetic identified, framing them as potential overlooked international crimes. This overview helps us see how, in a general sense, there seems to be a pattern whereby the seriousness or potential criminality of aesthetically unfamiliar harms is downgraded or obscured altogether. From pre-ICL colonial-era atrocities, to more recent or ongoing forms of oppression and mass harm causation, one can see aesthetics at work modulating the visibility and perceived seriousness of harms in relation to how closely they adhere to the atrocity aesthetic. In order to also provide a more granular analysis of the dynamics involved in backgrounding unspectacular harms in a particular situation, the following chapter closely examines the dichotomy between highly visible/broadly recognized forms of atrocity commission in Khmer Rouge-era Cambodia, and less visible/backgrounded ones, focusing most closely on the work of the ECCC. This granular analysis helps elucidate the interplay between the aesthetic familiarity of atrocity processes, power dynamics, and politics of recognition and resource allocation within the realm of international criminal justice.

5

Visible and Invisible International Crimes

Cambodia and Beyond

Introduction

Thus far, this book has argued that longstanding, widely shared understandings of atrocities as horrific spectacles have influenced the selective recognition of the forms genocide, crimes against humanity, and war crimes may take. The previous chapter introduced four examples of harms that tend to both fail to conform to the atrocity aesthetic and be relegated to the periphery of international criminal justice, despite potentially involving ICL violations. These harms are those associated with the causation and/or enforcement of famine conditions; large-scale corruption, interference with life-sustaining aid, and socioeconomic oppression and rights violations. As discussed in the previous chapter, these topics has been traditionally viewed as peripheral, rather than core subjects of ICL; framed as root causes or collateral consequences of "real" atrocity crimes, rather than potential means of commission.

The previous chapter focused on these general arguments concerning the potential applicability of ICL to famine, corruption, aid interference and socioeconomic rights violations, along with a doctrinal analysis of the substance of ICL with an eye to identifying opportunities to address unspectacular forms of mass harm causation. The chapter concluded that ICL seems to be constructed in a way allowing for its application to a diverse array of harm causation modalities, despite its current narrow focus on instantiations of international crimes conforming closely to the atrocity aesthetic. Both the doctrine and the literature examined demonstrate a certain flexibility within ICL, seemingly allowing for its application to novel forms of mass harm causation.

In order to ground the hypothetical forecasting of ICL's general applicability to heretofore unaddressed mass harms, this chapter considers ICL's applicability to a variety of real-world situations involving the production of mass suffering and/or death through relatively slow, unspectacular forms of harm causation. Again, as with the previous chapter, because these harms have largely been presumed to have been noncriminal, or at least not serious enough to warrant prosecution, this analysis is necessarily primarily one of rough forecasting, rather than definitive conclusions. This is the best one can do as an individual, especially given the complex, resource-intensive nature of ICL investigatory and adjudicatory processes. Nonetheless, even with these tempered expectations, this chapter identifies various examples of situations that, upon careful analysis, appear to have involved the commission of one or more international crimes, yet failed to conform to the atrocity aesthetic. These potential crimes have also been afforded comparatively scant attention, especially in comparison to more spectacular forms of atrocity, despite often being comparably massive in scale and gravity, suggesting that their aesthetic unfamiliarity has contributed to, or at least facilitated their relative invisibility, socially and legally, as potential international crimes.

At this juncture, a note on methodology and depth of analysis is warranted. Even the most obvious, aesthetically paradigmatic international crimes are thoroughly complex social phenomena, tied up as they are in time, place, history, culture, overlapping forms of violence, and the like. As such, it is impossible to provide a granular analysis of every situation referenced in this chapter, for reasons of both length and feasibility. Given this reality and the fact that my broader argument is that there exists a repetitive tendency to only see certain harms as potentially criminal that pervades ICL, it is important to identify various examples where aesthetics may play a role in ongoing processes of denial and/or minimization of atrocity crimes.

However, a closer analysis is also helpful for us to consider how aesthetic and other factors (political, practical, social, other) interact to push certain harms to the forefront, while relegating others to the background, irrespective of gravity, victim preference, or, arguably, prosecutorial feasibility. As such, this chapter first provides an in-depth look at the dynamics of recognizing and ranking the relative importance of varying forms of atrocity commission in the context of post-atrocity Cambodia, with an emphasis on the selection of what individuals and crimes were deemed essential to be addressed by the ECCC. This more granular analysis demonstrates that, regardless of scale, gravity, number of victims (or for that matter, seeming victim preferences), the ECCC deemed the most familiar perpetrators and forms of atrocity violence as those whose prosecution was essential. While various factors shaped who and what the Court did and did not investigate and prosecute, not the least of which being power dynamics and the Cambodian government's transparent (and ultimately successful) efforts to prevent trials in Cases 003 and 004, I contend that aesthetics played a meaningful role in constructing notions of what crimes and suspects were essential prosecutorial targets.

After spending some time delving into the process of recognizing and prioritizing international crimes in post-atrocity Cambodia, this chapter steps back and identifies a broad range of additional situations wherein the potential criminality of mass harms brought about through slow, attritive, or otherwise unspectacular methods has been obscured or artificially downgraded in terms of perceived gravity. These situations are discussed in far less depth, as my intention is not to assert that each of them definitively involved the commission of international crimes (indeed, some of the situations discussed occurred before crimes against humanity and/or genocide even existed in international law). Instead, the goal in discussing these various situations, ranging from pre-Nuremberg atrocities to recent and even ongoing unspectacular atrocity processes, is to invite us to think more expansively and creatively about the dynamics of international crime commission and the many forms genocide, crimes against humanity, and war crimes might take.

This analysis demonstrates that certain manifestations of culpable mass harm causation, such as, for example, the longstanding persecution of Rohingya populations in Myanmar since at least the 1970s, are difficult to recognize and conceptualize as potential international crimes, at least until such time as unfamiliar forms of atrocity violence begin to be accompanied by more highly visible and familiar ones, as has been the case in Myanmar. Moreover, in other circumstances, the criminality of slow, attritive, or otherwise aesthetically unfamiliar forms of atrocity commission, such as the enforcement of famine conditions in Khmer Rouge-era Cambodia, may remain obscured or at least deprioritized, even when committed within the context of a widely recognized general instance of genocide or mass atrocity. Finally, in other circumstances, potential international crimes may be viewed as noncriminal altogether, at least in mainstream discourses. Consequently, while far from being unilaterally determinative in terms of shaping ICL's extreme selectivity, aesthetic considerations appear to modulate the fluctuating visibility and perceived gravity of varying forms of atrocity violence. Through this analysis, this chapter demonstrates how dominant representations and understandings of atrocity and international crime, along with legal practices and discourses associated with ICL, inform and reinforce the notion that all instances of international crimes will manifest themselves as highly visible, intuitively recognizable horrific spectacles.[1]

Spectacular and Everyday Atrocities in Khmer Rouge-era Cambodia

On April 17, 1975, following a bitter five-year civil war, the Khmer Rouge swept into power in Cambodia.[2] The regime proceeded to set about radically altering the structure of Cambodian society, brutalizing the civilian population in the process. This brutalization took many forms, ranging from familiar manifestations of atrocity, such as beatings, mass imprisonment, torture, and executions, to an array of oppressive policies that combined to produce trauma and death incrementally over time.[3] These policies dictated virtually all aspects of the daily lives of civilians and were backed up by the

[1] In this regard, ICL is but one arena of representation wherein notions of atrocity, mass violence, and international crime are formed and reformed continually over time. However, it is an arena possessing considerable authority, along with a veneer of technocratic competence and political neutrality.

[2] For a basic overview of this history, see Khamboly Dy, *A History of Democratic Kampuchea 1975 – 1979* (Documentation Center of Cambodia, 2007). For more detailed histories, see, for example, Ben Kiernan, *The Pol Pot Regime: Race, Power, and Genocide in Cambodia under the Khmer Rouge, 1975–79*, 3rd ed. (Yale University Press, 2008); Elizabeth Becker, *When the War was Over: Cambodia and the Khmer Rouge Revolution* (Public Affairs, 1998). For a broader history of Cambodia, see David Chandler, *A History of Cambodia*, 4th ed. (Westview Press, 2008).

[3] The term "trauma" is subject to a wide array of understandings, ranging from physical traumas, to psychological traumas. The severity of harm being referred to also varies widely. Throughout this book, "trauma" is used to refer solely to experiences involving suffering that rising to the level of being "inhumane" according to ICL, by involving "great suffering, or serious injury to body or to mental or physical health." See generally *Prosecutor* v. *Lukić and Lukić, 98–32/1-T, July 20, 2009*, ICTY, para. 960 (stating that, to rise to the level of an inhumane act under ICL, an "act or omission must have caused serious mental or physical suffering or injury or constituted a serious attack on human dignity."). For historical overviews of the Khmer Rouge period, see, for example, Chandler, *History of Cambodia*; Becker, *When the War was Over*; Kiernan, *Pol Pot Regime.* Elsewhere, I have argued that the famine Cambodians endured during the Khmer Rouge period was a direct result of these policies and appears to have involved the commission of crimes against humanity by senior Khmer Rouge leaders. Randle C. DeFalco, "Justice and Starvation in Cambodia: International Criminal Law and the Khmer Rouge Famine," LLM Thesis, University of Toronto (2013); Randle C. DeFalco, "Accounting for Famine at the Extraordinary Chambers in the Courts of Cambodia: The Crimes against Humanity of Extermination, Inhumane Acts and Persecution" (2011) 5 *International Journal of Transitional Justice* 142–158.

ever-present threat of imprisonment, torture, and/or summary execution. When the regime was ultimately ousted by invading Vietnamese forces in January 1979, somewhere between 1.2 and 2.8 million Cambodians had perished over a period of approximately three years and eight months.[4] Demographers appointed by the ECCC, along with several scholars, estimate that roughly half of this massive death toll can be attributed to the regime's oppressive social and economic policies, as opposed to direct acts of interpersonal violence (i.e. executions, torture, and other forms of "violent" killing in a narrow sense of the word).[5] These deaths were caused, for the most part, attritively over time, through a combination of the effects of endemic famine, disease, denial of basic medical care, and overwork.[6]

These basic facts – of mass trauma and death, brought about through a mix of extreme forms of physical violence and the enforcement of exceptionally harsh living conditions – encapsulate the

4 The aggregate death toll (or, in technical terms, the aggregate number of "excess" deaths) of the Khmer Rouge era is subject to a wide range of estimates, attributable to a preexisting lack of reliable demographic statistical figures and exacerbated by strong political and ideological forces at work. In 2009, demographers appointed by the ECCC surveyed available death toll estimates and concluded the "most likely" total death toll of the Khmer Rouge era to be between 1.747 and 2.2 million victims. Ewa Tabeau and Kheam They, "Khmer Rouge Victims in Cambodia, April 1975 – January 1979: A Critical Assessment of Major Estimates," Office of the Co-Investigating Judges, ECCC, 2009, p. 70. More recently, Patrick Heuveline, using computer simulations, estimated that there is a 95 percent certainty that the death toll fell somewhere between 1.2 and 2.8 million, with a nearly 70 percent chance that the death toll was between 1.5 and 2.25 million victims. Patrick Heuveline, "The Boundaries of Genocide: Quantifying the Uncertainty of the Death Toll during the Pol Pot Regime in Cambodia (1975–79)" (2015) 69 *Population Studies* 201–218.

5 Tabeau and They, "Khmer Rouge Victims in Cambodia," 70. Heuveline similarly estimates that there is a 95 percent likelihood that 728,000 to 1.455 million deaths were caused through the commission of violence, narrowly defined. Heuveline, "Boundaries of Genocide," 214. Based on his estimate of 1.2 to 2.8 million aggregate deaths in the same likelihood range, this would result in a "non-violent" death toll of between 472,000 and 1.345 million victims. Heuveline refers to "policies of population displacement, forced labor, and restricting the availability of food and medicines" as "non-violent" sources of mortality under the Khmer Rouge. Ibid., 202. James Tyner identifies a "developing" consensus that "direct" and "indirect" death tolls during the Khmer Rouge period were proportional. James A. Tyner, "State Sovereignty, Bioethics, and Political Geographies: The Practice of Medicine under the Khmer Rouge" (2012) 30 *Environment and Planning D: Society and Space* 842–860: 852.

6 Heuveline, "Boundaries of Genocide," 202. For more information on these causes of death see generally James A. Tyner and Stian Rice, "To Live and Let Die: Food, Famine, and Administrative Violence in Democratic Kampuchea, 1975–1979" (2015) 48 *Political Geography* 1–10; James A. Tyner, "Dead Labor, Landscapes, and Mass Graves: Administrative Violence during the Cambodian Genocide" (2014) 52 *Geoforum* 70–77.

Khmer Rouge experience in Cambodia. When one delves into this history beyond the surface, to determine with more precision how the Khmer Rouge brought about such devastation, and who might be legally responsible, criminally or otherwise, the mutually reinforcing nature of the various modalities of oppression and harm causation enforced on the civilian population by the regime becomes even more apparent. During the reign of the Khmer Rouge, policy edicts emanated from the regime's "Party Center," a rough designation collectively denoting an evolving set of key authority figures in the regime primarily drawn from its "Standing" and "Central" Committees, themselves dominated by Pol Pot and a select group of close confidants.[7] These top Khmer Rouge leaders engaged in violent internal purges of party ranks repeatedly throughout their relatively short time in power.[8] Any Khmer Rouge official whose loyalty to the Party Center came to be questioned, or whose local power derived from loyalties independent of the Party Center's patronage network, was subject to increased suspicion and was likely to be purged.[9] Against this backdrop of suspicion and the ever-present threat of execution, the regime set about to radically overhaul Cambodian society on a remarkably aggressive timetable, despite taking over

[7] The term "Party Center" is used by Ben Kiernan to refer "members of the Standing Committee of the Central Committee with national responsibility, not specifically responsible for a regional area such as one of the Zones of the country." Kiernan, *Pol Pot Regime*, 93, note 7. For the purposes of the present inquiry, the term is used to generally refer to the highest echelons of the Khmer Rouge leadership apparatus. For an overview of the Khmer Rouge command and communication structures, see *Case 001, Case No. 001/18-07-2007/ ECCC/TC, Doc. No. E188, July 26, 2010*, ECCC, paras. 199–302. As the ECCC Trial Chamber found, "'Party Centre' was a nebulous term: sometimes it was used in a collective sense to describe an entire 'level within the Party hierarchy', and sometimes it was used to designate a specific entity or body within the upper echelon of the CPK [Communist Party of Kampuchea, i.e. the Khmer Rouge] (such as the Central Committee, the Standing Committee or one of its connected offices, or even POL Pot himself)." Ibid., para. 205 (internal citations omitted).

[8] For detailed analyses of the Khmer Rouge's internal purges, see Kiernan, *Pol Pot Regime*, 59–96, 313–356, 368–376, and 411–427; Alexander Laban Hinton, *Why Did They Kill? Cambodia in the Shadow of Genocide* (University of California Press, 2005), 96–169.

[9] The Khmer Rouge itself was an amalgamation of various revolutionary movements, and many mid- and senior-level Khmer Rouge officials and military leaders had preexisting loyalty and patronage networks outside of their status within the Khmer Rouge movement itself. These leaders, such as Ros Nhim and Sao Phim, tended to be the targets of internal purges during the Khmer Rouge period. For an overview of such purges, see generally Kiernan, *Pol Pot Regime*. For an analysis of Cambodian patronage networks and the role they played in mass killing, including internal purges, under the Khmer Rouge, see Hinton, *Why Did They Kill?*, 96–169.

a nation devastated by five years of civil war and a haphazard, yet massive American bombing campaign.[10]

The policy edicts of the Party Center created nationwide living conditions that soon began to produce mass suffering and death. The regime first closed Cambodia's borders and expelled all foreigners and foreign organizations, resulting in an immediate cessation of all humanitarian aid work in the country.[11] The government also forcibly evacuated Cambodia's cities, most notably the capital, Phnom Penh, dispersing the civilian population throughout the countryside according to where the Party Center deemed human labor to be most needed.[12] The conditions of these transfers were harsh. Most evacuees had to travel vast distances on foot and without proper provisions, resulting in food shortages and diseases weakening the population and causing many deaths along the way.[13]

On arrival at their assigned destination, evacuees were put to forced labor under appalling conditions, primarily in rice fields or at construction sites, where bridges, dams, and other infrastructure projects were built with near-exclusive reliance on manual labor.[14] Most areas that received evacuees lacked the necessary housing, sanitation, medical, and food production infrastructure to support the new arrivals. Consequently, many new arrivals lived in makeshift housing or slept out in the open.[15] Under these conditions, diseases quickly began to spread and continued to ravage the civilian population essentially unchecked throughout the duration of the Khmer Rouge's relatively brief time in power.

According to the Party Center's policy of "independence self-mastery," Cambodian society was to be overhauled without significant foreign aid

[10] For an overview of the Khmer Rouge's plans to overhaul Cambodian society, see generally, DeFalco, "Justice and Starvation in Cambodia," 27–45. For an overview of the United States bombing of Cambodia, see Taylor Owen and Ben Kiernan, "Bombs over Cambodia" (October 2006) *The Walrus* 62–69.

[11] For an overview of the expulsion of all foreigners from Cambodia after the Khmer Rouge seized power, see generally Kiernan, *Pol Pot Regime*, 39–44.

[12] For example, in 1976, 500,000 to 800,000 Cambodian civilians were sent to the country's Northwest Zone, where the regime deemed that additional labor forces were needed to achieve rice production quotas, which were especially high in the area. The areas these evacuees were sent to utterly lacked the capacity to house and feed them, creating especially high mortality rates. For an account of this forced relocation and its consequences, see generally ibid., 216–250.

[13] For an overview of the evacuation of Phnom Penh, See *Case 002, Case File No. 002/19-09-2007/ECCC/TC, Doc. No. E313, August 7, 2014*, ECCC, paras. 459–500.

[14] See generally DeFalco, "Justice and Starvation in Cambodia," 27–43.

[15] For example, see Kiernan's discussion of the mass forced evacuation of civilians to Northwestern Cambodia under the Khmer Rouge. Kiernan, *Pol Pot Regime*, 216–250.

or trade, save for with a short list of allied countries, primarily China.[16] The revolution was to maintain this defiant independence by "standing" (i.e. relying nearly exclusively) on rice production to sustain the civilian population, provision the military, *and* as the primary source of national income through export.[17] In essence, rice replaced money as the currency of the regime, which had banned markets, and soon thereafter, currency, shortly after taking power. Indeed, the very notion of private property was abolished and everything within Cambodia, from natural resources, to personal possessions, became the property of the regime, known in the countryside only collectively as the ominous and faceless *Angkar* ("organization").[18]

The regime's ban on all vestiges of "privatism" encompassed ownership of items such as medicine and cooking provisions, the cultivation of subsistence gardens, and the very acts of cooking or eating outside of communal dining halls. Even foraging for Cambodia's then-abundant wild food sources was forbidden as a vestige of forbidden privatism.[19] Consequently, the civilian population was forcibly made completely reliant on the regime itself for food, shelter, medical care, and other basic provisions, as it was a serious transgression, punishable by possible imprisonment, torture, and/or execution, to take independent action to sustain oneself or others. The regime's overarching policy of independence self-mastery also drove additional edicts that had disastrous human consequences. For instance, the already weakened medical care sector was replaced by the regime with a system of makeshift "hospitals" where untrained, often illiterate, teenage party members

[16] For a discussion of the Khmer Rouge concept of independence self-mastery, see DeFalco, "Justice and Starvation in Cambodia," 32–39; *Case 002, Case File No. 002/19-09-2007/ECCC/TC, Doc. No. E313, August 7, 2014*, ECCC, paras. 736–738.

[17] For a discussion of the Khmer Rouge regime's plan to "stand" on agriculture, see DeFalco, "Justice and Starvation in Cambodia," 35–40; *Case 002, Case File No. 002/19-09-2007/ECCC/TC, Doc. No. E313, August 7, 2014*, ECCC, para. 782 ("Based on the principle of self-reliance, priority was given to building irrigation projects, expanding the rice fields, and developing those industrial activities that served the development of agriculture.") (internal citations omitted).

[18] See Dy, *History*; Kiernan, *Pol Pot Regime*, 58 et seq.; *Case 002, Case File No. 002/19-09-2007/ECCC/TC, Doc. No. E313, August 7, 2014*, ECCC, paras. 128, 221–222.

[19] For information on the Khmer Rouge's ideology surrounding collectivism and their aversion to what they perceived as vestiges of "privatism" see generally, Hinton, *Why Did They Kill?*, 126–169; Kosal Path and Angeliki Kanavou, "Converts, Not Ideologues? The Khmer Rouge Practice of Thought Reform in Cambodia, 1975–1978" (2015) 20 *Journal of Political Ideologies* 304–332.

practiced a form of health care that amounted to little more than human experimentation.[20]

The rice production envisioned by the Party Center that would support the population and military while simultaneously funding the overhaul of Cambodia's infrastructure required nearly tripling the country's rice yield, from one, to three tons average per hectare.[21] The phrase "three tons per hectare" became a party mantra, repeatedly referenced in party propaganda, mentioned at party meetings, and adopted as a party slogan for local officials to disseminate among the masses.[22] This radical scaling up of rice production was manifestly impossible, especially on the aggressive timescale set out by the regime, and rice production targets were not met with any regularity while the Khmer Rouge held power. And yet, the Party Center viewed any failures to achieve these manifestly impossible production targets necessarily as products of subversion, sabotage, or laziness.[23] This is where the Party Center's paranoia and propensity for extreme violence came into play as a means of reinforcing the devastation being wrought by their disastrous socioeconomic policies. Mass internal purges of regime cadres tended to occur in areas where local officials enjoyed some degree of autonomous support, such as along Cambodia's eastern border, and/or where officials questioned or voiced opposition to the Party Center's impossible to meet rice production demands.[24] Thus, everyone, from local laborers, to Party officials, had to play their role in

[20] See Laura Vilim, "'Keeping Them Alive, One Gets Nothing; Killing Them, One Loses Nothing': Prosecuting Khmer Rouge Medical Practices as Crimes against Humanity," 2010, http://d.dccam.org/Abouts/Intern/Laura_PT1.pdf. The "medicine" administered in these hospitals was in reality, typically an unsanitary concoction of coconut juice and various plant extracts, injected randomly into victims already suffering from severe maladies, such as malaria and dysentery, compounded by endemic undernutrition and outright starvation. For analyses of Khmer Rouge medical practices, see generally DeFalco, "Justice and Starvation in Cambodia," 50–52; Tyner, "State Sovereignty, Bioethics, and Political Geographies," 847–852.

[21] See DeFalco, "Justice and Starvation in Cambodia," 36–37.

[22] See ibid., 35–39; *Case 002, Case File No. 002/19-09-2007/ECCC/TC, Doc. No. E313, August 7, 2014*, ECCC, paras. 604–609.

[23] For an overview of how the Khmer Rouge leadership shifted blame for its deeply flawed policies, see DeFalco, "Justice and Starvation in Cambodia," 52–72.

[24] For a discussion of how such purges were used by the Party Center to both enforce its socioeconomic policies and shift blame for the inevitable shortcomings of such policies to hidden "enemies" of the revolution, see ibid., 52–61. For analyses of the Khmer Rouge's internal purges, see David Chandler, *Voices from S-21: Terror and History in Pol Pot's Secret Prison* (University of California Press, 1999); Hinton, *Why Did They Kill?*; Kiernan, *Pol Pot Regime.*

remaining steadfastly dedicated to the Party Center's absurd policies and goals in order to reduce the likelihood of being purged.

The degree of suffering wrought by the Khmer Rouge regime through its oppressive policies cannot be conveyed by a mere recitation of the estimated number of victims who ultimately died of starvation, overwork, or wholly preventable and/or treatable diseases. Enduring the kinds of slow processes of attrition and starvation inflicted by the Khmer Rouge regime on the civilian population under its control produces extreme suffering and life-altering physical and mental traumas, among both those who ultimately die and survivors alike. In this way, the ravages of hunger, overwork, and lack of medical care, along with the ever-present threat of violence, represent a uniquely universal experience shared by all Cambodian civilians (and many former Khmer Rouge cadres) under the Khmer Rouge regime.[25] Those who survived, even those who managed to avoid being physically beaten or tortured, still experienced severe physical and mental traumas stemming from their experiences under the regime, and untreated post-traumatic stress disorder (PTSD) and other mental health problems continue to plague survivor populations and their descendants.[26]

[25] Conditions did vary throughout Cambodia under the Khmer Rouge, but famine, forced labor, forced communal eating, denial of basic medical care, and other sources of suffering were the widespread products of national policy edicts issued by the Khmer Rouge central leadership. For an overview of how various Khmer Rouge policies produced mass death in Cambodia, see DeFalco, "Justice and Starvation in Cambodia"; Tyner and Rice, "To Live and Let Die"; Tyner, "Dead Labor"; James A. Tyner, *The Politics of Lists: Bureaucracy and Genocide under the Khmer Rouge* (West Virginia Press, 2018).

[26] See Youk Chhang, Beth Van Schaack, and Daryn Reicherter, eds., *Cambodia's Hidden Scars: Trauma Psychology in the Wake of the Khmer Rouge* (Documentation Center of Cambodia, 2011). Recent research has found evidence that elderly Cambodians, virtually all of whom lived through the Khmer Rouge era, experience especially high rates of disability as they age. Experiences of prior trauma are likely a contributing factor to this increased disability rate. See Zachary Zimmer, "Disability and Active Life Expectancy among Older Cambodians" (2006) 2 *Asian Population Studies* 133–148. A survey conducted by the United State National Institute of Health found post-traumatic stress disorder (PTSD) to be "epidemic" among Cambodian immigrants in Long Beach, California, most of whom were in Cambodia during the Khmer Rouge period. United States Institute of Mental Health, "PTSD, Depression Epidemic among Cambodian Immigrants," August 2, 2005. There is also evidence that PTSD and trauma have intergenerational effects. See, for example, Cécile Rousseau, Aline Drapeau, and Robert Platt, "Family Trauma and Its Association with Emotional and Behavioral Problems and Social Adjustment in Adolescent Cambodian Refugees" (1999) 23 *Child Abuse and Neglect* 1263–1273; Richard F. Mollica et al., "The Enduring Mental Health Impact of Mass Violence: A Community Comparison Study of Cambodian Civilians Living in Cambodia and Thailand" (2014) 60 *International Journal of Social Psychiatry* 6–20; Nigel P. Field, Sophear Muong, and Vannavuth Sochanvimean, "Parental Styles in

Just as the scale of suffering and death in Cambodia under the Khmer Rouge cannot be reduced to a recitation of an estimated death toll, neither can the modalities through which such suffering and death were produced be neatly disaggregated into a discrete set of mutually exclusive causal categories. Any attempt to do so risks ignoring the fact that the regime produced mass trauma and death through a complex set of mutually reinforcing processes that unfolded dynamically over significant spans of time and space to decimate the population under its control. Local Khmer Rouge officials were routinely forced to choose between critiquing or failing to meet the impossible production demands of the Party Center, and overworking and underfeeding the civilian workforce in order to remit enough rice or other goods to the regime to avoid potentially deadly suspicion. Certain Khmer Rouge officials did complain that the production targets dictated by the Party Center were impossible to achieve. Such dissidents were mostly killed, along with their entire family, their subordinates, and the families of their subordinates, in a series of brutal purges.[27] Others worked the civilian population under their control past the brink of overwork and starvation, while obsessively stockpiling rice to assuage the ever-suspicious Party Center. When production shortfalls inevitably occurred, local Khmer Rouge officials were also incentivized to blame such shortfalls on subversive networks attempting to undermine the revolution in order to shift blame away from themselves (while remaining careful not to criticize the Party Center), further fueling the paranoia and violence of the regime.[28]

the Intergenerational Transmission of Trauma Stemming from the Khmer Rouge Regime in Cambodia" (2013) 83 *American Journal of Orthopsychiatry* 483–494.

[27] See Kiernan, *Pol Pot Regime*, 59–96, 313–356, 368–376, 411–427; Hinton, *Why Did They Kill?*, 96–169. For an analysis of S-21 prison, where purged high-level party officials were sent to be tortured into confessing to concocted subversive activities, see Chandler, *Voices from S-21*. For examples of specific Khmer Rouge officials who apparently complained about the regime's extreme policies and associated living condition repercussions, and were shortly thereafter purged, such as Mok Heng, Hou Yuon, Chin Suon, Hu Nim, Koy Thuon, Chum Narith, Nhim Ros, and Sao Phim, see DeFalco, "Justice and Starvation in Cambodia," 52–62.

[28] See generally DeFalco, "Justice and Starvation in Cambodia," 52–62. For example, after assuming control of the North Zone of Cambodia in April of 1976 after the Zone's previous leader had been purged, newly installed Zone Secretary Ke Pauk sent a telegram to the Party Center that reported on "the enemy, the masses, and cultivation in the northern zone" and stated that "[t]he enemy says that the revolution is too strict. They oppose the idea of cooperatives and the construction of new dikes. They also complain about starvation." To combat these "enemies," Ke Pauk informed the Center that he "advised regions to investigate the above-mentioned enemy activities closely. We have already arrested the former cooperative chiefs. In addition to these actions, the enemy has

Civilians, meanwhile, were placed in an even worse predicament. If they assiduously followed the regime's commands by working ceaselessly and not seeking to procure sufficient food, rest, or medicine, this still did not guarantee they would not be beaten, arrested, or even executed, and those who followed this strategy were very likely to waste away and die from a mix of disease, starvation, and overwork. Those who complained about rations or living conditions, or who otherwise resisted party policies, were far more likely to be executed. Those who clandestinely sought out additional food or medicine through illicit trade, foraging, or by "stealing" crops, also risked imprisonment, torture, and execution. Thus, all paths led inexorably to deprivation and a greatly increased likelihood of death, with the choices along the way mostly affecting only the immediate cause of such suffering and potential death. All these sources of precarity, trauma, and risk of death, can be traced directly back to the Party Center and the upper echelons of the Khmer Rouge leadership.

Amid these Orwellian circumstances, causes of trauma and death were both cumulative and overdetermined in nature, rendering efforts to neatly categorize harms according to a single, discrete cause (execution, overwork, famine, disease, torture, denial of medical care, etc.) necessarily an exercise in elision and oversimplification. Execution victims may have been killed only because they stole food in efforts to avoid starving to death, while victims of disease often died of relatively minor illnesses whose deleterious effects were exacerbated by overwork, starvation, and denial of medical care.

In their totality, the socioeconomic policies of the Khmer Rouge Party Center directly traumatized virtually every civilian living in Cambodia from 1975 to 1979 and killed somewhere between 470,000 and 1.34 million of these victims.[29] Despite this staggering toll, whether at the high or low end of estimates, standard narratives of atrocity and mass killing in Khmer Rouge-era Cambodia tend to foreground the spectacularly horrific, aesthetically familiar forms of violence and abuse committed by the regime in the form of mass executions, violent internal purges, mass imprisonment, and the widespread use of torture. In the process, harms caused by the Party Center's socioeconomic policy edicts are implicitly presented as either noncriminal collateral consequences flowing from more traditional atrocities, or as somehow less serious or central to the criminality of the Khmer Rouge regime.

a hidden network, which we are investigating. We will take appropriate measures to deal with this." Ibid., 57, quoting "Telegram 94" (2003) 2nd Quarter *Searching for the Truth: Magazine of the Documentation Center of Cambodia* 11.

[29] See generally Tabeau and They, "Khmer Rouge Victims in Cambodia"; Tyner, "State Sovereignty, Bioethics, and Political Geographies," 852.

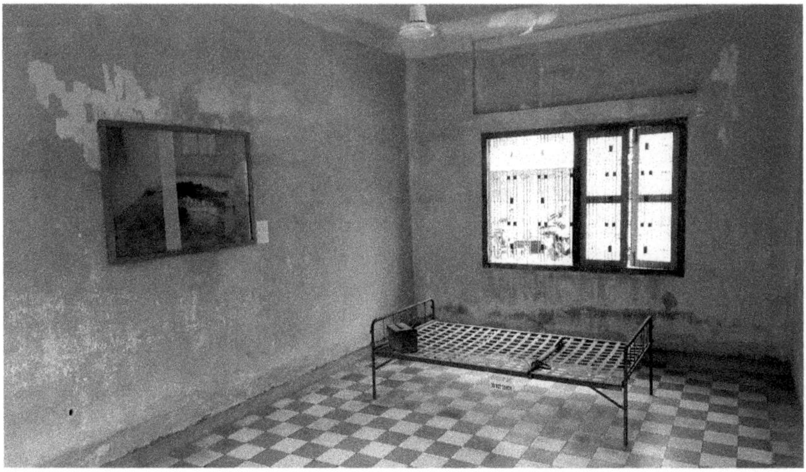

Figure 5.1 Former torture and interrogation room, *Tuol Sleng* prison, Cambodia[32]

One way to illustrate this dominant view is to simply conduct an internet image search of terms such as "Cambodia" and "atrocity," or "genocide." Such a search returns page after page of graphic, often quite visceral, images of violence and its aftermath. The images that are returned primarily depict Khmer Rouge guerillas wielding weaponry, mounds of human bones and skulls, and images of sullen detainees who were photographed prior to their execution at *Tuol Sleng* S-21 prison on the outskirts of Phnom Penh (see Figure 5.1).[30] Such spectacular violence left behind material, visceral reminders of its horror in Cambodia in the form of thousands of mass graves, and so-called dark tourism sites of former prisons, execution sites, and the like.[31] The bones, skulls, mass graves, and other visceral remnants of Khmer Rouge-era atrocities have

[30] "S-21" was the code name given to the prison by the Khmer Rouge. The prison itself was converted from a school that operated on the site before the Khmer Rouge regime. *Tuol Sleng* roughly translates as "poisonous hill" as *Tuol* refers to a high-lying area of land and *Sleng* is a term used to refer to two kinds of poisonous trees in Cambodia. For more on the etymology of the term *Tuol Sleng*, see Post Staff, "The 'Poisonous Hill' that was Toul Sleng" (May 2, 1997) *Phnom Penh Post*, www.phnompenhpost.com/national/poisonous-hill-was-toul-sleng. Throughout this book "S-21" and "*Tuol Sleng*" are used interchangeably. For a detailed analysis of the workings of S-21 prison, see Chandler, *Voices from S-21*.

[31] The two most prominent examples of such tourist sites are S-21 *Tuol Sleng* prison, and the *Choeung Ek* killing field and mass grave site. However, many other similar, yet less well-known sites exist or are in development. Examples include Pol Pot's cremation and grave site and the former residence of Khmer Rouge commander Ta Mok.

[32] Author's photo (2018).

undoubtedly helped the "Cambodian Genocide" enter into the canon of widely accepted, highly visible twentieth-century atrocities.

However, as Susan Sontag argues, such horrific images of atrocity may haunt us, but they do little to help us understand.[33] Along these lines, Valerie Hartouni traces the increasing role of aesthetic representation in understandings of atrocity crimes to the graphic imagery that emerged at the close of World War II of the Holocaust. These shocking images, of bodies piled in heaps and gaunt, ghost-like concentration camp internees, helped create the impetus for the creation of ICL itself and later played a central evidentiary role in the trial of Adolph Eichmann in Jerusalem.[34] This imagery has, according to Hartouni, helped produce a current situation where Nazi atrocities are treated as "both a benchmark and an aberration" in understanding atrocity and totalitarian violence.[35] This imagery has given rise to what Hartouni describes as a set of "myths" concerning the nature of mass atrocity and genocide that "are inextricably tied to and reinforced viscerally by the atrocity imagery that emerged with the liberation of the concentration camps."[36] Such imagery, according to Hartouni, grounds a "visual rhetoric that now circumscribes the moral and political fields and powerfully assists in contemporary mythmaking about how we know genocide and what counts as such."[37] Thus, applied to the Cambodian context, following the combined insights from Sontag and Hartouni, these images, and the actual bones, skulls, and bloodstains they depict, may indeed haunt us; however, the "ghosts" that haunt us when we are exposed to them are not only those of Cambodia's Khmer Rouge era, but also those from the Holocaust, Rwandan Genocide, and other prominent atrocities, as representations of such events have come to represent *all* atrocity events. This grounding of understandings of atrocity in an expectation of visceral aesthetic representation is summed up nicely by Sontag, as a state of affairs within which "the very notion of atrocity," brings with it the "expectation of photographic evidence."[38]

[33] Susan Sontag, *Regarding the Pain of Others* (Farrar, Straus & Giroux, 2003).

[34] Valerie Hartouni, *Visualizing Atrocity: Arendt, Evil, and the Optics of Thoughtlessness* (New York University Press, 2012). For example, Hartouni argues that "Atrocity images from the [WWII] period, especially the now iconic images of the liberation of the concentration camps, contribute to and reinforce viscerally what these scholars assert as a matter of fact – that the Holocaust is at the limit of knowledge and feeling." Ibid., 13.

[35] Ibid., 10. Along these lines see also Rebecca Jinks, *Representing Genocide: The Holocaust as Paradigm?* (Bloomsbury, 2016).

[36] Hartouni, *Visualizing Atrocity*, 21.

[37] Ibid., 22.

[38] Sontag, *Regarding the Pain of Others*, 83.

Meanwhile, other physical reminders of the suffering and death of atrocity events such as the Khmer Rouge period in Cambodia, either present themselves much more ambiguously, or are marked by absences, rather than material reminders of past violence. For example, various sites of forced labor, such as Trapeang Thma dam (see Figure 5.2) in Northwestern Cambodia (present-day Banteay Meanchey province), where suffering was intense and death rates quite high during the Khmer Rouge regime, may be experienced as quiet, beautiful, and peaceful. Material remnants of the mass suffering and death that occurred at such locations may be marked solely by seemingly neutral objects or other reminders. For example, the only reminders of the violence that occurred at Trapeang Thma dam are mounds of earth and sluice gates, which were dug out and constructed painstakingly by hand and at the cost of thousands of lives. The violent pasts of this landscape only become

Figure 5.2 Trapeang Thma dam, December 2013[39]

[39] Photo reproduced courtesy of the Documentation Center of Cambodia. Photo appears in Dalin Lorn, "A Trip to Trapeang Thma Dam in Banteay Meanchey Province, December 20–22, 2013," *Documentation Center of Cambodia* (2013), http://d.dccam.org/Projects/Radio/pdf/A_Trip_to_Trapeang_Thmar_Dam_Banteay_Meanchey_province.pdf. The author was present during this trip. The dam itself is multiple kilometers long and approximately three meters wide, broad enough for a car to drive along it.

apparent when properly contextualized, in sharp contrast to the many paradigmatic atrocity sites in Cambodia, where visitors are confronted by visceral reminders of prior acts of violence and killing.

The difficulty of visualizing the Trapeang Thma dam as a site of atrocity reflects the difficulty of conceptualizing suffering brought about through deprivation of access to basic subsistence needs as an affirmative form of harm causation that is actively perpetrated. While other, more familiar atrocities closely resemble domestic forms of criminality, albeit on a larger scale, atrocities committed through socioeconomic or other attritive means, including those in Cambodia, are harder to conceptualize as "crimes." Such unfamiliar atrocities lack discrete, identifiable moments of direct harm causation that are intuitively identifiable as criminal in nature. Many other atrocities, including many of those committed by the Khmer Rouge regime itself, are conversely, highly visible and self-evidently "criminal" in nature.[40] Thus, harms in Cambodia brought about through the Khmer Rouge Party Center's policy edicts and the violence of its bureaucracy,[41] remain at the periphery of shared understandings of the atrocities of this dark period of Cambodian history.

Aesthetics and Selectivity at the ECCC

The subtle foregrounding of forms of harm causation conforming to the atrocity aesthetic in social understandings of the Khmer Rouge experience in Cambodia is also reflected in the operations of the ECCC to date, in terms of both its prioritization of cases, suspects, and charges, and assessments of relative culpability between potential suspects. While the issue of the scope of the crimes and suspects the Court would investigate and prosecute have been controversial since the ECCC's inception, aesthetic considerations have arguably played a significant role in social, political, and legal decisions as to what suspects and crimes have been deemed essential versus expendable. Thus, I do not mean to suggest that aesthetic familiarity has been the driving force in determining what issues the ECCC has and has not addressed. Clearly, among the most salient factors in this regard has been the Cambodian government's persistent, ultimately successful efforts to block certain cases from proceeding. Rather, I argue that the horrific

40 Indeed, this deep-seated tendency toward material objects, remains, or crime sites also appears to influence local practices of memorialization of Khmer Rouge atrocities. See Savina Sirik, *Everyday Experiences of Genocide Survivors in Landscapes of Violence in Cambodia* (Documentation Center of Cambodia, 2016).

41 Tyner and Rice, "To Live and Let Die."

spectacularity of crimes committed at locations such as *Tuol Sleng* prison and the *Choeung Ek* "killing fields" have helped these sites become emblematic of the Khmer Rouge period and inflated their relative prominence and perceived gravity in relation to crimes committed through more mundane means, such as harsh socioeconomic policies. In some instances, this has led to certain potential international crimes being ignored altogether, or even implicitly situated as being noncriminal in nature, by being framed as root causes or collateral consequences of more familiar forms of atrocity commission.

The ECCC was created, following protracted negotiations between the Cambodian government and UN, with a mandate to prosecute former Khmer Rouge "senior leaders" and other individuals considered "most responsible" for the crimes of the Khmer Rouge era.[42] The Court, which began operations in 2006, has focused almost exclusively on familiar, physically violent crimes. The Court's first trial, that of S-21 commandant Kaing Guek Eav alias "Duch," solely addressed crimes related to the operation of S-21 prison.[43] Meanwhile, Case 002, against Nuon Chea and Khieu Samphan, the two most senior former Khmer Rouge leaders still alive at the time (Nuon Chea died, post-trial judgment, in 2019), has been bifurcated into a series of trials.[44] The first Case 002 trial (Case 002/01) focused exclusively on allegations related to the events immediately following the Khmer Rouge's seizure of power in 1975, most notably the forced evacuation of Phnom Penh and summary executions of individuals associated with the previous regime.[45]

While the second Case 002 trial judgment (Case 002/02) addresses living and working conditions, it does so only in relation to a handful of specific locations, rather than addressing such issues from a nationwide perspective.[46] The ECCC has also announced that there will be no further

[42] UN-Cambodia, Agreement between the United Nations and the Royal Government of Cambodia Concerning the Prosecution under Cambodian Law of Crimes committed during the Period of Democratic Kampuchea, June 6, 2003, in force April 29, 2005, 2329 UNTS 117, Art. 1. For an explanation and analysis of this provision, see Sergey Vasiliev, "ECCC Appeals: Appraising the Supreme Court Chamber's Interventions" (2020) 18 *Journal of International Criminal Justice* 723–745: 738–743.

[43] *Case 001, Case No. 001/18-07-2007/ECCC/TC, Doc. No. E188, July 26, 2010*, ECCC.

[44] For an explanation and analysis of the decision to sever Case 002 into a series of trials, see Sarah Williams, "The Severance of Case 002 at the ECCC: A Radical Trial Management Technique or a Step Too Far?" (2015) 13 *Journal of International Criminal Justice* 815–843.

[45] See *Case 001, Case No. 001/18-07-2007/ECCC/TC, Doc. No. E188, July 26, 2010*, ECCC.

[46] See generally *Case 002/02, 002/19-09-2007/ECCC/TC, Doc. No. E465, November 16, 2018*, ECCC.

trials in Case 002.[47] Thus, over a decade into the operation of the Court, questions relating to the Khmer Rouge leaders' potential criminal culpability for subjecting the entire nation's civilian population under their control to radically substandard living conditions remain unclear and largely unaddressed. While the suffering attendant to such living conditions has been acknowledged by the ECCC in passing, such conditions tend to mostly be presented as a collateral consequence of the regime's penchant for violence, rather than related, yet independent modalities of harm causation and potential crime commission.

In addition to the ECCC's prioritization of charges to pursue, the Court has also prioritized the prosecution of suspects implicated most directly in aesthetically familiar forms of atrocity commission. A comparison between convicted accused Duch in Case 001 and suspect Im Chaem in Case 004 provides a concrete example of how aesthetic considerations may influence assessments of gravity and culpability within ICL. Case 001 solely concerned the operations of S-21 prison and its nearby execution site, *Choeung Ek*.[48] The case against Im Chaem, meanwhile, concerned the operations of various prisons, as well as living and working conditions at worksites and in cooperative villages in Northwestern Cambodia.[49] Even though the allegations against Im Chaem appear to have involved harms of at the very least, a comparable (if not significantly greater) seriousness to those addressed in Case 001, the ECCC's Co-Investigating Judges dismissed the case against her, finding that she did not qualify as a "most responsible" individual, despite the fact that Duch was previously found to be among those "most responsible."[50] The two judges only reached this agreement after cycling through numerous International Co-Investigating Judges whose efforts to investigate Cases 003 and 004 were stymied by the Cambodian government, National

[47] ECCC, "Trial Chamber Reduces Scope of Case 002," Press Release, February 17, 2017, www.eccc.gov.kh/en/articles/press-release-trial-chamber-reduces-scope-case-002.

[48] *Case 001, Case No. 001/18-07-2007/ECCC/TC, Doc. No. E188, July 26, 2010*, ECCC. For an overview of S-21 and its role during the Khmer Rouge period in Cambodia, see Chandler, *Voices from S-21*.

[49] See *Case 004/1, Case No. 004/1/07-09-2009-ECCC- OCIJ, Doc. No. D308/3, July 10, 2017*, ECCC. For an overview of the charges against Im Chaem, see Sara Ochs, "In Need of Prosecution: The Role of Personal Jurisdiction in the Khmer Rouge Tribunal" (2019) 55 *Stanford Journal of International Law* 117–154: 131–143.

[50] *Case 004/1, Case No. 004/1/07-09-2009-ECCC- OCIJ, Doc. No. D308/3, July 10, 2017*, ECCC. For a critique of this finding and its rule of law implications for contemporary Cambodia, see Randle C. DeFalco, "The Uncertain Relationship between International Criminal Law Accountability and the Rule of Law in Post-Atrocity States: Lessons from Cambodia" (2018) 42 *Fordham International Law Journal* 1–60; see also Ochs, "In Need of Prosecution."

Co-Investigating Judge You Bunleng, and much of the Cambodian staff working at the Court.[51]

As I and other commentators have argued elsewhere, the ECCC's finding that the case could be dismissed against Im Chaem because she does not qualify as either a "senior" former Khmer Rouge leader or person "most responsible" for the crimes committed by the regime, amounts to little more than a thin legal façade.[52] The Cambodian government has openly opposed the prosecution of Im Chaem (or, for that matter, any of the suspects investigated in Cases 003 and 004), the ECCC has operated in a perpetual fiscal crisis, and there seems to be little appetite to push for further trials on the part of the UN and key donor states.[53]

[51] The ECCC is a hybrid Court based on Cambodia's civil law domestic system, adopted through colonization from the French civil law system. Each position at the Court is staffed by both an international UN appointee, and a "national" (i.e., Cambodian) appointee. For more on the complex organization of the ECCC and associated rules, see generally John D. Ciorciari and Anne Heindel, *Hybrid Justice: The Extraordinary Chambers in the Courts of Cambodia* (University of Michigan Press, 2014). For discussions of efforts to stymie and block Cases 003 and 004 from proceeding, see, for example, see Randle C. DeFalco, "Cases 003 and 004 at the Khmer Rouge Tribunal: The Definition of 'Most Responsible' Individuals According to International Criminal Law" (2014) 8 *Genocide Studies and Prevention* 45–65; DeFalco, "Uncertain Relationship"; Ochs, "In Need of Prosecution." This observation is not intended as a disparagement of the ECCC's Cambodian judges and staff members, who would risk serious consequences, professionally and even personally, if they were seen as resisting the perceived desire of the ruling Cambodia People's Party to prevent Cases 003 and 004 from proceeding to trial. See Alexandra Kent, "Friction and Security at the Khmer Rouge Tribunal" (2013) 28 *SOJOURN: Journal of Social Issues in Southeast Asia* 299–328: 305 (observing that "National court staff [at the ECCC] lead lives within relatively inflexible networks from which exclusion is attended by considerable risk."). See also ibid., 305–319.

[52] DeFalco, "Uncertain Relationship"; Ochs, "In Need of Prosecution," 121 ("One of the Tribunal's most notable flaws and the latest potential embodiment of the Cambodian government's political interference is the ECCC's unworkable application of its personal jurisdiction."). Legal expert Anne Heindel, who has written extensively on the ECCC described the decision to dismiss the case against Im Chaem as "a farce and pretense of justice to spend so much money convicting only [Duch, Nuon Chea, and Khieu Samphan] – a foregone conclusion – while pretending that the process was independent and not limited by politics for a decade." Quoted in Julia Wallace, "The Bucolic Life of a Cambodian Grandmother Accused of Mass Killings" (February 24, 2017) *New York Times*, www.nytimes.com/2017/02/24/world/asia/cambodia-khmer-rouge-im-chaem.html.

[53] See generally DeFalco, "Cases 003 and 004." For an overview of the Cambodian government's interference with the work of the ECCC, especially in relation to Cases 003 and 004, see Open Society Justice Initiative, "Dead End at Cambodia's Khmer Rouge Tribunal: Next Steps for the UN," April 29, 2020, www.justiceinitiative.org/uploads/9e0af740-d7b6-4c70-ba0c-96df88328b2c/briefing-eccc-end0304-20200429.pdf. On the ECCC's perpetual funding crisis, see Rachel Killean, "Compromised Justice: The Road to the ECCC," in

Moreover, suggestions of investigatory irregularities that could come to light if the cases were to proceed to trial have made actors invested in the Court's success and maintaining the validity and perceived legitimacy of the judgments in Cases 001 and 002, leery of pushing too hard for trials.[54] Thus, the shuttering of the cases against Im Chaem and her co-suspects in Cases 003 and 004 appear to be the product of a confluence of power politics, fiscal considerations, and an overarching desire to protect the Court's perceived legitimacy.[55] While these familiar stumbling blocks for the anti-impunity movement undoubtedly were driving forces behind the decision to shutter Cases 003 and 004, aesthetic considerations also arguably played an important role as well, by helping to frame what suspects and charges were deemed essential, versus expendable. In the process, the ECCC has shaped its legacy in terms of what Rachel Killean refers to as its "selective recognition" of harms, victims, and perpetrators within the context of Khmer Rouge-era atrocities.[56]

What harms and potential suspects were deemed nonnegotiable by key actors supporting the Court was bound to be important from the outset of the negotiations to set up the ECCC. The Cambodian government, deeply invested in a simplistic "rescue narrative," whereby members of the dominant Cambodian People's Party are framed as saving the nation from the scourge of the Khmer Rouge,[57] has always preferred a narrow focus, whereby the atrocities of the Khmer Rouge era are laid at the doorstep of a handful of already well-known individuals – primarily Pol Pot and the original Cases 001 and 002 accused: Nuon Chea, Ieng Sary, Ieng Thirith, and Duch.[58] As we will see, the centrality of S-21 prison and other sites of horrific violence to shared understandings of atrocity in

Rachel Killean, ed., *Victims, Atrocity and International Criminal Justice: Lessons from Cambodia* (Taylor and Francis, 2018), 40–63: 52.

54 See Amanda Mortwedt Oh, "A House Divided against Itself Cannot Stand: The Case for Ending the Extraordinary Chambers in the Courts of Cambodia" (2012) 10 *University of St. Thomas Law Journal* 502–532.

55 Of course, the equation of the securing of convictions with "doing justice" and enhancing institutional legitimacy raise troubling questions about the goals of ICL and institutions such as the ECCC.

56 Killean, "Compromised Justice," 40; see also Rachel Killean, "Constructing Victimhood at the Khmer Rouge Tribunal: Visibility, Selectivity and Participation" (2018) 24 *International Review of Victimology* 273–296.

57 Kirsten Ainley, "Transitional Justice in Cambodia: The Coincidence of Power and Principle," in Renée Jeffery and Hun Joon Kim, eds., *Transitional Justice in the Asia-Pacific* (Cambridge University Press, 2013), 125–156: 149.

58 See generally, ibid; David Scheffer, *All the Missing Souls: A Personal History of the War Crimes Tribunals* (Princeton University Press, 2012), 341–406.

Cambodia have aided in the backgrounding of novel harms, such as those attendant to famine and living conditions, despite the fact that such harms were responsible for roughly half of the total Khmer Rouge era death toll and otherwise victimized far more Cambodians (indeed, virtually the entire civilian population) than the commission of more familiar, directly violent forms of atrocity commission.

S-21 Prison and Shared Understandings of the "Killing Fields" of Cambodia

Tuol Sleng "S-21" prison (see Figures 5.1, 5.3, 5.4) is in what were the outskirts of Phnom Penh during the Khmer Rouge regime. This prison was discovered by invading Vietnamese soldiers and several journalists accompanying them in January 1979 amid the chaos of the Khmer Rouge's hasty retreat.[59]

Figure 5.3 Entrance to S-21 prison, January 10, 1979[60]

[59] For a description of S-21 and its discovery, see, for example, Cathy J. Schlund-Vials, *War, Genocide, and Justice: Cambodian American Memory Work* (University of Minnesota Press, 2012), 27–30.

[60] Photo reproduced courtesy of the Documentation Center of Cambodia.

The prison operated as the nerve center of the Khmer Rouge state security apparatus. As an institution, the primary role of S-21 was the manufacture of evidence validating the paranoia and suspicion of the Khmer Rouge Party Center, while also shifting the blame away from the regime leadership for its disastrous policies.[61] Under the supervision of Duch, guards at S-21 systematically tortured detainees until they "confessed" to predetermined anti-revolutionary acts. This house of horrors has become symbolic of the broader atrocities of the Khmer Rouge regime itself, as it, along with the *Choeung Ek* "killing fields" where at least 12,272 S-21 prisoners were executed, continue to operate as major tourist attractions.[62]

The horrors of S-21 have been well documented, including photographically, a rarity for the Khmer Rouge era, and the visceral nature of such documentation has been integral to the institution's central place in the history of the Khmer Rouge period. Duch and his subordinates abandoned S-21 shortly before the Vietnamese military entered Phnom Penh. Those who discovered S-21 were drawn to the site by the smell of bloated, decaying corpses. The journalists in the party visually documented what they found, producing haunting photographic images and recording silent video footage of torture implements and the mutilated bodies of several final victims, some

Figure 5.4 Visitors at the entrance to *Tuol Sleng* prison[63]

[61] See generally, Chandler, *Voices from S-21*.

[62] The ECCC Trial Chamber found that "[d]ue to the inaccuracy of the existing record, the Chamber finds that it is not possible to quantify the precise number of the detainees who died and were executed. On the basis of the Revised S-21 Prisoner List, the Chamber quantifies this number to be no fewer than 12,272 detainees." *Case 001, Case No. 001/18-07-2007/ECCC/TC, Doc. No. E188, July 26, 2010*, ECCC, para. 340.

[63] Author's photo (2018).

of them still chained to the metal bed frames where they had been tortured to death.[64] They also found a significant portion of Duch's notes, which he had kept fastidiously, and had neglected to destroy before fleeing. These notes carefully document the workings of what historian David Chandler describes as a highly organized "total institution" of torture and execution.[65]

The large body of graphic evidence of the horrific violence perpetrated at S-21 that has been preserved and displayed at the prison site itself and elsewhere, operate as material testaments to the cruelty of the Khmer Rouge regime. Along with the photographs and video footage shot by the journalists who happened upon S-21 in 1979, there exists a large body of iconic photographs of S-21 prisoners.[66] This haunting gallery of victims exists because, unlike any other prison at the time in Cambodia, a photograph was taken of each prisoner when they entered S-21. Almost every photographed prisoner is wearing the same black clothes and has a number pinned to them. These photographs evoke iconic Holocaust imagery of concentration camp inmates wearing striped clothing and the numerical branding of such victims with tattoos. As Figure 5.5 shows, exhibits of these photographs still stand at S-21 and have also been, not uncontroversially, displayed abroad, including, for example, at the Royal Ontario Museum in 2013.[67]

Conditions at S-21 and specific forms of torture committed there are also graphically depicted in paintings in Figure 5.6 by artists Bou Meng and Vann Nath, two of the handful of victims imprisoned at S-21 who survived.[68]

[64] This footage may be viewed at the Documentation Center of Cambodia's public information room at 66 Preah Sihanouk Boulevard, Phnom Penh, Cambodia, upon request. Photographs taken by Vietnamese photographer Ho Van Tay upon discovering S-21 on January 10, 1979, including those of the decaying corpses of the prison's final victims who were tortured to death days before, are also archived at the Documentation Center. Documentation Center of Cambodia, "Photos for the Khmer Rouge Secret Prison S-21," January 10, 1979, http://d.dccam.org/Archives/Photographs/Photos_from_Khmer_Rouge_Secret_Prison_S-21/index.html.

[65] See Chandler, *Voices from S-21.*

[66] These photographs are displayed at the current *Tuol Sleng* Museum and may be viewed online. See Yale University Genocide Studies Program, "Gallery of S-21 Prisoner Photographs," 2013, https://gsp.yale.edu/cgp/gallery/cts.

[67] Royal Ontario Museum, "Observance and Memorial: Photographs from S-21, Cambodia," www.rom.on.ca/en/exhibitions-galleries/exhibitions/observance-and-memorial-photographs-from-s-21-cambodia.

[68] Both men survived largely because they were artists, as they were assigned tasks utilizing their artistic skills.

Figure 5.5 Visitors viewing images of S-21 victims[69]

Choeung Ek, an otherwise empty field several kilometers outside of Phnom Penh where S-21 prisoners were regularly executed en masse in front of pre-dug mass graves, is also a tourist destination. Visitors to the site, often referred to as Cambodia's "killing fields," are first confronted by a multistory Buddhist stupa, encased in glass and containing neatly arranged stacks of thousands of human skulls of victims killed at the site. Informational plaques point out a tree where infants were executed by having their heads smashed and note the clothing and bone fragments from execution victims one can identify still being slowly churned out of the earth.

As sites of highly visible, visceral atrocity violence, S-21 and *Choeung Ek* serve as integral points of reference underlying social understandings of the Khmer Rouge experience in Cambodia. These sites, however, are not necessarily representative of the Khmer Rouge experience for many

[69] Author's photo (2018).

Figure 5.6 Poster displaying reproductions of artwork created by survivors of S-21[70]

victims and survivors. Although at least 12,272 people were mistreated and executed at S-21 and *Choeung Ek*,[71] this prison was, despite the horrific crimes perpetrated at it, but one aspect of Cambodia's experiences of atrocity under the Khmer Rouge, as it was one of an estimated nationwide network of 196 prisons established during the Khmer Rouge.[72] Some of these prisons were smaller, while others far larger than S-21 in terms of both total numbers of prisoners and execution victims.[73] The two factors that made S-21 unique were that it received all foreign nationals and high-value prisoners who were to be tortured into confessing to predetermined anti-revolutionary acts, and everyone who entered the prison had already been sentenced to death.[74] Likewise, *Choeung Ek* was not the sole, or largest, mass execution site created during the reign of the Khmer Rouge in Cambodia. As of 2005, DC-

[70] Author's photo (2018).

[71] See *Case 001, Case No. 001/18-07-2007/ECCC/TC, Doc. No. E188, July 26, 2010*, ECCC, para. 340. The true number is likely well over 20,000 victims.

[72] The Documentation Center of Cambodia (DC-Cam) has identified and mapped these prisons. See Pong-Rasy Pheng, "DK Prison" (February 18, 2008) *Documentation Center of Cambodia*, http://d.dccam.org/Projects/Maps/List_of_DK_Prisons_Most_Updated.pdf.

[73] See ibid; Hinton, *Why Did They Kill?*.

[74] See generally Chandler, *Voices from S-21*. For an overview of the nationwide prison and execution system created by the Khmer Rouge regime, see Meng-Try Ea, *The Chain of Terror: The Khmer Rouge Southwest Zone Security System* (Documentation Center of Cambodia, 2005), 1–17.

Cam had identified over 19,000 mass grave sites believed to date to the Khmer Rouge era.[75] While some of these grave sites contain the remains of as few as four individuals who died during the Khmer Rouge era, DC-Cam has identified and mapped numerous mass graves containing at least as many victims, and in some cases, many more, than those killed at *Choeung Ek*.[76]

More importantly, as discussed previously, executions and direct physical violence at prisons and execution sites form only one aspect of the complex web of processes through which the Khmer Rouge brutalized and killed. Approximately half of the regime's victims died from causes other than executions and other forms of direct, physical violence.[77] While forced labor, overwork, and famine are quite often mentioned as aspects of the "Cambodian Genocide," the graphic imagery from S-21 and *Choeung Ek* – photos of mutilated bodies, piles of skulls, and the like – have become the dominant imagery used to represent the horrors of the Khmer Rouge era. Images of emaciated civilian workers and photos of forced manual labor are often depicted as well, but such imagery, and in turn, relevant processes of mass harm causation, tend to be treated as collateral consequences of Khmer Rouge regime's penchant for shocking violence, rather than as forms of atrocity violence in and of themselves.

Nonetheless, S-21, *Choeung Ek*, and the physical remnants and remains at these sites continue to serve as emblems – aesthetically and conceptually – of the experience of mass violence and atrocity in Cambodia under the Khmer Rouge.[78] Visceral reminders of horrific violence, quite often images of the skeletal remains of victims, most often from S-21 or *Choeung Ek*, predominate in "book covers, film posters, tourist brochures, maps and sign boards, as well as numerous original works of art," related to the Khmer Rouge period, "often coupled with the haunting term 'the killing fields', as well as 'mug shots' of [S-21] prisoners destined for execution."[79] The prison has also served as a focal point of legal proceedings at the ECCC. Indeed,

[75] Pong-Rasy Pheng, "Burial" (February 18, 2008) *Documentation Center of Cambodia*.

[76] Ibid.

[77] See, for example, Tabeau and They, "Khmer Rouge Victims in Cambodia"; Heuveline, "Boundaries of Genocide."

[78] Helen Jarvis, "Powerful Remains: The Continuing Presence of Victims of the Khmer Rouge Regime in Today's Cambodia" (2015) 1 *Human Remains and Violence: An Interdisciplinary Journal* 36–55: 48 ("The mug shots from S-21 and the skulls from the mass graves have become ubiquitous icons, consistently attracting attention and providing the strongest and most enduring images of the Khmer Rouge regime and forming the basis for foreigners' and new generations of Cambodians' understanding.").

[79] Ibid., 36.

from the outset, one point of agreement was that Duch, who had been located and identified as the former commander of S-21 by a journalist in 1999[80] and subsequently arrested and held in pretrial detention without being charged at a Cambodian military facility for the duration of the long negotiation process culminating in the 2006 creation of the ECCC, would be prosecuted.[81]

While Duch's crimes are more obvious, spectacular and notorious in nature, and, hence, aesthetically familiar than those Im Chaem has been accused of, the role played by Im Chaem, and other similarly situated Khmer Rouge officials, was arguably far more instrumental in broader atrocity processes occurring throughout the country than that of Duch. Moreover, the acts of such individuals may have caused far more suffering and death than Duch's clearly heinous actions, as his authority was wholly circumscribed to the operation of S-21. It was the actions of willing, even enthusiastic party functionaries such as Im Chaem that were integral to Cambodian civilians being oppressed, overworked, and killed by the thousands in sacrifice to the regime's goals. The acts of these individuals fueled the deadly mixture of overconfidence, paranoia, and willingness to sacrifice any number of lives in the service of the revolution, which combined to kill well over one million Cambodians and traumatize several million more.[82]

Everyday, banal acts of violence and oppression, however, often fail to manifest themselves in ways that conform to our expectations of drama, spectacle, and horror when it comes to atrocities. Actions such as packaging rice, depicted in Figure 5.7, appear mundane at first glance. While a reasonably informed observer may well understand that the photo depicts forced labor, the depiction of the neutral-seeming act of packaging rice fails to convey to the viewer the quite deadly realities of resource allocation under the Khmer Rouge. This rice, despite being the product of civilian labor, was viewed as being the exclusive property of the revolution, to be doled out, or exported, according solely to the needs of the revolution itself, as determined by the Party Center.[83] Even this and other rare photographs like Figure 5.8 depicting actual forced labor during the Khmer Rouge period fail to directly convey, in a visceral sense, the extreme suffering and mass

[80] Philippa Fogarty, "Duch: Symbol of Khmer Rouge Horror" *BBC News*, www.bbc.com/news/world-asia-pacific-10685769.

[81] See Scheffer, *All the Missing Souls*, 367, 404–405.

[82] David Chandler, a scholar of Cambodian history, has aptly referred to these dynamics as a "volatile mixture of hubris, paranoia, and wishful thinking." Chandler, *Voices from S-21*, 44.

[83] On this subject, see generally DeFalco, "Justice and Starvation in Cambodia," 27–46.

Figure 5.7 Laborers packaging rice during the Khmer Rouge period[84]

death resulting from the cumulative effect of overwork, denial of access to sufficient food, denial of medical care, and poor sanitation practices. These harms are more difficult to capture and convey the wrongfulness of, when compared to representations of other forms of violence, such as images of torture implements, brutalized bodies, and mounds of skulls.

The horrific straightforwardness and wealth of evidence in relation to crimes at S-21, along with the fact that Duch was already in the custody of the Cambodian government when the ECCC was created, combined to make Duch the sole accused in the Court's first ever case. Duch, who rather candidly admitted his role as commandant of S-21, but, for the most part, denied any legal responsibility for the crimes committed at the prison, was convicted of various international crimes by the ECCC Trial Chamber, and such convictions were ultimately upheld on appeal.[85] Duch was given a life sentence by the ECCC Supreme Court Chamber and eventually died in prison in 2020.

[84] Photo reproduced courtesy of the Documentation Center of Cambodia.

[85] See *Case 001, Case No. 001/18-07-2007/ECCC/TC, Doc. No. E188, July 26, 2010*, ECCC; *Case 001, Case No. 001/18-07-2007-ECCC/SC, Doc. No. F28, February 3, 2012*, ECCC.

Figure 5.8 Forced labor at a dam construction site in Cambodia, 1976[86]

Case 001, and the spectacular violence it focused on, can be contrasted with the experience in relation to former ECCC Case 004 suspect Im Chaem, who had the charges against her dismissed.[87] As noted previously, because the ECCC was designed to pursue only limited prosecutions, language seemingly restricting the Court's personal jurisdiction to former Khmer Rouge "senior leaders" and other individuals considered "most responsible" for relevant crimes, was inserted into the Court's foundational legal documents.[88] The term "most responsible" is widely believed to have

[86] Photo reproduced courtesy of the Documentation Center of Cambodia. The photograph depicts forced labor at the 1st January Dam worksite. Alleged crimes committed in relation to this specific worksite are addressed to a limited degree by the ECCC in Case 002/02. See *Case 002/02, 002/19-09-2007/ECCC/TC, Doc. No. E465, November 16, 2018*, ECCC, paras. 1430–1712.

[87] See *Case 004/01, Case No. 004/1/07-09-2009-ECCC-OCIJ, Doc. No. D308/3, July 10, 2017*, ECCC. The ECCC utilizes civil law criminal procedure, according to which the prosecution initiates a case by forwarding an introductory submission to investigative judges, who then take carriage of the investigation, ultimately issuing a closing order that determines if a suspect will be sent to trial and if so, for what specific charges. For more information on the law applicable to the ECCC, see generally Ciorciari and Heindel, *Hybrid Justice*.

[88] See UN-Cambodia, Agreement, Art. 1.

been inserted specifically with Duch in mind, as he was clearly not a senior leader within the Khmer Rouge hierarchy, solely holding authority within the confines of S-21.[89] Both the Trial and Supreme Court Chambers of the ECCC eventually held that Duch qualifies as "most responsible" despite defense arguments to the contrary.[90]

While this holding, that the ECCC Co-Prosecutors and Co-Investigating Judges did not err in considering Duch a "most responsible" individual, is in itself reasonable given Duch's major role in operating S-21, it appears incompatible with the later finding that Im Chaem (and other suspects in Cases 003 and 004 for that matter) is *not* a most responsible individual.[91] The ECCC has only released a redacted version of the Closing Order wherein the Co-Investigating Judges dismissed the charges against Im Chaem, precluding a detailed analysis of their reasoning.[92] However, an analysis of the unredacted portions of the decision and the ultimate choice to find Im Chaem not among those "most responsible" in light of generally available evidence is highly questionable in light of their previous determination that Duch *does qualify* as a most responsible individual. There exists compelling evidence that Im Chaem was both more senior, and at least as responsible as Duch for atrocity crimes, if not more so. Within the Khmer Rouge hierarchy Im Chaem held real, if localized, authority after being placed in charge of Preah Net Preah district in Banteay Meanchey province during a 1977 purge of the area.[93]

89 For summaries and analyses of the negotiations leading to the creation of the ECCC, see Ciorciari and Heindel, *Hybrid Justice*, 14–40; Steve Heder, "A Review of the Negotiations Leading to the Establishment of the Personal Jurisdiction of the Extraordinary Chambers in the Courts of Cambodia," August 1, 2011, www.cambodiatribunal.org/sites/default/files/A%20Review%20of%20the%20Negotiations%20Leading%20to%20the%20Establishment%20of%20the%20Personal%20Jurisdiction%20of%20the%20ECCC.pdf; Scheffer, *All the Missing Souls*, 341–406.

90 See *Case 001, Case No. 001/18-07-2007-ECCC/SC, Doc. No. F28, February 3, 2012*, ECCC, paras. 22, 62–79. It is worth noting that both Chambers viewed assessments of who qualifies as a senior leader or most responsible individual as falling within the discretion of the Co-Prosecutors and Co-Investigating Judges, bounded by a good-faith test. For a discussion of these findings, see Vasiliev, "ECCC Appeals," 738–743.

91 *Case 004/1, Case No. 004/1/07-09-2009-ECCC- OCIJ, Doc. No. D308/3, July 10, 2017*, ECCC.

92 Ibid.

93 See generally, DeFalco "Cases 003 and 004," 56. Im Chaem freely admits that she was placed in charge of Preah Net Preah and that she associated with Ta Mok, a notorious Khmer Rouge figure, often referred to as "the butcher" due to the brutality of his methods. See Wallace, "Bucolic Life." Ta Mok was captured by Cambodian government forces in 1999 and died in pretrial detention in 2006.

While Duch was intimately involved in the systematic execution of at least 12,272 victims (with the actual number most likely being over 20,000 victims), many of whom were tortured before being killed,[94] Im Chaem appears to have held effective decision-making authority over prisons, worksites, and cooperatives where far more people were executed or died from a combination of disease, famine, overwork, lack of sanitation, the denial of medical care, and outright execution.[95]

The main prison Im Chaem is alleged to have held authority over is that of Phnom Trayoung. Like most of the prisons established by the Khmer Rouge, Phnom Trayoung prison was located in a rural area in Cambodia's Northwest, rather than Cambodia's capital city, and has not been preserved. Like other prisons and mass grave sites throughout the country, no systematic forensic analysis has been conducted in relation to this prison. Hence, there is a lack of clear information regarding the total number of victims killed at Phnom Trayoung, with some estimates placing the number of victims killed at the prison and nearby execution sites during the Khmer Rouge period as high as 40,000.[96] However, this high estimate, as with lower ones, placing the death toll in the neighborhood of 4,000 victims, amounts to little more than an educated guess, based on interviews with survivors, rather than any detailed forensic analysis. Nonetheless, what is clear is that Phnom Trayoung was a significant prison during the Khmer Rouge period where thousands of victims were imprisoned in terrible conditions, subjected to forced labor, and otherwise mistreated, with a large number eventually being executed.[97]

The Co-Investigating Judges found that Im Chaem was placed in charge of Preah Net Preah district, where Phnom Trayoung prison was situated,

[94] See *Case 001, Case No. 001/18-07-2007/ECCC/TC, Doc. No. E188, July 26, 2010*, ECCC, para. 340.

[95] Preah Net Preah is located in Banteay Meanchey province in Northwestern Cambodia, where living conditions were especially harsh during the Khmer Rouge regime and death rates from famine and other associated causes were especially high. Im Chaem is alleged to have held authority over Phnom Trayoung prison, where anywhere from several thousand, to 40,000 victims were killed. See Wallace, "Bucolic Life." Journalist Douglas Gillison, meanwhile, estimates that the case against Im Chaem concerns approximately 50,000 total deaths, and many more victims who survived. Douglas Gillison, "Crime Scenes of the Khmer" (February 27, 2012) *The Investigative Fund*, www.typeinvestigations.org/investigation/2012/02/27/crime-scenes-khmer.

[96] Wallace, "Bucolic Life"; see also *Case 004/1, Case No. 004/1/07-09-2009-ECCC- OCIJ, Doc. No. D308/3, July 10, 2017*, ECCC, para. 127 (citing a Documentation Center of Cambodia report estimating 40,000 victims).

[97] See generally *Case 004/1, Case No. 004/1/07-09-2009-ECCC- OCIJ, Doc. No. D308/3, July 10, 2017*, ECCC, paras. 127–139; Wallace, "Bucolic Life."

sometime in 1977 and remained in power until January 1979, when Vietnamese troops ousted the Khmer Rouge from power.[98] Moreover, although Im Chaem has denied any knowledge of the workings of Phnom Trayoung,[99] other evidence, including statements by potential witnesses, suggests that Im Chaem did indeed have authority over the prison while in charge of Preah Net Preah district. For example, in a 2011 interview, Thip Samphatt, a survivor of the Khmer Rouge period now living in a village near Preah Net Preah district, told DC-Cam interviewers that in August 1978 he was arrested and sent to Phnom Trayoung prison.[100] After being arrested, Samphatt was shown a letter by the prison chief, a man named Souen. This letter had, according to Samphatt, been "stamped and signed by *Yeay* [grandmother] Im Chaem" alleging that Samphatt and two other men he had been arrested with had "betrayed the revolution and therefore had to give their blood to the revolution" (i.e. be executed).[101] Samphatt was only spared because Souen was fond of him and sent Samphatt to a labor camp instead of having him executed. Many others were not so fortunate, as Samphatt himself witnessed the mass execution of approximately ninety fellow prisoners while held at Phnom Trayoung prison.[102] This is but one example of evidence strongly suggesting Im Chaem's supervisory powers over Phnom Trayoung prison. Moreover, Im Chaem herself has admitted that she took power in the area in 1977, despite denying any authority over the prison.[103] Indeed, despite dismissing the charges against her, the Co-Investigating Judges held that there exists compelling evidence suggesting that Im Chaem exercised regional authority at the sector level in the Northwest Zone, and discretionary local power as secretary of Preah Net Preah district.[104] The Judges found that Im Cham had "overall control" of the district, and that this encompassed authority over worksites and prisons, including the discretionary power to order

98 *Case 004/1, Case No. 004/1/07-09-2009-ECCC- OCIJ, Doc. No. D308/3, July 10, 2017,* ECCC, paras. 156–160.

99 "Statement of IM Chaem (DC-Cam)," ECCC, Doc. No. E305/13.23.330, www.eccc.gov.kh/sites/default/files/documents/courtdoc/2015-06-11%2013%3A07/E305_13.23.330_EN.PDF, 34–35.

100 Interview summarized in, Dany Long, "Promoting Accountability Project Interviews with El Pheap, Youk Neam, Bin Nann, Rin Kheng and Thip Samphatt: Field Trip Note" (September 2011) *Documentation Center of Cambodia.*

101 Ibid.

102 Ibid.

103 See Wallace, "Bucolic Life."

104 *Case 004/1, Case No. 004/1/07-09-2009-ECCC- OCIJ, Doc. No. D308/3, July 10, 2017,* ECCC, paras. 154–172.

arrests.[105] In wielding this authority, Im Chaem had the power to manage work assignments and conditions in cooperatives on a day-to-day basis.

Thus, it appears that Im Chaem's supervisory authority over the workings of Phnom Trayoung prison from mid-1977 through to the end of the Khmer Rouge regime in early 1979 could be established. Thus, like Duch, Im Chaem appears to have been the local figure with authority over the day-to-day operations of a major Khmer Rouge-era prison. Unlike Duch, while she was likely not intimately involved in the day-to-day activities of Phnom Trayoung, Im Chaem's authority over the prison appears to have encompassed discretionary powers to arrest and release prisons, and order (or halt) executions. Duch was under standing orders to execute every prisoner that entered S-21. If he did not do so, he would have been executed himself, evidenced by the fact that S-21 personnel regularly became inmates themselves at S-21 destined for execution at *Choeung Ek*. Im Chaem, however, a trusted confidant of high-placed Khmer Rouge official Ta Mok, appears to have enjoyed a degree of latitude in interpreting and enforcing the regime's plans and orders.

Many factors likely contributed to the decision to declare Im Chaem as not among those "most responsible" for the crimes of the Khmer Rouge era, despite Duch's inclusion in this category. As Thierry Cruvellier points out, "in Duch, the perfect soldier of the revolution, the [Cambodian] government and the [ECCC both] found the perfect villain to make into a symbol of justice."[106] The Cambodian government has also long been vocally opposed to Cases 003 and 004 and actively worked to impede the cases from moving forward to trials.[107] The Court itself, meanwhile, has operated amid a continual funding crisis and steadily waning international interest since it began operations. Various anonymous former ECCC staffers and observers have stated that the Court's central objective has been to reach judgments in Cases 001 and 002 and to protect the perceived legitimacy of these cases at all costs.[108]

105 Ibid., para. 174.

106 Thierry Cruvellier, "The Khmer Rouge's Perfect Villain" (February 8, 2012) *New York Times*, www.nytimes.com/2012/02/09/opinion/the-khmer-rouges-perfect-villain.html.

107 See, for example, Kuch Naren, "Hun Sen Warns of Civil War if ECCC Goes Beyond 'Limit'" (February 27, 2015) *The Cambodia Daily*, https://english.cambodiadaily.com/news/hun-sen-warns-of-civil-war-if-eccc-goes-beyond-limit-78757; DeFalco, "Cases 003 and 004"; Oh, "House Divided against Itself Cannot Stand"; Open Society Justice Initiative, "Dead End at Cambodia's Khmer Rouge Tribunal."

108 These sentiments have been expressed to the author repeatedly in discussions with relevant actors, commentators, and experts. For a sampling of such statements made

In this complicated legal-political situation, one typical of ICL prosecutions, the atrocity aesthetic operates subtly in the background to facilitate the false notion that finding Duch among those most responsible does not essentially require the same finding in relation to Im Chaem and other similar suspects (and potential, uninvestigated suspects). Indeed, aesthetic considerations are arguably central to the notion that, despite wielding a greater degree of authority and autonomy, and being implicated in what could very well prove to be far more deaths than Duch if a trial were to be conducted, Im Chaem's relative culpability is somehow lesser than that of Duch. As the regime's specialist torturer and day-to-day supervisor of S-21, Duch makes an ideal and familiar ICL villain, one whose culpability is quite apparent in relation to relevant crimes. And yet, unlike Im Chaem, Duch had extremely little, if any, power to change the ultimate outcome for any of the victims sent to the prison.

Im Chaem, meanwhile, is alleged to have had the power to order the execution *or* release of prisoners at Phnom Trayoung, and to dictate living and working conditions in the villages within Preah Net Preah district and at worksites such as Trapeang Thma dam, at least to some degree. She exercised this authority in a manner that significantly worsened conditions in Preah Net Preah after her arrival, resulting in many thousands of additional deaths in the area. The decision to drop the case against her before trial means we may never know the full extent of Im Chaem's authority and culpability.

The ECCC's heavy focus on aesthetically familiar atrocity crimes thus far, and the widespread agreement that Duch should be prosecuted before the ECCC, while the prosecution of Im Chaem and the other suspects in Cases 003 and 004 are considered optional, may also be seen more broadly as partially attributable to the particularized aesthetics of atrocity in Cambodia and the heavy emphasis therein on crimes occurring at S-21 and *Choeung Ek*. The highly visible, oft-graphic nature of the horrific crimes committed at S-21 and *Choeung Ek* in the form of photographs and paintings, bones, skulls, and clothing fragments helped to make the prosecution of these crimes at the ECCC seem essential. The same can be said for crimes attendant to the forced evacuation of Phnom Penh in April 1975, an event that was extensively documented with photographic evidence, much of it depicting Khmer Rouge guerrillas, often young teenagers, brandishing

anonymously by relevant ECCC actors, see Oh, "House Divided against Itself Cannot Stand."

weapons and issuing orders to bewildered city occupants.[109] To a lesser extent, internal purges, mass executions, and the creation of a nationwide network of prisons have also been seen as essential subjects to address, even if symbolically.

Conversely, what was likely the largest source of suffering and death under the Khmer Rouge – the slow physical and mental deterioration of the civilian population as they were systematically overworked, underfed, prevented from feeding themselves, and denied basic medical care – has been treated as a largely peripheral, potentially noncriminal issue. A trial of Im Chaem could have provided a representative case for the Court to delve much more deeply into the potential criminality of these conditions of daily life enforced on Cambodians by the Khmer Rouge and the degree to which local and/or regional leaders were liable for any such criminality. These slower, less spectacular forms of everyday violence have, however, been viewed as too complicated, too large (or somewhat paradoxically, not serious enough), or too structural in nature, to be addressed head-on by the ECCC. Yet, such explanations do not fully explain this preoccupation with aesthetically familiar forms of atrocity in dominant narratives of the Khmer Rouge experience in Cambodia, including those emanating from the ECCC. As I argue elsewhere, causation and culpability for such unfamiliar atrocity processes, especially the enforcement of famine conditions, including in the Khmer Rouge context, may be as direct (if not moreso) than for acts of direct violence, while also involving far more victims.[110] In the Cambodian context, the Khmer Rouge Party Center dictated quite specific socioeconomic policies for the entire country, triggering and perpetuating mass death through starvation, overwork, and ill-treatment, yet in many cases deferred local security policies, including decisions of whom to arrest and execute, to local authorities.[111]

In light of these realities, simplicity, directness, and ease of prosecution arguably cannot fully explain the backgrounding of unfamiliar atrocity processes in Cambodia. Instead, such arguments about legality and feasibility provide cover for the insertion of power politics and unacknowledged biases, including those grounded in aesthetic assumptions

109 See, for example, Sydney Schanberg, "Millions Uprooted as Communists Impose a 'Peasant Revolution'" (May 9, 1975) *New York Times*, www.pulitzer.org/article/phnom-penh-becomes-echo-chamber-silent-streets.

110 See DeFalco, "Justice and Starvation in Cambodia"; DeFalco, "Accounting for Famine."

111 On this delegation of rights and obligations to arrest and execute individuals falling into categories of perceived "enemies" of the revolution according to the Party Center, see, for example, Ea, *Chain of Terror*, 16–17.

concerning what is and is not atrocity violence, into assessments of what counts as an international crime and which crimes are most important. Thus, we can see how shared understandings of atrocity, international crime, mass violence, and criminal harm causation – intertwined as they are at the ECCC and within ICL more generally – influence both notions of what forms genocide, crimes against humanity, and war crimes may take, and assessments of relative degrees of gravity, culpability, and symbolic importance in determining which prosecutions are deemed essential and, more importantly, which are not. In Cambodia, the predominance of familiar sites and forms of atrocity, especially S-21 prison and the *Choeung Ek* killing site, in the construction of socio-legal imaginaries of Cambodia's "killing fields" has facilitated the ECCC's narrow focus on spectacularly violent forms of criminality and in doing so, helped the Court to obfuscate the legal incompatibility of the prosecution of Duch as a "most responsible" individual, and the deeming of the suspects in Cases 003 and 004 including Im Chaem, as *not* among those "most responsible."

Visible and Invisible Atrocity Harms: Beyond Cambodia

The backgrounding of harms attendant to famine, living conditions, and other forms of slow, attritive, unspectacular harm causation under the Khmer Rouge in discourses of atrocity and international criminal justice described above is far from an outlier. History is replete with examples of situations wherein various overlapping forms of oppression and abuse combine to produce suffering and death on a massive scale. How atrocity, both as a broad social concept, and as a term used to refer to the general subject matter of ICL, is understood deeply shapes how such histories are framed, especially concerning the assignment of culpability and responsibility. Familiar, spectacularly horrific atrocity processes tend to be remembered and memorialized as unequivocally wrongful, manifestly criminal actions. In contrast, slower, less spectacular forms of atrocity commission are more likely to be overlooked, misremembered, or downgraded in terms of their seriousness, by being discussed in less condemnatory terms, or treated as root causes, regrettable mistakes ("mere" negligence), or collateral consequences of "real" atrocities involving the commission of genocide, crimes against humanity, and/or war crimes.

This selective recognition of mass harms extends to the labeling of potential atrocities even before Nuremberg and the advent of the body of law we now know as ICL. As discussed in Chapter 2, shared understandings of the notion of atrocity have been imbued with aesthetic aspects since well before ICL came into being. What has, and has not, been branded as an atrocity (and post-Nuremberg, an international crime) has largely reflected prevailing power arrangements, often facilitated by aesthetic biases. This downgrading and obfuscating effect shapes both the historical narratives of pre-Nuremberg forms of atrocity violence that would now violate ICL, as well as more recent forms of mass harm causation that arguably involved the commission of genocide, crimes against humanity, and/or war crimes.

Obscured and Downgraded Pre-Nuremberg Atrocities

One major example of the downplaying of certain forms of large-scale violence and harm causation in historical narratives is that of certain forms of colonial violence. Historical narratives concerning the oppression and mass killing of Indigenous populations in settler-colonial nations such as Canada, the United States, and Australia are prime examples of aesthetic factors aiding and abetting the denial and erasure of extremely large-scale atrocity processes sustained over time. The ability to downgrade the seriousness of the wrongdoing committed against Indigenous populations, as well as harms they suffered, through the refusal to use terms such as genocide or atrocity, or to unnecessarily qualify such terms (e.g. the use of the term "cultural" genocide to refer to a seemingly non-legal (i.e. not "real") form of genocide), facilitates ongoing processes of denial by settler-colonial nations and their citizens, of the degree to which their current globally privileged position is at least partially attributable to the obtainment of power and wealth through the commission of actions that currently constitute genocide, crimes against humanity, and/or war crimes. In many colonial circumstances, slower, attritive processes of persecuting, killing, and displacing Indigenous communities formed the interstitial material connecting more visible intermittent acts of direct violence against such communities, such as massacres and the like.[112] Once this

[112] See, for example, Patrick Wolfe, "Settler Colonialism and the Elimination of the Native" (2006) 8 *Journal of Genocide Research* 387–409; Damien Short, "Australia: A Continuing Genocide?" (2010) 12 *Journal of Genocide Research* 45–68; Andrew Woolford and Jeff Benvenuto, "Canada and Colonial Genocide" (2015) 17 *Journal of Genocide Research* 373–390; Kiera L. Ladner, "Political Genocide: Killing Nations through Legislation and Slow-Moving Poison," in Andrew Woolford, Jeff Benvenuto, and Alexander Laban Hinton, eds., *Colonial Genocide in Indigenous North America* (Duke University Press, 2014), 226–245; Andrew Basso, "Toward a Theory of Displacement Atrocities: The Cherokee Trail of Tears, the Herero Genocide, and the Pontic Greek Genocide" (2016) 10 *Genocide Studies and Prevention* 5–29; Kjell Anderson,

connective tissue is conceptually framed as (perhaps) regrettable, but noncriminal, it becomes more difficult to recognize the full scope and scale of the broader, multigenerational series of atrocities committed against Indigenous populations that arguably remain ongoing to this day.

A localized and discrete example of the role of unfamiliar atrocity processes deployed against Indigenous populations was the mass displacement of Native American Cherokee peoples from their traditional lands from 1838 to 1839, an event that has come to be known as the "Trail of Tears."[113] During this period, at least 16,000 members of the Cherokee nation were forcibly displaced to areas in Oklahoma. The transfer was conducted without sufficient resources, causing thousands of deaths along the way. Those who survived arrived in Oklahoma during the winter without enough provisions or food, causing thousands of additional deaths. In all, between 4,000 and 8,000 of the 16,000 Cherokees forcibly removed from their territory were killed.[114] The fact that this process of producing mass suffering and death lacked identifiable, discrete acts of physical killing continues to assist in the obfuscation of the culpability of those responsible for this quite direct form of atrocity violence. What was a planned, wholly intentional process of violent displacement causing mass death and suffering was able to be rebranded and misremembered as an unfortunate mistake in the otherwise noble task of American nation-building. The fact that this very nation-building project was one carried out almost wholly through the commission of acts currently qualifying as extremely serious international crimes (inter alia, aggression, the crimes against humanity of extermination, persecution, inhumane acts, enslavement, apartheid, etc., along with genocide) becomes obscured as the violence of the project is disaggregated and disconnected. The net result is a series of seemingly unconnected "mistakes" or, worse, legally neutral "wars" between settlers and Native American nations with war crimes committed on both sides. Of course, the focus remains on decontextualized, individual instances of horrific violence, committed by both sides. Lost is the fact that any such crimes were committed within the context of what in the post-Nuremberg era can be described as a series of criminally "aggressive" wars, waged by settler communities against various sovereign nations.

One can see the same downgrading effect operating in the misremembering of histories of slavery in the United States and elsewhere. While, of

"Colonialism and Cold Genocide: The Case of West Papua" (2015) 9 *Genocide Studies and Prevention* 9–25.

113 Basso, "Toward a Theory of Displacement Atrocities."

114 Ibid., 22.

course, enslavement is now itself a crime against humanity, the focus on slavery as America's "original sin" tends to highlight the brutality of many plantation owners and the high mortality rates of enslaved peoples. While, of course, these factors were horrific and more than worthy of condemnation as "atrocities," this narrow focus divides the institution of the transatlantic slave trade into a series of individual bad acts, now recognizable as international crimes. What is much too often ignored is the suffering of the many generations of people who lived all or most of their lives while enslaved, regardless of whether they were otherwise violently mistreated. The very status of being enslaved, regardless of attendant material conditions, itself involves a daily form of extreme violence that was both perpetrated and suffered by individuals. Every person significantly and knowingly involved in the institution of slavery, regardless of whether they participated in acts of direct interpersonal violence, would be liable for crimes against humanity at the very least under current formulations of ICL. Yet, seemingly passive (or even certain forms of active, such as the actual owning of slaves) participation in slavery, especially by otherwise revered American founders, is somehow excused as an unfortunate error in judgment, rather than quite active and knowing participation in what is now among the most serious crimes in existence.[115]

Another example of this dichotomy between familiar and unfamiliar processes of atrocity is the events that took place in present-day Namibia from 1904 to 1908, when German colonial forces put down an uprising by the Herero and Nama people in what was then German South West Africa.[116] This uprising followed years of colonial oppression and violence. Herero forces were decisively defeated by the German military at the 1904 Battle of Waterberg.[117] After defeating the Herero and Nama militarily, German forces displaced the remaining Herero and Nama populations into the Namib and Kalahari deserts. The victorious Germans then guarded the borders of the desert to prevent the Herero and Nama from escaping. The Germans also guarded water-wells and poisoned the wells they left unguarded.[118] The net result was that of "the 50,000 or 60,000" Herero and Nama "displaced to the desert, by 1908 only

[115] Along these lines, see Ibram X. Kendi, *Stamped from the Beginning: The Definitive History of Racist Ideas in America* (Nation Books, 2016).

[116] See Basso, "Toward a Theory of Displacement Atrocities"; Aaron Akinyemi, "The Forgotten Genocide" (January 31, 2010) *The Guardian*, www.theguardian.com/commentisfree/2010/jan/31/genocide-namibia.

[117] Akinyemi, "Forgotten Genocide."

[118] Basso, "Toward a Theory of Displacement Atrocities," 23.

3,000 escaped to neighbouring countries safely."[119] The massacre of Herero and Nama fighters by the German military largely conforms to the atrocity aesthetic, involving direct killing en masse. This battle, however, may have been a traditional military engagement, and hence, may not have involved the commission of what we now know as international crimes.[120] Herero and Nama victims of intentional acts of persecution and mass killing through displacement into the desert, however, are less well-remembered victims of atrocity violence, despite being the victims most accurately characterized as such under currently prevailing ICL. Andrew Basso presents the actions committed against the Cherokee during the Trail of Tears, and Herero and Nama people by German military, along with similar oppression and mass killing of Pontic Greeks in the Ottoman Empire from 1916 to 1918 and 1919 to 1923, as examples of what he refers to as "displacement" atrocities, which he frames as an oft-overlooked modality of genocide and atrocity violence.[121]

Another example of an oft-overlooked historical atrocity is the *Holodomor* ("extermination by hunger") famine in Soviet-controlled Ukraine. Under Stalin, as part of the Soviet Union's "Russification" plan, millions of people in the Ukraine died of hunger and famine-related diseases from 1932 to 1933, leading many to label this an atrocity.[122] Nonetheless, the *Holodomor* is among the least prominent atrocities of the twentieth century. Even the Holocaust, often viewed as the prototypical mass atrocity event, involved harms brought about through economic oppression, forced confinement, and other processes, along with massacres and mass executions.[123] In the case of the Holocaust, many of these processes of

[119] Ibid. An additional 17,000 Herero prisoners were sent to labor camps where approximately 6,000 of them died.

[120] Leaving aside the fact that the entire broader colonial project was one of waging a succession of aggressive wars.

[121] Basso, "Toward a Theory of Displacement Atrocities."

[122] See generally Robert Conquest, *The Harvest of Sorrow: Soviet Collectivization and the Terror-Famine*, reprint ed. (Oxford University Press, 1987); David Marcus, "Famine Crimes in International Law" (2003) 97 *American Journal of International Law* 245–281: 252–255; Rebekah Moore, "'A Crime against Humanity Arguably without Parallel in European History': Genocide and the 'Politics' of Victimhood in Western Narratives of the Ukrainian Holodomor" (2012) 58 *Australian Journal of Politics and History* 367–379.

[123] For example, Helen Fein observes that:

> [w]hile the historiography of genocide often focuses on the numbers directly killed-by execution, gassing, or burning in mass graves outside cities and villages and in extermination camps, many victims die from starvation and disease induced by elevated vulnerability following deportation (usually

atrocity, even ones which were socioeconomic in nature, were made highly visible by the practices of the Nazi regime, in the form of the construction of ghettos, and the marking of Jewish businesses and bodies themselves with the yellow star and, later, tattooed numbers in concentration camps. These few examples are but a handful of the wide array of atrocities that have been pushed to the periphery of historical narratives, or been treated as mistakes, or regrettable errors in judgment, rather than quite knowing and often purposive acts of mass killing and abuse that were actively perpetrated.

Post-Nuremberg Obscured Unspectacular Atrocities

While the historical examples referenced in the previous section all took place before World War II and, hence, before ICL as we now know it existed, and the Khmer Rouge period ended nearly four decades ago, many other, more recent examples exist of various potential international crimes being committed through unspectacular and/or unfamiliar means, yet downgraded or ignored in terms of their potential criminality. In the reporting and analysis of such events, and within rare actual ICL prosecutions, harm causation processes have tended to be simplified and conceptually flattened to conform to the atrocity aesthetic.

One prime example of such invisibility was the suffering of minority populations in Myanmar prior to the commencement of repeated spectacular acts of violence against them. Over multiple decades the government and military in Myanmar have engaged in highly organized efforts to marginalize and/or forcibly remove various ethnic minority groups, especially Rohingya Muslims, producing large-scale suffering and greatly increased mortality rates.[124] Only recently, since Rohingyas and members of other minority groups have been subjected to sustained violent attacks, have the plight of

> under harsh conditions) and enforced concentration in overcrowded camps and ghettoes. This is true even in genocide characterized by industrial killing in camps, like the Holocaust, where an estimated 700,000 Jews or 13.7 percent of the total number of those who perished, did so from hunger and diseases attributable to starvation and poor living conditions in ghettos.

Helen Fein, "Genocide by Attrition 1939–1993: The Warsaw Ghetto, Cambodia, and Sudan: Links between Human Rights, Health, and Mass Death" (1997) 2 *Health and Human Rights* 10–45: 12.

124 See, for example, Akm Ahsan Ullah, "Rohingya Refugees to Bangladesh: Historical Exclusions and Contemporary Marginalization" (2011) 9 *Journal of Immigrant and Refugee Studies* 139–161; Maung Zarni and Alice Cowley, "The Slow-Burning Genocide of Myanmar's Rohingya" (2014) 23 *Pacific Rim Law and Policy Journal* 683–752.

these groups become widely discussed using the rhetoric of ICL, even rising to the level that the ICC has opened an investigation into potential crimes crossing onto the territory of Bangladesh, and the International Court of Justice ordering provisional anti-genocide measures as it assesses Myanmar's potential state responsibility.[125] Also in Myanmar, as referenced earlier, several scholars argue that the government's actions of refusing to accept and properly distribute humanitarian aid following Cyclone Nargis in 2008 amounted to the commission of crimes against humanity.[126] Again, these acts were not predominantly framed through the lenses of atrocity and ICL, but were rather viewed as potential human rights violations, rather than potential individually culpable violations of ICL.

North Korea is another location where intermittent acts of violence have been interspersed with long-term social and economic oppression that has produced mass death and suffering through a host of relatively banal means.[127] Grace Kang argues that, as of 2007, high-level members of the North Korean dictatorship appeared to have committed the crime against humanity of extermination by enforcing famine conditions on the civilian population under their control.[128] Conducting a similar analysis, Rhoda

[125] See, for example, David Mathieson, "Perilous Plight: Burma's Rohingya Take to the Seas" (May 26, 2009) *Human Rights Watch*, www.hrw.org/report/2009/05/26/perilous-plight/burmas-rohingya-take-seas; Matthew Smith, "'All You Can Do Is Pray': Crimes against Humanity and Ethnic Cleansing of Rohingya Muslims in Burma's Arakan State" (April 22, 2013) *Human Rights Watch*, www.hrw.org/report/2013/04/22/all-you-can-do-pray/crimes-against-humanity-and-ethnic-cleansing-rohingya-muslims; UN Human Rights Council, "Situation of Human Rights of Rohingya Muslims and Other Minorities in Myanmar," UN Doc. A/HRC/32/18, June 20, 2016; Azeem Ibrahim, *The Rohingyas: Inside Myanmar's Hidden Genocide* (Hurst, 2016); *Application of the Convention on the Prevention and Punishment of the Crime of Genocide (The Gambia* v. *Myanmar), General List No. 178, Order, January 23, 2020*, ICJ.

[126] See, for example, Stuart Ford, "Is the Failure to Respond Appropriately to a Natural Disaster a Crime against Humanity? The Responsibility to Protect and Individual Criminal Responsibility in the Aftermath of Cyclone Nargis" (2010) 38 *Denver Journal of International Law and Policy* 227–276; Eamon Aloyo, "Improving Global Accountability: The ICC and Nonviolent Crimes against Humanity" (2013) 2 *Global Constitutionalism* 498–530; Josh Scheinert, "Refusal to Save Lives: A Perspective from International Criminal Law" (2013) 13 *International Criminal Law Review* 627–663.

[127] For an overview of this famine, see Rhoda E. Howard-Hassmann, *State Food Crimes* (Cambridge University Press, 2016), 61–71; see also Marzuki Darusman, "End of Mission Statement to Japan of the Special Rapporteur on the Situation of Human Rights in the Democratic People's Republic of Korea," January 22, 2016, www.ohchr.org/EN/NewsEvents/Pages/DisplayNews.aspx?NewsID=16981&LangID=E.

[128] Grace M. Kang, "A Case for the Prosecution of Kim Jong Il for Crimes against Humanity, Genocide, and War Crimes" (2006) 38 *Columbia Human Rights Law Review* 51–114: 85.

Howard-Hassmann concludes that members of the North Korean dictatorship appear to have "merely" committed the crime against humanity of other inhumane acts by enforcing famine conditions.[129] A 2014 report by a UN commission of inquiry, meanwhile, found that in North Korea, "international crimes appear to be intrinsic to the fabric of the state" and that Kim Jong-Un and other high-level North Korean officials appear to have committed crimes against humanity repeatedly against "starving civilian populations."[130] Again, the dominant framing of atrocities in North Korea focuses on familiar, spectacular processes of commission, such as the execution of dissidents and conditions in prison camps where dissidents and perceived enemies of the state are sent for reeducation.

In the context of Zimbabwe, meanwhile, Howard-Hassmann argues that systemic oppression by the Mugabe government from 2000 to 2009 involved the commission of crimes against humanity.[131] Howard-Hassmann argues that, while Mugabe's land redistribution policies were ostensibly aimed at combatting the legacies of colonialism, in practice, land and resources were redistributed along partisan lines, primarily to Mugabe's political allies.[132] The result of these and other policies, enforced by violence, was mass suffering and death amid a precipitous rise in the HIV/AIDS infection rate and famine conditions.[133] Howard-Hassmann and Eamon Aloyo both argue that this situation involved the commission of the crime against humanity of other inhumane acts by Mugabe and other high-level government figures.[134] While Mugabe's complicated legacy involves numerous allegations of malfeasance and human rights violations related to living conditions nationally, acts of violence and massacres

[129] Rhoda E. Howard-Hassmann, "State-Induced Famine and Penal Starvation in North Korea" (2012) 7 *Genocide Studies and Prevention* 147–165: 158.

[130] UN Commission of Inquiry on Human Rights in the Democratic People's Republic of Korea, "Report of the Detailed Findings of the Commission of Inquiry on Human Rights in the Democratic People's Republic of Korea," UN Doc. A/HRC/25/CRP.1, February 7, 2014, paras. 1162, 1164.

[131] Rhoda E. Howard-Hassmann, "Mugabe's Zimbabwe, 2000–2009: Massive Human Rights Violations and the Failure to Protect" (2010) 32 *Human Rights Quarterly* 898–920. To a large degree this sentiment is shared by Eamon Aloyo, see Aloyo, "Improving Global Accountability," 505–506. For another perspective, see John D. Kraemer, Dhrubajyoti Bhattacharya, and Lawrence O. Gostin, "Blocking Humanitarian Assistance: A Crime against Humanity?" (2008) 372 *The Lancet* 1203–1205.

[132] Howard-Hassmann, "Mugabe's Zimbabwe," 899–906.

[133] For an overview of these conditions and their causation, see Howard-Hassmann, *State Food Crimes*, 78–91.

[134] Howard-Hassmann, "Mugabe's Zimbabwe," 906–909; Aloyo, "Improving Global Accountability," 505–506.

against perceived political enemies such as occurred in Matabeleland in the 1980s, are typically presented as the central "atrocities" Mugabe bore responsibility for.[135] While perhaps the net harms associated with the massacres, when up to 20,000 people were killed by government and government-affiliated forces,[136] were greater than those related to Mugabe's disastrous socioeconomic policies, again we see the former being dominantly framed as atrocities, and the latter largely being viewed primarily as seemingly less serious, and less direct human rights violations.

Also in relation to corruption and mismanagement, in Nigeria, from 1998 to 2007, Peter Odili, then-Governor of Nigeria's Rivers State, allegedly engaged in corruption and election-fixing, misappropriating huge sums of money in bribes, kickbacks and misappropriation of public funds, resulting in poverty, increased morality rates, and widespread suffering.[137] Ben Bloom argues that available evidence indicates that, during this period, Odili and others committed the crime against humanity of other inhumane acts by engaging in these and other acts of grand corruption that directly caused widespread inhumane conditions.[138] Once again, these types of harms are often cast as noncriminal human rights, rule of law, and/or development concerns, rather than potential products of criminal actions. In this regard, when it comes to "atrocity crimes" in Nigeria, the primary focus, including in the ICC's longstanding preliminary examination in the country, continues to be the shocking acts of violence committed by the Boko Haram militant group.[139] Again, this is not intended as an assertion

[135] See, for example, Stuart Doran, "New Documents Claim to Prove Mugabe Ordered Gukurahundi Killings" (May 19, 2015) *The Guardian*, www.theguardian.com/world/2015/may/19/mugabe-zimbabwe-gukurahundi-massacre-matabeleland; Stephen McLoughlin and Maartje Weerdesteijn, "Eliminating Rivals, Managing Rivalries: A Comparison of Robert Mugabe and Kenneth Kaunda" (2016) 9 *Genocide Studies and Prevention* 116–136: 120 ("mass atrocities were committed there between 1980 and 1988, through the torture and massacring of members of the Ndebele minority group").

[136] See, for example, Doran, "New Documents"; McLoughlin and Weerdesteijn, "Eliminating Rivals"; Shari Eppel, "'Bones in the Forest' in Matabeleland, Zimbabwe: Exhumations as a Tool for Transformation" (2014) 8 *International Journal of Transitional Justice* 404–425: 407–408.

[137] See Ben Bloom, "Criminalizing Kleptocracy? The ICC as a Viable Tool in the Fight against Grand Corruption" (2014) 29 *American University International Law Review* 627–671: 640–648, 659–665.

[138] Ibid., 659–667.

[139] See ICC Office of the Prosecutor, "Situation in Nigeria: Article 5 Report," August 5, 2013, www.icc-cpi.int/iccdocs/PIDS/docs/SAS%20-%20NGA%20-%20Public%20version%20Article%205%20Report%20-%2005%20August%202013.PDF; ICC Office of the Prosecutor, "Report on Preliminary Examination Activities: 2018," December 5, 2018, www.icc-cpi.int/itemsDocuments/181205-rep-otp-PE-ENG.pdf, 55–62.

that potential international crimes such as those identified by Bloom are necessarily more serious or worthy of attention and prosecution than those committed by Boko Haram and certain Nigerian military units. Rather, the point is merely that the aesthetically familiar atrocities are viewed as international crimes, while the harm-causing behaviors described by Bloom tend to be viewed as inherently noncriminal in nature.

In Somalia, famine, exacerbated by actions restricting food-aid deliveries and other living condition issues resulted in approximately 260,000 deaths from 2010 to 2012.[140] The Al-Shabaab militant group has been accused of committing crimes against humanity through their role in producing and thereafter enforcing famine conditions in areas under their control by killing foreign-aid workers, confiscating food aid, and preventing civilians from fleeing famine-plagued areas.[141] More recently, journalist Alex Perry has accused the Somali government and their US military advisors of the war crime of intentionally using starvation of civilians as a method of warfare by impeding humanitarian food relief efforts destined for areas controlled by the Al-Shabaab militant group in 2011.[142] As with the situation in Nigeria, the horrific violence committed by Al-Shabaab has been widely framed as involving the commission of international crimes, while the same group's arguably direct and knowing causal role in not only creating famine conditions, but thereafter actively enforcing such conditions by preventing civilians from fleeing areas they controlled and refusing to allow food aid to be delivered on an as-needed basis has been viewed as condemnable, and violative of human rights and humanitarian law, but not necessarily rising to the level of an international crime. Once again, in this context, unfamiliar

[140] See BBC News, "Somalia Famine 'Killed 260,000 People'," May 2, 2013, www.bbc.com/news/world-africa-22380352; Gerald Martone and Maureen Shawn Kennedy, "Scenes from Somalia" (2012) 112 *American Journal of Nursing* 38–39.

[141] See, for example, Andrew Jillions, "The (in)Justice of Famine: Is al-Shabaab Guilty of a Crime against Humanity?" (August 15, 2011) *Justice in Conflict*, http://justiceinconflict.org/2011/08/15/the-injustice-of-famine-is-al-shabaab-guilty-of-a-crime-against-humanity; Jens David Ohlin, "Somalia Famine: 'Crime against Humanity'?," August 12, 2011, www.cnn.com/2011/OPINION/08/12/ohlin.somalia.crimes/index.html; Matt Bryden, "Somalia's Famine Is Not Just a Catastrophe, It's a Crime" (October 2011) *Enough Project*, https://enoughproject.org/files/Bryden_SomaliaFamine%20Brief_final_0.pdf; Human Rights Watch, "Somalia: End War Crimes to Help Tackle Famine," August 14, 2011, www.hrw.org/news/2011/08/14/somalia-end-war-crimes-help-tackle-famine.

[142] CBC, "Somalia 2011 Famine was a U.S.-Created War Crime, says Journalist Alex Perry," January 18, 2016, www.cbc.ca/radio/thecurrent/the-current-for-january-18–2016–1.3408273/somalia-2011-famine-was-a-u-s-created-war-crime-says-journalist-alex-perry-1.3408302.

harms have been largely cast as collateral consequences of armed conflict and the commission of more aesthetically familiar forms of atrocity violence.

In Sudan, as referenced previously, socioeconomic oppression and the imposition of terrible living conditions marked by famine and the spread of disease have been central aspects of the alleged genocidal campaign waged by former Sudanese President Omar al-Bashir and his allies in both Darfur and the Nuba Mountains.[143] Within the context of the Darfur region, such processes of harm causation have been framed as international crimes by the ICC Office of the Prosecutor (OTP). The prosecution alleges that between September 2003 and January 2005 in the Darfur region of Sudan certain ethnic groups were systematically attacked as part of a genocidal plan carried out by al-Bashir and others. More specifically, the prosecution further alleges that an integral part of this genocidal plan was the use of "[m]ethods of destruction other than direct killings" against targeted groups, including "destruction of their means of survival in their homeland; systematic displacement from their homes into inhospitable terrain where some died as a result of thirst, starvation and disease; usurpation of the land and denial and hindering of medical and other humanitarian assistance needed to sustain life in [internally displaced persons] camps."[144] These indirect methods of killing were more deadly than more familiar acts of direct violence, as the OTP estimates that 83,000 out of 118,142 total civilian victims (roughly 70 percent) died from indirect causes, including injury, starvation, lack of water, or poor living conditions in refugee camps.[145] Samuel Totten argues that similar tactics were used by the Sudanese

[143] See, for example, Fein, "Genocide by Attrition"; Alex de Waal, "Reflections on the Difficulties of Defining Darfur's Crisis as Genocide" (2007) 20 *Harvard Human Rights Journal* 25–33; Jenny Edkins, "The Criminalization of Mass Starvations: From Natural Disaster to Crime against Humanity," in Stephen Devereux, ed., *The New Famines: Why Famines Persist in an Era of Globalization* (Routledge, 2007), 50–65; *Situation in Darfur, Sudan, Annex A: Public Redacted Version of Prosecution's Application under Article 58 filed on 14 July 2008, 14 July 2008, ICC-02/05–157-AnxA*, ICC; Samuel Totten, *Genocide by Attrition: The Nuba Mountains of Sudan* (Transaction, 2012).

[144] *Situation in Darfur, Sudan, Annex A: Public Redacted Version of Prosecution's Application under Article 58 filed on 14 July 2008, 14 July 2008, ICC-02/05–157-AnxA*, ICC, para. 172.

[145] Ibid., para. 111. While the figures provided by the ICC Office of the Prosecutor remain allegations and not necessarily proven facts, they are illustrative of the basic fact that many human beings died in Darfur during the relevant period and that a large proportion of such deaths were not immediately caused by the application of direct physical violence against victims.

government as part of a genocidal campaign waged against minority groups in Sudan's Nuba Mountains in the late 1980s and early 1990s.[146]

Thus far, al-Bashir and his alleged co-perpetrators have managed to avoid arrest through deft political maneuvering, although after being ousted from power, there is increasing talk of al-Bashir being prosecuted at the ICC or elsewhere.[147] While still in power, al-Bashir and the Sudanese government were, at times, able to decrease international scrutiny of their efforts to gain control over Darfur by reducing their reliance on direct, armed attacks in the area, by both relying on proxy paramilitary groups and tactics of displacing victims into harsh desert areas.

In December 2016, then UN Secretary General Ban Ki-moon reported to the UN Security Council that "no major armed conflict [occurred] in Darfur" during the preceding months, linking this development to an overall marginal improvement in living conditions.[148] The Secretary General, however, also observed that there still exists a pressing need to address the "root causes" of violence in Darfur.[149] Meanwhile, only later in his report, under the heading of the "humanitarian situation" in Darfur, does the Secretary General mention that 97,000 new verified internally displaced persons were documented over the same time period, and that "[h]umanitarian actors also continued to face bureaucratic impediments in the form of delays and rejections of intra-state travel permits, in particular for areas in which internally displaced persons affected by [recent armed conflict] reportedly settled."[150] Thus, while al-Bashir and his co-indictees continued to cause mass suffering and death in Darfur, their decreasing reliance on the direct commission of acts of violence helped them to, over time, conceptually move atrocity and genocide in Darfur toward becoming a past event, rather than an ongoing process. Given the increased likelihood that al-Bashir and/or certain of his key allies and co-indictees may actually be prosecuted by the ICC in the relatively near future, it will be interesting to see what harms the prosecution and the Court itself prioritize in any trials that take place.

146 Totten, *Genocide by Attrition.*

147 Aljazeera News, "Sudan Protest Group Has 'No Objection' to Handing Bashir to ICC" (November 4, 2019) *Aljazeera*, www.aljazeera.com/news/2019/11/sudan-protest-group-objection-handing-bashir-icc-191104064608367.html.

148 UN Security Council, "Report of the Secretary-General on the African Union-United Nations Hybrid Operation in Darfur," UN Doc. S/2016/1109, December 23, 2016, para. 2.

149 Ibid.

150 Ibid., paras. 24–25, 29.

The above-mentioned examples are not intended to represent an exhaustive list. Nor should this illustrative list be interpreted as asserting that each one of these examples definitively did (or did not) involve the commission of international crimes according to current ICL. Rather, these examples have been provided to illustrate that there are a wide variety of mass harms that reasonable scholarship argues should be viewed through the rubrics of atrocity and ICL. Additional potential examples abound, ranging from many other forms of historical and ongoing colonial violence and dispossession, to actions closer to home in the Global North, such as Donald Trump's potential liability for intentionally misleading the US public concerning the seriousness of the coronavirus pandemic, while affirmatively blocking the distribution of masks by the postal service.[151] These and many other situations, when carefully scrutinized, might produce surprising results in terms of ICL's potential applicability. Of course, given ICL's still-evolving, oft-doctrinally unclear nature, certain of these harm causation processes may be included or excluded from ICL more definitively in the future. This raises important questions concerning how we are to interpret and apply ICL and, in doing so, whether we are to focus our energies on the largest harms (in terms of the number of victims affected and the severity of their suffering), or the ones that we (in the Global North) find to be the ugliest and most upsetting.

The production of mass suffering and death through this wide variety of unspectacular, unfamiliar means is also not likely to cease any time soon. In 2016, Secretary-General Ban Ki-moon accused the Syrian government, rebel forces, and Islamic State militants, all of committing the war crime of using

[151] Josh Dawsey, Felicia Sonmez, and Paul Kane, "Trump Acknowledges He Intentionally Downplayed Deadly Coronavirus, Says Effort was to Reduce Panic" (September 9, 2020) *Washington Post*, www.washingtonpost.com/politics/trump-reaction-woodward-interview-coronavirus/2020/09/09/fc21e67e-f2ca-11ea-b796-2dd09962649c_story.html; Tony Romm, Jacob Bogage, and Lena H. Sun, "Newly Revealed USPS Documents Show an Agency Struggling to Manage Trump, Amazon and the Pandemic" (September 18, 2020) *Washington Post*, www.washingtonpost.com/us-policy/2020/09/17/usps-trump-coronavirus-amazon-foia. For an analysis of the Trump administration's failures to take action to contain the coronavirus within the context of international law related to genocide, concluding that *mens rea* issues would prevent any attempts at prosecution, see John Heieck, "Trump's Coronavirus Response: Genocide By Default?" (May 15, 2020) *Opinio Juris*, http://opiniojuris.org/2020/05/15/trumps-coronavirus-response-genocide-by-default. For a discussion of how a systematic failure to deal with a public health emergency, such as the COVID-19 pandemic, could rise to the level of the crime against humanity of other inhumane acts, see David J. Scheffer, "Is It a Crime to Mishandle a Public Health Response?" (April 22, 2020) *Council on Foreign Relations*, www.cfr.org/article/it-crime-mishandle-public-health-response.

starvation as a weapon within the context of ongoing food crises in Madaya and other parts of Syria.[152] In early 2017, meanwhile, the UN Food and Agriculture Organization officially declared that areas of South Sudan are experiencing "man-made" famine conditions.[153] Climate change and the coronavirus pandemic have also both created newfound humanitarian challenges and the potential for escalating resource conflicts. If ICL is to operate to prevent powerful actors from abusing victims en mass, it is imperative that it not be applied in a manner that privileges the most powerful, by ignoring their contributions to mass suffering and death when caused through means we do not tend to associate with crime and criminality.

Overall, these situations discussed in this chapter, from Cambodia to South Sudan and beyond, demonstrate the complex, causally multifaceted nature of atrocities. Many of these situations have been socially conceptualized as atrocities, and some of them, such as Khmer Rouge-era Cambodia, North Korea, and events in the Darfur region of Sudan, have, to some extent, even been legally characterized as international crimes. Yet, even when broader situations are placed within the rubrics of atrocity and ICL, there exists a tendency to connect unfamiliar atrocity processes with more familiar ones in order to conceptually validate them. Accordingly, starvation and the spread of disease in Cambodia are linked to the Khmer Rouge's tendencies toward extreme violence and the presence of overseers at work sites. In Darfur, the seemingly calculated expulsion of members of certain ethnic groups into the desert is linked to violent attacks on villages, the expropriation of livestock, and poisoning of drinking wells. In North Korea, state policies enforcing famine conditions on the civilian population are viewed in tandem with the regime's practice of executing perceived traitors and preventing emigration through violence. When these links are absent (or themselves, largely invisible), such as was the case for decades in Myanmar, or the Nuba Mountains, where victims were oppressed and killed primarily through attritive means, until such situations boil over into the production of horrific spectacles of violence, they tend to occupy

[152] UN Web Services Section, "Full Transcript of Secretary-General's Press Encounter Following Briefing to the General Assembly on His Priorities for 2016," January 14, 2016, www.un.org/sg/offthecuff/index.asp?nid=4316.

[153] Food and Agriculture Organization of the UN, "Famine Hits Parts of South Sudan," February 20, 2017, www.fao.org/news/story/en/item/471251/icode. For an analysis of this famine and its causes, see Siobhán O'Grady, "South Sudan's Man-Made Famine" (February 27, 2017) *Foreign Policy*, http://foreignpolicy.com/2017/02/27/south-sudans-man-made-famine.

a position at the periphery of ICL, or to be primarily viewed as noncriminal "root causes," or collateral consequences of conflict and atrocity.[154] The upshot is that these aesthetic biases and politics incentivize the commission of atrocities through means that are slow and unspectacular in nature, as such means tend to be both cost-effective and help those responsible to avoid being branded authors of atrocities, whether or not they face any realistic possibility of being prosecuted.[155]

Conclusion

Atrocities are complex social phenomena that may take many different forms and involve many different causal mechanisms. Such processes can, and regularly do, involve methods of harm causation, such as the creation or enforcement of famine conditions, corrupt acts causing enormous damage to groups of people, or interference with humanitarian aid, that are slow, attritive, and not readily apparent as involving the potential commission of genocide, crimes against humanity, and/or war crimes, despite at times, involving acts properly characterizable as such upon more careful consideration. These situations fail to fit neatly within dominant understandings of atrocity as the imagined general subject matter of ICL. This awkwardness of fit is evidenced by a common tendency to either view harms brought about through slow, aesthetically unfamiliar and unspectacular means, as being situated outside the reach of ICL, or to connect such harms to more familiar forms of atrocity violence, by framing them as (often noncriminal) root causes or collateral consequences of more familiar crimes. This backgrounding process cannot be attributed wholly to ICL's general selectivity and jurisdictional gaps, or the triaging of case selection according

[154] See, for example, Fabricio Guariglia, "COVID-19 Symposium: COVID-19 and International Criminal Law" (April 4, 2020) *Opinio Juris*, http://opiniojuris.org/2020/04/04/covid-19-symposium-covid-19-and-international-criminal-law (observing that "[e]pidemics and international crimes, more often than not, feed from the same toxic elements: systemic poverty, lack of education, of basic services, of state protection, of respect for individual rights, including the most basic socio-economic human rights").

[155] For example, Basso provides four reasons why the commission of atrocity through displacement may be selected as the "optimal mode of destruction" by actors with genocidal intentions, including: "cost-effectiveness . . ., the ability to lessen psychological strains on individual perpetrators, the pervasive social disruption among victim groups, and veiling the public." Basso, "Toward a Theory of Displacement Atrocities," 11. For a similar argument see generally Sheri P. Rosenberg and Everita Silina, "Genocide by Attrition: Silent and Efficient," in Joyce Apsel and Ernesto Verdeja, eds., *Genocide Matters: Ongoing Issues and Emerging Perspectives* (Routledge, 2013), 106–126.

to assessments of gravity. Indeed, as evidenced by the ECCC experience in Cambodia, especially visible atrocity crimes, ones involving the production of horrific, viscerally shocking evidence, may be prioritized over less aesthetically familiar crimes, despite involving fewer victims. The remaining chapters in this book explore some of the ramifications of this aesthetic bias within ICL.

6

The Costs of Invisibility

An Incomplete List

Introduction

Thus far, this book has argued that aesthetic considerations have shaped shared understandings of what constitutes genocide, crimes against humanity, and war crimes, resulting in the backgrounding of atrocities committed through aesthetically unfamiliar means, especially those that are slow and unspectacular in nature. One may very well accept this assertion yet view it as relatively inconsequential in terms of the role such aesthetic biases play in contributing to the shortcomings of ICL, or in their broader material effects. Given the rarity of ICL prosecutions, pointing out an additional set of instances where the perpetration of atrocity crimes goes unpunished may be dismissed as merely adding to the veritable mountain of such crimes that are never formally investigated and prosecuted.

This chapter argues that the effects of the social and legal invisibility of aesthetically unfamiliar atrocity processes goes far beyond merely adding to the so-called impunity gap that afflicts international criminal justice. It does so by demonstrating how the aesthetic biases toward horrifically spectacular crimes not only undermines the goals and values ascribed to ICL itself, but also contributes to a variety of negative outcomes that go far beyond missed prosecutorial opportunities. Indeed, I view the failure to prosecute international crimes committed through means failing to conform to the atrocity aesthetic as one of the *least* significant outcomes of the aesthetic biases of international criminal justice. As I touch upon in the conclusion, ICL's myopic focus on horrifically spectacular crimes raises a host of troubling questions concerning what harms are prioritized and whose interests are served by international criminal justice. This chapter considers some of these implications, specifically those relating to theories of punishment, and ICL's role in shaping historical memory, transitional justice, peacebuilding, human rights, and global justice more broadly.

Aesthetic Biases and the Aims of International Criminal Law

ICL is not underlaid by any clearly elucidated set of normative commitments, but, like most legal regimes, rests on a complex patchwork of goals and justifications ascribed to it. The variation of these goals and justifications is especially broad in ICL, including aims related to "retribution, deterrence, rehabilitation, truth-telling, incapacitation, expressivism, and reconciliation."[1] One consequence of this loading up of expectations is that the stated purposes of ICL vacillate, swinging between retributive, consequentialist, and other proposed criminal law (and other) justifications.[2] As the following analysis demonstrates, regardless of one's viewpoint concerning what the proper purposes of ICL are, such purposes are undermined the myopic focus on crimes conforming closely to the atrocity aesthetic.

Retributivism

Retributivist theories of criminal punishment are premised on the notion that there exists a moral imperative to punish those who commit crimes, irrespective of whether such punishment serves any broader social purpose.[3] The extreme harms associated with the commission of

[1] Mark A. Drumbl, "Accountability for System Criminality" (2010) 8 *Santa Clara Journal of International Law* 373–382: 380. For an overview of proposed justifications for ICL, see Nancy Amoury Combs, "Seeking Inconsistency: Advancing Pluralism in International Criminal Sentencing" (2016) 41 *Yale Journal of International Law* 1–49: 3–5.

[2] The preamble of the Rome Statute embodies this vacillation, repeatedly referencing the gravity of international crimes and seeming moral imperative to punish those responsible through battling impunity, while also explicitly stating the utilitarian goals of deterrence and the maintenance of international peace and security. See Rome Statute of the International Criminal Court, Rome, July 17, 1998, in force July 1, 2002, 2187 UNTS 3, preamble. Moreover, the increasing reliance on positioning victims as one of the beneficiaries of ICL has gestured toward alternative justice models, such as restorative ones. On ICL's gesturing toward restorative justice, see Kamari Maxine Clarke, "'We Ask for Justice You Give Us Law': The Rule of Law, Economic Markets and the Reconfiguration of Victimhood," in Christian De Vos, Sara Kendall, and Carsten Stahn, eds., *Contested Justice: The Politics and Practice of International Criminal Court Interventions* (Cambridge University Press, 2015), 272–301.

[3] This characterization is, of course, a rather simplistic one, as there exist various permutations of retributive theories of criminal punishment. For more information on retributivism and its contemporary permutations, see generally Mark D. White, ed., *Retributivism: Essays on Theory and Policy* (Oxford University Press, 2011). For a discussion of retributive theory in relation to atrocity crimes, see Mark A. Drumbl, "Collective Violence and Individual Punishment: The Criminality of Mass Atrocity" (2004) 99 *Northwestern University Law Review* 539–610: 577–588.

international crimes are often invoked as creating a deep moral imperative for criminal punishment, thus justifying ICL, though oft-intertwined with utilitarian deterrence sentiments.[4] This invocation of the gravity of international crimes as demanding criminal prosecution is reflected in the Rome Statute's preambular reference to the fact that during the twentieth century "millions of children, women and men have been victims of unimaginable atrocities that deeply shock the conscience of humanity."[5] While this statement arguably evinces aspects of utilitarian and expressivist sentiment, it merges such sentiments with an overarching emphasis on the wrongfulness and gravity of international crimes.

At first glance, given the gravity and moral wrongfulness of most international crimes, ICL seems eminently justifiable as a retributivist criminal justice exercise. However, the glaring severity of atrocity crimes also complicates retributivist theories of justice, as such crimes may very well be of a gravity and wrongfulness that transcends the boundaries of retributive justice. After all, it seems impossible to mete out criminal sanctions that are appropriate and "just" against individuals implicated in abusing and murdering hundreds, thousands, or even millions of victims.[6] This paradox, of the strong moral argument for retributivist criminal justice following the commission of international crimes, yet the seeming impossibility of adequate punishment, has long been a point of difficulty for ICL theorists. For example, on one hand, Hannah Arendt argues that the "radical evil" of atrocities demand their direct criminalization under international law.[7] In correspondence with Karl Jaspers, however, Arendt expresses

[4] For example, in the second sentence of his famous opening statement at Nuremberg, Justice Jackson highlights the gravity of the crimes at issue, stating that "[t]he wrongs which we seek to condemn and punish have been so calculated, so malignant, and so devastating, that civilization cannot tolerate their being ignored, because it cannot survive their being repeated." PBS, "Opening Statement Nuremberg Trials, 1945," November 21, 1945, www.pbs.org/wnet/supremecourt/personality/sources_document12.html.

[5] Rome Statute, preamble. For a rather extreme version of such a focus on gravity, see *Prosecutor* v. *Sesay, Kallon, and Gbao, SCSL—2004-15-PT, July 5, 2004, The Opening Statement of Prosecutor David M. Crane with Mr. Abdul Tejan-Cole, Trial Attorney,* SCSL (Prosecutor David Crane claiming that "the pure evil of the [relevant] deeds of destruction are so horrific, terrible, and devastating in their scope, words in any language do not describe the offences.").

[6] On this subject, see Drumbl, "Collective Violence," 577–588.

[7] See Hannah Arendt, *The Human Condition*, 2nd ed. (University of Chicago Press, 1958), 241.

the view that such crimes may also, because of their awfulness and scale, "explode the limits" of the criminal law.[8]

Regardless of one's position concerning whether individual punishment for participating in the commission of atrocities is deontologically feasible, the current aesthetic myopia of international criminal justice is arguably unjustifiable from a deontological retributivist perspective. Such selectivity is unjustifiable because it inserts factors that are both legally *and* morally irrelevant into processes of recognizing, prioritizing, and selecting whom to punish for the commission of genocide, crimes against humanity, and/or war crimes. At first glance, this emphasis on shock and gravity may appear natural, even wholly appropriate, in terms of assessing the severity of relevant crimes. Yet, as Margaret deGuzman reminds us, when it comes to international crimes, assessments of relative gravity may be much more complicated and unclear than commonly assumed.[9] Assessments of gravity are grounded in highly subjective personal values and routinely present challenging philosophical questions. For example, how does one compare the relative wrongfulness of the commission of acts of sexual violence, to acts of mass killing, to acts of more generalized inhumane treatment affecting thousands more victims?[10] These are difficult and oft-confounding questions.

These fine-grained, admittedly complex and subjective assessments of gravity are not, however, the main reason why I find the prioritization of harms conforming to the atrocity aesthetic troubling from a deontological perspective. What troubles me more is the possibility that, by inserting aesthetic considerations, of shock, spectacle, and visceral horror, into assessments of what constitutes an international crime and which crimes are most demanding of attention and prosecution, the negative emotions and discomfort experienced by those exposed to such crimes, but

[8] Hannah Arendt and Karl Jaspers, *Hannah Arendt/Karl Jaspers: Correspondence, 1926–1969*, Lotte Kohler and Hans Saner, eds., trans. Robert Kimber and Rita Kimber (Harcourt Brace Jovanovich, 1992), 54.

[9] Margaret M. deGuzman, "Gravity and the Legitimacy of the International Criminal Court" (2009) 32 *Fordham International Law Journal* 1400–1465; see also Margaret M. deGuzman, *Shocking the Conscience of Humanity: Gravity and the Legitimacy of International Criminal Law* (Oxford University Press, 2020).

[10] For a discussion of gravity within the context of expressing collective "outrage" and how this process is necessarily tied up in nonlegal constitutive questions, see Nikolas M. Rajkovic, "What Is a 'Grave' International Crime? The Rome Statute, Durkheim and the Sociology of Ruling Outrages" (2020) 16 *Loyola University Chicago International Law Review* 65–86.

otherwise unaffected by them, may creep into assessments of culpability and gravity. That is, the degree of discomfort experienced, and outrage expressed by members of remote constituencies, primarily those in the Global North, whose governments collectively exercise an outsized degree of control over international criminal justice institutions, when exposed to horrific spectacles of violence, seems to operate as an (unacknowledged) factor in assessing the relative gravity of potential international crimes. Consequently, otherwise unaffected individuals who are confronted by stories and images of atrocities that "assault their eyes," offend their sensibilities, and cause them emotional discomfort, risk becoming a kind of secondary class of "victims" of international crimes, by having their discomfort factor into the prioritization (and perhaps even baseline recognition) of international crimes.

Considering that constituencies whose opinions are most likely to actually influence international criminal justice policies and practices tend to be clustered in the Global North, far removed from the world's most vulnerable populations, mostly clustered in the Global South, who face the greatest risks of being victimized by atrocity crimes, implicitly factoring in such discomfort as a quasi-harm flowing from the commission of genocide, crimes against humanity, or war crimes exposes ICL to further allegations of various forms of bias. Thus, while assessing the moral wrongfulness of an atrocity crime according to the shocking displays of violence and suffering it produces may conform to moral intuitions and resonate with the emotional reactions elicited among those exposed to such crimes, such reactionary emotional assessments risk inserting factors that are arguably morally irrelevant and that may entail deeply troubling ramifications into processes of recognizing and prioritizing international crimes.

Thus, for example, as discussed in the previous chapter, while on one level it may feel intuitively appropriate to prioritize the prosecution of an individual such as Duch over that of other potential suspects, such as Im Chaem, given the centrality of S-21 prison to the legacy of the Khmer Rouge period, such a decision arguably undermines the retributive legitimacy of the ECCC. Retributivist theories focus primarily on the harms caused by a perpetrator and their degree of causal responsibility for such harms in determining moral and legal culpability. Unless we are to place those physically removed from, yet exposed to, atrocity violence into the category of victim, a move I consider wholly improper, there is no place for aesthetic considerations within processes of assessing gravity and culpability. From a retributive perspective, the means involved in the production of harm are wholly inconsequential, aside from variations in the degree of suffering they produce. For example, in terms of both causation and moral blameworthiness, it is irrelevant if a perpetrator commits murder by shooting a victim in the head with a gun, versus locking them in a room and allowing them to die from starvation, dehydration, exposure, or the like. Indeed, in the latter case, because the victim suffers more pain and for much longer than the victim immediately killed by a gunshot to the head, if anything, the person responsible is arguably *more* culpable than the shooter. Thus, the insertion of visibility biases into assessments of what constitutes an international crime, and the culpability of those potentially responsible for such crime(s), undermines potential retributive justifications for ICL punishment.

Consequentialism and the Risk of Deterrence "Slippage"

The aesthetic biases of international criminal justice also negatively affect the potential utilitarian purposes served by ICL. The main utilitarian purpose ascribed to ICL, or for that matter criminal prosecutions in general, is that of deterrence.[11] Deterrence is typically subdivided into specific and general deterrence. Specific deterrence refers to criminal sanctions, especially incarceration, deterring a perpetrator from committing further criminal acts. General deterrence refers to the broader social deterrent effect criminalization and prosecution of harmful conduct may have. Deterrence, especially general deterrence, like retributivism, is central to standard justifications invoked by advocates of ICL. The notion that the prosecution of prior atrocity crimes may help deter the commission of future atrocities is, for example, evident in both Justice Jackson's oft-quoted statement that "civilization cannot tolerate [the atrocities of World War II] being ignored, because it cannot survive their being repeated" in his famous opening address at Nuremberg, and the preambular language of the Rome Statute, which explicitly links the fight against impunity for international crimes with their prevention.[12]

[11] For example, Stuart Ford argues that the prevention of future international crimes should be the "primary focus" of ICL institutions, "because [prevention] has both an extremely high value when it does occur and we now have good evidence that courts can prevent violations." Stuart Ford, "A Hierarchy of the Goals of International Criminal Courts" (2018) 27 *Minnesota Journal of International Law* 179–244. For a discussion of deterrence-based consequentialist justifications proposed for ICL. See Drumbl, "Collective Violence," 588–592.

[12] PBS, "Opening Statement." One of the lines of the Rome Statute's preamble lists as one of the goals of the state parties to the ICC, a "[d]etermin[ation] to put an end to impunity for the perpetrators of [international] crimes and thus to contribute to the prevention of such crimes." Rome Statute, preamble.

The degree to which ICL produces any deterrent effect is, however, unclear, and any deterrent effect ICL serves is certainly not currently demonstrably direct or substantial.[13] Most recently, Stuart Ford, surveying a number of empirical studies, argues that the ICC should be viewed as currently succeeding in its mission, because the Court's "principal goal is to prevent violations of international criminal law and it is already doing that."[14] Regardless of the ultimate degree to which ICL produces a deterrent effect, now, or may produce such an effect at some point in the future, such deterrence is, and will continue to be, diminished, or in some situations, extinguished altogether, in relation to forms of atrocity that fail to be recognized *as international crimes*. This creates risks of both overstating ICL's current deterrent effects, and that any such effect ICL does have, will be undermined, which I refer to as a risk of deterrence "slippage."

[13] There is an ongoing debate concerning whether ICL prosecutions produce any deterrent effect and if so, to what degree. See, for example, David Wippman, "Atrocities, Deterrence, and the Limits of International Justice" (1999) 23 *Fordham International Law Journal* 473–488; Payam Akhavan, "Beyond Impunity: Can International Criminal Justice Prevent Future Atrocities?" (2001) 95 *American Journal of International Law* 7–31; Tom Buitelaar, "The ICC and the Prevention of Atrocities: Criminological Perspectives" (2016) 17 *Human Rights Review* 285–302: 285; Kate Cronin-Furman, "Managing Expectations: International Criminal Trials and the Prospects for Deterrence of Mass Atrocity" (2013) 7 *International Journal of Transitional Justice* 434–454. Cronin-Furman argues that because mass atrocity commission tends to be motivated by varying "logics" that this changes the dynamic of deterrence within ICL and that "given the comparative lack of certainty and severity of sanction represented by the [ICC's] prosecutions, as well as the selection of perpetrators with powerful incentives to offend, current prosecutorial policy is not well-targeted at producing a deterrent effect." Ibid., 434. For the argument that ICL prosecutions do not deter, and indeed, may even encourage atrocity commission in certain circumstances, see Julian Ku and Jide Nzelibe, "Do International Criminal Tribunals Deter or Exacerbate Humanitarian Atrocities?" (2006) 84 *Washington University Law Review* 777–833. However, in contrast, see, for example, Hyeran Jo and Beth A. Simmons, "Can the International Criminal Court Deter Atrocity?" (2016) 70 *International Organization* 443–475 (finding empirical evidence that prosecutions at the ICC do produce a limited degree of deterrence for government actors, along with rebel groups that seek legitimacy). More generally, Kathryn Sikkink and Hunjoon Kim contend that empirical evidence suggests that "human rights prosecutions," including ICL prosecutions, do produce broad, if limited, normative deterrent effects. See Hunjoon Kim and Kathryn Sikkink, "Explaining the Deterrence Effect of Human Rights Prosecutions for Transitional Countries" (2010) 54 *International Studies Quarterly* 939–963; see also Kathryn Sikkink, *The Justice Cascade: How Human Rights Prosecutions are Changing World Politics* (Norton, 2011).

[14] Stuart Ford, "Can the International Criminal Court Succeed? An Analysis of the Empirical Evidence of Violence Prevention" (2020) 43 *Loyola of Los Angeles International and Comparative Law Review* 101–123: 122.

First, there is the risk that, by ignoring a subset of important, yet less visible international crimes, analyses of the degree to which ICL performs a deterrent effect will be skewed and incomplete. For example, the degree to which one agrees with Ford's assertion that the ICC is currently succeeding at preventing ICL "violations" is contingent to a significant degree on what forms of harm causation one views as being potentially violative of ICL in the first place. For his part, Ford argues that the ICC deters "violence," without defining the term. The closest Ford comes is to refer to "murder, rape and widespread property destruction" as "the sort of violence associated with violations of ICL."[15] While Ford does claim that "[t]here are people alive today who would not be alive if the [ICC] did not exist," again this claim remains partially contingent on how one counts suffering and death. From a more critical perspective, an argument may be made that Ford's orientation fails to account for the harms (and potentially numerous excess deaths) attributable to the degree to which ICL's myopic focus on individual culpability facilitates an obscuring of more widespread, and overall, more deadly forms of structural violence, or otherwise noncriminal sources of mass suffering and excess death.[16] I would add that it is unclear the degree to which Ford's analysis is able to (or if it is even possible to) account for the possibility that to some extent harm causation and even killing, has not been deterred, but rather certain spectacular *forms and means* of harm causation have been deterred. Thus, both noncriminal mass harms ignored (and, arguably, thereby encouraged) by the current myopic focus on ICL as the preferred, often sole means used to address mass harms, and criminal mass harms not recognized as such, fail to figure into the empirical studies Ford

[15] Ibid., 107 (internal citations omitted).

[16] Along these lines, see, for example, Frédéric Mégret, "What Sort of Global Justice Is 'International Criminal Justice'?" (2015) 13 *Journal of International Criminal Justice* 77–96: 80–81 (observing that while "it is entirely logically possible that the worst international offence would be the fact of 'deliberately tolerating conditions of relievable poverty' . . . this is clearly not the case [and] in fact, international criminal justice largely ignores questions of economic justice that are otherwise so prominent in the work of global justice scholars"); Tor Krever, "International Criminal Law: An Ideology Critique" (2013) 26 *Leiden Journal of International Law* 701–723: 723 ("Blinkered attention to individual criminal responsibility and pious celebration of ICL as the solution to violence or conflict narrow our field of vision and prevent us from seeing, let alone challenging, that wider context."); see also Karen Engle, "Anti-Impunity and the Turn to Criminal Law in Human Rights" (2015) 100 *Cornell Law Review* 1069–1128 (critiquing the recent turn to criminal prosecutions, especially through ICL, as the preferred method of enforcing human rights by, inter alia, noting the harms excluded from this approach).

analyzes, creating a risk that if one redefines "violence," ICL and the ICC might arguably be complicit in certain forms of violence.[17]

In sum, the current focus on horrifically spectacular crimes undermines the deterrent potential of ICL because the types of powerful, collective actors who perpetrate the vast majority of international crimes almost always have the capacity to commit such crimes not only on a fundamentally larger scale than domestic criminal actors, but also through a much wider array of means.[18] That is, such actors may choose to oppress, persecute, and kill through either aesthetically familiar forms of atrocity violence, such as mass executions, the creation of concentration camps, or the like, or through other, less visible methods, such as socioeconomic oppression, the enforcement of famine conditions, or the like, which may produce equally disastrous results, yet are less likely to be broadly recognized as potentially criminal in nature.

Precisely because such alternative forms of harm causation are unlikely to be broadly conceptualized as international crimes, a risk of deterrence "slippage" is created. I use the term "slippage" to convey the risk that any deterrent effect produced by ICL may be undermined by the ability of those contemplating the commission of atrocities to obscure the criminality of their actions through the selection of alternative, aesthetically unfamiliar means of perpetration. Indeed, such choices may be made in the sincere, yet erroneous belief that relevant harm-producing actions will not even violate ICL, but merely run afoul of legal interests perceived (rightly or wrongly) as being less serious, such as those provided for by international human rights law. Although ignorance of the law is not generally a valid excuse for violations of criminal law, including ICL, if

[17] A full analysis of whether and how ICL and the ICC may or may not contribute to or encourage certain forms of violence and oppression is outside the scope of this book. One example of such a possibility is that the ICC may be, contrary to the intentions of those involved in the Court's workings, complicit in the reproduction of racist tropes framing Black and/or Arab men as especially prone to violence by exclusively charging Black and/or Arab men (along with one Black woman) for at least the first twenty years of the Court's operational life span. Frédéric Mégret and I raise this possibility elsewhere. See Randle C. DeFalco and Frédéric Mégret, "The Invisibility of Race at the ICC: Lessons from the US Criminal Justice System" (2019) 7 *London Review of International Law* 55–87. Of course, it may be exceedingly difficult to assess such arguably "violent" unanticipated effects of the work of the ICC and other ICL institutions empirically.

[18] On the inherently collective nature of atrocity perpetration, see, for example, Jens David Ohlin, "Organizational Criminality," in Elies van Sliedregt and Sergey Vasiliev, eds., *Pluralism in International Criminal Law* (Oxford University Press, 2014), 107–127; Drumbl, "Collective Violence"; Kirsten Ainley, "Excesses of Responsibility: The Limits of Law and the Possibilities of Politics" (2011) 25 *Ethics and International Affairs* 407–431.

this misperception of the substance and applicability of ICL reflects broader social understandings of atrocity and international crime, such beliefs may eventually become self-authenticating through practices of legality associated with ICL and international criminal justice more broadly. Moreover, while ignorance of the law is not an excuse, the principle of legality, or in ICL, *nullum crimen sine lege* is grounded in the concept of fair warning.[19] ICL jurisprudence has, borrowing from the European Court of Human Rights, held that relevant criminal law prohibitions must be both "accessible" to an accused and the application of such laws to the actions grounding the accused's liability must be "foreseeable."[20] The latter requirement, of foreseeability, may become an obstacle to efforts to prosecute unspectacular atrocity crimes should ICL's myopic focus on a subset of aesthetically familiar crimes continue.

One can look to any variety of situations and see this slippage effect in action. Given the choice, it is clearly preferable for actors not to be viewed as implicated in the commission of international crimes, regardless of whether or not ICL performs any straight-line deterrent effect. Aside from whether ICL prosecutions are ever pursued, if a particular situation becomes dominantly socially framed as a "genocide" or "atrocity," such framing helps such situation gain attention as a pressing global justice issue and creates a relative degree of urgency in relation to the need to take some form of action. Those responsible, meanwhile, may be branded "enemies of humankind" (*hostis humani generis*). By utilizing relatively slow, aesthetically unfamiliar methods of mass killing, abuse, and/or oppression, powerful actors may evade the scrutiny, and potential material ramifications, such as sanctions, trade restrictions, or the like, associated with being branded as international criminals.

For example, in Myanmar, the military dictatorship actively and intentionally oppressed Rohingya Muslim populations and other minority groups for decades.[21] Much of this oppression was effectuated through socioeconomic, and other slow, attritive

[19] See Darryl Robinson, "The Identity Crisis of International Criminal Law" (2008) 21 *Leiden Journal of International Law* 925–963.

[20] See Jared L. Watkins and Randle C. DeFalco, "Joint Criminal Enterprise and the Jurisdiction of the Extraordinary Chambers in the Courts of Cambodia" (2010) 63 *Rutgers Law Review* 193–273: 200–204.

[21] See generally Akm Ahsan Ullah, "Rohingya Refugees to Bangladesh: Historical Exclusions and Contemporary Marginalization" (2011) 9 *Journal of Immigrant and Refugee Studies* 139–161; Maung Zarni and Alice Cowley, "The Slow-Burning Genocide of Myanmar's Rohingya" (2014) 23 *Pacific Rim Law and Policy Journal* 683–752; Azeem Ibrahim, *The Rohingyas: Inside Myanmar's Hidden Genocide* (Hurst, 2016).

means.[22] While the junta was regularly accused of human rights violations in relation to their actions toward minority populations during this period, the plight of the Rohingya was not dominantly conceptualized as a situation involving the large-scale commission of international crimes. In recent years, however, the government of Myanmar, despite moving toward a more democratic system for a time, has encouraged, and even participated in, violent attacks by the Buddhist majority against minority groups, especially Rohingya Muslims. These attacks, and the spectacle of Rohingya victims fleeing Myanmar on overcrowded boats, being forced into overcrowded displaced person camps, having their villages razed, and being subjected to horrific acts of interpersonal and sexual violence, have led to an increased tendency to use the language of ICL in describing the plight of the Rohingya population and the potential culpability of members of Myanmar's government.[23] The increasing spectacularity of the violence committed against Rohingya populations has arguably played a significant contributory role in the instigation of legal proceedings at both the ICC and the International Court of Justice, the latter of which found sufficient evidence to order the Myanmar government to undertake provisional measures to halt and/or prevent the commission of genocide against the Rohingya.[24]

While the recent spate of violent attacks against Rohingya and other minority groups in Myanmar is, of course, reprehensible, the victimization of the Rohingya, involving the likely commission of well-established international crimes, is nothing new, dating back to Myanmar gaining independence in 1948 or at least the military junta's seizure of power in 1962.[25] Scholars, such as Azeem Ibrahim, Maung Zarni, and Alice

[22] Zarni and Cowley, "Slow-Burning Genocide."

[23] See, for example, David Mathieson, "Perilous Plight: Burma's Rohingya Take to the Seas" (May 26, 2009) *Human Rights Watch*, www.hrw.org/report/2009/05/26/perilous-plight/burmas-rohingya-take-seas; Matthew Smith, "'All You Can Do Is Pray': Crimes against Humanity and Ethnic Cleansing of Rohingya Muslims in Burma's Arakan State" (April 22, 2013) *Human Rights Watch*, www.hrw.org/report/2013/04/22/all-you-can-do-pray/crimes-against-humanity-and-ethnic-cleansing-rohingya-muslims; UN Human Rights Council, "Situation of Human Rights of Rohingya Muslims and other Minorities in Myanmar," UN Doc. A/HRC/32/18, June 20, 2016.

[24] See *Situation in the People's Republic of Bangladesh/Republic of the Union of Myanmar, Decision Pursuant to Article 15 of the Rome Statute on the Authorisation of an Investigation into the Situation in the People's Republic of Bangladesh/Republic of the Union of Myanmar, ICC-01/19, November 14, 2019*, ICC; *Application of the Convention on the Prevention and Punishment of the Crime of Genocide (The Gambia* v. *Myanmar), General List No. 178, Order, January 23, 2020*, ICJ.

[25] Ibrahim, *Rohingyas*, 1–10. Zarni and Cowley, meanwhile, argue that Rohingya Muslims "have been subject to a state-sponsored process of destruction" since 1978. Zarni and Cowley, "Slow-Burning Genocide," 683.

Cowley, who have attempted to draw much broader temporal boundaries around the continuing atrocities being committed against the Rohingya population, highlight the unfamiliarity of longstanding forms of atrocity committed against the Rohingya, by describing the situation as a "hidden" or "slow-burning" genocide.[26] Thus, the situation in Myanmar has, for decades, exemplified how the criminality of relatively slow, aesthetically unspectacular forms of atrocity violence may be downgraded in terms of perceived gravity and urgency.

Similar processes of obscuring the criminality, or downgrading the severity, of mass harm causation processes failing to conform to the atrocity aesthetic can also be observed elsewhere. For example, it is more difficult to conceptualize corrupt acts in Nigeria's Rivers State, the South African government's refusal to accept prenatal HIV/AIDS medicine, or socioeconomic policies of the Khmer Rouge regime, as atrocities worthy of ICL scrutiny, despite the fact that all three situations may well have involved both enormous harms and the commission of well-established international crimes.[27] While currently, the risk of aesthetic bias shaping ICL's selectivity and thereby undermining deterrence within the realm of ICL is limited by ICL's already extreme generalized selectivity, moving forward, when and if ICL becomes less generally selective, deterrence slippage may become a more significant problem. In the meantime, it is important to recognize that situations broadly conceptualized as genocides or atrocities, for better or worse, are treated as the most important and urgent global justice issues and therefore attract the lion's share of attention and resources at the expense of less familiar mass harms.

The Expressive Role of International Criminal Law

As previously indicated, traditional criminal law justifications of retribution and deterrence fit awkwardly when applied to ICL.[28] The harms

[26] Ibrahim, *Rohingyas*; Zarni and Cowley, "Slow-Burning Genocide."

[27] See generally See Ben Bloom, "Criminalizing Kleptocracy? The ICC as a Viable Tool in the Fight against Grand Corruption" (2014) 29 *American University International Law Review* 627–671; Josh Scheinert, "Refusal to Save Lives: A Perspective from International Criminal Law" (2013) 13 *International Criminal Law Review* 627–663; Randle C. DeFalco, "Accounting for Famine at the Extraordinary Chambers in the Courts of Cambodia: The Crimes against Humanity of Extermination, Inhumane Acts and Persecution" (2011) 5 *International Journal of Transitional Justice* 142–158.

[28] On the general limitations of the usefulness of drawing theoretical analogies between ICL and domestic criminal law regimes when it comes to justification and punishment, see

involved in many international crimes, routinely involving killing on a massive scale, may transcend the limits of retributive moral desert. Moreover, the often relatively light sentences imposed by ICL institutions, and the idiosyncratic sentencing practices of such institutions, further disrupt traditional retributive rationales for criminal punishment.[29] The widespread skepticism of ICL's deterrent effect, meanwhile, makes traditional utilitarian criminal law justifications, particularly those grounded in general deterrence, ring somewhat hollow.

These limitations have likely contributed to an increasing embrace of expressive theories of punishment within the realm of ICL.[30] Expressivism is grounded in the notion that one of the central aims of criminal law is the promotion of certain normative values.[31] As such,

Robert D. Sloane, "The Expressive Capacity of International Punishment: The Limits of the National Law Analogy and the Potential of International Criminal Law" (2007) 43 *Stanford Journal of International Law* 39–94: 39–42.

[29] On the inconsistency within ICL sentencing, see generally Drumbl, "Collective Violence"; Margaret M. deGuzman, "Harsh Justice for International Crimes?" (2014) 39 *Yale Journal of International Law* 1–35; Joseph W. Doherty and Richard H. Steinberg, "Punishment and Policy in International Criminal Sentencing: An Empirical Study" (2016) 110 *American Journal of International Law* 49–81; Barbora Hola and Hollie Nyseth Brehm, "Punishing Genocide: A Comparative Empirical Analysis of Sentencing Laws and Practices at the International Criminal Tribunal for Rwanda (ICTR), Rwandan Domestic Courts, and Gacaca Courts" (2016) 10 *Genocide Studies and Prevention* 59–80. For an argument that sentencing consistency ought not to be viewed as desirable, see Combs, "Seeking Inconsistency."

[30] For a helpful overview of the expressivist turn within ICL in recent years, see Barrie Sander, "The Expressive Turn of International Criminal Justice: A Field in Search of Meaning" (2019) 32 *Leiden Journal of International Law* 851–872. For examples of explicit expressive proposals, see Diane Marie Amann, "Group Mentality, Expressivism, and Genocide" (2002) 2 *International Criminal Law Review* 93–143; Sloane, "Expressive Capacity"; Margaret M. deGuzman, "Choosing to Prosecute: Expressive Selection at the International Criminal Court (2012) 33 *Michigan Journal of International Law* 265–320; Saira Mohamed, "Deviance, Aspiration, and the Stories We Tell: Reconciling Mass Atrocity and the Criminal Law" (2015) 124 *Yale Law Journal* 1628–1689. Other justifications provided are often grounded in some form of expressivism, such as norm projection or didactic functions. For example, Mirjan Damaška locates the "primacy" of the didactic function of ICL. Mirjan Damaška, "What Is the Point of International Criminal Justice?" (2008) 83 *Chicago-Kent Law Review* 329–365. Frédéric Mégret, meanwhile, argues, albeit indirectly, that expressivism is central to the actual function of ICL, claiming that ICL is a form of distributive justice, which assigns stigma selectively to certain forms of behavior. Frédéric Mégret, "Practices of Stigmatization" (2013) 76 *Law and Contemporary Problems* 287–318.

[31] See, for example, Diane Marie Amann, "Message as Medium in Sierra Leone" (2001) 7 *ILSA Journal of International and Comparative Law* 237–245: 238. ("Expressive theories look not so much at whether a law deters or whether a law punishes, but at the message we get from a law. The message understood, rather than the message intended, is critical.

expressivism views the role of criminal prosecution and punishment as communicative in nature, expressing a society's opprobrium to certain behaviors by stigmatizing those who engage in such behaviors.[32]

The attractiveness of an expressive justification for ICL is easily grasped given the general social opprobrium to mass killing and abuse. Consequently, ICL may be viewed from an expressivist perspective as a vehicle for expressing and propagating social opposition to the commission of atrocities and the impunity of those who participate in them. While, in a general sense, the propagation of social opprobrium to the commission of atrocities is a worthwhile endeavor, the selectivity of ICL both generally, and specifically flowing from its aesthetic biases, operates to warp such messaging. As Frédéric Mégret points out, the operation of ICL, including its selectivity of application, has significant distributive justice ramifications.[33] Mégret argues elsewhere that it is stigma, "both an expression of the inherent moral blameworthiness assigned to the perpetrators of certain heinous acts and a way of constituting the society that assigns this blameworthiness," that is distributed through ICL.[34] Thus, one may view the operation of ICL as a process of selectively assigning extreme stigma to certain actions.[35] From this perspective, the aesthetic biases of international criminal justice may be seen as influencing the normative values expressed through ICL, problematically suggesting in

Expressivism tells us that a harmful message in itself causes harm; therefore, when we evaluate whether an action done was good or bad, we should look at the message that the action was understood to convey."), citing Dan M. Kahan, "The Secret Ambition of Deterrence" (1999) 113 *Harvard Law Review* 413–500; Elizabeth S. Anderson and Richard H. Pildes, "Expressive Theories of Law: A General Restatement" (2000) 148 *University of Pennsylvania Law Review* 1503–1575. See also Sander, "Expressive Turn," 852 ("Although expressivism encompasses a range of ideas from different disciplines, the animating assumption shared by most strands of expressivist thought is simple: social practices carry meanings and transmit messages quite apart from their consequences.") (internal citations omitted).

32 Joel Feinberg characterizes expressive justifications for criminal law as grounded in the fact that "[p]unishment is a conventional device for the expression of attitudes of resentment and indignation, and of judgments of disapproval and reprobation, either on the part of the punishing authority himself or of those 'in whose name' the punishment is inflicted. Punishment, in short, has *a symbolic significance* largely missing from other kinds of penalties." Joel Feinberg, "The Expressive Function of Punishment" (1965) 49 *The Monist* 397–423: 400 (emphasis in original). See also Drumbl, "Collective Violence," 592–595.

33 Mégret, "What Sort of Global Justice," 77–96.

34 Mégret, "Practices of Stigmatization," 290.

35 In a general sense, international crimes are viewed as more serious than other forms of injustice, such as human rights violations.

the process that mass killing and abuse brought about through means that are not spectacularly horrific (and hence not intuitively recognizable *as* international crimes in the first place) are somehow less worthy of stigma.

The flipside of stigmatization is, of course, toleration, and the current tendency to broadly conceptualize aesthetically unfamiliar forms of atrocity violence as necessarily situated outside the purview of ICL problematically suggests that such forms of harm causation, regardless of their scale and severity, or the potential culpability of those who brought about such harms, are somehow more tolerable than more familiar, aesthetically gruesome atrocities. This toleration implicates ICL in the much broader tendency of international law to prioritize the experiences and lives of certain individuals and communities over others and to marginalize social, distributive, and economic questions of justice.[36] Thus, in an expressivist sense, ICL may operate to present a subset of horrifically spectacular forms of violence and abuse as the world's most serious and pressing global justice issues, exacerbating certain already troubling consequences of ICL's current predominance within global justice discourses.

The victims of manifestations of genocide, crimes against humanity, and war crimes failing to conform to the atrocity aesthetic tend to be drawn from already vulnerable and marginalized populations. These populations are largely clustered in the Global South,[37] and lack sufficient social, legal, and political capital to gain security in terms of both their subsistence needs and physical surroundings. Such populations, and in particular, the sources of their suffering, are often already routinely obscured from popular sightlines.[38] As Chris Tenove observes, ICL

[36] For example, Mégret notes that international criminal justice largely ignores questions of economic justice that are otherwise so prominent in the work of global justice scholars." Mégret, "What Sort of Global Justice," 81.

[37] In this context, the term "Global South" is not used simply as a geographic descriptor, but as a concept grounded in a "networked" understanding of power. One that "attempts to mediate between territorialist and deterritorialist models through a nonterritorial socio-spatial mapping of inequity" and which consequently "conceive[s] of subaltern political collectivities not through a focus on the transnational experience and legacy of European colonization but through a shared experience of the negative effects of capitalist globalization." Ann Garland Mahler, *From the Tricontinental to the Global South: Race, Radicalism, and Transnational Solidarity* (Duke University Press, 2018), 34.

[38] In this vein, on the socially constructed visibility of different bodies and their experiences, see generally Monica J. Casper and Lisa Jean Moore, *Missing Bodies: The Politics of Visibility* (New York University Press, 2009), 10–14; Michel Foucault, *The History of Sexuality Volume I: An Introduction*, trans. Robert Hurley (Pantheon Books, 1978);

institutions "are selective about who receives victim status," and this selectivity of recognition itself has "very complex and variegated effects" that depend highly on context.[39] By expressing the sentiment that everyday forms of oppression that fail to shock us do not merit ICL's attention, the aesthetic biases of international criminal justice subtly help condone the current global stratification in terms of the importance of human lives (indeed, arguably extending to the very recognition of the humanity of certain groups), and recognition of experiences of harm, trauma, and victimhood.[40]

Beyond International Criminal Law: The Broader Effects of Aesthetic Bias

The reach of international criminal justice goes far beyond the narrow confines of ICL, or even international law more generally for that matter. For better or worse, ICL casts a rather long shadow, exerting a great deal of influence over historical narratives and practices in adjacent fields, such as human rights, transitional justice, and peacebuilding.[41]

Achille Mbembe, "Necropolitics" (2003) 15 *Public Culture* 11–40; Sylvia Wynter, "Unsettling the Coloniality of Being/Power/Truth/Freedom: Toward the Human, After Man, Its Overrepresentation–An Argument" (2003) 3 *The New Centennial Review* 257–337.

[39] Chris Tenove, "International Criminal Justice and the Empowerment or Disempowerment of Victims," in Morten Bergsmo, Mark Klamberg, Kjersti Lohne, and Christopher B. Mahony, eds., *Power in International Criminal Justice* (Torkel Opsahl Academic EPublisher, 2020), 743–778: 744.

[40] In the words of Judith Butler, these forces may contribute to the determination of "bodies that matter." Butler famously uses this turn of phrase within an entirely different context, that of gender identity politics. Judith Butler, *Bodies that Matter: On the Discursive Limits of "Sex"* (Routledge, 2011). Despite focusing on a completely different subject matter, Butler's insight that legal and other "regulatory [social] schemas are not timeless structures, but historically revisable criteria of intelligibility which produce and vanquish bodies that matter" helps us to understand how ICL shapes and narrates what victims, harms, and perpetrators are recognized and thereby made to "matter." Ibid., xxii. Jill Stauffer, meanwhile, describes this failure to listen to victims as a process of double abandonment by humanity, whereby victims of mass violence and oppression are first abandoned by humanity through being directly victimized and again abandoned by having their experiences not fully recognized or ignored altogether. See Jill Stauffer, *Ethical Loneliness: The Injustice of Not Being Heard* (Columbia University Press, 2015).

[41] See generally, Christine Schwöbel, "The Comfort of International Criminal Law" (2013) 24 *Law and Critique* 169–191; Engle, "Anti-Impunity"; Sarah M.H. Nouwen and Wouter G. Werner, "Monopolizing Global Justice: International Criminal Law as Challenge to Human Diversity" (2015) 13 *Journal of International Criminal Justice* 157–176; Sander, "Expressive Turn," 851–852.

Consequently, the aesthetic selectivity of international criminal justice not only undermines the retributive, consequentialist, and expressive functions (or at least potential) of ICL, but may also produce broader problematic repercussions outside the realm of ICL itself. Such repercussions flow directly from how international crimes are framed within ICL, as whether a specific situation is viewed as implicating ICL often has a significant role in dictating the content of dominant historical discourses, and the allocation of resources to human rights, transitional justice, peacebuilding projects, and other forms of redress and social reconstruction. Such projects are overwhelmingly pursued much more vigorously, and with greater resources, in the aftermath of the commission of recognized atrocity crimes. Human rights, meanwhile, are also increasingly viewed through the lens of ICL, especially the increasingly ubiquitous mantra of "anti-impunity."[42] One consequence of this emphasis on ICL is that the repercussions of ICL's aesthetic selectivity are not strictly limited to ICL itself, but seep into adjacent legal regimes and broader attitudes toward how to improve global justice and redress large-scale wrongs.

The remainder of this chapter explores the role aesthetic considerations play in narrating histories of oppression and abuse and perpetuating the backgrounding of questions of structural and socioeconomic justice, especially within discourses of human rights, transitional justice, and peacebuilding. This analysis demonstrates that social preferences for aesthetics of dramatic spectacle and ease of recognition are not unique to ICL, but rather appear to similarly influence these related disciplines. Moreover, because ICL has become the primary normative environment within which concepts such as atrocity, genocide, mass violence, and the like, are socially constructed, the aesthetic biases of international criminal justice play a significant role in perpetuating a continuing broader blindness to structural and socioeconomic questions of justice afflicting human rights, transitional justice, peacebuilding, and other fields, disciplines, and epistemologies of global justice.

Historical Memory

Shared understandings of atrocity grounded in notions of what constitutes genocide, crimes against humanity, and war crimes have significant ramifications for dominant historical narratives, helping to maintain

[42] See Engle, "Anti-Impunity."

hegemonic, yet oft-inaccurate, narratives of conflict and violence that cater to existing global power arrangements. In this regard, because one of the main objectives commonly ascribed to ICL is the establishment of an accurate historical record of periods of atrocity, and the special legitimacy commonly ascribed to legal fact-finding processes, international criminal justice often plays a major role in shaping social memory.[43] Actually producing an accurate, integrated truth, especially a singular one, of what occurred during the tumult and chaos of atrocity is, however, a quite difficult, if not impossible, task.[44] Moreover, the form of criminal adjudication, given that the sole purpose of a criminal trial is the determination of the guilt or innocence of the accused, is arguably ill-suited to the production of broad, fully informed historical narratives.[45]

Regardless of whether or not ICL is actually any good at producing accurate historical narratives of atrocities, social and legal understandings of what constitutes genocide and atrocity play a major role in shaping how histories of large-scale oppression and violence are remembered and historically documented. As demonstrated previously, a correlation exists between forgotten or hidden histories of mass killing and abuse, and forms of harm causation failing to conform to the atrocity aesthetic. For example, histories of atrocities, including acts that would now legally constitute very serious international crimes including genocide and/or crimes against humanity, such as those committed against Herero and Nama victims in present-day Namibia between 1904 and 1908 by confining them to unlivable desert areas, the Cherokee "Trail of

[43] See generally Marina Aksenova, "Symbolism as a Constraint on International Criminal Law" (2017) 30 *Leiden Journal of International Law* 475–499: 494; Lawrence Douglas, *The Memory of Judgment: Making Law and History in the Trials of the Holocaust* (Yale University Press, 2001); see also Sander, "Expressive Turn," 854–855; Barrie Sander, "History on Trial: Historical Narrative Pluralism Within and Beyond International Criminal Courts" (2018) 67 *International and Comparative Law Quarterly* 547–576.

[44] On the "pluralism" of truths in relation to histories of atrocity, see Mark A. Drumbl, "The Curious Criminality of Mass Atrocity: Diverse Actors, Multiple Truths, and Plural Responses," in Elies van Sliedregt and Sergey Vasiliev, eds., *Pluralism in International Criminal Law* (Oxford University Press, 2014), 68–103; Sander, "History on Trial."

[45] For critiques of ICL's suitability for truth-telling and the production of accurate historical narratives, see Drumbl, "Curious Criminality"; Martti Koskenniemi, "Between Impunity and Show Trials" (2002) 6 *Max Planck Yearbook of United Nations Law* 1–32; Richard Ashby Wilson, "Judging History: The Historical Record of the International Criminal Tribunal for the former Yugoslavia" (2005) 27 *Human Rights Quarterly* 908–942; Aksenova, "Symbolism as a Constraint," 494. However, some scholars argue that the structure of ICL prosecutions allows for them to contribute meaningfully to the establishment of accurate historical records. See, for example, Ruti G. Teitel, *Transitional Justice* (Oxford University Press, 2000), 69–118.

Tears" forced relocation from 1838 to 1839, or many other processes of slow, yet far-reaching projects of violence and domination may be misremembered as non-atrocities, downgrading their perceived seriousness in terms of both the harms involved and their present-day legacies. Moreover, ongoing, largely bureaucratic acts of violence and oppression, such as that committed against vulnerable migrant populations, continue to have their seriousness downgraded and relevant culpabilities obscured.[46]

According to this flawed logic, specific acts, such as the poisoning of wells in Namibia and the use of violence to prevent starving and dehydrated Herero and Nama victims from escaping the desert, may amount to atrocities, but the broader, holistic set of processes involved in killing and abusing such victims may be inaccurately viewed as largely non-criminal in nature. For example, there exists a common misconception that some, oft-unnecessary qualifier, such as "political" or "cultural," needs to be added to the concept of genocide for it to be used to describe the systematic destruction and domination of Indigenous populations in North America and elsewhere to facilitate settler-colonialism.[47] Such discourses affect how both previous and ongoing settler-colonial processes are acknowledged and addressed.

These qualifiers are used to denote that within these contexts, the concept of genocide as a legally defined crime is *not* being invoked. This is especially

[46] See, for example, Ioannis Kalpouzos and Itamar Mann, "Banal Crimes against Humanity: The Case of Asylum Seekers in Greece" (2015) 16 *Melbourne Journal of International Law* 1-28.

[47] See, for example, Kiera L. Ladner, "Political Genocide. Killing Nations through Legislation and Slow-Moving Poison," in Andrew Woolford, Jeff Benvenuto, and Alexander Laban Hinton, eds., *Colonial Genocide in Indigenous North America* (Duke University Press, 2014), 226–245. For a broader overview of the debate in Canada surrounding usage of the term "cultural genocide" in relation to treatment of Aboriginal populations, see Joseph Brean, "'Cultural Genocide' of Canada's Indigenous Peoples Is a 'Mourning Label', Former War Crimes Prosecutor Says" (January 15, 2016) *National Post*, http://news.nationalpost.com/news/canada/cultural-genocide-of-canadas-indigenous-people-is-a-mourning-label-former-war-crimes-prosecutor-says. For a discussion of the US context in this regard, see Chris Mato Nunpa, "Historical Amnesia: The 'Hidden Genocide' and Destruction of Indigenous Peoples in the United States," in Alexander Laban Hinton, Thomas La Pointe, and Douglas Irvin-Erickson, eds., *Hidden Genocides: Knowledge, Power, Memory* (Rutgers University Press, 2014), 96–108. In Nunpa's words, "At the time of initial contact (1492), there were approximately sixteen million Native Peoples within 'the continental United States', and four centuries later, there were only 237,196 Native People, according to the 1900 U.S. Census. This represents a 98.5 percent population decline, if one says it nicely. If one says it not so nicely, then this represents a 98.5 percent extermination rate." Ibid., 97.

curious considering that often such situations would represent paradigmatic examples of genocide, including in a strictly legal sense, if committed now. This linguistic reluctance is itself deeply political. For example, the Armenian Genocide has by now entered the pantheon of widely accepted twentieth-century genocides, despite having occurred well before genocide as a concept, legal or otherwise, even existed. The widespread acknowledgment of the Armenian Genocide, and the ongoing political implications of such designation, suggests that such "history wars"[48] are less about temporality and the problems represented by the retroactive forecasting of criminal liability to an era before relevant crimes existed, and more so reflective of a certain desire among those who currently benefit from power, privilege, and wealth, to downgrade the scale of the atrocities committed in past (or ongoing) processes of securing the land, resources, and other forms of capital upon which such wealth was accumulated. Aesthetic assumptions help societies to avoid this discomfort of acknowledging the full realities of their collective pasts, rife with atrocity commission as they so commonly are, by helping to perpetuate the myth that such atrocities were isolated, regrettable mass killing events, rather than longstanding, multifaceted processes aimed at accumulating land, wealth, and resources through interrelated forms of violence and domination.

Historical nomenclature is also not limited solely to abstract debates and practices of memorialization but often has significant continuing social and political implications. This importance also extends to how victim groups are labeled, as researchers have found a correlation between the failure to acknowledge prior atrocities and continuing oppression.[49] As an example, one need not look any further than the situation in Turkey, where Armenian, Assyrian, and other populations continue to be oppressed, and the government has long denied that these groups were victims of genocide.[50] The same can be said of dominant

[48] David B. MacDonald, "Canada's History Wars: Indigenous Genocide and Public Memory in the United States, Australia and Canada" (2015) 17 *Journal of Genocide Research* 411–431.

[49] See, for example, Riccardo Armillei, Nikki Marczak, and Panayiotis Diamadis, "Forgotten and Concealed: The Emblematic Cases of the Assyrian and Romani Genocides" (2016) 10 *Genocide Studies and Prevention* 98–120 (noting a correlation between a lack of acknowledgement of the fact that atrocities were committed against Romani populations during the Holocaust and Assyrian populations in Turkey during the Armenian Genocide, and the continuing persecution of these groups).

[50] On this subject, see generally Shelley Burleson and Alberto Giordano, "Spatiality of the Stages of Genocide: The Armenian Case" (2016) 10 *Genocide Studies and Prevention* 39–58.

discourses within settler-colonial nations such as the United States and Canada, wherein the minimization of the scale of atrocities committed against Indigenous and African-American populations operate to buttress arguments that the oppression suffered by such groups is now over, and no affirmative steps therefore need be taken to address the continuing effects of "past" violence.[51]

Transitional Justice and Peacebuilding

Whether a historical narrative is broadly understood as involving acts of atrocity also has far-reaching repercussions for activities related to human rights, transitional justice, and peacebuilding.[52] Each of these fields is influenced by ICL because atrocity crimes are viewed as the most serious human rights transgressions possible. Consequently, once a country or region becomes a widely acknowledged atrocity site, new sources of funding and resources become available to civil society actors and social justice activists located there, creating material incentives for

[51] This assertion is not meant to suggest that the violence and oppression committed against groups such as Native and African American populations is wholly a product of the denial of past violence. These and many other populations continue to experience active, present forms of oppression and violence as well, although these active harms are often intertwined with longer histories of abuse.

[52] The term "transitional justice" does not have a universally agreed-upon definition, but, in a general sense, "refers to the ways countries emerging from periods of conflict and repression address large scale or systematic human rights violations so numerous and so serious that the normal justice system will not be able to provide an adequate response." International Center for Transitional Justice, "Transitional Justice Factsheet," (2009) www.ictj.org/about/transitional-justice. Another influential definition views transitional justice as "the conception of justice associated with periods of political change, characterized by legal responses to confront the wrongdoings of repressive predecessor regimes." Ruti G. Teitel, "Transitional Justice Genealogy" (2003) 16 *Harvard Human Rights Journal* 69–94: 69. For the purposes of the present inquiry, the term transitional justice is used to generally refer to any and all efforts to pursue justice in the wake of large-scale oppression or harm causation. The term "peacebuilding" meanwhile:

> first emerged in 1970s through the work of Johan Galtung who called for the creation of peacebuilding structures to promote sustainable peace by addressing the "root causes" of violent conflict and supporting indigenous capacities for peace management and conflict resolution. Since then, the term Peacebuilding has covered a multidimensional exercise and tasks ranging from the disarming of warring factions to the rebuilding of political, economic, judicial and civil society institutions.

UN Peacebuilding Support Office, "UN Peacebuilding: an Orientation" (September 2010), p. 5, www.un.org/peacebuilding/sites/www.un.org.peacebuilding/files/documents/peacebuilding_orientation.pdf.

actors seeking to engage with local histories of oppression and injustice to frame such histories within the rubric of ICL.[53]

For example, in 2017, the US Agency for International Development (USAID) Bureau for Democracy, Conflict, and Humanitarian Assistance announced that $16 million of funding would be distributed to support "activities that mitigate conflict and promote reconciliation by bringing together individuals of different ethnic, religious, or political backgrounds from areas of civil conflict and war."[54] While the USAID call for applications states that "[p]rograms that provide opportunities for adversaries to address issues, reconcile differences, promote greater understanding and mutual trust, and work on common goals with regard to potential, ongoing, or recent conflict will receive consideration for funding," only organizations working in an enumerated group of eleven "post-conflict" countries were even permitted to submit grant applications.[55] Each of

[53] For example, preliminary empirical research suggests that ICL projects tend to attract far more funding than other transitional justice mechanisms, such as truth commissions. See William Muck and Eric Wiebelhaus-Brahm, "External Transitional Justice Funding: Introducing a New Dataset" (2016) 11 *Journal of Peacebuilding and Development* 66–71. The fact that forms of harm causation that tend not to be conceptualized as atrocity crimes, such as socioeconomic ones, also tend to be marginalized within the literature and practice of transitional justice lends support to the general conclusion that there exists a material incentive for actors seeking funding for transitional justice projects to frame the past harms they seek to address as atrocities. On the backgrounding of forms of harm causation failing to conform to the atrocity aesthetic within the realm of transitional justice, see, for example, Louise Arbour, "Economic and Social Justice for Societies in Transition" (2007) 40 *New York University Journal of International Law and Politics* 1–27; Zinaida Miller, "Effects of Invisibility: In Search of the 'Economic' in Transitional Justice" (2008) 2 *International Journal of Transitional Justice* 266–291; Ruben Carranza, "Plunder and Pain: Should Transitional Justice Engage with Corruption and Economic Crimes?" (2008) 2 *International Journal of Transitional Justice* 310–330; Ismael Muvingi, "Sitting on Powder Kegs: Socioeconomic Rights in Transitional Societies" (2009) 3 *International Journal of Transitional Justice* 163–182; Amanda Cahill-Ripley, "Foregrounding Socio-Economic Rights in Transitional Justice: Realising Justice for Violations of Economic and Social Rights" (2014) 32 *Netherlands Quarterly of Human Rights* 183–213. For a critique of the ramifications flowing from the fact that virtually all transitional justice projects are externally funded, see Ismael Muvingi, "Donor-Driven Transitional Justice and Peacebuilding" (2016) 11 *Journal of Peacebuilding and Development* 10–25. For a similar critique within the field of ICL, see Sara Kendall, "Donors' Justice: Recasting International Criminal Accountability" (2011) 24 *Leiden Journal of International Law* 585–606.

[54] USAID, "Notice of Funding Opportunity: Request for Applications Number RFA-OAA-17-000011," 2017.

[55] Ibid., 5. Eligible countries include Bangladesh, Bosnia-Herzegovina, Central African Republic, Colombia, Democratic Republic of Congo, Georgia, Liberia, Indonesia, Nigeria, Peru, South Africa, and Thailand.

these countries is a well-established site of recent, highly visible periods of violent conflict and/or genocide and atrocity.

The aesthetic selectivity of ICL influences not only *where* transitional justice and peacebuilding are pursued but also *how* they are pursued, what harms are prioritized, and how resources dedicated to redress are allocated. Along these lines, Zinaida Miller argues:

> Transitional justice as both literature and practice offers more than just a set of neutral instruments for the achievement of the goals of justice, truth and reconciliation. It also serves to narrate conflict and peace, voice and silence, tolerable structural violence and intolerable physical atrocity. Ultimately, transitional justice is a definitional project, explaining who has been silenced by delineating who may now speak.[56]

As Miller points out, one consequence of this narrative role of transitional justice is that, "[d]espite its claims to exposure, revelation and memorialization, the project of transitional justice may simultaneously perpetuate invisibility and silence," especially in relation to questions of economic inequality and structural violence.[57] Miller's observations again raise troubling questions regarding whose lives, experiences, and stories are valued. Miller's usage of visibility as an organizing theme also reflects the similar role aesthetic assumptions play within transitional justice as they do within ICL. Indeed, such aesthetic politics of recognition and redress appear to operate symbiotically within these two fields, mutually reinforcing the incorrect notion that all forms of mass harm causation will be spectacularly visible and aesthetically self-evident.[58]

Recently, a growing number of scholars have begun to advocate for broader, more holistic approaches to transitional justice. Pádraig McAuliffe describes this shift as a "transformative turn," which he links

[56] Miller, "Effects of Invisibility," 266–267.

[57] Ibid., 267. On the general meaning of the term "structural violence" see Johan Galtung, "Violence, Peace and Peace Research" (1969) 6 *Journal of Peace Research* 167–191. On the meaning of structural violence within the realm of transitional justice, see generally Krista Thomason, "Transitional Justice as Structural Justice," in Claudio Corradetti, Nir Eisikovits, and Jack Volpe Rotondi, eds., *Theorizing Transitional Justice* (Ashgate, 2015), 71–80.

[58] On the incorrectness of this assumption that socioeconomic issues are inherently structural in terms of their causal dynamics and thus, less direct than other forms of harm causation and rights violations, see Evelyne Schmid and Aoife Nolan, "'Do No Harm'? Exploring the Scope of Economic and Social Rights in Transitional Justice" (2014) 8 *International Journal of Transitional Justice* 362–382; Evelyne Schmid, *Taking Economic, Social and Cultural Rights Seriously in International Criminal Law* (Cambridge University Press, 2015).

with the liberation of transitional justice from its "legalist beginnings."[59] Thus, according to McAuliffe and numerous other scholars, transitional justice's overly narrow focus stems at least partially from its grounding in legal mechanisms, the most notable of which being ICL.[60] The general assertion made by McAuliffe and others that legal mechanisms, especially those grounded in criminal law, offer but one of a wide variety of approaches to justice-seeking in the aftermath of social upheaval and pervasive injustice is undoubtedly true. However, the aesthetic biases of international criminal justice exacerbate the degree to which transitional justice's close associations with ICL blind it to certain forms of harm causation. Moreover, such presumptions may render situations altogether invisible within transitional justice and peacebuilding, obscuring the presence of systemic oppression and killing processes that manifest themselves non-spectacularly.

Human Rights

The field of human rights experiences a similar set of material and normative repercussions stemming from the aesthetic biases of international criminal justice to those of transitional justice and peacebuilding. As ICL has become increasingly prominent, human rights have undergone what Karen Engle describes as a "turn to criminal law."[61] Although she acknowledges that, for the most part, the linking of human

[59] See, for example, Pádraig McAuliffe, *Transformative Transitional Justice and the Malleability of Post-Conflict States* (Edward Elgar, 2017), 2–3.

[60] Ibid; see also, for example, Cahill-Ripley, "Foregrounding Socio-Economic Rights," 189 ("It is evident that violations of economic and social rights have been ignored or sidelined within transitional justice as they are not viewed as a legitimate concern for prosecutorial justice or are deemed too difficult an issue for criminal accountability."); Rosemary Nagy, "Transitional Justice as Global Project: Critical Reflections" (2008) 29 *Third World Quarterly* 275–289: 276. ("Although there is no single definition of transitional justice, I suggest that predominant views construct human rights violations fairly narrowly to the exclusion of structural and gender-based violence. There is a privileging of legal responses which are at times detrimentally abstracted from lived realities.").

[61] Engle, "Anti-Impunity", 1070. For an overview of how this turn occurred, see ibid., 1073–1079. For an analysis of the role that the emergence of the field of transitional justice played in the shift in human rights away from "naming and shaming" practices and toward an emphasis on accountability, see Paige Arthur, "How 'Transitions' Reshaped Human Rights: A Conceptual History of Transitional Justice" (2009) 31 *Human Rights Quarterly* 321–367. Human Rights Watch, for example, "considers international justice – accountability for genocide, war crimes, and crimes against humanity – to be an essential element of building respect for human rights." Human Rights Watch, "International Justice," www.hrw.org/topic/international-justice.

rights with criminal law, especially ICL, has been viewed as a positive development, Engle has deep concerns that such linkages may play into a broader entrenching of neoliberalism.[62] As with the concerns voiced by transitional justice scholars, Engle and other human rights scholars are wary that by linking human rights with criminal prosecutions, the visibility and recognition of socioeconomic and structural human rights violations will be impaired.[63]

Thus, as ICL is increasingly integrated with human rights, normatively and legally, the tendency for ICL's own blindnesses to background socioeconomic and other unspectacular, less obvious forms of mass harm causation are likely to bleed into similar preferences for spectacle and simplicity within human rights. The turn to criminal law also has arguably perpetuated the longstanding bias against economic, social, and cultural rights within human rights itself. Human rights lawyers and activists have worked against the division between civil/political and economic/social/cultural rights and the prioritization of the former over the latter, for decades.[64] Aesthetic factors play into this divide. For example, Wendy Hesford argues that what she terms the "human rights spectacle" shapes "discourses of vision and violation" within the internationalist human rights movement.[65] Other scholars, such as Hilary Charlesworth and Benjamin Authers, make similar arguments, alluding to the allure of the aesthetics of spectacle in arguing that the label "crisis," a term that is, like atrocity, definitionally capacious and ambiguous, gives "power" to human rights law.[66] Charlesworth and Authers argue that one effect of this preoccupation with crisis within human rights is that "the absence of crisis language can make some human rights violations appear quotidian, a part of everyday life and less urgent to redress than crisis-generated rights," while noting that "[e]conomic, social, and cultural rights, for example, are only infrequently depicted as the subjects of legal crisis."[67] A host of other scholars have made similar arguments concerning the prioritization of civil and political human rights over

[62] Engle, "Anti-Impunity," 123.
[63] Ibid., 1112–1127.
[64] For an overview of this schism in human rights, see Dustin N. Sharp, ed., *Justice and Economic Violence in Transition* (Springer, 2014), 38–40.
[65] Wendy S. Hesford, *Spectacular Rhetorics: Human Rights Visions, Recognitions, Feminisms* (Duke University Press, 2011), 7.
[66] Benjamin Authers and Hilary Charlesworth, "The Crisis and the Quotidian in International Human Rights Law" (2013) 44 *Netherlands Yearbook of International Law* 19–39.
[67] Ibid., 21.

economic, social, and cultural human rights.[68] Sonja Starr extends Charlesworth's general argument, framing international law itself as foundationally a discipline of crisis, to the realm of ICL, arguing that international law's broader focus on crisis helps obfuscate the criminality of economic atrocities such as extreme corruption.[69]

These permutations of aesthetic biases operating to influence ICL-adjacent fields such as human rights, while in some ways distinct from those I argue operate within ICL, are nonetheless, to some degree, interlinked with, and perpetuated by, the aesthetic biases of international criminal justice. The same preference for easily recognizable horrific spectacles embedded in shared understandings of atrocity and international crime also helps background questions of socioeconomic justice within transitional justice and peacebuilding, and economic, social, and cultural rights violations within human rights law. Indeed, Evelyne Schmid draws a direct connection between the failure to take economic, social, and cultural rights issues seriously within ICL, and their continued backgrounding in human rights law and discourse more generally.[70] Tine Destrooper, meanwhile, has found empirical support for the notion that, in Cambodia, the ECCC's near-exclusive focus on atrocities characterizable primarily as civil and political human rights violations has helped perpetuate the backgrounding of social, economic, and cultural rights in contemporary human rights discourses within the country.[71] This is especially concerning in light of the fact that so many of Cambodia's most pressing contemporary human rights shortcomings are tied up in socioeconomic issues such as land ownership and labor organizing

[68] See, for example, Shedrack C. Agbakwa, "A Path Least Taken: Economic and Social Rights and the Prospects of Conflict Prevention and Peacebuilding in Africa" (2003) 47 *Journal of African Law* 38–64; Arbour, "Economic and Social Justice"; Susan Marks, "Human Rights and Root Causes" (2011) 74 *The Modern Law Review* 57–78; Philip Alston, "Phantom Rights: The Systemic Marginalization of Economic and Social Rights" (August 4, 2016) *Open Democracy*, www.opendemocracy.net/openglobalrights/philip-alston/phantom-rights-systemic-marginalization-of-economic-and-social-rights.

[69] Sonja Starr, "Extraordinary Crimes at Ordinary Times: International Justice Beyond Crisis Situations" (2007) 101 *Northwestern University Law Review* 1257–1314, 1260–1271, citing Hilary Charlesworth, "International Law: A Discipline of Crisis" (2002) 65 *Modern Law Review* 377–392.

[70] Schmid, *Taking Economic, Social and Cultural Rights Seriously*, 77.

[71] Tine Destrooper, "Accountability for Human Rights Violations in Cambodia: Mapping the Indirect Effects of Transitional Justice Mechanisms" (2018) 19 *Asia-Pacific Journal on Human Rights and the Law* 113–139; see also Tine Destrooper, "Neglecting Social and Economic Rights Violations in Transitional Justice: Long-Term Effects on Accountability" (2018) 37 *Journal of Current Southeast Asian Affairs* 95–124.

rights. Larissa van den Herik, meanwhile, characterizes economic, social, and cultural rights issues as a "blind spot" within ICL.[72] Schmid, van den Herik, and others have identified areas of overlap between economic, social, and cultural rights violations and the commission of international crimes.[73] More recently, Barrie Sander highlights the importance of "revealing blind spots in anti-impunity frameworks," in order to "trigger changes within anti-impunity institutions" including encouraging the "thematic prosecutions in response to traditionally under-prosecuted social, cultural, environmental, and economic forms of violence."[74] Arguably, one of the main reasons why these areas of potential overlap remain underexplored in the practice of ICL is that they invariably involve aesthetically unfamiliar forms of atrocity violence, creating a troubling positive feedback loop between the notion that economic, social, and cultural rights are not "real" (i.e. legally enforceable) human rights and the myopic focus on spectacles within not only ICL, but also transitional justice, human rights, peacebuilding, and other fields related to addressing large-scale harms and/or rights violations.

Conclusion

This chapter has argued that the aesthetic biases of ICL have repercussions that go far beyond a general failure to prosecute a subset of relatively unfamiliar and unspectacular international crimes. Rather,

[72] Larissa van den Herik, "Economic, Social, and Cultural Rights: International Criminal Law's Blind Spot?," in Eibe H. Riedel, Gilles Giacca, and Christophe Golay, eds., *Economic, Social, and Cultural Rights in International Law: Contemporary Issues and Challenges* (Oxford University Press, 2014), 343–366.

[73] See ibid.; Schmid, *Taking Economic, Social and Cultural Rights Seriously*, 316. ICL scholars Carsten Stahn and Robert Cryer, along with van den Herik, agree with Schmid's general argument that international crimes may be committed through methods that also amount to economic, social, and cultural rights violations. See European Journal of International Law, "Book Discussion: Taking Economic, Social and Cultural Rights Seriously in International Criminal Law" (March 16, 2016) *EJIL Talk!: Blog of the European Journal of International Law*, www.ejiltalk.org/book-discussion-taking-economic-social-and-cultural-rights-seriously-in-international-criminal-law-a-response-to-cryer-stahn-and-van-den-herik.

[74] Barrie Sander, "The Anti-Impunity Mindset," in Morten Bergsmo, Mark Klamberg, Kjersti Lohne and Christopher B. Mahony, eds., *Power in International Criminal Justice* (Torkel Opsahl Academic EPublisher, 2020), 325-355, 354, citing Barrie Sander, "Addressing the Economic Dimensions of Mass Atrocities: International Criminal Law's Business or Blind Spot?" (June 8, 2015) *Justice in Conflict*, https://justiceinconflict.org/2015/06/08/addressing-the-economic-dimensions-of-mass-atrocities-international-criminal-laws-business-or-blind-spot.

the failure to acknowledge the gravity and/or baseline criminality of such atrocity processes undermines the retributive, utilitarian, and expressive functions of ICL, distorts historical memory, and contributes to the broader backgrounding of socioeconomic justice issues within discourses of transitional justice, peacebuilding, human rights, and global justice more broadly.

ICL's myopic focus on crimes conforming to the atrocity aesthetic undermines its retributive credentials by inserting morally irrelevant considerations into assessments of gravity and individual culpability. This myopic focus also creates a risk of undermining any deterrent effect ICL may have, now or in the future, by allowing powerful actors to commit atrocities with impunity so long as they utilize means that are banal, bureaucratic, or otherwise fail to aesthetically resemble paradigmatic atrocity crimes. The expressive functions of ICL are similarly impaired, as this myopic focus expresses the problematic notion that slow, relatively unspectacular processes of mass killing, oppression, and abuse – processes that may be seen as less offending of the sensibilities of constituencies in the Global North – are somehow more tolerable than more familiar, more spectacular ones that cause feelings of revulsion and horror.

Meanwhile, ICL's aesthetic biases similarly contribute to the backgrounding of socioeconomic and structural rights and justice issues within the realms of transitional justice, peacebuilding, and human rights, by subtly diverting attention and resources away from forms of harm causation failing to conform to the atrocity aesthetic. This diversion process helps perpetuate the notion that economic, social, and cultural human rights violations are necessarily less serious and less worthy of redress than violations of civil and political rights. Thus, in sum, a host of negative normative and material consequences flow from the aesthetic biases of international criminal justice, expanding well beyond the confines of ICL itself. Indeed, such collateral consequences are likely far more important to broader questions of global justice and the material conditions of life of much of the world's most vulnerable populations than any effect such biases have within the relatively narrow confines of the ICC, or other international criminal justice institutions.

7

Aesthetic Bias and Legal Legitimacy

An Interactional Assessment

The previous chapter explored some of the repercussions of the backgrounding of unspectacular, everyday atrocities within international criminal justice. This chapter, returning to interactional legal theory, considers the implications of such selectivity for the legal legitimacy of ICL itself. Such considerations are important for two reasons. First, the need to protect ICL's legal legitimacy is often presented as a reason why ICL accountability should not be pursued for nontraditional modalities of atrocity commission. Second, in a more general sense, such an examination helps us understand how unacknowledged biases affect the legal legitimacy of ICL. Through an analysis of how the aesthetic biases of ICL affect adherence to a selection of Fuller's criteria of legality, this chapter demonstrates that, from an interactional perspective of international lawmaking and legality, rather than protecting the legal legitimacy of ICL, the continuing myopic focus on aesthetically familiar forms of atrocity commission actually impairs ICL's legitimacy as a putative independent international legal regime.

Legality and Legitimacy: An Interactional Perspective

As discussed in Chapter 1, interactional legal theory represents a social constructivist account of lawmaking, legal legitimacy, and compliance at the international level developed by Jutta Brunnée and Stephen Toope.[1] According to interactional theory, the distinguishing feature of international *law* that differentiates it from "other types of social ordering is not form, but adherence to specific criteria of legality."[2] Thus, per interactionalism, "[w]hen norm creation meets these criteria and is matched with norm application that also satisfies the legality requirements," actors are "able to pursue their purposes and organize their interactions

1 See generally Jutta Brunnée and Stephen J. Toope, *Legitimacy and Legality in International Law: An Interactional Account* (Cambridge University Press, 2010).

2 Ibid., 6.

through law."[3] Conversely, regardless of whether norms and rules are formally labeled international "law" or not, if Fuller's legality criteria are not substantially satisfied in their creation or application, the result cannot be properly labeled "law," but is, instead, some other, nonlegal form of rulemaking or social ordering.

Within this context, Brunnée and Toope view legal legitimacy as something that, rather than being inherent in a particular form of rulemaking, instead fluctuates dynamically based on a variety of factors. Legal legitimacy may be strengthened and maintained through robust practices of legality, evolve through recalibration of shared understandings and their instantiation into the law, or erode through a lack of support. Moreover, according to interactionalism, legal legitimacy is not merely an ephemeral goal that is pursued for wholly abstract reasons, but when established, engenders habitual adherence, a phenomenon Fuller refers to as "fidelity."[4] As such, interactional legal theory seeks to peer into the inner workings of what Martti Koskenniemi refers to as the "mystery" of legal obligation.[5]

From an interactional legal theory perspective, shared understandings that ground social norms are the raw material from which law is created. Once a discernible, widely shared rule or norm is developed, in order for it to become interactional international law, Brunnée and Toope argue it must be instantiated into law in "substantial" accordance with Fuller's eight criteria of legality, which require that laws be:

1. general;
2. promulgated;
3. nonretroactive;
4. clear;
5. noncontradictory of one another;
6. possible to follow;
7. relatively constant (or stable); and
8. actually, to some extent, followed by those who are subject to them (i.e. there must exist a significant degree of "congruence" between the law and official action).[6]

[3] Ibid., 6–7.
[4] Ibid., 7.
[5] Martti Koskenniemi, "The Mystery of Legal Obligation" (2011) 3 *International Theory* 319–325.
[6] Jutta Brunnée and Stephen J. Toope, "Interactional International Law: An Introduction" (2011) 3 *International Theory* 307–318: 310. As mentioned previously, these criteria are drawn from Lon Fuller's work on the internal morality of law. Lon L. Fuller, *The Morality of Law* (Yale University Press, 1969).

Only once a potential international legal norm or rule is instantiated into law in substantial accordance with these criteria may such rule or norm be properly labeled international "law" according to interactional theory. The initial process of instantiation, however, is far from the end of the story according to interactional theory. Instead, interactionalism views international lawmaking as a dynamic, perpetual process, with relevant legal norms never becoming fully settled, but evolving dynamically and requiring constant support in the form of recognition, reaffirmation, and application, processes Brunnée and Toope describe as "practices of legality."[7] This chapter demonstrates how the tendency to background aesthetically unfamiliar forms of atrocity violence within ICL entails not only a host of negative collateral ramifications for historical memory, transitional justice, peacebuilding, and human rights, as discussed in the previous chapter, but, from an interactional perspective, undermines the specifically legal legitimacy of ICL from the perspective of interactional theory.

Aesthetic Biases and the Legal Legitimacy of International Criminal Law

Aesthetic biases affect lawmaking and legal legitimacy vis-à-vis ICL in various ways. As discussed in Chapter 2, ICL was conceived of largely as a project to repress, through the technique of criminal prosecution, instances of especially large-scale harm causation, often referred to as "atrocities." Since its founding, ICL has remained normatively linked to an aesthetics of horrific spectacle, to the point that it is commonly assumed that *all* atrocity harms will manifest themselves as such spectacles. This normative linkage has been reproduced over time and when seeking to identify potential international crimes, relevant actors are apt to seek out familiar forms of spectacular atrocity violence. In the process, forms of mass harm causation failing to conform to this dominant atrocity aesthetic model are less likely to be identified as potential international crimes or prioritized if recognized.

This cycle produces a host of legal legitimacy implications for ICL. First, because aesthetic considerations influence social learning processes, they affect the development of widely shared understandings concerning what the subject matter of ICL is, and what forms international crimes may take. Rather than developing a set of general, widely

[7] Brunnée and Toope, *Legitimacy and Legality*, 121–122, 56, 85, 216, 270, 347.

agreed-upon criteria concerning what the basic elements of international crimes are, shared understandings of atrocity and international crime have coalesced around a particular aesthetic model as a prima facie means of identification. This aesthetically grounded understanding of atrocity violence oversimplifies the complex causal realities of actual processes of mass killing, oppression, and abuse in the real world, and is not necessarily dictated by the doctrinal substance of ICL itself, as demonstrated in Chapters 4 and 5. In the remainder of this chapter, I demonstrate how, from an interactional legal theory perspective, aesthetic biases in the recognition of international crimes undermines the legal legitimacy of ICL by considering how such biases affect ICL's adherence to the legality criteria of generality, promulgation, nonretroactivity, clarity, stability, and congruence between the law and official action.

Generality

The legality criterion of generality requires that legal norms be "general," that is, "prohibiting, requiring, or permitting certain conduct."[8] This requirement is grounded in the notion that law must be evenhanded and cannot descend into hyper-specificity requiring constant explanation.[9] As discussed in Chapter 3, ICL's multiple layers of selectivity undermine its generality in practice. It is one thing to say that anyone who participates in an international crime could theoretically be prosecuted and, thus, ICL is general in its application.[10] However, practically speaking, there are broad swaths of the globe where impunity for atrocity participation is the rule, rather than the exception. This state of affairs impairs ICL's generality, as it remains abundantly clear that certain individuals enjoy functional immunity from the reach of ICL.[11]

[8] Brunnée and Toope, "Interactional International Law," 310.

[9] In this regard, Fuller observes that "[i]f we observe that the power of law normally expresses itself in the application of general rules, we can think of no better explanation of this than to say that the supreme legal power can hardly afford to post a subordinate at every street corner to tell people what to do." Fuller, *Morality of Law*, 147.

[10] Theoretically, even if an international crime occurs in a state that does not provide for domestic criminal liability for international crimes and which is not a state party to the ICC, such crime could be prosecuted through either the UN Security Council referring the situation to the ICC, or a domestic court invoking universal jurisdiction. However, in practice, these processes are exceptionally rare occurrences.

[11] For example, despite abundant evidence that the US military engaged in systematic torture in Guantanamo Bay and elsewhere in prosecuting the "War on Terror," there

ICL's generality is further impaired by the lack of clear rules concerning how prosecuting authorities will select which situations, suspects, and crimes to investigate and prosecute. Prosecutors at the ICC and other ICL institutions, despite being reliant on other authorities, states, and institutions to assist them in investigating crimes, arresting suspects, and funding their work, nonetheless wield a great deal of discretionary power. The bounds of such discretion are especially broad at the ICC, which is the first court with general jurisdiction over ICL, but the exercise of prosecutorial discretion has also engendered controversy at the ICTY, ICTR, and ECCC.[12] At the ECCC, for example, as discussed in Chapter 5, the question of how many suspects would be prosecuted has been a source of considerable controversy since the Court's inception.[13] In the Rwandan context, although the government pledged full accountability, this pledge created its own set of selectivity problems, as over 120,000 suspects languished in pretrial detention for years awaiting trial.[14] Meanwhile, the Rwandan Government blocked the ICTR from

has never been any serious suggestion that senior Bush administration officials will ever be held accountable for such atrocities. For an overview of the implications of the war on terror for the legal prohibition on torture under international law, see Brunnée and Toope, *Legitimacy and Legality*, 220–270. Similarly, despite abundant evidence that under the direction of Henry Kissinger, the US Nixon administration committed various crimes against humanity and war crimes by carpet-bombing Cambodia indiscriminately from 1965–1973, the pursuit of ICL charges against Kissinger or other relevant individuals has never been seriously contemplated. For an overview of the bombing, and an analysis of its extremely indiscriminate manner, see Taylor Owen and Ben Kiernan, "Bombs over Cambodia" (October 2006) *The Walrus* 62–69.

[12] For an overview of the limited personal jurisdiction regimes of the ICC, ICTY, SCSL, and ECCC, and resulting selectivity guidelines developed at each institution, see generally Randle C. DeFalco, "Cases 003 and 004 at the Khmer Rouge Tribunal: The Definition of 'Most Responsible' Individuals According to International Criminal Law" (2014) 8 *Genocide Studies and Prevention* 45–65: 46–55. At the ICC, the Office of the Prosecutor has issued periodic public guidelines outlining its internal policies in selecting situations to investigate. See ICC Office of the Prosecutor, "Policy Paper on Case Selection and Prioritisation," September 15, 2016, www.icc-cpi.int/itemsDocuments/20160915_OTP-Policy_Case-Selection_Eng.pdf.

[13] See Kirsten Ainley, "Transitional Justice in Cambodia: The Coincidence of Power and Principle," in Renée Jeffery and Hun Joon Kim, eds., *Transitional Justice in the Asia-Pacific* (Cambridge University Press, 2013), 125–156; David Scheffer, *All the Missing Souls: A Personal History of the War Crimes Tribunals* (Princeton University Press, 2012), 341–406; Ciorciari, John D. and Anne Heindel, *Hybrid Justice: The Extraordinary Chambers in the Courts of Cambodia* (University of Michigan Press, 2014), 14–40.

[14] Shannon E. Powers, "Rwanda's Gacaca Courts: Implications for International Criminal Law and Transitional Justice" (2011) 15 *American Society of International Law Insights*, www.asil.org/insights/volume/15/issue/17/rwanda%E2%80%99s-gacaca-courts-implications-international-criminal-law-and.

investigating atrocities allegedly committed by Rwandan Patriotic Front forces who were under the command of current Rwandan President Paul Kagame when they entered Rwanda and brought an end to the genocide in 1994.[15] The ICTY experienced similar controversies concerning the selection of what individuals would be investigated and prosecuted, especially in relation to the decision not to pursue investigations into potential war crimes committed during the NATO bombing campaign.[16]

Thus far, this discretion has not been bounded by any comprehensive set of legal principles, but has only been subjected to broad and highly subjective tests of good faith and comparative assessments of gravity.[17] The exercise of this discretion has been predictably fraught with political pressure, influence, and subjected to a great deal of critique. Thus, even within their sphere of influence, it remains impossible for international prosecutors to apply ICL in a truly evenhanded manner, as there are no guidelines they can follow which clearly delineate whom they should prosecute and in what order.

While the overall selectivity of ICL undermines its generality in practice, the aesthetic biases of ICL further impair its generality. These biases do so by inserting a set of unacknowledged aesthetic considerations into already contentious processes of ICL case selection, especially when it comes to assessments of comparative gravity. Thus, while doctrinally, ICL is theoretically applicable to all situations involving the commission of genocide, crimes against humanity, war crimes, and other recognized international crimes, in practice, aesthetically grounded assumptions limit ICL's perceived applicability to a subset of such crimes substantially conforming to the atrocity aesthetic. The net result is a form of aesthetic bias that exacerbates the general selectivity of ICL. It does so in a way that adds an arguably unnecessary layer of specificity, by narrowing ICL's perceived applicability to a subset of highly visible, easily recognizable manifestations of international crimes. In doing so, general prohibitions (e.g. do not participate in mass killing) impliedly become more specific (e.g. do not participate in mass killing through horrifically violent

[15] Larissa van den Herik, "International Criminal Law as a Spotlight and Black Holes as Constituents of Legacy" (2016) 110 *AJIL Unbound* 209–213.

[16] For an overview of this controversy, see Paolo Benvenuti, "The ICTY Prosecutor and the Review of the NATO Bombing Campaign against the Federal Republic of Yugoslavia" (2001) 12 *European Journal of International Law* 503–530.

[17] See Margaret M. deGuzman, *Shocking the Conscience of Humanity: Gravity and the Legitimacy of International Criminal Law* (Oxford University Press, 2020); Margaret M. deGuzman, "Gravity and the Legitimacy of the International Criminal Court" (2009) 32 *Fordham International Law Journal* 1400–1465.

means). It is this unstated layer of additional specificity that arguably impairs the legality criteria of generality in the practice of ICL.[18]

Promulgation

A second legality requirement affected by ICL's aesthetic selectivity is that of promulgation, which requires that laws be "accessible to the public, enabling actors to know what the law requires."[19] In comparison to domestic jurisdictions, processes of legal promulgation at the international level tend to be less straightforward, as there is no single authority presumed to be the lawgiver, but a horizontal authority structure made up of sovereign states and influenced by a host of other relevant actors. While international law is becoming increasingly codified in the form of various treaties, conventions, and the like, customary rules of international law, general principles of law, and so-called soft-law norms remain important.[20]

The doctrinal substance of ICL reflects these various sources of international law. While each of the various hybrid or international courts and tribunals, from Nuremberg to the ICC, has been created through treaties or other codified processes, much of the substance of ICL has been developed and refined incrementally over time through adjudication, and judges regularly look to customary law in determining the substance of ICL. Nevertheless, despite the fact that over time a wealth of published ICL treaties, statutes, opinions, judgments, and the like has in some ways promulgated the outlines of ICL as an independent legal regime, this body of legal sources has yet to fully coalesce into a coherent body of law.[21]

[18] For example, as discussed previously, aesthetic factors appear to have assisted the ECCC Co-Investigating Judges in placing a legal gloss on the decision to dismiss the case against Im Chaem by obscuring the seriousness of such allegations in relation to the crimes former S-21 prison commander Duch was convicted of in Case 001. See Randle C. DeFalco, "The Uncertain Relationship between International Criminal Law Accountability and the Rule of Law in Post-Atrocity States: Lessons from Cambodia" (2018) 42 *Fordham International Law Journal* 1–60: 34–58.

[19] Brunnée and Toope, "Interactional International Law," 310.

[20] On these and other acknowledged sources of international law, see Brunnée and Toope, *Legitimacy and Legality*, 47.

[21] For example, formulations of crimes against humanity vary across ICL institutions and have yet to be codified in any multilateral agreement aside from the Rome Statute, which does not necessarily reflect customary international law. Certain legal scholars have been advocating for a multilateral treaty codifying the customary law of crimes against humanity for decades. See, for example, M. Cherif Bassiouni, "Crimes against Humanity: The Need for a Specialized Convention" (1994) 31 *Columbia Journal of Transnational Law* 457–494. Indeed, efforts to codify ICL more generally predate World War II. See Jessica Lynn Corsi, "An Argument for Strict Legality in

To some degree, however, aesthetic biases concerning the forms international crimes may take, arguably undermine the degree to which ICL can be viewed as being properly promulgated. Such biases do so because they play a significant role in the development of shared understandings of what constitutes an international crime, yet because aesthetic assumptions in this regard remain unacknowledged, they themselves have not in any way been recognized, let alone inserted into the substance of ICL itself. This lack of acknowledgment demonstrates how, within the realm of ICL, a shared understanding (i.e. that international crimes will manifest themselves as horrific spectacles) appears to exist which is arguably relatively strong, stable, and widely agreed-on (albeit implicitly). Nonetheless, while this understanding arguably affects the functioning of ICL, as it concerns the very subject matter this body of international law is meant to address, it remains wholly extralegal in that it reflects an assumption not necessarily grounded in the doctrinal substance of ICL. As such, the current myopic focus within ICL practice on international crimes substantially conforming to the atrocity aesthetic arguably impairs the interactional legality criterion of promulgation by shaping practices of legality without undergoing any recognizable process of promulgation into the law itself.

Nonretroactivity

A third criterion of legality undermined by the aesthetic myopia of ICL in practice is that of nonretroactivity, which requires legal norms to be wholly "prospective, enabling [those subject to the law] to take the law into account in their decision making."[22] This requirement is grounded in the idea of fair notice, and tends to be strongly enforced in criminal law regimes, where the stakes are especially high for those subjected to the law, as their physical liberty is often at risk.[23] In the realm of ICL specifically, this requirement is expressed through the maxim *nullum crimen sine lege* ("no crime without law"), which operates as an affirmative defense.[24] In ICL jurisprudence, in order to survive a *nullum crimen*

International Criminal Law" (2018) 49 *Georgetown Journal of International Law* 1321–1381: 1378–1381.

22 Brunnée and Toope, "Interactional International Law," 310.

23 For a discussion of the notion of fair warning and its implications for ICL, see Darryl Robinson, "A Cosmopolitan Liberal Account of International Criminal Law" (2013) 26 *Leiden Journal of International Law* 127–153.

24 The phrase *nullum crimen sine lege* is used interchangeably with the term "legality" as a means of referring to the prohibition on retroactive criminalization within the realm of ICL. To avoid confusion, this book exclusively uses the terminology of *nullum crimen sine lege*. For

challenge, the specific law alleged as being applied retroactively must be found to have existed at the time of the alleged offense, in a form sufficiently clear and accessible to the specific accused.[25] In terms of existence of the legal provision being challenged, the law must simply be found to have existed at the time the accused is alleged to have violated it.[26] Determining the existence of the law requires turning to the traditional sources of international law, as laid out in Article 38 of the Statute of the International Court of Justice.[27] The law's applicability to the accused's actions must also have been foreseeable at the time of the alleged offense, and be promulgated in a form accessible to the accused in particular.[28]

While the current formulation of the *nullum crimen* principle provides protection against the retroactive application of ICL, the principle of nonretroactivity was a source of a great deal of controversy at early ICL institutions, such as the IMT and the International Military Tribunal for the Far East (IMTFE). These institutions were quite loose in their

an overview of the requirements of the doctrine of legality under ICL, see Antonio Cassese, *International Criminal Law*, 2nd ed. (Oxford University Press, 2008), 36–38; Beth Van Schaack, "The Principle of Legality in International Criminal Law" (2009) 103 *Proceedings of the Annual Meeting (American Society of International Law)* 101–104.

25 *Prosecutor* v. *Vasiljević, IT-98-32-T, November 29, 2002*, ICTY, para. 198 (stating that an offense must be defined "with sufficient clarity for it to have been foreseeable and accessible, taking into account the specificity of customary international law."); see also *Prosecutor* v. *Milutinović, IT-99-37-AR72, May 21, 2003*, ICTY, para. 21. The twin inquiries of specificity and accessibility are sometimes grouped as subsets of the requirement that the law was defined with sufficient "clarity" at the relevant time. See *Streletz, Kessler and Krenz* v. *Germany, Application Nos. 34044/96, 35532/97 and 44801/98, March 22, 2001*, ECtHR, para. 91 (stating that to assess the principle of *nullum crimen sine lege*, the proper assessment is "whether, at the time when they were committed, the [relevant] acts constituted offences defined with sufficient accessibility and foreseeability under international law."). Thus, the principle of *nullum crimen* under ICL protects not only the legality criteria of nonretroactivity, but also those of promulgation and clarity in requiring accessibility, clarity, and foreseeability.

26 See *Prosecutor* v. *Norman, SCSL-2004-14-AR72(E), May 31, 2004*, SCSL, para. 8 (holding that the question to be answered in response to a defense argument that the law did not exist is whether the relevant provision of ICL "was recognized as a crime entailing individual criminal responsibility under customary international law at the time of the acts alleged in the indictment against the accused.").

27 See generally *Streletz, Kessler and Krenz* v. *Germany, Application Nos. 34044/96, 35532/97 and 44801/98, March 22, 2001*, ECtHR; *Prosecutor* v. *Vasiljević, IT-98-32-T, November 29, 2002*, ICTY, para. 198.

28 See generally Jared L. Watkins and Randle C. DeFalco, "Joint Criminal Enterprise and the Jurisdiction of the Extraordinary Chambers in the Courts of Cambodia" (2010) 63 *Rutgers Law Review* 193–273: 202–204. For a judicial discussion of these factors, see *Prosecutor* v. *Milutinović, IT-99-37-AR72, May 21, 2003*, ICTY, paras. 40–42.

adherence to the principle against retroactive criminalization.[29] The IMT, for example, famously held that "the maxim *nullum crimen sine lege* is not a limitation of sovereignty, but is in general a principle of justice," going on to state:

> To assert that it is unjust to punish those who in defiance of treaties and assurances have attacked neighboring states without warning is obviously untrue, for in such circumstances the attacker must know that he is doing wrong, and so far from it being unjust to punish him, it would be unjust if his wrong were allowed to go unpunished. Occupying the positions they did in the Government of Germany, the defendants, or at least some of them must have known of the treaties signed by Germany, outlawing recourse to war for the settlement of international disputes; they must have known that they were acting in defiance of all international law when in complete deliberation they carried out their designs of invasion and aggression. On this view of the case alone, it would appear that the maxim [*nullum crimen sine lege*] has no application to the present facts.[30]

This passage encapsulates the IMT's relatively fast and loose approach to the principle of nonretroactivity. At the time of the IMT judgment, ICL was, of course, far from fully formed, and arguably new legal concepts, such as that of crimes against humanity, were constructed and applied by the IMT in one fell swoop.[31]

Over time, as the doctrinal substance of ICL has become increasingly codified and elucidated in a massive body of jurisprudence, criticisms of ICL grounded in *nullum crimen* arguments have become less common. The nonretroactivity principle, however, remains central to debates concerning whether ICL can and should be applied to novel forms of harm causation, especially those not conforming to the atrocity aesthetic, such as the creation or enforcement of famine conditions and other relatively slow or attritive processes of mass harm causation.[32] Such concerns tend to be

[29] For an overview of the legality principle at the IMT and other early ICL institutions see generally Beth Van Schaack, "Crimen Sine Lege: Judicial Lawmaking at the Intersection of Law and Morals" (2008) 97 *Georgetown Law Journal* 119–192: 125–133.

[30] International Military Tribunal, *Trial of the Major War Criminals before the International Military Tribunal, Nuremberg 14 November 1945 – 1 October 1946*, 42 vols. (International Military Tribunal, 1947), vol. 1, p. 219.

[31] See generally Van Schaack, "Crimen Sine Lege," 125–133.

[32] See, for example, J. Solomon Bashi, "Prosecuting Starvation in the Extraordinary Chambers in the Courts of Cambodia" (2011) 29 *Wisconsin International Law Journal* 34–69: 39–40 (expressing concern that the defense of *nullum crimen sine lege* could block certain attempts to prosecute Khmer Rouge officials for crimes predicated on their roles in causing famine). For critiques of these arguments, see Evelyne Schmid, *Taking Economic, Social and Cultural Rights Seriously in International Criminal Law*

deeply grounded in a rather formalistic approach, one that helps demonstrate how aesthetic biases influence how key actors conceptualize international crimes. Many advocates call for codification of new, issue-specific ICL provisions directly criminalizing certain types of harm causing behavior such as corrupt practices or famine causation, as opposed to the application of existing provisions to new methods of commission.[33]

Thus, certain interpretations of the principle of *nullum crimen sine lege* might be viewed as a legal barrier to the prosecution of international crimes committed through novel, unspectacular, and/or unfamiliar means. In this way, arguments against the application of ICL to novel forms of mass harm causation are at times, couched in the protection of the legal legitimacy of ICL by preventing the retroactive criminalization of novel forms of harm causation. The argument that ICL may run afoul of the *nullum crimen* principle, while generally true in relation to certain vague areas of the law, has, however, no special applicability in relation to discussions concerning extant ICL's applicability to novel factual scenarios. This is because the argument that declining to pursue ICL accountability for novel forms of harm causation safeguards the legality of ICL confuses potential *means* of committing crimes with criminal sanctions themselves. The principle of nonretroactivity operates solely in relation to the *law* and not in relation to whether there exist analogous examples of successful ICL prosecutions based on substantially the same *method* of commission.[34]

While it is true that nonretroactivity is a foundational principle of both Fuller's internal morality of law and basic liberal criminal law theory, it is a principle grounded in concept of fair warning and not

(Cambridge University Press, 2015), 71–73; Randle C. DeFalco, "Conceptualizing Famine as a Subject of International Criminal Justice: Toward a Modality-Based Approach" (2017) 38 *University of Pennsylvania Journal of International Law* 1113–1187: 1178.

[33] For examples of such calls for codification, see David Marcus, "Famine Crimes in International Law" (2003) 97 *American Journal of International Law* 245–281 (advocating for the creation of new famine-specific crimes that criminalize famine causing ("faminogenic") behavior); Ndiva Kofele-Kale, "The Right to a Corruption-Free Society as an Individual and Collective Human Right: Elevating Official Corruption to a Crime under International Law" (2000) 34 *International Lawyer* 149–178 (advocating for new corruption-specific international crimes). The proposed international crime of "ecocide" is another example of this push to create new issue-specific international crimes.

[34] For an illustration of this distinction in practice at the international level, see, for example, *Prosecutor* v. *Milutinović, IT-99-37-AR72, May 21, 2003*, ICTY, para. 38 (discussing the requirements of specificity and foreseeability at the international level and concluding that the doctrine of legality prevents a court from "creating new law or interpreting existing law beyond the reasonable limits of acceptable clarification.").

a ban on the application of the law to new facts.[35] From an interactional legal theory perspective, while ICL's previously fast and loose (in)fidelity to the principle of nonretroactivity may have impaired ICL's legality, the pursuit of ICL accountability beyond harms conforming to the atrocity aesthetic would not impair the legality of ICL in any general sense. That is, so long as the actual legal provisions used were well established when the relevant events took place and the accused had fair warning that ICL prohibited their actions. Indeed, to hold that the *nullum crimen* principle forbids prosecuting individuals for well-established international crimes, utilizing well-established modes of liability, albeit through novel forms of commission, would further undermine the legality criteria of generality, by rendering ICL overly specific in a manner far beyond its doctrinal substance.

Thus, in sum, while at first glance it may seem that ICL's recurrent failure to be applied to novel forms of commission that are banal, bureaucratic, or otherwise unspectacular in nature protects the perceived legitimacy of international criminal justice, from an interactional perspective, one can argue the inverse is actually the case. The failure to prosecute novel means of committing existing crimes is not a product of scrupulous adherence to the principle of nonretroactivity. All such failure does is to perpetuate an aesthetic bias that remains independent from ICL's doctrinal substance, and to lend credence to the unsubstantiated assumption that ICL simply cannot be applied to novel factual scenarios. While arguably, this is presently the case, it bears noting, however, that this conclusion may be in the process of being eroded. This is because, while the provisions of ICL themselves that may apply to a situation involving the commission of atrocities through unfamiliar means are by now, relatively clear and quite accessible, as such modalities of harm causation continue to be systemically backgrounded within ICL practice, it may become less foreseeable that these forms of mass killing and abuse actually may violate ICL. Indeed, one could argue that all that is required to transform the atrocity aesthetic from a source of bias to an aspect of ICL itself, is to promulgate this limitation into the substance of ICL.

35 At the international level, the concept of fair warning is manifested in the twin requirements of "accessibility" and "foreseeability" at the heart of the doctrine of *nullum crimen sine lege*. See Watkins and DeFalco, "Joint Criminal Enterprise," 200–203.

Clarity

The third criterion of legality implicated by the aesthetic biases of ICL is that of clarity, which requires that the law be clear enough for those subject to it to be able to "understand what is permitted, prohibited, or required by law."[36] While, in a general sense, as demonstrated in Chapter 3, ICL continues to suffer from a lack of clarity in certain key areas, from a bird's eye perspective, when limited to genocide, crimes against humanity, and war crimes, along with its core specialized modes of liability, ICL can be seen as broadly criminalizing large-scale harm causation, particularly in relation to abuses committed against civilians and other noncombatants. The increasingly large body of ICL jurisprudence and its codification in international legal instruments such as the Genocide Convention, Geneva Conventions, various ad hoc tribunal treaties and statutes, and the Rome Statute, have, to some degree advanced the clarity of ICL.[37]

While it may be true that the doctrinal substance of ICL has generally become progressively clearer since Nuremberg, from an interactional legal theory perspective, such adherence appears to be both overstated and undermined in practice through the myopic focus on aesthetically familiar means of commission. The various zones of ambiguity that persist within ICL render the boundaries of ICL liability hazy and unclear. Moreover, the insertion of aesthetic considerations into processes of recognizing potential international crimes impairs the clarity of ICL. It does so by rendering it more difficult to assess how the law might actually be applied to a given situation, as it remains unclear why and how the selection of specific harm causation methods by perpetrator groups legally matter. Thus, when we assess, for instance, Donald Trump's potential ICL liability for knowingly worsening the suffering and death caused by the coronavirus pandemic, the law seems unclear. On the one hand, Trump, along with other key members of his administration, took affirmative steps that they knew would encourage the spread

36 Brunnée and Toope, "Interactional International Law," 310.

37 Indeed, ICL is now at times referred to as a mature or near-mature legal system. For an example of such a sentiment, see, for example, Van Schaack, "Crimen Sine Lege," 189 ("Although codification will never be complete, the rate of change is slowing significantly. As a maturing system of law, most of the next phase of the evolution of ICL will happen at the outer edges of doctrine, where the implications of new ideas are perhaps less dramatic. As a result, there will be less and less space for judges to build upon the ICL edifice."). It bears noting that the significant differences in the substance of the various efforts to codify ICL may also, to some extent, undermine its clarity.

of the virus and sicken and kill an untold number of Americans, numbering at the very least well into the thousands. The affirmative steps he took with such knowledge were varied, but key steps among them were those of blocking the postal service from distributing masks nationwide, and intentionally downplaying the seriousness of the virus to the American public in various statements he knew were untrue at the time.[38] Yet, Trump's actions may not seem "criminal" in nature, in an intuitive sense, and it is unclear how ICL might apply. There is a strong possibility that assumptions, partially grounded in aesthetic biases, concerning the noncriminality of "policy" decisions or "mere" misleading statements, or a discomfort in assigning criminal liability for the causation of additional excess deaths during a pandemic, may color how relevant legal provisions are interpreted. Thus, by being grounded in a myopic focus on acts that appear intuitively criminal, the atrocity aesthetic bias of ICL clouds our ability to assess how the law might apply to less obvious examples, thereby undermining the clarity of ICL.

Stability

A fourth criterion of legality undermined by ICL's aesthetic selectivity is that of stability, which requires that the demands of the law "must remain relatively constant" over time.[39] While aesthetic biases do not directly impair the stability of ICL, they do, to a degree, affect the stability of the law in a broad sense by contributing to a certain, unstable reactivity in the development and application of ICL. Questions of when, where, and to whom ICL will be applied have always been contingent primarily on political factors and power dynamics, rather than "neutral" legal assessments, despite efforts by ICL actors to separate "law" and "politics."[40]

[38] See, for example, Josh Dawsey, Felicia Sonmez, and Paul Kane. "Trump Acknowledges He Intentionally Downplayed Deadly Coronavirus, Says Effort was to Reduce Panic" (September 9, 2020) *Washington Post*,www.washingtonpost.com/politics/trump-reaction-woodward-interview-coronavirus/2020/09/09/fc21e67e-f2ca-11ea-b796-2dd09962649c_story.html; Tony Romm, Jacob Bogage, and Lena H. Sun, "Newly Revealed USPS Documents Show an Agency Struggling to Manage Trump, Amazon and the Pandemic" (September 18, 2020) *Washington Post*,www.washingtonpost.com/us-policy/2020/09/17/usps-trump-coronavirus-amazon-foia; David J. Scheffer, "Is It a Crime to Mishandle a Public Health Response?" (April 22, 2020) *Council on Foreign Relations*, www.cfr.org/article/it-crime-mishandle-public-health-response.

[39] Brunnée and Toope, "Interactional International Law," 310.

[40] See, for example, Tor Krever, "Unveiling (and Veiling) Politics in International Criminal Trials," in Christine Schwöbel, ed., *Critical Approaches to International Criminal Law: An Introduction* (Routledge, 2014), 117–137.

Even in its doctrinal development, ICL has proceeded reactively, as the law has been shaped to address the specificities of a succession of high-profile atrocity events deemed most important and most deserving of criminal sanction. From the Holocaust, to the Rwandan Genocide and a host of more recent atrocities, ICL has strained to calibrate itself to the perceived needs at hand. Of course, commitments to legality and the "rule of law" have constrained the degree to which ICL could be adapted to suit each instance deemed worthy of its application.[41] Within the spaces where ICL is made malleable to at least some degree, discretion is conferred on relevant actors, allowing aesthetic biases to creep in.

These biases are especially powerful in affecting the development of the critically important consensus-building involved in the social selection of instances wherein impunity for those participating in atrocity crimes may be tolerable, versus when accountability is viewed as an absolute imperative. For example, the horrific stories and imagery that emerged from Rwanda and the Balkans during the 1990s clearly played a major role in creating the necessary political climate for the ICTR and ICTY to be created. The same can be said of the graphic images of child soldiers and victims missing limbs in Sierra Leone, and the social furor around the issue of "blood diamonds" and their role in fueling the Sierra Leonean civil war in relation to the creation of the SCSL. The film *The Killing Fields* and the graphic evidence of atrocity on display in Cambodia at sites such as S-21 and *Choeung Ek*, meanwhile, clearly helped fuel the creation of the ECCC. At the ICC, indictments of Omar al-Bashir and others in Sudan followed global protests concerning the Darfuri genocide, and the search for Joseph Kony intensified after the "Kony 2012" campaign went viral on social media. More recently, the spectacles of violence being committed against Rohingya populations in Myanmar

[41] For examples of arguments framing the ICC, as a "pillar" of the global rule of law, see, for example, Australian Magna Carta Institute, "The ICC and Challenges to International Rule of Law," December 12, 2016, www.ruleoflaw.org.au/the-icc-challenges-international-rule-of-law ("[t]he International Criminal Court (ICC) is a pillar of the international rule of law"); Sang-Hyun Song, "The Role of the International Criminal Court in Ending Impunity and Establishing the Rule of Law" (2012) *UN Chronicle*, www.un.org/en/chronicle/article/role-international-criminal-court-ending-impunity-and-establishing-rule-law. Of course, some view ICL as generally failing to adhere to the rule of law. For a more skeptical view assessing ICL's internal commitment to core rule of law principles, see Markus D. Dubber, "Common Civility: The Culture of Alegality in International Criminal Law" (2011) 24 *Leiden Journal of International Law* 923–936: 923 (arguing that, from an external perspective, ICL appears to operate more so as an "as an ethical – administrative enterprise rather than a legal one").

have arguably played a key role in the recent surge in calls for accountability and proceedings being initiated at both the ICC and the International Court of Justice.

This contingency unsettles the stability of ICL because it makes the law's evolution unpredictable and subject to extralegal considerations that themselves, remain unacknowledged. New norms may emerge rather rapidly when social opprobrium to a shocking practice or event is properly leveraged, as has been the case concerning the relatively rapid development of ICL in relation to its applicability to the use of child soldiers, and sexual and gender-based violence.[42] Alternatively, the law's applicability may be left unsettled and unclear in relation to forms of mass harm causation that fail to gain broader social visibility and deemed importance, thereby undermining the stability of ICL.

Congruence between the Law and Official Action

Finally, and perhaps most importantly, the application of ICL consistently fails to exhibit substantial "congruence between legal norms and the actions of officials operating under the law."[43] This general failure is arguably exacerbated by ICL's aesthetic biases. The "congruence" requirement is a bedrock component of most rule of law formulations, and is essential to Fuller's understanding of reciprocity between lawgivers and those governed by laws.[44] This notion of reciprocity, as interpreted by Brunnée and Toope, "means that law givers must be able to expect that citizens will 'accept as law and generally observe' the promulgated body of rules."[45] This notion of reciprocity does not require that the law be perfectly followed at all times, but rather that officials empowered by or tasked with applying the law, along with those subject to it, generally behave as if they are constrained by the law's requirements.

For example, in the realm of criminal law, the principle of congruence does not require that laws criminalizing murder deter all would-be murderers perfectly, but rather that officials who shape the law or are

[42] See Dianne Luping, "Investigation and Prosecution of Sexual and Gender-Based Crimes before the International Criminal Court" (2009) 17 *American University Journal of Gender, Social Policy and the Law* 431–496; Mark A. Drumbl, *Reimagining Child Soldiers in International Law and Policy* (Oxford University Press, 2012). This is not to suggest that either of these issues do not merit being treated as international crimes.

[43] Brunnée and Toope, "Interactional International Law," 310.

[44] See generally Ibid., 311; Fuller, *Morality of Law*.

[45] Brunnée and Toope, "Interactional International Law," 311, quoting Lon L. Fuller, "Human Interaction and the Law" (1969) 14 *American Journal of Jurisprudence* 1–36: 24.

empowered by it (police, lawyers, judges, etc.) behave as if they are also bound by the law and that those subject to the law generally refrain from intentionally killing others, or at least expecting to do so without incurring criminal sanction. Thus, according to a Fullerian view of legality, a private citizen who commits a murder, yet somehow evades capture, does not necessarily undermine the legality of the criminal law regime that he has managed to evade. Conversely, if a police officer commits a murder and behaves as if the law regarding murder simply does not apply to him, that he is somehow exempt because of his official position in relation to the criminal law, this would have the effect of impairing the legality of the prohibition on murder.[46] So too would a situation wherein an officer randomly chooses what murders he will investigate, or a court haphazardly prosecutes certain murder cases, while dismissing others. As Brunnée and Toope note, this notion of reciprocity maps well onto the horizontal authority structure of international law, wherein legal obligations flow primarily from reciprocal agreement among sovereign states.[47]

As a general matter, ICL struggles mightily with enforcement and selectivity problems. Thus, in a quite general sense, legal practices within the realm of ICL arguably fail regularly to substantially conform to the legality criterion of congruence. Despite ICL's explicitly universalist aspirations and theoretically worldwide applicability, in a practical sense, ICL remains narrowly applicable to select pockets of time and space within which the proper combination of jurisdictional competencies (subject matter, temporal, personal, etc.), political will, and sufficient resources to actually pursue accountability converge. These pockets have proven consistently to exist only in exceptional circumstances, with impunity for atrocity crimes stubbornly remaining the general rule to which accountability continues to represent a rare exception. Aside from exposing ICL to all manner of allegations of enforcement bias, its extremely selective application also exposes it to accusations of illegitimacy as a putative legal regime. This tension, between ICL's explicitly universalist aspirations, and its decidedly particular, highly circumscribed application, one could argue is, in itself, fatal to any claim ICL may make to legal legitimacy from an interactional perspective.

[46] This also explains the pernicious rule of law ramifications of the recent spate of police killings of unarmed Black men in the United States that have not been treated as homicides despite manifestly violating relevant criminal laws concerning culpable forms of killing.

[47] Brunnée and Toope, "Interactional International Law," 311.

Of course, various political and social forces shape the selective application of ICL. Each of these forces that narrow ICL's applicability from its potential to as-practiced reality arguably undermines ICL's adherence to the criteria of congruence to some degree. Hence, the degree to which aesthetic biases affect international crime recognition also represents one such normative force, one that operates to shape and constrain where and how ICL is applied by influencing shared understandings of what kinds of situations ICL may address. The resultant subtle narrowing of the focus of ICL in practice may be framed as contributing to the more general lack of congruence between ICL's supposed universality and its actual particularized application.

Conclusion

The effect of the aesthetic biases of international criminal justice on the legal legitimacy of ICL represents a novel case study for interactional legal theory, involving a situation wherein a set of unacknowledged, aesthetic (and hence, nonlegal) considerations shape shared understandings of the subject matter of an international legal regime, yet have not been explicitly recognized, let alone instantiated into the substance of the regime, in this case ICL itself. This situation highlights the importance, and dangers, of nonlinear social learning processes in the development of shared understandings and law at the international level. Through social interaction, ICL actors appear to have embraced and reproduced a widely shared understanding concerning the nature of atrocity violence steeped in an aesthetics of horrific spectacle. This understanding – of international crimes as "atrocity" crimes, and atrocities as horrific spectacles of violence – appears to have seeped into the vocabulary and rhetoric of ICL, without itself being recognized, let alone instantiated into the substance of the law. By treating the production of horrific spectacles as an intrinsic characteristic of all instances of the commission of genocide, crimes against humanity, and/or war crimes, this aesthetic bias is treated not as influencing the selective recognition of international crimes and application of ICL, but rather as flowing from the doctrinal substance of ICL itself, creating a self-affirming feedback loop. This feedback loop, over time, has made it seem obvious that it is in the very nature of international crimes to announce themselves spectacularly, despite the absence of any serious legal or criminological substantiation of this assumed intrinsic spectacularity.

While this insight helps confirm the central role that social interaction and nonlinear, nonpurposive social learning processes play in shaping the normative contours of ICL, it also highlights the potentially troubling legal ramifications of such processes. Shared understandings that are developed through such processes, though they may be more inclusive in terms of the number of actors involved, may shape deeper social understandings of relevant legal rules, and influence relevant legal practices, without ever actually being themselves acknowledged, let alone instantiated into the substance of a relevant international legal regime. This dynamic is exemplified by the grounding of shared understandings of international crime in a particular aesthetic model of atrocities as familiar horrific spectacles.

This chapter has argued that, from an interactional legal theory perspective, the failure of ICL to engage with novel, aesthetically unfamiliar forms of mass harm causation, rather than safeguarding the legality of ICL, actually works to impair ICL's legal legitimacy by undermining various criteria of legality. This argument is not meant to be interpreted as denying ICL any claim to legal legitimacy, as Fuller, as well as Brunnée and Toope view legality as a phenomenon that exists in degrees along a spectrum, rather than a binary assessment.[48] This chapter has instead argued that, when one assesses the legality of ICL as a system from the perspective of interactional legal theory, ICL's various forms of selectivity and zones of ambiguity stand out as major impediments to ICL achieving a high degree of legal legitimacy. ICL's lack of generality, clarity, and congruence between the law and official action are often dismissed as enforcement problems, rather than issues affecting the very legitimacy and legality of ICL itself. From the practice-based perspective of interactional legal theory,

[48] Fuller asserts that, contrary to others, he is of the view that law can "half exist" or exist in degrees of imperfection. He notes that, for all other fields of inquiry, the "normal expectation would be of some performance falling between zero and a theoretical perfection" but that somehow law is thought of in different terms, finding it "truly astounding to what an extent there runs through modern legal thinking in legal philosophy the assumption that law is like a piece of inert matter – it is there or not there." Fuller, *Morality of Law*, 122–123. Fuller makes a parallel argument in relation to entire legal regimes, stating that "both rules of law and legal systems can and do half exist. This condition results when the purposive effort necessary to bring them into full being has been, as it were, only half successful." Ibid., 122. Fuller leaves "uncertain the precise point at which a legal system can be said to have come into being. I see no reason to pretend to see black and white where reality presents itself in shades of gray. Certainly, there is little point in imposing on the situation some definitional fiat, by saying, for example, that we shall consider law to exist only where there are courts." Ibid., 131. See also Brunnée and Toope, *Legitimacy and Legality*, 22–23.

however, these shortcomings cannot be so neatly separated from assessments of ICL's legal legitimacy. Because the selectivity and ambiguity of ICL significantly impair at least three of Fuller's criteria of legality (generality, clarity, and congruence), ICL cannot be viewed as a mature or perfected system of international law from an interactional perspective. While I am hesitant to conclude that ICL currently exists as a minimally legitimate system of international law, a final determination of this essentially subjective assessment is not essential at this juncture. Rather, this chapter has simply demonstrated that the aesthetic selectivity of ICL, and the politics of visibility flowing therefrom, operate to exacerbate the legality shortcomings associated with ICL's more general selectivity and doctrinal ambiguity by operating as an additional, unacknowledged layer of selectivity of application, thereby further obscuring ICL's normative aims and doctrinal boundaries, and further undermining its claims to legal legitimacy.

8

Conclusion

Addressing the Many Forms of Atrocity Crimes

Reporting on the 1963 trial of Adolph Eichmann in Jerusalem, Hannah Arendt famously coined the phrase "the banality of evil" to describe what she perceived to be Eichmann's fundamental ordinariness as a human being, despite having been a central figure in the Holocaust.[1] This observation, which has been repeated to the point of cliché, was quite controversial when Arendt first made it, despite the fact that she nonetheless supported the prosecution (and execution) of Eichmann. Central to Arendt's conclusion regarding the potential banality of individuals who participate in extreme forms of atrocity violence was the fact that Eichmann himself was, in Arendt's view, a wholly unremarkable career bureaucrat, an average person in so many ways, and yet a willing, key participant in the Holocaust.

Much has been written on Arendt's views on the potential banality of those who participate in mass atrocity.[2] There is also an extensive literature theorizing how and why individuals choose to participate in horrific acts of atrocity violence.[3] Significantly less attention has been paid to the potential banality of the forms atrocities themselves may take. While it has become widely accepted that perpetrators of mass violence may not necessarily all be zealous true believers of hateful ideologies, but may participate in atrocities for a variety of motivations, such as social or economic advancement, this book has argued that insufficient attention has been paid to the possibility that atrocities themselves may, in certain circumstances, themselves be banal in nature. In the words of Mark Drumbl, rather than

[1] Hannah Arendt, *Eichmann in Jerusalem: A Report on the Banality of Evil* (Penguin Classics, 2006).

[2] See, for example, David Luban, "Hannah Arendt as a Theorist of International Criminal Law" (2011) 11 *International Criminal Law Review* 621–641.

[3] See, for example, Alette Smeulers, Maartje Weerdesteijn, and Barbora Holá, eds., *Perpetrators of International Crimes: Theories, Methods, and Evidence* (Oxford University Press, 2019).

"unitary" phenomena, mass atrocities are "metastasized – and often messy – agglomerations of many local tragedies, small-scale decisions, and parochial horrors."[4]

This book represents an effort to explore the potential banality and "messiness" of atrocity as they relate to the relationship between how processes of mass killing, abuse, and oppression actually unfold, as compared to how such processes are imagined to unfold in the dominant social and legal imaginaries that have shaped the trajectory of ICL thus far. Along these lines, rather than focusing on the characteristics of the actors involved in the commission of such atrocities, be they victims, perpetrators, victim-perpetrators, bystanders, or others, I have focused on the messiness, and, at times, banality, of the processes through which genocide, crimes against humanity, and war crimes may themselves be committed. I have done so through the lens of Jutta Brunnée and Stephen Toope's interactional theory of international lawmaking and legality. Utilizing this social constructivist theory of international norm development and lawmaking, I have argued that the norm development processes involved in the social construction of widely shared understandings of atrocity as the primary subject matter of ICL have been deeply influenced by aesthetic considerations, producing a politics of recognition grounded in an aesthetics of horrific spectacle. I have argued that forms of mass harm causation committed through means that are slow, banal, and/or bureaucratic in nature, and, hence, tend not to conform to this dominant "atrocity aesthetic" model, despite at times involving the commission of well-established international crimes, tend to be viewed as collateral causes or consequences of international crimes, rather than potential means of committing them.

The assumption that all international crimes will necessarily involve the production of horrific spectacles of violence is both inaccurate and problematic. It is inaccurate because it places limits on how we perceive and interpret ICL that is itself not grounded in law, but rather reflects

[4] Mark A. Drumbl, "The Curious Criminality of Mass Atrocity: Diverse Actors, Multiple Truths, and Plural Responses," in Elies van Sliedregt and Sergey Vasiliev, eds., *Pluralism in International Criminal Law* (Oxford University Press, 2014), 68–103: 101. Drumbl, for example, elsewhere questions the sharp line that is commonly assumed to separate victims and perpetrators of atrocity crimes, and the ability to arrive at a singular, objective "truth" of events as complex and messy as those involving the commission of atrocity crimes. See Mark A. Drumbl, "Victims Who Victimise" (2016) 4 *London Review of International Law* 217–246. Drumbl refers specifically to the collapse of the perpetrator/victim divide embodied in the figure of the Kapo, who were concentration camp prisoners appointed by the Nazis to fulfill various functions within the camps themselves. Ibid., 220.

unstated and untested assumptions concerning the intrinsic qualities of international crime commission. It is problematic because, in limiting our perception of what forms genocide, crimes against humanity, and war crimes might take, it helps to obscure the wrongfulness and potential criminal culpability of those who knowingly participate in causing mass suffering and/or death through means that are slow, banal, or otherwise unspectacular in nature. I find this blind spot to be especially troubling given that it caters to power and privilege, by allowing certain, especially powerful actors, to abuse and/or kill, even on a potentially massive scale, with impunity simply by utilizing processes of harm causation that are less shocking and revulsive to external audiences, even if actual victims experience them quite violently.

The aesthetic biases of ICL entail implications that go far beyond questions of who and what crimes are formally investigated and prosecuted at international courts and tribunals. Chapter 6 explored some of these implications by considering how the aestheticized selectivity of recognizing and assessing the gravity of potential international crimes warps historical narratives, influences how and where (and how well-funded) transitional justice and peacebuilding efforts are pursued, and contributes to the broader backgrounding of structural justice, especially socioeconomic and distributive justice issues. Chapter 7 considered the legitimacy implications for ICL as a putative legal regime from the perspective of interactional legal theory, arguing that the tendency to background or ignore altogether a subset of unspectacular international crimes impairs ICL's adherence to certain key criteria of legality, thereby undermining its legal legitimacy. These implications, while significant, are far from the only ramifications flowing from ICL's myopic focus on spectacular harms. The atrocity aesthetic also raises questions concerning ICL's determinacy, relationships to power and sovereignty, recognition of suffering and relative valuation of human lives, and whose interests the international criminal justice project does (and should) serve.

As a body of criminal law, ICL is often presumed, or at least expected, to be relatively clearer and more determinative than other areas of international law, given its implications for those investigated for and accused of international crimes. As demonstrated in Chapter 3, ICL may not be quite so clear and unambiguous as it is often presumed to be. Despite the proliferation of codified ICL and related jurisprudence since the 1990s, areas of ambiguity and lack of clarity persist. While this book looked at how these key zones of ambiguity have facilitated the unquestioned reproduction of aestheticized assumptions concerning the forms international crimes may take, helping ground shared understandings of international crime in the atrocity aesthetic model described in Chapter 2, one could also situate ICL within the longstanding indeterminacy debate concerning international law more generally.[5] Specifically, as proponents of the indeterminacy thesis generally frame international law as little more than an edifice, surface, or language for power and politics to operate on or through, one can see how aesthetic politics of the recognition of international crimes could lend credence to the indeterminacy thesis' application to ICL, an area of international law that has, thus far, not been a central area of analysis within determinacy debates.

In terms of power and sovereignty, given that only especially powerful actors, especially those wielding state authority, tend to have the ability to abuse and kill en masse through either spectacularly violence or unspectacular, banal-seeming processes of harm causation, what does the myopic focus on the former tell us about the relationships between ICL, sovereignty, and power? ICL has long been framed as operating to limit sovereignty and power, by criminalizing certain harmful behaviors even when committed by state actors against their own subjects. If one accepts the central thesis of this book – that international criminal justice overwhelmingly focuses its energies on a subset of highly visible, spectacularly violent crimes at the expense of other forms of atrocity and international crime commission – it seems to follow that one could make the argument that ICL actually operates to protect sovereign states, by criminalizing forms of violence that they do not have a monopoly on (i.e. direct, interpersonal violence), while tolerating equally (and at times, more so) destructive forms of violence that, for the most part, are only available to states and other especially powerful, highly organized entities. This would seem to undermine claims that ICL limits traditional state sovereignty.

Relatedly, in terms of how human lives are valued, the aesthetic biases of ICL raise significant questions concerning Michel Foucault's notion of biopolitics and Achille Mbembe's related notion of necropolitics. These concepts help us to see how life may be facilitated or, in the words of Foucault "disallowed" to the point of death, through biopolitical processes, which Foucault describes as the "administration of bodies and calculated management of life."[6] Foucault views this "management" of lives as a central facet of the modern technologies and forms of

[5] See generally, for example, Martti Koskenniemi, *From Apology to Utopia: The Structure of International Legal Argument* (Cambridge University Press, 2005).

[6] Michel Foucault, *The History of Sexuality Volume I: An Introduction*, trans. Robert Hurley (Random House, 1978), 140–145.

governance.[7] When viewed in this way, the international criminal justice project itself can be framed as a "necropolitical" enterprise, one that acknowledges and seeks to discipline, through the technique of criminal prosecutions, a subset of "contemporary forms of subjugation of life to the power of death."[8] Framed thusly, ICL might be viewed as a necropolitical enterprise, one which regulates certain forms of biopower, while ignoring others, and in the process valuing certain lives and experiences over others by selectively expressing collective "outrage" through criminalization.[9]

Finally, and again relatedly, the aesthetic biases of ICL raise troubling questions concerning what the unstated, perhaps even unrecognized purpose(s) of international criminal justice may be, and whose interests it serves. Given the malleability of the concept of gravity and the central role of elite technocrats drawn from the Global North in interpreting it,[10] one can imagine how biases of constituencies in the Global North can color how ICL is deployed and who it serves as its primary audience and imagined constituency.[11] If atrocities are understood as real-world tragedies, one can frame the pursuit of international criminal justice as a vehicle for pursuing the relief of catharsis, not solely (or even arguably, primarily) for the victims and societies directly affected, but also (and perhaps primarily) for those of us in the Global North who experience the discomfort and negative emotions associated with witnessing atrocities from afar, and perhaps even feel tangentially responsible in some small way. This dynamic may implicate ICL in the reproduction of tropes of the "savage" Global South and the "civilized"

[7] Ibid., 138.

[8] Achille Mbembe, "Necropolitics" (2003) 15 *Public Culture* 11–40: 39.

[9] On the expression of collective "outrage" within the context of ICL and the operation of the ICC specifically, see Nikolas M. Rajkovic, "What Is a 'Grave' International Crime? The Rome Statute, Durkheim and the Sociology of Ruling Outrages" (2020) 16 *Loyola University Chicago International Law Review* 65–86.

[10] See ibid., 68 (describing "an elite class of international criminal lawyers as managers of the gravity threshold").

[11] On the question of constituencies and voice within ICL, see generally Immi Tallgren, "Who are 'We' in International Criminal Law? On Critics and Membership," in Christine Schwöbel-Patel, ed., *Critical Approaches to International Criminal Law: An Introduction* (Routledge, 2014), 71–95; Immi Tallgren, "The Voice of the International: Who Is Speaking?" (2015) 13 *Journal of International Criminal Justice* 135–155; Frédéric Mégret, "In Whose Name? The ICC and the Search for Constituency," in Carsten Stahn, Sarah Kendall, and Christian M. de Vos, eds., *Contested Justice: The Politics and Practice of International Criminal Court Interventions* (Cambridge University Press, 2015), 23–45.

Global North.[12] Moreover, this dynamic exposes ICL to allegations that not only does this body of law focus myopically on violence in the Global South, but also that what forms of such violence are recognized is dictated by what constituencies in the Global North view *as* violence. This raises the troubling possibility that one of the primary functions ICL actually serves is to operate as a salve, to remedy the discomfort we in the Global North feel when exposed to horrific forms of violence in the Global South, while allowing us to continue to ignore the root causes of such violence, along with other less discomforting forms of mass harm causation (and our relation thereto), even if potentially criminal in nature.

Ultimately, along with these and other potential problematic ramifications, the fact that aesthetic biases in favor of spectacle and simplicity influence how we understand international crime commission challenges certain foundational assumptions underlying the project of international criminal justice itself. While scholars such as Arendt and Drumbl, along with many others, have identified the limitations of legal processes – especially criminal prosecutions – in accounting for the scale and complexities presented by mass atrocities, I have argued that their general insight, that atrocity crimes can, and do, depart radically from ordinary criminality, is equally applicable to the *means* through which such crimes are committed. Thus, somewhat paradoxically, I have argued that one of the reasons international crimes are properly viewed as being so extraordinary in relation to "ordinary" domestic crimes is that they may be committed through processes that may, at first glance, appear decidedly ordinary, even banal in nature.

Consequently, just as the figure of the perpetrator of atrocity has been complicated by Arendt and others, and the suitability of ICL as a response to the moral, legal, and ethical "murkiness" of atrocity situations has been complicated by Drumbl[13] and others, I believe there exists a pressing need to critically reexamine and complicate social and legal understandings concerning the forms international crimes may take and the means through which they may be committed. That is, there exists a need to step back and reconsider the very notion of what an atrocity is with a more critical eye, while remaining open to the possibility that international crimes may manifest themselves in ways that may depart radically from

[12] See Makau Mutua, "Savages, Victims, and Saviors: The Metaphor of Human Rights" (2001) 42 *Harvard International Law Journal* 201–245.

[13] Drumbl, "Victims Who Victimise," 220.

our intuitive understandings of them. In doing so, we may discover that, just as Eichmann's seemingly ordinary, highly bureaucratic nature defied stereotypical notions of mass murderers, so too may the oft-bureaucratic nature of certain processes of mass killing and abuse themselves defy stereotypes of atrocities as intuitively recognizable, highly visible spectacles of horrific violence and evildoing. While doing so may somewhat undermine what Christine Schwöbel-Patel refers to as the "comfort" of ICL,[14] by complicating its seeming moral clarity, and may exacerbate the degree to which certain atrocity crimes, in the words of Arendt, "explode the limits of the law,"[15] it is only by acknowledging the true complex and often messy nature of atrocity situations, and grappling with the implications of such complexity and messiness, that we may be able to formulate more suitable and effective methods of responding to atrocity violence, both within and beyond the confines of ICL.

[14] On ICL as a source of comfort, see Christine Schwöbel, "The Comfort of International Criminal Law" (2013) 24 *Law and Critique* 169–191.

[15] Hannah Arendt and Karl Jaspers, *Hannah Arendt/Karl Jaspers: Correspondence, 1926–1969*, Lotte Kohler and Hans Saner, eds., trans. Robert Kimber and Rita Kimber (Harcourt Brace Jovanovich, 1992), 54.

BIBLIOGRAPHY

Books

Arendt, Hannah, *The Human Condition*, 2nd ed. (University of Chicago Press, 1958).

Eichmann in Jerusalem: A Report on the Banality of Evil (Penguin Classics, 2006).

Arendt, Hannah and Karl Jaspers, *Hannah Arendt/Karl Jaspers: Correspondence, 1926–1969*, Lotte Kohler and Hans Saner (eds.), trans. Robert Kimber and Rita Kimber (Harcourt Brace Jovanovich, 1992).

Aristotle, *The Poetic of Aristotle*, trans. Henry James Pye (John Stockton Piccadilly, 1788).

Aristotle, George Whalley, John Baxter, and Patrick Atherton, *Aristotle's Poetics* (McGill-Queen's University Press, 1997).

Bass, Gary, *Stay the Hand of Vengeance: The Politics of War Crimes Tribunals* (Princeton University Press, 2014).

Becker, Elizabeth, *When the War Was Over: Cambodia and the Khmer Rouge Revolution* (Public Affairs, 1998).

Brunnée, Jutta and Stephen J. Toope, *Legitimacy and Legality in International Law: An Interactional Account* (Cambridge University Press, 2010).

Butler, Judith, *Frames of War: When Is Life Grievable?* (Verso, 2009).

Bodies that Matter: On the Discursive Limits of "Sex" (Routledge, 2011).

Card, Claudia, *The Atrocity Paradigm: A Theory of Evil* (Oxford University Press, 2002).

Casper, Monica J. and Lisa Jean Moore, *Missing Bodies: The Politics of Visibility* (New York University Press, 2009).

Cassese, Antonio, *International Criminal Law*, 2nd ed. (Oxford University Press, 2008).

Chandler, David, *Voices from S-21: Terror and History in Pol Pot's Secret Prison* (University of California Press, 1999).

A History of Cambodia, 4th ed. (Westview Press, 2008).

Chhang, Youk, Beth Van Schaack, and Daryn Reicherter (eds.), *Cambodia's Hidden Scars: Trauma Psychology in the Wake of the Khmer Rouge* (Documentation Center of Cambodia, 2011).

Ciorciari, John D. and Anne Heindel, *Hybrid Justice: The Extraordinary Chambers in the Courts of Cambodia* (University of Michigan Press, 2014).

Clark, Phil, *Distant Justice: The Impact of the International Criminal Court on African Politics* (Cambridge University Press, 2018).

Conquest, Robert, *The Harvest of Sorrow: Soviet Collectivization and the Terror-Famine* (Oxford University Press, 1987).

Cryer, Robert, *Prosecuting International Crimes: Selectivity and the International Criminal Law Regime* (Cambridge University Press, 2005).

De Waal, Alex, *Mass Starvation: The History and Future of Famine* (Policy Press, 2017).

Debord, Guy, *The Society of the Spectacle*, trans. Donald Nicholson-Smith (Zone Books, 1994).

deGuzman, Margaret M., *Shocking the Conscience of Humanity: Gravity and the Legitimacy of International Criminal Law* (Oxford University Press, 2020).

Devereux, Stephen (ed.), *The New Famines: Why Famines Persist in an Era of Globalization* (Routledge, 2006).

Douglas, Lawrence, *The Memory of Judgment: Making Law and History in the Trials of the Holocaust* (Yale University Press, 2001).

Drumbl, Mark A., *Atrocity, Punishment and International Law* (Cambridge University Press, 2007).

Reimagining Child Soldiers in International Law and Policy (Oxford University Press, 2012).

Dy, Khamboly, *A History of Democratic Kampuchea 1975–1979* (Documentation Center of Cambodia, 2007).

Ea, Meng-Try, *The Chain of Terror: The Khmer Rouge Southwest Zone Security System* (Documentation Center of Cambodia, 2005).

Fein, Helen, *Accounting for Genocide: Victims–and Survivors–of the Holocaust* (Free Press, 1979).

Fisher, Kirsten, *Moral Accountability and International Criminal Law: Holding Agents of Atrocity Accountable to the World* (Routledge, 2013).

Foucault, Michel, *The History of Sexuality Volume I: An Introduction*, trans. Robert Hurley (Pantheon Books, 1978).

Discipline and Punish: The Birth of the Prison, 2nd ed., trans. Alan Sheridan (Vintage Books, 1995).

Friedrich, Ernst, *War against War*, 3rd ed., trans. Douglas Kellner (Spokesman Press, 2014).

Fuller, Lon L., *The Morality of Law* (Yale University Press, 1969).

Hartouni, Valerie, *Visualizing Atrocity: Arendt, Evil, and the Optics of Thoughtlessness* (New York University Press, 2012).

Hesford, Wendy S., *Spectacular Rhetorics: Human Rights Visions, Recognitions, Feminisms* (Duke University Press, 2011).

Hinton, Alexander Laban, *Why Did They Kill? Cambodia in the Shadow of Genocide* (University of California Press, 2005).

Hinton, Alexander Laban, Thomas La Pointe, and Douglas Irvin-Erickson (eds.), *Hidden Genocides: Power, Knowledge, Memory* (Rutgers University Press, 2014).

Howard-Hassmann, Rhoda E., *State Food Crimes* (Cambridge University Press, 2016).

Ibrahim, Azeem, *The Rohingyas: Inside Myanmar's Hidden Genocide* (Hurst, 2016).

International Military Tribunal, *Trial of the Major War Criminals before the International Military Tribunal, Nuremberg 14 November 1945 – 1 October 1946*, 42 vols. (International Military Tribunal, 1947).

Jain, Neha, *Perpetrators and Accessories in International Criminal Law: Individual Modes of Responsibility for Collective Crimes* (Hart, 2014).

Jinks, Rebecca, *Representing Genocide: The Holocaust as Paradigm?* (Bloomsbury, 2016).

Kant, Immanuel, *Critique of Judgment*, trans. J. H. Bernard (Hafner, 1951).

Kendi, Ibram X., *Stamped from the Beginning: The Definitive History of Racist Ideas in America* (Nation Books, 2016).

Kiernan, Ben, *Blood and Soil: A World History of Genocide and Extermination from Sparta to Darfur* (Yale University Press, 2007).

The Pol Pot Regime: Race, Power, and Genocide in Cambodia under the Khmer Rouge, 1975–79, 3rd ed. (Yale University Press, 2008).

Koskenniemi, Martti, *From Apology to Utopia: The Structure of International Legal Argument* (Cambridge University Press, 2005).

May, Larry, *Crimes against Humanity: A Normative Account* (Cambridge University Press, 2005).

McAuliffe, Pádraig, *Transformative Transitional Justice and the Malleability of Post-Conflict States* (Edward Elgar, 2017).

Minow, Martha, *Between Vengeance and Forgiveness: Facing History after Genocide and Mass Violence* (Beacon Press, 1998).

Moeller, Susan, *Compassion Fatigue: How the Media Sell Disease, Famine, War and Death* (Routledge, 1999).

Nixon, Rob, *Slow Violence and the Environmentalism of the Poor* (Harvard University Press, 2011).

Nuttall, Anthony D., *Why Does Tragedy Give Pleasure?* (Oxford University Press, 2001).

Ó Gráda, Cormac, *Famine: A Short History* (Princeton University Press, 2009).

O'Keefe, Roger, *International Criminal Law* (Oxford University Press, 2015).

Osiel, Mark, *Making Sense of Mass Atrocity* (Cambridge University Press, 2009).

Ramji, Jaya and Beth van Schaack (eds.), *Bringing the Khmer Rouge to Justice: Prosecuting Mass Violence before the Cambodian Courts* (Mellen Press, 2005).

Robinson, Darryl, *Justice in Extreme Cases: Criminal Law Theory Meets International Criminal Law* (Cambridge University Press, 2020).

Rodenhäuser, Tilman, *Organizing Rebellion: Non-State Armed Groups under International Humanitarian Law, Human Rights Law, and International Criminal Law* (Oxford University Press, 2018).

Sadat, Leila Nadya (ed.), *Forging a Convention for Crimes against Humanity* (Cambridge University Press, 2011)

Sands, Phillipe, *East West Street: On the Origins of "Genocide" and "Crimes against Humanity"* (Knopf, 2016).

Scheffer, David, *All the Missing Souls: A Personal History of the War Crimes Tribunals* (Princeton University Press, 2012).

Schlund-Vials, Cathy J., *War, Genocide, and Justice: Cambodian American Memory Work* (University of Minnesota Press, 2012).

Schmid, Evelyne, *Taking Economic, Social and Cultural Rights Seriously in International Criminal Law* (Cambridge University Press, 2015).

Schwöbel-Patel, Christine, *Marketing Global Justice: The Political Economy of International Criminal Law* (Cambridge University Press, 2021).

Sharp, Dustin N. (ed.), *Justice and Economic Violence in Transition* (Springer, 2014).

Sikkink, Kathryn, *The Justice Cascade: How Human Rights Prosecutions are Changing World Politics* (Norton, 2011).

Sirik, Savina, *Everyday Experiences of Genocide Survivors in Landscapes of Violence in Cambodia* (Documentation Center of Cambodia, 2016).

Smeulers, Alette and Fred Grünfeld, *International Crimes and Other Gross Human Rights Violations* (Brill Nijhoff, 2011).

Smeulers, Alette, Maartje Weerdesteijn, and Barbora Holá (eds.), *Perpetrators of International Crimes: Theories, Methods, and Evidence* (Oxford University Press, 2019).

Sontag, Susan, *Regarding the Pain of Others* (Farrar, Straus and Giroux, 2003).

Stauffer, Jill, *Ethical Loneliness: The Injustice of Not Being Heard* (Columbia University Press, 2015).

Teitel, Ruti G., *Transitional Justice* (Oxford University Press, 2000).

TIME, *Time 100 Photographs: The Most Influential Images of All Time* (Time Inc. Books, 2016).

Totten, Samuel, *Genocide by Attrition: The Nuba Mountains of Sudan* (Transaction, 2012).

Tyner, James A., *The Politics of Lists: Bureaucracy and Genocide under the Khmer Rouge* (West Virginia Press, 2018).

Wenger, Étienne, *Communities of Practice: Learning, Meaning, and Identity* (Cambridge University Press, 1998).

White, Mark D. (ed.), *Retributivism: Essays on Theory and Policy* (Oxford University Press, 2011).

Journal Articles, Book Sections, and Periodicals

Agbakwa, Shedrack C., "A Path Least Taken: Economic and Social Rights and the Prospects of Conflict Prevention and Peacebuilding in Africa" (2003) 47 *Journal of African Law* 38–64.

Ainley, Kirsten, "Excesses of Responsibility: The Limits of Law and the Possibilities of Politics" (2011) 25 *Ethics and International Affairs* 407–431.

"Transitional Justice in Cambodia: The Coincidence of Power and Principle," in Renée Jeffery and Hun Joon Kim (eds.), *Transitional Justice in the Asia-Pacific* (Cambridge University Press, 2013), 125–156.

Aisenberg, Eugene et al., "Defining Violence," in Todd I. Herrenkohl et al. (eds.), *Violence in Context: Current Evidence on Risk, Protection, and Prevention* (Oxford University Press, 2010), 13–22.

Akhavan, Payam, "Beyond Impunity: Can International Criminal Justice Prevent Future Atrocities?" (2001) 95 *American Journal of International Law* 7–31.

Aloyo, Eamon, "Improving Global Accountability: The ICC and Nonviolent Crimes against Humanity" (2013) 2 *Global Constitutionalism* 498–530.

Amann, Diane Marie, "Message as Medium in Sierra Leone" (2001) 7 *ILSA Journal of International and Comparative Law* 237–245.

"Group Mentality, Expressivism, and Genocide" (2002) 2 *International Criminal Law Review* 93–143.

Ambos, Kai, "The ICC and Common Purpose: What Contribution Is Required under Article 25 (3)(d)?," in Carsten Stahn (ed.), *The Law and Practice of the International Criminal Court* (Oxford University Press, 2015), 592–607.

"The Overall Function of International Criminal Law: Striking the Right Balance between the Rechtsgut and the Harm Principles: A Second Contribution Toward a Consistent Theory of ICL" (2015) 9 *Criminal Law and Philosophy* 301–329.

Anderson, Elizabeth S. and Richard H. Pildes, "Expressive Theories of Law: A General Restatement" (2000) 148 *University of Pennsylvania Law Review* 1503–1575.

Anderson, Kjell, "Colonialism and Cold Genocide: The Case of West Papua" (2015) 9 *Genocide Studies and Prevention* 9–25.

Arbour, Louise, "Economic and Social Justice for Societies in Transition" (2007) 40 *New York University Journal of International Law and Politics* 1–27.

Armillei, Riccardo, Nikki Marczak, and Panayiotis Diamadis, "Forgotten and Concealed: The Emblematic Cases of the Assyrian and Romani Genocides" (2016) 10 *Genocide Studies and Prevention* 98–120.

Arthur, Paige, "How 'Transitions' Reshaped Human Rights: A Conceptual History of Transitional Justice" (2009) 31 *Human Rights Quarterly* 321–367.

Authers, Benjamin and Hilary Charlesworth, "The Crisis and the Quotidian in International Human Rights Law" (2013) 44 *Netherlands Yearbook of International Law* 19–39.

Bantekas, Ilias, "Corruption as an International Crime and Crime against Humanity: An Outline of Supplementary Criminal Justice Policies" (2006) 4 *Journal of International Criminal Justice* 466–484.

Bashi, J. Solomon, "Prosecuting Starvation in the Extraordinary Chambers in the Courts of Cambodia" (2011) 29 *Wisconsin International Law Journal* 34–69.

Bassiouni, M. Cherif, "Crimes against Humanity: The Need for a Specialized Convention" (1994) 31 *Columbia Journal of Transnational Law* 457–494.

Basso, Andrew, "Toward a Theory of Displacement Atrocities: The Cherokee Trail of Tears, the Herero Genocide, and the Pontic Greek Genocide" (2016) 10 *Genocide Studies and Prevention* 5–29.

Benvenuti, Paolo, "The ICTY Prosecutor and the Review of the NATO Bombing Campaign against the Federal Republic of Yugoslavia" (2001) 12 *European Journal of International Law* 503–530.

Bloom, Ben, "Criminalizing Kleptocracy? The ICC as a Viable Tool in the Fight against Grand Corruption" (2014) 29 *American University International Law Review* 627–671.

Bloxham, Donald and A. Dirk Moses, "Editors' Introduction: Changing Themes in the Study of Genocide," in Donald Bloxham and A. Dirk Moses (eds.), *The Oxford Handbook of Genocide Studies* (Oxford University Press, 2010), 1–16.

Boas, Gideon, "What Is International Criminal Justice?," in Gideon Boas, Michael P. Scharf, and William Schabas (eds.), *International Criminal Justice: Legitimacy and Coherence* (Edward Elgar, 2012), 1–24.

Bohrer, Ziv, "International Criminal Law's Millennium of Forgotten History" (2016) 34 *Law and History Review* 393–485.

"British Atrocities in India," February 1809, *Irish Magazine and Monthly Asylum for Neglected Biography* 52–54.

Brunnée, Jutta and Stephen J. Toope, "Interactional International Law: An Introduction" (2011) 3 *International Theory* 307–318.

"The Rule of Law in an Agnostic World: The Prohibition on the Use of Force and Humanitarian Exceptions," in Wouter Werner, Marieke de Hoon, and Alexis Galan (eds.), *Koskenniemi and his Critics* (Cambridge University Press, 2015), 137–166.

Burleson, Shelley and Alberto Giordano, "Spatiality of the Stages of Genocide: The Armenian Case" (2016) 10 *Genocide Studies and Prevention* 39–58.

Cahill-Ripley, Amanda, "Foregrounding Socio-Economic Rights in Transitional Justice: Realising Justice for Violations of Economic and Social Rights" (2014) 32 *Netherlands Quarterly of Human Rights* 183–213.

Carranza, Ruben, "Plunder and Pain: Should Transitional Justice Engage with Corruption and Economic Crimes?" (2008) 2 *International Journal of Transitional Justice* 310–330.

Cassese, Antonio, "The Nexus Requirement for War Crimes" (2012) 10 *Journal of International Criminal Justice* 1395–1417.

Charlesworth, Hilary, "International Law: A Discipline of Crisis" (2002) 65 *Modern Law Review* 377–392.

Chattaraman, Veena et al., "Form 'Defines' Function: Neural Connectivity between Aesthetic Perception and Product Purchase Decisions in an fMRI Study" (2016) 15 *Journal of Consumer Behaviour* 335–347.

Chatterjee, Anjan, "Prospects for a Cognitive Neuroscience of Visual Aesthetics" (2004) 4 *Bulletin of Psychology and the Arts* 55–59.

"Neuroaesthetics: A Coming of Age Story" (2010) 23 *Journal of Cognitive Neuroscience* 53–62.

Chehtman, Alejandro, "Contemporary Approaches to the Philosophy of Crimes against Humanity" (2014) 14 *International Criminal Law Review* 813–835.

"A Theory of International Crimes: Conceptual and Normative Issues," in Kevin Jon Heller, Frédéric Mégret, Sarah MH Nouwen, Jens David Ohlin, and Darryl Robinson (eds.), *The Oxford Handbook of International Criminal Law* (Oxford University Press, 2020), 317–340.

Clark, Roger S., "Weapons of Mass Destruction," in Dinah L. Shelton (ed.), *Encyclopedia of Genocide and Crimes against Humanity* (Macmillan Reference, 2005), 1151–1155.

Clarke, Kamari Maxine, "'We Ask for Justice You Give Us Law': The Rule of Law, Economic Markets and the Reconfiguration of Victimhood," in Christian De Vos, Sara Kendall, and Carsten Stahn (eds.), *Contested Justice: The Politics and Practice of International Criminal Court Interventions* (Cambridge University Press, 2015), 272–301.

Conley-Zilkic, Bridget and Alex de Waal, "Setting the Agenda for Evidence-Based Research on Ending Mass Atrocities" (2014) 16 *Journal of Genocide Research* 55–76.

Corsi, Jessica Lynn, "An Argument for Strict Legality in International Criminal Law" (2018) 49 *Georgetown Journal of International Law* 1321–1381.

Cronin-Furman, Kate, "Managing Expectations: International Criminal Trials and the Prospects for Deterrence of Mass Atrocity" (2013) 7 *International Journal of Transitional Justice* 434–454.

Damaška, Mirjan, "What Is the Point of International Criminal Justice?" (2008) 83 *Chicago-Kent Law Review* 329–365.

Danner, Allison Marston and Jenny S. Martinez, "Guilty Associations: Joint Criminal Enterprise, Command Responsibility, and the Development of International Criminal Law" (2005) 93 *California Law Review* 75–169.

de Waal, Alex, "A Re-assessment of Entitlement Theory in the Light of the Recent Famines in Africa" (1990) 21 *Development and Change* 469–490.

"Reflections on the Difficulties of Defining Darfur's Crisis as Genocide" (2007) 20 *Harvard Human Rights Journal* 25–33.

"On Famine Crimes and Tragedies" (2008) 372 *The Lancet* 1538–1539.

DeFalco, Randle C., "The Right to Food in Gaza: Israel's Obligations under International Law" (2009) 35 *Rutgers Law Record* 11–22.

"Accounting for Famine at the Extraordinary Chambers in the Courts of Cambodia: The Crimes against Humanity of Extermination, Inhumane Acts and Persecution" (2011) 5 *International Journal of Transitional Justice* 142–158.

"Contextualizing Actus Reus under Article 25 (3)(d) of the ICC Statute: Thresholds of Contribution" (2013) 11 *Journal of International Criminal Justice* 715–735.

"Cases 003 and 004 at the Khmer Rouge Tribunal: The Definition of 'Most Responsible' Individuals According to International Criminal Law" (2014) 8 *Genocide Studies and Prevention* 45–65.

"Conceptualizing Famine as a Subject of International Criminal Justice: Toward a Modality-Based Approach" (2017) 38 *University of Pennsylvania Journal of International Law* 1113–1187.

"The Uncertain Relationship between International Criminal Law Accountability and the Rule of Law in Post-Atrocity States: Lessons from Cambodia" (2018) 42 *Fordham International Law Journal* 1–60.

DeFalco, Randle C. and Frédéric Mégret, "The Invisibility of Race at the ICC: Lessons from the US Criminal Justice System" (2019) 7 *London Review of International Law* 55–87.

deGuzman, Margaret M., "Gravity and the Legitimacy of the International Criminal Court" (2009) 32 *Fordham International Law Journal* 1400–1465.

"Choosing to Prosecute: Expressive Selection at the International Criminal Court" (2012) 33 *Michigan Journal of International Law* 265–320.

"Harsh Justice for International Crimes?" (2014) 39 *Yale Journal of International Law* 1–35.

Destrooper, Tine, "Accountability for Human Rights Violations in Cambodia: Mapping the Indirect Effects of Transitional Justice Mechanisms" (2018) 19 *Asia-Pacific Journal on Human Rights and the Law* 113–139.

"Neglecting Social and Economic Rights Violations in Transitional Justice: Long-Term Effects on Accountability" (2018) 37 *Journal of Current Southeast Asian Affairs* 95–124.

Doherty, Joseph W. and Richard H. Steinberg, "Punishment and Policy in International Criminal Sentencing: An Empirical Study" (2016) 110 *American Journal of International Law* 49–81.

Drumbl, Mark A., "Collective Violence and Individual Punishment: The Criminality of Mass Atrocity" (2004) 99 *Northwestern University Law Review* 539–610.

"Accountability for Property Crimes and Environmental War Crimes: Prosecution, Litigation, and Development," April 4, 2009, *International Center for Transitional Justice.*

"Accountability for System Criminality" (2010) 8 *Santa Clara Journal of International Law* 373–382.

"The Curious Criminality of Mass Atrocity: Diverse Actors, Multiple Truths, and Plural Responses," in Elies van Sliedregt and Sergey Vasiliev (eds.), *Pluralism in International Criminal Law* (Oxford University Press, 2014), 68–103.

"Victims Who Victimise" (2016) 4 *London Review of International Law* 217–246.

Eberechi, Ifeonu, "'Rounding Up the Usual Suspects': Exclusion, Selectivity, and Impunity in the Enforcement of International Criminal Justice and the African Union's Emerging Resistance" (2011) 4 *African Journal of Legal Studies* 51–84.

Eboe-Osuji, Chile, "Kleptocracy: A Desired Subject of International Criminal Law that Is in Dire Need of Prosecution by Universal Jurisdiction," in Evelyn A. Ankumah and Edward K. Kwakwa (eds.), *African Perspectives on International Criminal Justice* (Africa Legal Aid, 2005), 121–132.

"Crimes against Humanity: Directing Attacks against a Civilian Population" (2006) 2 *African Journal of Legal Studies* 118–129.

Edkins, Jenny, "The Criminalization of Mass Starvations: From Natural Disaster to Crime against Humanity," in Stephen Devereux (ed.), *The New Famines: Why Famines Persist in an Era of Globalization* (Routledge, 2007), 50–65.

Engle, Karen, "Anti-Impunity and the Turn to Criminal Law in Human Rights" (2015) 100 *Cornell Law Review* 1069–1128.

Fein, Helen, "Explanations of Genocide" (1990) 38 *Current Sociology* 32–50.

"Genocide by Attrition 1939–1993: The Warsaw Ghetto, Cambodia, and Sudan: Links between Human Rights, Health, and Mass Death" (1997) 2 *Health and Human Rights* 10–45.

Feinberg, Joel, "The Expressive Function of Punishment" (1965) 49 *The Monist* 397–423.

Field, Nigel P., Sophear Muong, and Vannavuth Sochanvimean, "Parental Styles in the Intergenerational Transmission of Trauma Stemming from the Khmer Rouge Regime in Cambodia" (2013) 83 *American Journal of Orthopsychiatry* 483–494.

Finzsch, Norbert, "War, Violence, and Population: Making the Body Count" (2011) 13 *Journal of Genocide Research* 187–189 (book review).

Ford, Stuart, "Is the Failure to Respond Appropriately to a Natural Disaster a Crime against Humanity? The Responsibility to Protect and Individual

Criminal Responsibility in the Aftermath of Cyclone Nargis" (2010) 38 *Denver Journal of International Law and Policy* 227–276.

"A Hierarchy of the Goals of International Criminal Courts" (2018) 27 *Minnesota Journal of International Law* 179–244.

"Can the International Criminal Court Succeed? An Analysis of the Empirical Evidence of Violence Prevention" (2020) 43 *Loyola of Los Angeles International and Comparative Law Review* 101–123.

Fuller, Lon L., "Human Interaction and the Law" (1969) 14 *American Journal of Jurisprudence* 1–36.

Galtung, Johan, "Violence, Peace and Peace Research" (1969) 6 *Journal of Peace Research* 167–191.

Greenwalt, Alexander K. A., "The Pluralism of International Criminal Law" (2011) 86 *Indiana Law Journal* 1063–1130.

Groome, Dermot, "The Church Abuse Scandal: Were Crimes against Humanity Committed?" (2011) 11 *Chicago Journal of International Law* 439–503.

Halliwell, Stephen, "Katharsis," in Donald M. Borchert (ed.), *The Encyclopedia of Philosophy*, 2nd ed. (Macmillan Reference, 2006), 44.

Hamilton, Rebecca, "User-Generated Evidence" (2018) 57 *Columbia Journal of Transnational Law* 1–61.

Haque, Adil Ahmad, "Group Violence and Group Vengeance: Toward a Retributivist Theory of International Criminal Law" (2005) 9 *Buffalo Criminal Law Review* 273–328.

Harms, Brian C., "Holding Public Officials Accountable in the International Realm: A New Multi-Layered Strategy to Combat Corruption" (2000) 33 *Cornell International Law Journal* 159–209.

Heath, J. Benton, "Disasters, Relief, and Neglect: The Duty to Accept Humanitarian Assistance and the Work of the International Law Commission" (2010) 43 *New York University Journal of International Law and Policy* 419–477.

Heller, Kevin Jon, "What Is an International Crime? (A Revisionist History)" (2017) 58 *Harvard International Law Journal* 353–420.

Heuveline, Patrick, "The Boundaries of Genocide: Quantifying the Uncertainty of the Death Toll during the Pol Pot Regime in Cambodia (1975–79)" (2015) 69 *Population Studies* 201–218.

Hola, Barbora and Hollie Nyseth Brehm, "Punishing Genocide: A Comparative Empirical Analysis of Sentencing Laws and Practices at the International Criminal Tribunal for Rwanda (ICTR), Rwandan Domestic Courts, and Gacaca Courts" (2016) 10 *Genocide Studies and Prevention* 59–80.

Howard-Hassmann, Rhoda E., "Mugabe's Zimbabwe, 2000–2009: Massive Human Rights Violations and the Failure to Protect" (2010) 32 *Human Rights Quarterly* 898–920.

"State-Induced Famine and Penal Starvation in North Korea" (2012) 7 *Genocide Studies and Prevention* 147–165.

The Independent, "Atrocities in Congo" (1902) 1 *The Journal of Geography* 228–229.

Jappah, Jlateh Vincent and Danielle Taana Smith, "State Sponsored Famine: Conceptualizing Politically Induced Famine as a Crime against Humanity" (2012) 4 *Journal of International and Global Studies* 17–31.

Jarvis, Helen, "Powerful Remains: The Continuing Presence of Victims of the Khmer Rouge Regime in Today's Cambodia" (2015) 1 *Human Remains and Violence: An Interdisciplinary Journal* 36–55.

Jarvis, Michelle and Alan Tieger, "Applying the Genocide Convention at the ICTY: The Influence of Paradigms Past" (2016) 14 *Journal of International Criminal Justice* 857–877.

Jo, Hyeran and Beth A. Simmons, "Can the International Criminal Court Deter Atrocity?" (2016) 70 *International Organization* 443–475.

Jones, Adam, "Genocide and Structural Violence: Charting the Terrain," in Adam Jones (ed.), *New Directions in Genocide Research* (Routledge, 2012), 132–152.

Kahan, Dan M., "The Secret Ambition of Deterrence" (1999) 113 *Harvard Law Review* 413–500.

Kalpouzos, Ioannis and Itamar Mann, "Banal Crimes against Humanity: The Case of Asylum Seekers in Greece" (2015) 16 *Melbourne Journal of International Law* 1–28.

Kang, Grace M., "A Case for the Prosecution of Kim Jong II for Crimes against Humanity, Genocide, and War Crimes" (2006) 38 *Columbia Human Rights Law Review* 51–114.

Kapur, Ratna, "Precarious Desires and Ungrievable Lives: Human Rights and Postcolonial Critiques of Legal Justice" (2015) 3 *London Review of International Law* 267–294.

Kearney, Diana, "Food Deprivations as Crimes against Humanity" (2013) 46 *New York University Journal of International Law and Politics* 207–289.

Kendall, Sara, "Donors' Justice: Recasting International Criminal Accountability" (2011) 24 *Leiden Journal of International Law* 585–606.

Kennedy, David, "Spring Break" (1985) 63 *Texas Law Review* 1377–1423.

Kent, Alexandra, "Friction and Security at the Khmer Rouge Tribunal" (2013) 28 *SOJOURN: Journal of Social Issues in Southeast Asia* 299–328.

Khorakiwala, Ateya, "Staging the Modern Ruin: Beato's 'Sikander Bagh, Lucknow'" (2013) 41 *Thresholds: Journal of the MIT Department of Architecture* 138–145.

Killean, Rachel, "Compromised Justice: The Road to the ECCC," in Rachel Killean (ed.), *Victims, Atrocity and International Criminal Justice: Lessons from Cambodia* (Taylor and Francis, 2018), 40–63.

"Constructing Victimhood at the Khmer Rouge Tribunal: Visibility, Selectivity and Participation" (2018) 24 *International Review of Victimology* 273–296.

Kim, Hunjoon and Kathryn Sikkink, "Explaining the Deterrence Effect of Human Rights Prosecutions for Transitional Countries" (2010) 54 *International Studies Quarterly* 939–963.

Kofele-Kale, Ndiva, "Patrimonicide: The International Economic Crime of Indigenous Spoliation" (1995) 28 *Vanderbilt Journal of Transnational Law* 45–118.

"The Right to a Corruption-Free Society as an Individual and Collective Human Right: Elevating Official Corruption to a Crime Under International Law" (2000) 34 *International Lawyer* 149–178.

Koskenniemi, Martti, "Between Impunity and Show Trials" (2002) 6 *Max Planck Yearbook of United Nations Law* 1–32.

"The Mystery of Legal Obligation" (2011) 3 *International Theory* 319–325.

Kraemer, John D., Dhrubajyoti Bhattacharya, and Lawrence O. Gostin, "Blocking Humanitarian Assistance: A Crime against Humanity?" (2008) 372 *The Lancet* 1203–1205.

Krever, Tor, "International Criminal Law: An Ideology Critique" (2013) 26 *Leiden Journal of International Law* 701–723.

"Unveiling (and Veiling) Politics in International Criminal Trials," in Christine Schwöbel (ed.), *Critical Approaches to International Criminal Law: An Introduction* (Routledge, 2014), 117–137.

Ku, Julian, "How System Criminality Could Exacerbate the Weaknesses of International Criminal Law" (2010) 8 *Santa Clara Journal of International Law* 365–372.

Ku, Julian and Jide Nzelibe, "Do International Criminal Tribunals Deter or Exacerbate Humanitarian Atrocities?" (2006) 84 *Washington University Law Review* 777–833.

Ladner, Kiera L., "Political Genocide: Killing Nations through Legislation and Slow-Moving Poison," in Andrew Woolford, Jeff Benvenuto, and Alexander Laban Hinton (eds.), *Colonial Genocide in Indigenous North America* (Duke University Press, 2014), 226–245.

Law, Helen H., "Atrocities in Greek Warfare" (1919) 15 *The Classical Journal* 132–147.

Lieberman, Benjamin, "From Definition to Process: The Effects and Roots of Genocide," in Adam Jones (ed.), *New Directions in Genocide Research* (Routledge, 2012), 3–17.

Luban, David, "A Theory of Crimes against Humanity" (2004) 29 *Yale Journal of International Law* 85–167.

"Hannah Arendt as a Theorist of International Criminal Law" (2011) 11 *International Criminal Law Review* 621–641.

Luping, Dianne, "Investigation and Prosecution of Sexual and Gender-Based Crimes before the International Criminal Court" (2009) 17 *American University Journal of Gender, Social Policy and the Law* 431–496.

MacDonald, David B., "Canada's History Wars: Indigenous Genocide and Public Memory in the United States, Australia and Canada" (2015) 17 *Journal of Genocide Research* 411–431.

Mann, Itamar, "Border Violence as Crime" (2021) 42 *University of Pennsylvania Journal of International Law* 675-736.

Marcus, David, "Famine Crimes in International Law" (2003) 97 *American Journal of International Law* 245–281.

Marks, Susan, "Human Rights and Root Causes" (2011) 74 *The Modern Law Review* 57–78.

Martone, Gerald and Maureen Shawn Kennedy, "Scenes from Somalia" (2012) 112 *American Journal of Nursing* 38–39.

Mbembe, Achille, "Necropolitics" (2003) 15 *Public Culture* 11–40.

McCormack, Timothy L.H., "Selective Reaction to Atrocity: War Crimes and the Development of International Criminal Law" (1996) 60 *Albany Law Review* 681–732.

McLoughlin, Stephen and Maartje Weerdesteijn, "Eliminating Rivals, Managing Rivalries: A Comparison of Robert Mugabe and Kenneth Kaunda" (2016) 9 *Genocide Studies and Prevention* 116–136.

Mégret, Frédéric, "In Defense of Hybridity: Toward a Representational Theory of International Criminal Justice" (2005) 38 *Cornell International Law Journal* 725–751.

"Practices of Stigmatization" (2013) 76 *Law and Contemporary Problems* 287–318.

"In Whose Name? The ICC and the Search for Constituency," in Carsten Stahn, Sarah Kendall, and Christian M. de Vos (eds.), *Contested Justice: The Politics and Practice of International Criminal Court Interventions* (Cambridge University Press, 2015), 23–45.

"What Sort of Global Justice Is 'International Criminal Justice'?" (2015) 13 *Journal of International Criminal Justice* 77–96.

"The Anxieties of International Criminal Justice" (2016) 29 *Leiden Journal of International Law* 197–221.

Miller, Zinaida, "Effects of Invisibility: In Search of the 'Economic' in Transitional Justice" (2008) 2 *International Journal of Transitional Justice* 266–291.

Minow, Martha, "Naming Horror: Legal and Political Words for Mass Atrocities" (2007) 2 *Genocide Studies and Prevention* 37–41.

Mohamed, Saira, "Deviance, Aspiration, and the Stories We Tell: Reconciling Mass Atrocity and the Criminal Law" (2015) 124 *Yale Law Journal* 1628–1689.

Mollica, Richard F. et al., "The Enduring Mental Health Impact of Mass Violence: A Community Comparison Study of Cambodian Civilians Living in Cambodia and Thailand" (2014) 60 *International Journal of Social Psychiatry* 6–20.

Moore, Rebekah, "'A Crime against Humanity Arguably without Parallel in European History': Genocide and the 'Politics' of Victimhood in Western Narratives of the Ukrainian Holodomor" (2012) 58 *Australian Journal of Politics and History* 367–379.

Muck, William and Eric Wiebelhaus-Brahm, "External Transitional Justice Funding: Introducing a New Dataset" (2016) 11 *Journal of Peacebuilding and Development* 66–71.

Munteanu, Dana LaCourse, "Introduction," in Dana LaCourse Munteanu (ed.), *Tragic Pathos: Pity and Fear in Greek Philosophy and Tragedy* (Cambridge University Press, 2011), 1–26.

Mutua, Makau, "Savages, Victims, and Saviors: The Metaphor of Human Rights" (2001) 42 *Harvard International Law Journal* 201–245.

Muvingi, Ismael, "Sitting on Powder Kegs: Socioeconomic Rights in Transitional Societies" (2009) 3 *International Journal of Transitional Justice* 163–182.

"Donor-Driven Transitional Justice and Peacebuilding" (2016) 11 *Journal of Peacebuilding and Development* 10–25.

Nagy, Rosemary, "Transitional Justice as Global Project: Critical Reflections" (2008) 29 *Third World Quarterly* 275–289.

Nassehi, Armin, "Social Constructivism," in Austin Harrington, Barbara L. Marshall, and Hans-Peter Müller (eds.), *Encyclopedia of Social Theory* (Routledge, 2006), 98–100.

Neuborne, Burt, "The Legality of the American Bombing of Cambodia–The ACLU Position" (1973) 40 *Brooklyn Law Review* 1–34.

Neuner, Matthias, "The Notion of Continuous or Continuing Crimes in International Criminal Law," in Morten Bergsmo, Wolfgang Kaleck, and Kyaw Yin Hlaing (eds.), *Colonial Wrongs and Access to International Law* (Torkel Opsahl Academic EPublisher, 2020), 123–174.

Nollkaemper, André, "Systemic Effects of International Responsibility for International Crimes" (2010) 8 *Santa Clara Journal of International Law* 313–352.

Nouwen, Sarah, "International Criminal Law: Theory All Over the Place," in Anne Orford, Florian Hoffmann, and Martin Clark (eds.), *The Oxford Handbook of the Theory of International Law* (Oxford University Press, 2016), 738–761.

Nouwen, Sarah M.H. and Wouter G. Werner, "Monopolizing Global Justice: International Criminal Law as Challenge to Human Diversity" (2015) 13 *Journal of International Criminal Justice* 157–176.

Nunpa, Chris Mato, "Historical Amnesia: The 'Hidden Genocide' and Destruction of Indigenous Peoples in the United States," in Alexander Laban Hinton, Thomas La Pointe, and Douglas Irvin-Erickson (eds.), *Hidden Genocides: Knowledge, Power, Memory* (Rutgers University Press, 2014), 96–108.

Ocheje, Paul D., "Refocusing International Law on the Quest for Accountability in Africa: The Case Against the 'Other' Impunity" (2002) 15 *Leiden Journal of International Law* 749–779.

Ochs, Sara, "In Need of Prosecution: The Role of Personal Jurisdiction in the Khmer Rouge Tribunal" (2019) 55 *Stanford Journal of International Law* 117–154.

Oh, Amanda Mortwedt, "A House Divided against Itself Cannot Stand: The Case for Ending the Extraordinary Chambers in the Courts of Cambodia" (2012) 10 *University of St. Thomas Law Journal* 502–532.

Ohlin, Jens David, "Three Conceptual Problems with the Doctrine of Joint Criminal Enterprise" (2005) 5 *Journal of International Criminal Justice* 69–90.

"Group Think: The Law of Conspiracy and Collective Reason" (2007) 98 *Journal of Criminal Law and Criminology* 147–206.

"Joint Criminal Confusion" (2009) 12 *New Criminal Law Review* 406–419.

"Organizational Criminality," in Elies van Sliedregt and Sergey Vasiliev (eds.), *Pluralism in International Criminal Law* (Oxford University Press, 2014), 107–127.

"The One or the Many" (2015) 9 *Criminal Law and Philosophy* 285–299.

Osiel, Mark J., "Obeying Orders: Atrocity, Military Discipline, and the Law of War" (1998) 86 *California Law Review* 939–1129.

Owen, Taylor and Ben Kiernan, "Bombs over Cambodia," October 2006, *The Walrus* 62–69.

Owens, Peter B., Yang Su, and David A. Snow, "Social Scientific Inquiry into Genocide and Mass Killing: From Unitary Outcome to Complex Processes" (2013) 39 *Annual Review of Sociology* 69–84.

Panagia, Davide, "'Partage du Sensible': The Distribution of the Sensible," in Jean-Phillipe Deranty (ed.), *Jacques Rancière: Key Concepts* (Routledge, 2014), 95–103.

Path, Kosal and Angeliki Kanavou, "Converts, Not Ideologues? The Khmer Rouge Practice of Thought Reform in Cambodia, 1975–1978" (2015) 20 *Journal of Political Ideologies* 304–332.

Peskin, Victor, "Victor's Justice Revisited: Rwandan Patriotic Front Crimes and the Prosecutorial Endgame at the ICTR," in Scott Straus and Lars Waldorf (eds.), *Remaking Rwanda: State Building and Human Rights after Mass Violence* (University of Wisconsin Press, 2011), 173–183.

Rajkovic, Nikolas M., "What is a 'Grave' International Crime? The Rome Statute, Durkheim and the Sociology of Ruling Outrages" (2020) 16 *Loyola University Chicago International Law Review* 65–86.

Reeves, Eric, "Humanitarian Obstruction as a Crime against Humanity: The Example of Sudan" (2011) 54 *African Studies Review* 165–174.

Roberts, Christopher, "On the Definition of Crimes against Humanity and Other Widespread or Systematic Human Rights Violations" (2017) 20 *University of Pennsylvania Journal of Law and Social Change* 1–27.

Robinson, Darryl, "The Identity Crisis of International Criminal Law" (2008) 21 *Leiden Journal of International Law* 925–963.

"A Cosmopolitan Liberal Account of International Criminal Law" (2013) 26 *Leiden Journal of International Law* 127–153.

"Crimes against Humanity: A Better Policy on 'Policy'," in Carsten Stahn (ed.), *The Law and Practice of the International Criminal Court* (Oxford University Press, 2014), 705–730.

Rodenhäuser, Tilman, "Beyond State Crimes: Non-State Entities and Crimes against Humanity" (2014) 27 *Leiden Journal of International Law* 913–926.

Rosenberg, Sheri P., "Genocide Is a Process, Not an Event" (2012) 7 *Genocide Studies and Prevention* 16–23.

Rosenberg, Sheri P. and Everita Silina, "Genocide by Attrition: Silent and Efficient," in Joyce Apsel and Ernesto Verdeja (eds.), *Genocide Matters: Ongoing Issues and Emerging Perspectives* (Routledge, 2013), 106–126.

Roth, Kenneth, "Defending Economic, Social and Cultural Rights: Practical Issues Faced by an International Human Rights Organization" (2004) 26 *Human Rights Quarterly* 63–72.

Rottensteiner, Christa, "The Denial of Humanitarian Assistance as a Crime under International Law" (1999) 81 *International Review of the Red Cross* 555–582.

Rousseau, Cécile, Aline Drapeau, and Robert Platt, "Family Trauma and its Association with Emotional and Behavioral Problems and Social Adjustment in Adolescent Cambodian Refugees" (1999) 23 *Child Abuse and Neglect* 1263–1273.

Sadat, Leila Nadya, "Crimes against Humanity in the Modern Age" (2013) 107 *American Journal of International Law* 334–377.

Sander, Barrie, "History on Trial: Historical Narrative Pluralism within and Beyond International Criminal Courts" (2018) 67 *International and Comparative Law Quarterly* 547–576.

"The Expressive Turn of International Criminal Justice: A Field in Search of Meaning" (2019) 32 *Leiden Journal of International Law* 851–872.

"The Anti-Impunity Mindset," in Morten Bergsmo, Mark Klamberg, Kjersti Lohne and Christopher B. Mahony, eds., Power in International Criminal Justice (Torkel Opsahl Academic EPublisher, 2020), 325–355.

Sanikidze, Zurab, "The Level of 'Contribution' Required under Article 25 (3)(D)of the Rome Statute of the International Criminal Court" (2012) 83 *Revue Internationale de Droit Pénal* 221–232.

Sankey, Diana, "Toward Recognition of Subsistence Harms: Reassessing Approaches to Socioeconomic Forms of Violence in Transitional Justice" (2014) 8 *International Journal of Transitional Justice* 121–140.

Scheffer, David, "Genocide and Atrocity Crimes" (2006) 1 *Genocide Studies and Prevention* 229–250.

Scheinert, Josh, "Refusal to Save Lives: A Perspective from International Criminal Law" (2013) 13 *International Criminal Law Review* 627–663.

Schmid, Evelyne, "War Crimes Related to Violations of Economic, Social and Cultural Rights" (2011) 71 *Heidelberg Journal of International Law* 523–540.

Schmid, Evelyne and Aoife Nolan, "'Do No Harm'? Exploring the Scope of Economic and Social Rights in Transitional Justice" (2014) 8 *International Journal of Transitional Justice* 362–382.

Schneider, Joseph W., "Social Constructionism," in George Ritzer (ed.), *Encyclopedia of Social Theory* (Sage, 2005), 724–729.

Schwöbel, Christine, "The Comfort of International Criminal Law" (2013) 24 *Law and Critique* 169–191.

"The Market and Marketing Culture of International Criminal Law," in Christine Schwöbel (ed.), *Critical Approaches to International Criminal Law: An Introduction* (Routledge, 2014), 264–280.

Schwöbel-Patel, Christine, "Spectacle in International Criminal Law: The Fundraising Image of Victimhood" (2016) 4 *London Review of International Law* 247–274.

"The 'Ideal' Victim of International Criminal Law" (2018) 29 *European Journal of International Law* 703–724.

Sen, Amartya, "Ingredients of Famine Analysis: Availability and Entitlements" (1981) 96 *The Quarterly Journal of Economics* 433–464.

Serbyn, Roman and Raphael Lemkin, "Lemkin on Genocide of Nations" (2009) 7 *Journal of International Criminal Justice* 123–130.

Sharp, Dustin, "Addressing Economic Violence in Times of Transition: Toward a Positive-Peace Paradigm for Transitional Justice" (2011) 35 *Fordham International Law Journal* 780–814.

Shaw, Martin, "From Comparative to International Genocide Studies: The International Production of Genocide in 20th-Century Europe" (2012) 18 *European Journal of International Relations* 645–668.

Short, Damien, "Australia: A Continuing Genocide?" (2010) 12 *Journal of Genocide Research* 45–68.

Skogly, Sigrun I., "Crimes against Humanity–Revisited: Is There a Role for Economic and Social Rights?" (2001) 5 *International Journal of Human Rights* 58–80.

Sloane, Robert D., "The Expressive Capacity of International Punishment: The Limits of the National Law Analogy and the Potential of International Criminal Law" (2007) 43 *Stanford Journal of International Law* 39–94.

Slovic, Paul, "'If I Look at the Mass I will Never Act': Psychic Numbing and Genocide" (2007) 2 *Judgment and Decision Making* 79–95.

Slovic, Paul, David Zionts, Andrew K. Woods, Ryan Goodman, and Derek Jinks, "Psychic Numbing and Mass Atrocity," in Eldar Shafir (ed.), *The Behavioral Foundations of Public Policy* (Princeton University Press, 2013), 126–142.

Sluiter, Göran, "Chapeau Elements," in Leila Nadya Sadat (ed.), *Forging a Convention for Crimes against Humanity* (Cambridge University Press, 2011), 102–141.

Starr, Sonja, "Extraordinary Crimes at Ordinary Times: International Justice Beyond Crisis Situations" (2007) 101 *Northwestern University Law Review* 1257–1314.

Stewart, James G., "Overdetermined Atrocities" (2012) 10 *Journal of International Criminal Justice* 1189–1218.

Stolk, Sofia, "A Sophisticated Beast? On the Construction of an 'Ideal' Perpetrator in the Opening Statements of International Criminal Trials" (2018) 29 *European Journal of International Law* 677–701.

Straus, Scott, "What Is Being Prevented? Genocide, Mass Atrocity, and Conceptual Ambiguity in the Anti-Atrocity Movement," in Sheri P. Rosenberg, Tibi Galis, and Alex Zucker (eds.), *Reconstructing Atrocity Prevention* (Oxford University Press, 2016), 17–30.

Tallgren, Immi, "Who are 'We' in International Criminal Law? On Critics and Membership," in Christine Schwöbel-Patel (ed.), *Critical Approaches to International Criminal Law: An Introduction* (Routledge, 2014), 71–95.

"The Voice of the International: Who is Speaking?" (2015) 13 *Journal of International Criminal Justice* 135–155.

Teitel, Ruti G., "Transitional Justice Genealogy" (2003) 16 *Harvard Human Rights Journal* 69–94.

Tennyson, Lord Alfred, "The Charge of the Light Brigade," in Lord Alfred Tennyson (ed.), *The Charge of the Light Brigade and Other Poems* (Dover, 1992), 52.

Tenove, Chris, "International Criminal Justice and the Empowerment or Disempowerment of Victims," in Morten Bergsmo, Mark Klamberg, Kjersti Lohne, and Christopher B. Mahony (eds.), *Power in International Criminal Justice* (Torkel Opsahl Academic EPublisher, 2020), 743–778.

"The Sanitary Phase of the Siberian Atrocities" (April 12, 1890) 135 *The Lancet* 820.

Thomason, Krista, "Transitional Justice as Structural Justice," in Claudio Corradetti, Nir Eisikovits, and Jack Volpe Rotondi (eds.), *Theorizing Transitional Justice* (Ashgate, 2015), 71–80.

Tversky, Amos and Daniel Kahneman, "Judgment under Uncertainty: Heuristics and Biases" (1974) 185 *Science* 1124–1131.

Tyner, James A., "State Sovereignty, Bioethics, and Political Geographies: The Practice of Medicine under the Khmer Rouge" (2012) 30 *Environment and Planning D: Society and Space* 842–860.

"Dead Labor, Landscapes, and Mass Graves: Administrative Violence during the Cambodian Genocide" (2014) 52 *Geoforum* 70–77.

Tyner, James A. and Stian Rice, "To Live and Let Die: Food, Famine, and Administrative Violence in Democratic Kampuchea, 1975–1979" (2015) 48 *Political Geography* 1–10.

Tzouvala, Ntina, "New Approaches to International Law: The History of a Project" (2016) 27 *European Journal of International Law* 215–233.

Ullah, Akm Ahsan, "Rohingya Refugees to Bangladesh: Historical Exclusions and Contemporary Marginalization" (2011) 9 *Journal of Immigrant and Refugee Studies* 139–161.

Ussher, Clarence, "The Armenian Atrocities and the Jihad" (1916) 6 *The Muslim World* 140–143.

van den Herik, Larissa, "International Criminal Law as a Spotlight and Black Holes as Constituents of Legacy" (2016) 110 *AJIL Unbound* 209–213.

"Economic, Social, and Cultural Rights: International Criminal Law's Blind Spot?," in Eibe H. Riedel, Gilles Giacca, and Christophe Golay (eds.), *Economic, Social, and Cultural Rights in International Law: Contemporary Issues and Challenges* (Oxford University Press, 2014), 343–366.

Van Schaack, Beth, "Crimen Sine Lege: Judicial Lawmaking at the Intersection of Law and Morals" (2008) 97 *Georgetown Law Journal* 119–192.

"The Principle of Legality in International Criminal Law" (2009) 103 *Proceedings of the Annual Meeting (American Society of International Law)* 101–104.

Vasiliev, Sergey, "ECCC Appeals: Appraising the Supreme Court Chamber's Interventions" (2020) 18 *Journal of International Criminal Justice* 723–745.

Vernon, Richard, "What Is a Crime against Humanity?" (2002) 10 *Journal of Political Philosophy* 231–249.

Verpoorten, Marijke, "Detecting Hidden Violence: The Spatial Distribution of Excess Mortality in Rwanda" (2012) 31 *Political Geography* 44–56.

Wakabi, Wairagala, "Health and Humanitarian Situation Worsens in Somalia" (2007) 370 *The Lancet* 1201–1202.

Watkins, Jared L. and Randle C. DeFalco, "Joint Criminal Enterprise and the Jurisdiction of the Extraordinary Chambers in the Courts of Cambodia" (2010) 63 *Rutgers Law Review* 193–273.

Werth, Nicolas, "Keynote Address for the Holodomor Conference, Harvard Ukrainian Research Institute, 17–18 November 2008" (2008) 30 *Harvard Ukrainian Studies* xxix–xxxviii.

Williams, Sarah, "The Severance of Case 002 at the ECCC: A Radical Trial Management Technique or a Step Too Far?" (2015) 13 *Journal of International Criminal Justice* 815–843.

Wilson, Richard Ashby, "Judging History: The Historical Record of the International Criminal Tribunal for the Former Yugoslavia" (2005) 27 *Human Rights Quarterly* 908–942.

Wippman, David, "Atrocities, Deterrence, and the Limits of International Justice" (1999) 23 *Fordham International Law Journal* 473–488.

Wolfe, Patrick, "Settler Colonialism and the Elimination of the Native" (2006) 8 *Journal of Genocide Research* 387–409.

Woolford, Andrew and Jeff Benvenuto, "Canada and Colonial Genocide" (2015) 17 *Journal of Genocide Research* 373–390.

Wynter, Sylvia, "Unsettling the Coloniality of Being/Power/Truth/Freedom: Toward the Human, after Man, Its Overrepresentation–an Argument" (2003) 3 *The New Centennial Review* 257–337.

Xenakis, Ioannis and Argyris Arnellos, "Aesthetic Perception and Its Minimal Content: A Naturalistic Perspective" (2014) 5 *Frontiers in Psychology* 1–15.

Zarni, Maung and Alice Cowley, "The Slow-Burning Genocide of Myanmar's Rohingya" (2014) 23 *Pacific Rim Law and Policy Journal* 683–752.

Zimmer, Zachary, "Disability and Active Life Expectancy Among Older Cambodians" (2006) 2 *Asian Population Studies* 133–148.

Jurisprudence

Application of the Convention on the Prevention and Punishment of the Crime of Genocide (*The Gambia* v. *Myanmar*), General List No. 178, Order, January 23, 2020, ICJ.

Attorney General v. *Eichmann*, Criminal Case No. 40/61, December 11, 1961, District Court of Jerusalem.

Case 001, Case No. 001/18-07-2007/ECCC/TC, Doc. No. E188, July 26, 2010, ECCC.

Case 001, Case No. 001/18-07-2007-ECCC/SC, Doc. No. F28, February 3, 2012, ECCC.

Case 002/01, Case No. 002/19-09-2007/ECCC/TC, Doc. No. E313, August 7, 2014, ECCC.

Case 002/01, Case No.002/19-09-2007-ECCC/TC, Doc. No. E1/13.1, November 21, 2011, ECCC.

Case 004/1, Case No. 004/1/07-09-2009-ECCC- OCIJ, Doc. No. D308/3, July 10, 2017, ECCC.

Prosecutor v. *Akayesu*, ICTR-96-4-T, September 2, 1998, ICTR.

Prosecutor v. *al Bashir*, ICC-02/05-01/09, Second Warrant of Arrest for Omar Hassan Ahmad Al Bashir, July 12, 2010, ICC.
Prosecutor v. *Brđanin*, IT-99-36-A, April 3, 2007, ICTY.
Prosecutor v. *Jelisić*, IT-95-10-T, December 14, 1999, ICTY.
Prosecutor v. *Karadžić*, IT-95-5/18-T, March 24, 2016, ICTY.
Prosecutor v. *Karemera and Ngirumpatse*, ICTR-98-44-A, September 29, 2014, ICTR.
Prosecutor v. *Kayishema*, ICTR-95-1-T, May 21, 1999, ICTR.
Prosecutor v. *Krnojelac*, IT-97-25-T, March 15, 2002, ICTY.
Prosecutor v. *Krstić*, IT-98-33-T, August 2, 2001, ICTY.
Prosecutor v. *Krstić*, IT-98-33-A, April 19, 2004, ICTY.
Prosecutor v. *Kunarac, Kovac and Vukovic*, IT-96-23-A and IT-96-23/1-A, June 12, 2002, ICTY.
Prosecutor v. *Kupreškić*, IT-95-16-T, January 14, 2000, ICTY.
Prosecutor v. *Kvočka*, IT-98-30/1-T, November 2, 2001, ICTY.
Prosecutor v. *Lukić and Lukić*, 98-32/1-T, July 20, 2009, ICTY.
Prosecutor v. *Mbarushimana*, Decision on Confirmation of Charges, ICC-01/04-01/10, December 16, 2011, ICC.
Prosecutor v. *Mbarushimana*, Judgment on the Appeal of the Prosecutor against the Decision of Pre-Trial Chamber I of 16 December 2011 entitled "Decision on the Confirmation of Charges," ICC-01/04-01/10 OA4, May 30, 2012, ICC.
Prosecutor v. *Mbarushimana*, Separate Opinion of Judge Silvia Fernández de Gurmendi, ICC-01/04-01/10 OA4, May 30, 2012, ICC.
Prosecutor v. *Milutinović*, IT-99-37-AR72, May 21, 2003, ICTY.
Prosecutor v. *Musema*, ICTR-96-13-A, January 27, 2000, ICTR.
Prosecutor v. *Naletilić*, IT-98-34-T, March 31, 2003, ICTY.
Prosecutor v. *Norman*, SCSL-2004-14-AR72(E), May 31, 2004, SCSL.
Prosecutor v. *Ntakirutimana and Ntakirutimana*, ICTR-96-10-A & ICTR-96-17-A, December 13, 2004, ICTR.
Prosecutor v. *Sesay, Kallon, and Gbao*, SCSL—2004-15-PT, July 5, 2004, SCSL.
Prosecutor v. *Stakić*, IT-97-24-A, March 22, 2006, ICTY.
Prosecutor v. *Tadić*, IT-94-1-T, May 7, 1997, ICTY.
Prosecutor v. *Tadić*, IT-94-1-A, July 15, 1999, ICTY.
Prosecutor v. *Taylor*, SCSL-03-01-A, September 26, 2013, SCSL.
Prosecutor v. *Vasiljević*, IT-98-32-T, November 29, 2002, ICTY.
R. v. *Finta*, [1994] 1 SCR 701, Supreme Court of Canada.
Situation in Darfur, Sudan, Annex A: Public Redacted Version of Prosecution's Application under Article 58 filed on 14 July 2008, ICC-02/05-157-AnxA, July 14, 2008, ICC.
Situation in the People's Republic of Bangladesh/Republic of the Union of Myanmar, Decision Pursuant to Article 15 of the Rome Statute on the

Authorisation of an Investigation into the Situation in the People's Republic of Bangladesh/Republic of the Union of Myanmar, ICC-01/19, November 14, 2019, ICC.

Streletz, Kessler and Krenz v. *Germany*, Application Nos. 34044/96, 35532/97 and 44801/98, March 22, 2001, ECtHR.

Webpages and Internet Resources

Akinyemi, Aaron, "The Forgotten Genocide," January 31, 2010, *The Guardian*, www.theguardian.com/commentisfree/2010/jan/31/genocide-namibia.

Aljazeera News, "Sudan Protest Group Has 'No Objection' to Handing Bashir to ICC," November 4, 2019, www.aljazeera.com/news/2019/11/sudan-protest-group-objection-handing-bashir-icc-191104064608367.html.

Alston, Philip, "Phantom Rights: The Systemic Marginalization of Economic and Social Rights," August 4, 2016, *Open Democracy*, www.opendemocracy.net/openglobalrights/philip-alston/phantom-rights-systemic-marginalization-of-economic-and-social-rights.

American Bar Association, "Atrocity Crimes Initiative," www.americanbar.org/groups/human_rights/preventing-atrocities.

Anderson, Haley S., "Why Them? On the U.S. Sanctions against Int'l Criminal Court Officials," September 2, 2020, *Just Security*, www.justsecurity.org/72275.

Australian Magna Carta Institute, "The ICC and Challenges to International Rule of Law," December 12, 2016, www.ruleoflaw.org.au/the-icc-challenges-international-rule-of-law.

Baltermants, Dmitri, "Grief", TIME, *Time 100 Photographs: The Most Influential Images of All Time* (Time Inc. Books, 2016), 104.

BBC News, "Somalia Famine 'Killed 260,000 People'," May 2, 2013, www.bbc.com/news/world-africa-22380352.

Bensouda, Fatou, "Remarks at the Commemoration of the 20th Anniversary of the Adoption of the Rome Statute of the International Criminal Court," July 17, 2018, *International Criminal Court Officer of the Prosecutor*, www.icc-cpi.int/itemsDocuments/20180717-otp-speech.pdf.

Brean, Joseph, "'Cultural Genocide' of Canada's Indigenous Peoples is a 'Mourning Label', Former War Crimes Prosecutor Says," January 15, 2016, *National Post*, http://news.nationalpost.com/news/canada/cultural-genocide-of-canadas-indigenous-people-is-a-mourning-label-former-war-crimes-prosecutor-says.

Bryden, Matt, "Somalia's Famine is Not Just a Catastrophe, It's a Crime," October 2011, *Enough Project*, https://enoughproject.org/files/Bryden_SomaliaFamine%20Brief_final_0.pdf.

Burke, Jason and Philip Oltermann, "Germany Moves to Atone for 'Forgotten Genocide' in Namibia," December 25, 2016, *The Guardian*, www

.theguardian.com/world/2016/dec/25/germany-moves-to-atone-for-forgotten-genocide-in-namibia.

Calabresi, Massimo, "20 Years Later: The Bosnian Conflict in Photographs," April 5, 2012, *TIME Magazine*, http://time.com/3787440/bosnia.

CBC, "Somalia 2011 Famine was a U.S.-Created War Crime, says Journalist Alex Perry," January 18, 2016, www.cbc.ca/radio/thecurrent/the-current-for-january-18–2016–1.3408273/somalia-2011-famine-was-a-u-s-created-war-crime-says-journalist-alex-perry-1.3408302.

Cruvellier, Thierry, "The Khmer Rouge's Perfect Villain," February 8, 2012, *New York Times*, www.nytimes.com/2012/02/09/opinion/the-khmer-rouges-perfect-villain.html.

Darusman, Marzuki, "End of Mission Statement to Japan of the Special Rapporteur on the Situation of Human Rights in the Democratic People's Republic of Korea," January 22, 2016, *United Nations Office of the High Commissioner for Human Rights*, www.ohchr.org/EN/NewsEvents/Pages/DisplayNews.aspx?NewsID=16981&LangID=E.

Dawsey, Josh, Felicia Sonmez, and Paul Kane. "Trump Acknowledges he Intentionally Downplayed Deadly Coronavirus, Says Effort was to Reduce Panic," September 9, 2020, *Washington Post*, www.washingtonpost.com/politics/trump-reaction-woodward-interview-coronavirus/2020/09/09/fc21e67e-f2ca-11ea-b796-2dd09962649c_story.html.

DeFalco, Randle, "Sudan Announces Intention to Have al-Bashir and Others 'Appear' Before the ICC," February 13, 2020, *Just Security*, www.justsecurity.org/68643.

"Is Pompeo Unintentionally Helping Out the International Criminal Court?," March 25, 2020, *Just Security*, www.justsecurity.org/69362.

Documentation Center of Cambodia, "Our History," 2019, http://dccam.org/our-history.

Doran, Stuart, "New Documents Claim to Prove Mugabe Ordered Gukurahundi Killings," May 19, 2015, *The Guardian*, www.theguardian.com/world/2015/may/19/mugabe-zimbabwe-gukurahundi-massacre-matabeleland.

Eboe-Osuji, Chile, "Remarks at Opening Ceremony: 55th Ordinary Session of the Authority of Heads of State and Government of the Economic Community of West African States (ECOWAS)," June 29, 2019, *International Criminal Court Presidency*, www.icc-cpi.int/itemsDocuments/190629-ICC-President-remarks-ECOWAS-Summit-ENG.pdf.

European Journal of International Law, "Book Discussion: Taking Economic, Social and Cultural Rights Seriously in International Criminal Law," March 16, 2016, *EJIL Talk!: Blog of the European Journal of International Law*, www.ejiltalk.org/book-discussion-taking-economic-social-and-cultural-rights-seriously-in-international-criminal-law-a-response-to-cryer-stahn-and-van-den-herik.

Fenton, Roger, "Valley of the Shadow of Death," 1855, *J. Paul Getty Museum*, www.getty.edu/art/collection/objects/60602/roger-fenton-valley-of-the-shadow-of-death-english-april-23–1855.

Food and Agriculture Organization of the UN, "Famine Hits Parts of South Sudan," February 20, 2017, www.fao.org/news/story/en/item/471251/icode.

Getty Images, "Rwanda Genocide Stock Photos and Pictures," 2021, www.gettyimages.com/photos/rwanda-genocide?sort=mostpopular&mediatype=photography&phrase=rwanda%20genocide.

Gillison, Douglas, "Crime Scenes of the Khmer," February 27, 2012, *The Investigative Fund*, www.typeinvestigations.org/investigation/2012/02/27/crime-scenes-khmer.

Global Action against Mass Atrocity Crimes, "Prevention of Atrocities," www.gaamac.org/prevention-of-atrocities.

Global Centre for the Responsibility to Protect, "Defining the Four Mass Atrocity Crimes," August 15, 2018, www.globalr2p.org/publications/defining-the-four-mass-atrocity-crimes.

Global Rights Compliance, "The Crime of Starvation and Methods of Prosecution and Accountability," 2019, https://sites.tufts.edu/wpf/files/2019/06/The-Crimes-of-Starvation-and-Methods-of-Prosecution-and-Accountability.pdf.

Gray, Denis D., "Atrocity or Theme Park?," August 15, 2006, *MSNBC*, www.nbcnews.com/id/14363744/ns/travel/t/atrocity-or-theme-park.

Guariglia, Fabricio, "COVID-19 Symposium: COVID-19 and International Criminal Law", April 4, 2020, *Opinio Juris*, http://opiniojuris.org/2020/04/04/covid-19-symposium-covid-19-and-international-criminal-law.

Heder, Steve, "A Review of the Negotiations Leading to the Establishment of the Personal Jurisdiction of the Extraordinary Chambers in the Courts of Cambodia," August 1, 2011, *Cambodia Tribunal Monitor*,www.cambodiatribunal.org/sites/default/files/A%20Review%20of%20the%20Negotiations%20Leading%20to%20the%20Establishment%20of%20the%20Personal%20Jurisdiction%20of%20the%20ECCC.pdf.

Heieck, John, "Trump's Coronavirus Response: Genocide By Default?," May 15, 2020, *Opinio Juris*, http://opiniojuris.org/2020/05/15/trumps-coronavirus-response-genocide-by-default.

Heller, Kevin Jon, "The Rome Statute's Flawed Amendment Regime – Starvation in NIAC Edition," December 7, 2019, *Opinio Juris*, www.opiniojuris.org/2019/12/07/the-rome-statutes-flawed-amendment-regime-starvation-in-niac-edition.

Human Rights Watch, "Somalia: End War Crimes to Help Tackle Famine," August 14, 2011, www.hrw.org/news/2011/08/14/somalia-end-war-crimes-help-tackle-famine.

"International Justice," March 31, 2015, www.hrw.org/topic/international-justice.

"ICC: Kenya Deputy President's Case Ends," April 5, 2016, www.hrw.org/news/2016/04/05/icc-kenya-deputy-presidents-case-ends.

"Jordan: Bar Entry or Arrest Sudan's Bashir," March 26, 2017, www.hrw.org/news/2017/03/26/jordan-bar-entry-or-arrest-sudans-bashir.

ICC Office of the Prosecutor, "Prosecutorial Strategy 2009–2012," February 1, 2010, www.icc-cpi.int/Pages/item.aspx?name=otp-rep-strategy-2010.

"Policy Paper on Case Selection and Prioritisation," September 15, 2016, www.icc-cpi.int/itemsDocuments/20160915_OTP-Policy_Case-Selection_Eng.pdf.

ICTY, "The Tribunal – Establishment," www.icty.org/en/about/tribunal/establishment.

Independent International Commission of Inquiry on the Syrian Arab Republic, "Sieges as Weapons of War: Encircle, Starve, Surrender, Evacuate," May 29, 2018, www.ohchr.org/Documents/HRBodies/HRCouncil/CoISyria/PolicyPaperSieges_29May2018.pdf.

International Center for Transitional Justice, "Transitional Justice Factsheet," 2009, www.ictj.org/about/transitional-justice.

International Criminal Court, "Joining the International Criminal Court: Why Does it Matter?," 2018, www.icc-cpi.int/Publications/Joining-Rome-Statute-Matters.pdf.

Jillions, Andrew, "The (in)Justice of Famine: Is al-Shabaab guilty of a Crime against Humanity?," August 15, 2011, *Justice in Conflict*, http://justiceinconflict.org/2011/08/15/the-injustice-of-famine-is-al-shabaab-guilty-of-a-crime-against-humanity.

Kan, Leslie, "Spectacle," in *The University of Chicago Theories of Media Keyword Glossary*, https://csmt.uchicago.edu/glossary2004/spectacle.htm.

Lorn, Dalin, "A Trip to Trapeang Thma Dam in Banteay Meanchey Province, December 20–22, 2013," 2013, *Documentation Center of Cambodia*, http://d.dccam.org/Projects/Radio/pdf/A_Trip_to_Trapeang_Thmar_Dam_Banteay_Meanchey_province.pdf.

Mathieson, David, "Perilous Plight: Burma's Rohingya Take to the Seas," May 26, 2009, *Human Rights Watch*, www.hrw.org/report/2009/05/26/perilous-plight/burmas-rohingya-take-seas.

Merriam-Webster Dictionary, www.merriam-webster.com.

Museum of Modern Art, Alexander Gardner, "Home of a Rebel Sharpshooter, Gettysburg," in *Gardner's Photographic Sketchbook of the War* (1865), www.moma.org/learn/moma_learning/alexander-gardner-home-of-a-rebel-sharpshooter-gettysburg-from-gardners-photographic-sketchbook-of-the-war-1865.

Naren, Kuch, "Hun Sen Warns of Civil War if ECCC Goes Beyond 'Limit'," February 27, 2015, *Cambodia Daily*, www.cambodiadaily.com/news/hun-sen-warns-of-civil-war-if-eccc-goes-beyond-limit-78757.

O'Grady, Siobhán, "South Sudan's Man-Made Famine," February 27, 2017, *Foreign Policy*, http://foreignpolicy.com/2017/02/27/south-sudans-man-made-famine.

Obama, Barack, "Presidential Study Directive on Mass Atrocities," Presidential Study Directive No. 10, August 4, 2011, *The White House Office of the Press Secretary*, www.whitehouse.gov/the-press-office/2011/08/04/presidential-study-directive-mass-atrocities.

Ohlin, Jens David, "Somalia Famine 'Crime against Humanity'?," August 12, 2011, *CNN*, www.cnn.com/2011/OPINION/08/12/ohlin.somalia.crimes/index.html.

Open Society Justice Initiative, "Dead End at Cambodia's Khmer Rouge Tribunal: Next Steps for the UN," April 29, 2020, www.justiceinitiative.org/uploads/9e0af740-d7b6-4c70-ba0c-96df88328b2c/briefing-eccc-end0304-20200429.pdf.

Oxford University Press, *The Oxford English Dictionary*, 2016 online ed., www.oed.com.

Pasos Peace Museum, "Vann Nath,"2014, http://pasospeacemuseum.org/vann-nath.

PBS, "Opening Statement Nuremberg Trials, 1945," November 21, 1945, www.pbs.org/wnet/supremecourt/personality/sources_document12.html.

Pheng, Pong-Rasy, "Burial," February 18, 2008, *Documentation Center of Cambodia*, www.d.dccam.org/Projects/Maps/List_of_Burial_Site_Most_Updated.pdf.

"DK Prison," February 18, 2008, *Documentation Center of Cambodia*, http://d.dccam.org/Projects/Maps/List_of_DK_Prisons_Most_Updated.pdf.

Post Staff, "The 'Poisonous Hill' that was Toul Sleng," May 2, 1997, *Phnom Penh Post*, www.phnompenhpost.com/national/poisonous-hill-was-toul-sleng.

Powers, Shannon E., "Rwanda's Gacaca Courts: Implications for International Criminal Law and Transitional Justice," (2011) 15 *American Society of International Law Insights*, www.asil.org/insights/volume/15/issue/17/rwanda%E2%80%99s-gacaca-courts-implications-international-criminal-law-and.

Romm, Tony, Jacob Bogage, and Lena H. Sun, "Newly Revealed USPS Documents Show an Agency Struggling to Manage Trump, Amazon and the Pandemic," September 18, 2020, *Washington Post*, www.washingtonpost.com/us-policy/2020/09/17/usps-trump-coronavirus-amazon-foia.

Sander, Barrie, "Addressing the Economic Dimensions of Mass Atrocities: International Criminal Law's Business or Blind Spot?," June 8, 2015, *Justice in Conflict*, https://justiceinconflict.org/2015/06/08/addressing-the-economic-dimensions-of-mass-atrocities-international-criminal-laws-business-or-blind-spot.

Schanberg, Sydney, "Millions Uprooted as Communists Impose a 'Peasant Revolution'," May 9, 1975, *New York Times*, www.pulitzer.org/article/phnom-penh-becomes-echo-chamber-silent-streets.

Scheffer, David J., "Is It a Crime to Mishandle a Public Health Response?," April 22, 2020, *Council on Foreign Relations*, www.cfr.org/article/it-crime-mishandle-public-health-response.

Shelley, James, "The Concept of the Aesthetic," in Edward N. Zalta (ed.), *Stanford Encyclopedia of Philosophy* (2015), *Stanford University*, https://plato.stanford.edu/archives/win2015/entries/aesthetic-concept.

Smith, Adam M., "Dissecting the Executive Order on Int'l Criminal Court Sanctions: Scope, Effectiveness, and Tradeoffs," June 15, 2020, *Just Security*, www.justsecurity.org/70779.

Smith, Matthew, "'All You Can Do Is Pray': Crimes against Humanity and Ethnic Cleansing of Rohingya Muslims in Burma's Arakan State," April 22, 2013, *Human Rights Watch*, www.hrw.org/report/2013/04/22/all-you-can-do-pray/crimes-against-humanity-and-ethnic-cleansing-rohingya-muslims.

Song, Sang-hyun, "Keynote Remarks at Human Rights Council Side Event 'The International Criminal Court after 15 Years: Prospects for the Future'," September 10, 2013, *International Criminal Court Office of the Pres*idency, www.icc-cpi.int/Pages/item.aspx?name=2013–09–10-President-keynote-Geneva.

"The Role of the International Criminal Court in Ending Impunity and Establishing the Rule of Law," *UN Chronicle*, www.un.org/en/chronicle/article/role-international-criminal-court-ending-impunity-and-establishing-rule-law.

Stolk, Sofia, "Ntaganda at the ICC – Some Observations from the Public Gallery," September 14, 2015, *Vrije Universiteit Amsterdam School of Law Center for International Criminal Justice*, https://cicj.org/2015/09/the-opening-of-the-ntaganda-trial-at-the-icc-some-observations-from-the-public-gallery.

Sudan Tribune, "Sudan's Bashir Arrives in Jordan for Arab Summit," March 28, 2017, www.sudantribune.com/spip.php?article62037.

Taylor, Alan, "World War II: The Holocaust," October 16, 2011, *The Atlantic*, www.theatlantic.com/photo/2011/10/world-war-ii-the-holocaust/100170/.

TIME Magazine, "The Story of this Shocking Image from a Prison Camp in Bosnia Continues 25 Years Later," November 22, 2017, https://time.com/5034826/fikret-alic-time-cover-bosnia.

UN Peacebuilding Support Office, "UN Peacebuilding: an Orientation," September 2010, www.un.org/peacebuilding/sites/www.un.org.peacebuilding/files/documents/peacebuilding_orientation.pdf.

UN Web Services Section, "Full Transcript of Secretary-General's Press Encounter Following Briefing to the General Assembly on His Priorities for 2016," January 14, 2016, www.un.org/sg/offthecuff/index.asp?nid=4316.

Van Schaack, Beth, "The Int'l Criminal Court Executive Order: Global Reactions Compiled," September 1, 2020, *Just Security*, www.justsecurity.org/72256.

Vilim, Laura, "'Keeping Them Alive, One Gets Nothing; Killing Them, One Loses Nothing': Prosecuting Khmer Rouge Medical Practices as Crimes against Humanity," 2010, *Documentation Center of Cambodia*, http://d.dccam.org/Abouts/Intern/Laura_PT1.pdf.

Wallace, Julia, "The Bucolic Life of a Cambodian Grandmother Accused of Mass Killings," February 24, 2017, *New York Times*, www.nytimes.com/2017/02/24/world/asia/cambodia-khmer-rouge-im-chaem.html.

Yale University Genocide Studies Program, "Gallery of S-21 Prisoner Photographs," https://gsp.yale.edu/cgp/gallery/cts.

Statutes, Treaties, and Conventions

Convention on the Prevention and Punishment of the Crime of Genocide, Paris, December 9, 1948, in force January 12, 1951, 78 UNTS 277.

Geneva Convention for the Amelioration of the Condition of the Wounded and Sick in Armed Forces in the Field, Geneva, August 12, 1949, in force October 21, 1950, 75 UNTS 31.

Geneva Convention for the Amelioration of the Condition of Wounded, Sick and Shipwrecked Members of Armed Forces at Sea, Geneva, August 12, 1949, in force October 21, 1950, 75 UNTS 85.

Geneva Convention Relative to the Protection of Civilian Persons in Time of War, Geneva, August 12, 1949, in force October 21, 1950, 75 UNTS 287.

Geneva Convention Relative to the Treatment of Prisoners of War, Geneva, August 12, 1949, in force October 21, 1950, 75 UNTS 135.

Rome Statute of the International Criminal Court, Rome, July 17, 1998, in force July 1, 2002, 2187 UNTS 3.

Sierra Leone-UN, Agreement between the United Nations and the Government of Sierra Leone on the establishment of a Special Court for Sierra Leone, January 16, 2002, in force April 13, 2002, 2178 UNTS 137.

UN-Cambodia, Agreement between the United Nations and the Royal Government of Cambodia Concerning the Prosecution under Cambodian Law of Crimes committed during the Period of Democratic Kampuchea, June 6, 2003, in force April 29, 2005, 2329 UNTS 117.

USA-UK-USSR, Moscow Protocol, Moscow, USSR, October 30, 1943, in force November 1, 1943, 1943 For. Rel. (I) 749.

Documents and Other Sources

DeFalco, Randle C., "Justice and Starvation in Cambodia: International Criminal Law and the Khmer Rouge Famine," LLM Thesis, University of Toronto (2013).

Documentation Center of Cambodia, "List of Democratic Kampuchea Burial" (2005).

International Criminal Court Assembly of State Parties Working Group on Amendments, "Report of the Working Group on Amendments," Doc. ICC-ASP/17/35, November 29, 2018, ICC.

Long, Dany, "Promoting Accountability Project Interviews with El Pheap, Youk Neam, Bin Nann, Rin Kheng and Thip Samphatt: Field Trip Note," Documentation Center of Cambodia, September 2011.

Preparatory Commission for the International Criminal Court, "Report of the Preparatory Commission for the International Criminal Court, Addendum Part II, Finalized Draft Text of the Elements of Crimes," UN Doc. PCNICC/2000/1/Add.2, November 2, 2000.

"Statement of IM Chaem (DC-Cam)," ECCC, Doc. No. E305/13.23.330, April 6, 2012, www.eccc.gov.kh/sites/default/files/documents/courtdoc/2015-06-11%2013%3A07/E305_13.23.330_EN.PDF.

Stolk, Sofia, "A Solemn Tale of Horror: The Opening Statement of the Prosecution in International Criminal Trials," PhD thesis, Vrije Universiteit Amsterdam (2017).

Tabeau, Ewa and They Kheam, "Khmer Rouge Victims in Cambodia, April 1975 – January 1979: A Critical Assessment of Major Estimates," ECCC Office of the Co-Investigating Judges, 2009.

"Telegram 94," 2nd Quarter Searching for the Truth: Magazine of the Documentation Center of Cambodia, 2003, 11.

UN Commission of Inquiry on Human Rights in the Democratic People's Republic of Korea, "Report of the Detailed Findings of the Commission of Inquiry on Human Rights in the Democratic People's Republic of Korea," UN Doc. A/HRC/25/CRP.1, February 7, 2014.

UN High Commissioner for Human Rights, "Report of the United Nations High Commissioner for Human Rights containing the findings of the Group of Independent Eminent International and Regional Experts: Situation of Human Rights in Yemen, including Violations and Abuses since September 2014," UN Doc. A/HRC/39/43, August 17, 2018.

UN Human Rights Council, "Report of the Commission on South Sudan," UN Doc. A/HRC/37/71, March 13, 2018.

UN Human Rights Council, "Situation of Human Rights of Rohingya Muslims and other Minorities in Myanmar," UN Doc. A/HRC/32/18, June 20, 2016.

UN Office on Genocide Prevention and the Responsibility to Protect, "Framework of Analysis for Atrocity Crimes" United Nations, 2014.

UN Security Council, "Report of the Secretary-General on the African Union-United Nations Hybrid Operation in Darfur," UN Doc. S/2016/1109, December 23, 2016.

United States Institute of Mental Health, "PTSD, Depression Epidemic Among Cambodian Immigrants," US National Institute of Mental Health, August 2, 2005.

USAID, "Notice of Funding Opportunity: Request for Applications Number RFA-OAA-17–000011," 2017.

INDEX

For EU product safety concerns, contact us at Calle de José Abascal, 56–1°, 28003 Madrid, Spain or eugpsr@cambridge.org.

www.ingramcontent.com/pod-product-compliance
Ingram Content Group UK Ltd.
Pitfield, Milton Keynes, MK11 3LW, UK
UKHW022004220926
475880UK00004B/245
* 9 7 8 1 1 0 8 4 8 7 4 1 2 *